Nissan Micra
Owners Workshop Manual

M R Storey

Models covered

(4734 - 12AR2 - 240)

Micra Hatchback (K12 Series) with 1.0 litre (998cc), 1.2 litre (1240cc) & 1.4 litre (1386cc) petrol engines, including special/limited editions

Does NOT cover models with 1.6 litre petrol engine, diesel models or C+C Coupe Convertible

© Haynes Publishing 2013

ABCDE
FGHIJ
KLMNO
PQ

A book in the **Haynes Owners Workshop Manual Series**

ISBN **978 0 85733 570 8**

British Library Cataloguing in Publication Data
A catalogue record for this book is available from the British Library.

Printed in the USA

Haynes Publishing
Sparkford, Yeovil, Somerset BA22 7JJ, England

Haynes North America, Inc
861 Lawrence Drive, Newbury Park, California 91320, USA

Haynes Publishing Nordiska AB
Box 1504, 751 45 UPPSALA, Sverige

Contents

LIVING WITH YOUR NISSAN MICRA

Introduction   Page   0•4
Safety first!   Page   0•6

Roadside repairs

If your car won't start   Page   0•7
Jump starting   Page   0•8
Wheel changing   Page   0•9
Identifying leaks   Page   0•10
Towing   Page   0•10

Weekly checks

Introduction   Page   0•11
Underbonnet check points   Page   0•11
Engine oil level   Page   0•12
Coolant level   Page   0•12
Brake and clutch fluid level   Page   0•13
Washer fluid level   Page   0•13
Tyre condition and pressure   Page   0•14
Wiper blades   Page   0•15
Battery   Page   0•15
Electrical systems   Page   0•16

Lubricants and fluids

                                                 Page   0•17

Tyre pressures

                                                 Page   0•17

MAINTENANCE

Routine maintenance and servicing

Nissan Micra petrol models   Page   1•1
   Servicing specifications   Page   1•2
   Maintenance schedule   Page   1•3
   Maintenance procedures   Page   1•5

Contents

REPAIRS AND OVERHAUL

Engine and associated systems

Engine in-car repair procedures   Page   2A•1
Engine removal and overhaul procedures   Page   2B•1
Cooling, heating and ventilation systems   Page   3•1
Fuel system   Page   4A•1
Emission control and exhaust systems   Page   4B•1
Starting and charging systems   Page   5A•1
Ignition system   Page   5B•1

Transmission

Clutch   Page   6•1
Manual transmission   Page   7A•1
Automatic transmission   Page   7B•1
Driveshafts   Page   8•1

Brakes and suspension

Braking system   Page   9•1
Suspension and steering   Page   10•1

Body equipment

Bodywork and fittings   Page   11•1
Body electrical system   Page   12•1

Wiring diagrams   Page 12•17

REFERENCE

Dimensions and weights   Page REF•1
Conversion factors   Page REF•2
Buying spare parts   Page REF•3
Jacking and vehicle support   Page REF•4
Disconnecting the battery   Page REF•5
General repair procedures   Page REF•6
Vehicle identification   Page REF•7
Tools and working facilities   Page REF•8
MOT test checks   Page REF•10
Fault finding   Page REF•14
Glossary of technical terms   Page REF•26

Index   Page REF•31

The third incarnation of the Nissan Micra was first introduced into the UK in January 2003. With its distinctive high level headlights it at first seems a radical departure from the previous model. It has the big car look in a small package despite being only slightly wider and taller than the previous model (K11). Initially introduced with a choice of three engines (1.0, 1.2 and 1.4 litre) the 1 litre version was quickly discontinued. A diesel version is also available, and from 2005 a 1.6 litre petrol engine was introduced to the range (these engines are not covered by this manual).

Three- and five-door Hatchback models are available, as well as a C+C convertible (not covered by this manual). The range comprised five variants when first introduced (E, S, SE, SX and SVE). A facelift in late 2005 brought new bumpers and an updated dashboard, as well as revised model designations (E, S, Urbis, Sport, SE and SVE). October 2006 saw the introduction of special edition 'Active luxury' models and a further change in model designations (Activ, Initia and Spirita). In 2008 the range was rationalised to four options: Visia, Acenta, Tekna and Active Luxury.

As befits a modern supermini, the Micra offers high levels of passenger safety, with an impact-absorbing bodyshell, highly-rigid cabin, driver's and passenger airbags. Seat belt pretensioners are also standard throughout the range. Higher specification models also feature side airbags, curtain airbags and active headrests. The Micra has been awarded a four-star Euro NCAP safety rating.

All models have front-wheel-drive, with a five-speed manual transmission (or an optional Jatco four-speed automatic on 1.4 litre models). The front suspension is of conventional MacPherson strut type, incorporating lower arms, and an anti-roll bar; at the rear, a semi-independent beam axle is combined with compact under-floor springs to provide a more spacious load area.

The engines are all 16-valve twin cam engines, with variable inlet valve timing. These engines have chain driven camshafts and sequential fuel injection. A pre-catalytic converter oxygen sensor and a post-catalytic converter oxygen sensor are fitted to comply with the current EOBD standards for emissions control (EU4).

The Micra has a high equipment level, even at the lower end of the model range. All models have ABS and electronic brake distribution. Air conditioning is standard on all but the lowest models in the range. Higher specification models also feature climate control. Electric power steering and electric front windows are also standard throughout the range. Remote central locking is standard throughout the range. Some models feature Nissan's 'Intelligent key system' (I key). This system makes the mechanical key redundant – except for emergency use. Sensors within the car detect the proximity of the correct key fob and automatically unlock the doors. Starting is then a simple push of a button.

For the home mechanic, the Micra is a straightforward car to maintain and repair, since design features have been incorporated to reduce the actual cost of ownership to a minimum, and most of the items requiring frequent attention are easily accessible.

Your Nissan Micra manual

The aim of this manual is to help you get the best value from your car. It can do so in several ways. It can help you decide what work must be done (even should you choose to get it done by a garage). It will also provide information on routine maintenance and servicing, and give a logical course of action and diagnosis when random faults occur. However, it is hoped that you will use the manual by tackling the work yourself. On simpler jobs it may even be quicker than booking the car into a garage and going there twice, to leave and collect it. Perhaps most important, a lot of money can be saved by avoiding the costs a garage must charge to cover its labour and overheads.

The manual has drawings and descriptions to show the function of the various components so that their layout can be understood. Tasks are described and photographed in a clear step-by-step sequence.

References to the 'left' and 'right' of the car are in the sense of a person in the driver's seat, facing forwards.

Acknowledgements

Thanks are due to Draper tools Limited, who provided some of the workshop tools, and to all those people at Sparkford who helped in the production of this manual.

We take great pride in the accuracy of information given in this manual, but car manufacturers make alterations and design changes during the production run of a particular car of which they do not inform us. No liability can be accepted by the authors or publishers for loss, damage or injury caused by any errors in, or omissions from, the information given.

Working on your car can be dangerous. This page shows just some of the potential risks and hazards, with the aim of creating a safety-conscious attitude.

General hazards

Scalding

• Don't remove the radiator or expansion tank cap while the engine is hot.
• Engine oil, transmission fluid or power steering fluid may also be dangerously hot if the engine has recently been running.

Burning

• Beware of burns from the exhaust system and from any part of the engine. Brake discs and drums can also be extremely hot immediately after use.

Crushing

• When working under or near a raised vehicle, always supplement the jack with axle stands, or use drive-on ramps. *Never venture under a car which is only supported by a jack*.
• Take care if loosening or tightening high-torque nuts when the vehicle is on stands. Initial loosening and final tightening should be done with the wheels on the ground.

Fire

• Fuel is highly flammable; fuel vapour is explosive.
• Don't let fuel spill onto a hot engine.
• Do not smoke or allow naked lights (including pilot lights) anywhere near a vehicle being worked on. Also beware of creating sparks (electrically or by use of tools).
• Fuel vapour is heavier than air, so don't work on the fuel system with the vehicle over an inspection pit.
• Another cause of fire is an electrical overload or short-circuit. Take care when repairing or modifying the vehicle wiring.
• Keep a fire extinguisher handy, of a type suitable for use on fuel and electrical fires.

Electric shock

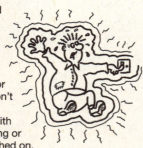

• Ignition HT and Xenon headlight voltages can be dangerous, especially to people with heart problems or a pacemaker. Don't work on or near these systems with the engine running or the ignition switched on.

• Mains voltage is also dangerous. Make sure that any mains-operated equipment is correctly earthed. Mains power points should be protected by a residual current device (RCD) circuit breaker.

Fume or gas intoxication

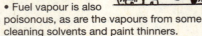

• Exhaust fumes are poisonous; they can contain carbon monoxide, which is rapidly fatal if inhaled. Never run the engine in a confined space such as a garage with the doors shut.
• Fuel vapour is also poisonous, as are the vapours from some cleaning solvents and paint thinners.

Poisonous or irritant substances

• Avoid skin contact with battery acid and with any fuel, fluid or lubricant, especially antifreeze, brake hydraulic fluid and Diesel fuel. Don't syphon them by mouth. If such a substance is swallowed or gets into the eyes, seek medical advice.
• Prolonged contact with used engine oil can cause skin cancer. Wear gloves or use a barrier cream if necessary. Change out of oil-soaked clothes and do not keep oily rags in your pocket.
• Air conditioning refrigerant forms a poisonous gas if exposed to a naked flame (including a cigarette). It can also cause skin burns on contact.

Asbestos

• Asbestos dust can cause cancer if inhaled or swallowed. Asbestos may be found in gaskets and in brake and clutch linings. When dealing with such components it is safest to assume that they contain asbestos.

Special hazards

Hydrofluoric acid

• This extremely corrosive acid is formed when certain types of synthetic rubber, found in some O-rings, oil seals, fuel hoses etc, are exposed to temperatures above 4000C. The rubber changes into a charred or sticky substance containing the acid. *Once formed, the acid remains dangerous for years. If it gets onto the skin, it may be necessary to amputate the limb concerned*.
• When dealing with a vehicle which has suffered a fire, or with components salvaged from such a vehicle, wear protective gloves and discard them after use.

The battery

• Batteries contain sulphuric acid, which attacks clothing, eyes and skin. Take care when topping-up or carrying the battery.
• The hydrogen gas given off by the battery is highly explosive. Never cause a spark or allow a naked light nearby. Be careful when connecting and disconnecting battery chargers or jump leads.

Air bags

• Air bags can cause injury if they go off accidentally. Take care when removing the steering wheel and trim panels. Special storage instructions may apply.

Diesel injection equipment

• Diesel injection pumps supply fuel at very high pressure. Take care when working on the fuel injectors and fuel pipes.

 Warning: Never expose the hands, face or any other part of the body to injector spray; the fuel can penetrate the skin with potentially fatal results.

Remember...

DO

• Do use eye protection when using power tools, and when working under the vehicle.

• Do wear gloves or use barrier cream to protect your hands when necessary.

• Do get someone to check periodically that all is well when working alone on the vehicle.

• Do keep loose clothing and long hair well out of the way of moving mechanical parts.

• Do remove rings, wristwatch etc, before working on the vehicle – especially the electrical system.

• Do ensure that any lifting or jacking equipment has a safe working load rating adequate for the job.

DON'T

• Don't attempt to lift a heavy component which may be beyond your capability – get assistance.

• Don't rush to finish a job, or take unverified short cuts.

• Don't use ill-fitting tools which may slip and cause injury.

• Don't leave tools or parts lying around where someone can trip over them. Mop up oil and fuel spills at once.

• Don't allow children or pets to play in or near a vehicle being worked on.

The following pages are intended to help in dealing with common roadside emergencies and breakdowns. You will find more detailed fault finding information at the back of the manual, and repair information in the main chapters.

If your car won't start and the starter motor doesn't turn

☐ Open the bonnet and make sure that the battery terminals are clean and tight.
☐ Switch on the headlights and try to start the engine. If the headlights go very dim when you're trying to start, the battery is probably flat. Get out of trouble by jump starting (see next page) using a friend's car.

If your car won't start even though the starter motor turns as normal

☐ Is there fuel in the tank?
☐ Has the engine immobiliser been deactivated? This should happen automatically, on inserting the ignition key. However, if a new key has been obtained (other than from a Nissan dealer), it may not contain the transponder chip necessary to deactivate the system.
☐ If it's a model with automatic transmission, the footbrake must be applied.
☐ Is there moisture on electrical components under the bonnet? Switch off the ignition, then wipe off any obvious dampness with a dry cloth. Spray a water-repellent aerosol product (WD-40 or equivalent) on ignition and fuel system electrical connectors like those shown in the photos. Pay special attention to the ignition coil wiring connectors.

A Check the condition and security of the battery connections.

B With the ignition off remove the air filter and throttle housing and check that the wiring connectors are securely connected to the four ignition coils.

C Check the plugs and wiring of all the critical engine connectors. Work around the engine bay methodically. Pay particular attention the crankshaft position sensor.

Check that electrical connections are secure (with the ignition switched off) and spray them with a water-dispersant spray like WD-40 if you suspect a problem due to damp

With the ignition off, check the fuses in the main fusebox, and the fusebox adjacent to the battery. On automatic transmission models, also check that the electronic transmission fuse No 14 in the main fusebox is correctly fitted.

Jump starting

When jump-starting a car using a booster battery, observe the following precautions:

✔ Before connecting the booster battery, make sure that the ignition is switched off.

✔ Ensure that all electrical equipment (lights, heater, wipers, etc) is switched off.

✔ Take note of any special precautions printed on the battery case.

✔ Make sure that the booster battery is the same voltage as the discharged one in the vehicle.

✔ If the battery is being jump-started from the battery in another vehicle, the two vehicles MUST NOT TOUCH each other.

✔ Make sure that the transmission is in neutral (or PARK, in the case of automatic transmission).

 HAYNES HiNT *Jump starting will get you out of trouble, but you must correct whatever made the battery go flat in the first place. There are three possibilities:*

1 *The battery has been drained by repeated attempts to start, or by leaving the lights on.*

2 *The charging system is not working properly (alternator drivebelt slack or broken, alternator wiring fault or alternator itself faulty).*

3 *The battery itself is at fault (electrolyte low, or battery worn out).*

1 Connect one end of the red jump lead to the positive (+) terminal of the flat battery

2 Connect the other end of the red lead to the positive (+) terminal of the booster battery.

3 Connect one end of the black jump lead to the negative (-) terminal of the booster battery

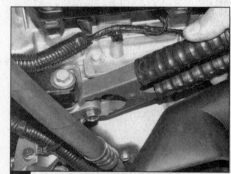

4 Connect the other end of the black jump lead to a bolt or bracket on the engine block, well away from the battery, on the vehicle to be started.

5 Make sure that the jump leads will not come into contact with the fan, drive-belts or other moving parts of the engine.

6 Start the engine using the booster battery and run it at idle speed. Switch on the lights, rear window demister and heater blower motor, then disconnect the jump leads in the reverse order of connection. Turn off the lights etc.

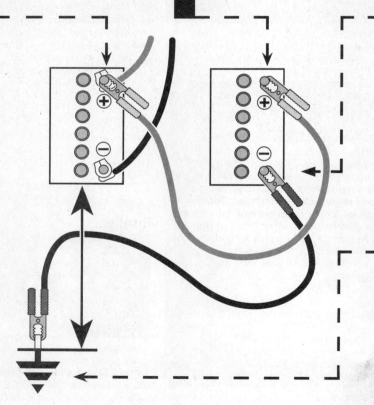

Wheel changing

 Warning: Do not change a wheel in a situation where you risk being hit by other traffic. On busy roads, try to stop in a lay-by or a gateway. Be wary of passing traffic while changing the wheel – it is easy to become distracted by the job in hand.

Preparation

- [ ] When a puncture occurs, stop as soon as it is safe to do so.
- [ ] Park on firm level ground, if possible, and well out of the way of other traffic.
- [ ] Use hazard warning lights if necessary.

- [ ] If you have one, use a warning triangle to alert other drivers of your presence.
- [ ] Apply the handbrake and engage first or reverse gear (or P on models with automatic transmission).

- [ ] Chock the wheel diagonally opposite the one being removed – a couple of large stones will do for this.
- [ ] If the ground is soft, use a flat piece of wood to spread the load under the jack.

Changing the wheel

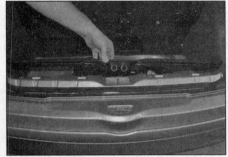

1 The spare wheel and tools are located in the luggage compartment, under the boot carpet. Push the sliding seat forward and lift up the carpet,

2 Unscrew the spare wheel retainer anti-clockwise, then lift out the spare wheel. The vehicle jack is stored next to the spare wheel, at the side of the wheel recess.

3 Prise off the wheel trim (where applicable) from the punctured wheel, using the end of the wheelbrace.

4 Use the wheelbrace to loosen each wheel nut by half a turn. On models with alloy wheels, one of the wheel nuts may be of the locking type – use the 'key' tool (a special socket usually provided in the glovebox) with the wheelbrace to undo this.

5 Place the spare wheel under the sill next to the jacking point as an emergency back up, should the vehicle slip off the jack. Locate the jack head below the jacking point nearest the wheel to be changed. The jacking points are an additional plate on the sill lower edge. Only use the jack on firm, level ground. Ensure that the slot in the jack head engages with the sill flange at the jacking point. Turn the jack handle clockwise until the wheel is raised clear of the ground.

7 Fit the spare wheel. Refit the wheel nuts, and tighten moderately with the wheelbrace. Lower the car to the ground, then finally tighten the wheel nuts in a diagonal sequence. Recover the punctured tyre and refit the wheel trim (where applicable). Ideally, the wheel nuts should be slackened and retightened to the specified torque at the earliest opportunity.

6 Remove the nuts and lift the punctured wheel clear. Place the wheel under the sill.

Finally...

- [ ] Remove the wheel chocks.
- [ ] Stow the jack and tools in the correct locations in the car.
- [ ] Check the tyre pressure on the wheel just fitted. If it is low, or if you don't have a pressure gauge with you, drive slowly to the nearest garage and inflate the tyre to the right pressure.
- [ ] The space-saver spare wheel is for temporary use only. Drive with extra care – limit yourself to a maximum of 50 mph, and to the shortest possible journeys, while it is fitted.
- [ ] Have the damaged tyre or wheel repaired as soon as possible.

Identifying leaks

Puddles on the garage floor or drive, or obvious wetness under the bonnet or underneath the car, suggest a leak that needs investigating. It can sometimes be difficult to decide where the leak is coming from, especially if the engine bay is very dirty already. Leaking oil or fluid can also be blown rearwards by the passage of air under the car, giving a false impression of where the problem lies.

 Warning: Most automotive oils and fluids are poisonous. Wash them off skin, and change out of contaminated clothing, without delay.

 The smell of a fluid leaking from the car may provide a clue to what's leaking. Some fluids are distinctively coloured. It may help to clean the car carefully and to park it over some clean paper overnight as an aid to locating the source of the leak. Remember that some leaks may only occur while the engine is running.

Sump oil

Engine oil may leak from the drain plug...

Oil from filter

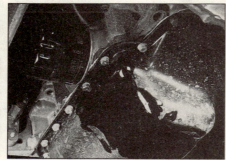

...or from the base of the oil filter.

Gearbox oil

Gearbox oil can leak from the seals at the inboard ends of the driveshafts.

Antifreeze

Leaking antifreeze often leaves a crystalline deposit like this.

Brake fluid

A leak occurring at a wheel is almost certainly brake fluid.

Towing

When all else fails, you may find yourself having to get a tow home – or of course you may be helping somebody else. Long-distance recovery should only be done by a garage or breakdown service. For shorter distances, DIY towing using another car is easy enough, but observe the following points:

☐ Use a proper tow-rope – they are not expensive. The vehicle being towed must display an ON TOW sign in its rear window.

☐ A front towing eye is located with the jack and wheelbrace in the luggage compartment (see *Wheel changing*). To fit the front towing eye, prise out the cover on the left-hand side of the front bumper, and remove it. Screw the towing eye in as far as it will go. Tighten the towing eye with the wheelbrace.

☐ The rear lashing eye (not designed for towing) is a conventional loop under the rear bumper.

☐ Always turn the ignition key to the 'On' position when the vehicle is being towed, so that the steering lock is released, and the direction indicator and brake lights work.

☐ Before being towed, release the handbrake and select neutral on the transmission. **Do not** attempt to tow models with automatic transmission.

☐ Note that greater-than-usual pedal pressure will be required to operate the brakes, since the vacuum servo unit is only operational with the engine running.

☐ The power steering will not operate without the engine running, so greater-than-usual steering effort will be required.

☐ The driver of the car being towed must keep the tow-rope taut at all times to avoid snatching.

☐ Make sure that both drivers know the route before setting off.

☐ Only drive at moderate speeds and keep the distance towed to a minimum. Drive smoothly and allow plenty of time for slowing down at junctions.

Introduction

There are some very simple checks which need only take a few minutes to carry out, but which could save you a lot of inconvenience and expense.

These *Weekly checks* require no great skill or special tools, and the small amount of time they take to perform could prove to be very well spent, for example:

☐ Keeping an eye on tyre condition and pressures, will not only help to stop them wearing out prematurely, but could also save your life.

☐ Many breakdowns are caused by electrical problems. Battery-related faults are particularly common, and a quick check on a regular basis will often prevent the majority of these.

☐ If your car develops a brake fluid leak, the first time you might know about it is when your brakes don't work properly. Checking the level regularly will give advance warning of this kind of problem.

☐ If the oil or coolant levels run low, the cost of repairing any engine damage will be far greater than fixing the leak, for example.

Underbonnet check points

A *Engine oil filler cap*

B *Engine oil level dipstick*

C *Brake and clutch fluid reservoir*

D *Washer fluid reservoir*

E *Coolant reservoir (expansion tank)*

F *Battery*

Engine oil level

Before you start

✔ Make sure that your car is on level ground.
✔ Check the oil level before the car is driven, or at least 5 minutes after the engine has been switched off.

HAYNES HiNT *If the oil is checked immediately after driving the vehicle, some of the oil will remain in the upper engine components, resulting in an inaccurate reading on the dipstick.*

The correct oil

Modern engines place great demands on their oil. It is very important that the correct oil for your car is used (see *Lubricants and fluids*).

Car care

● If you have to add oil frequently, you should check whether you have any oil leaks. Place some clean paper under the car overnight, and check for stains in the morning. If there are no leaks, then the engine may be burning oil.

● Always maintain the level between the upper and lower dipstick marks (see photo 3). If the level is too low, severe engine damage may occur. Oil seal failure may result if the engine is overfilled by adding too much oil.

1 The dipstick is located in a tube at the front of the engine on all engines (see *Underbonnet check points* for exact location). Withdraw the dipstick.

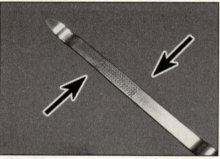
3 Note the oil level on the end of the dipstick, which should be within the 'hatched' area, between the upper (F) mark and the lower (L) mark. If the engine is very hot, the oil level may appear to be above the upper mark, owing to thermal expansion. Approximately 0.5 to 1.0 litre of oil will raise the level from the lower to the upper mark.

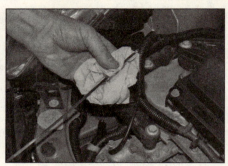
2 Using a clean rag or paper towel, wipe all the oil from the dipstick. Insert the clean dipstick into the tube as far as it will go, then withdraw it again.

4 Oil is added through the filler cap. Unscrew the filler cap, then top-up the level. A funnel may help to reduce spillage. Add the oil slowly, checking the level on the dipstick often. Don't overfill.

Coolant level

⚠ *Warning: Do not attempt to remove the expansion tank pressure cap when the engine is hot, as there is a very great risk of scalding. Do not leave open containers of coolant about, as it is poisonous.*

Car Care

● With a sealed-type cooling system, adding coolant should not be necessary on a regular basis. If frequent topping-up is required, it is likely there is a leak. Check the radiator, all hoses and joint faces for signs of staining or wetness, and rectify as necessary.

● It is important that antifreeze is used in the cooling system all year round, not just during the winter months. Don't top up with water alone, as the antifreeze will become diluted.

1 The expansion tank has F (full) and L (low) level markings. When cold, the level should be between the two marks. When the engine is hot, the level may rise slightly above the F mark.

2 If topping-up is necessary, wait until the engine is cold, then remove the cap on the expansion tank. Note that two different style expansion tanks are fitted.

3 Add a mixture of water and antifreeze to the expansion tank, until the coolant is up to the F mark. Use antifreeze of the same type (and colour) as that which is already in the system. Refit the cap securely.

Brake and clutch* fluid level

The brake fluid reservoir also supplies fluid to the clutch master cylinder.

Warning: Brake fluid can harm your eyes and damage painted surfaces, so use extreme caution when handling and pouring it. Do not use fluid which has been standing open for some time, as it absorbs moisture from the air, which can cause a dangerous loss of braking effectiveness.

Safety first!

● If the reservoir requires repeated topping-up, this is an indication of a fluid leak somewhere in the system, which should be investigated immediately.

● The fluid level in the reservoir will drop slightly as the brake pads wear down, but the fluid level must never be allowed to drop below the MIN mark.

● If a leak is suspected, the car should not be driven until the braking system has been checked. Never take any risks where brakes are concerned.

Before you start

✔ Make sure that the car is on level ground.
✔ Cleanliness is of great importance when dealing with the braking system, so take care to clean around the reservoir cap before topping-up. Use only clean brake fluid.

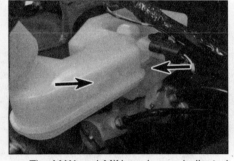

1 The MAX and MIN marks are indicated on the side of the reservoir, which is located right at the back of the engine compartment, on the driver's side. The fluid level must be kept between these two marks.

2 If topping-up is necessary, first wipe the area around the filler cap with a clean rag, then unscrew the cap. Take care not to lose the seal. When adding fluid, it's a good idea to inspect the reservoir. The fluid should be changed if it appears to be dark, or if dirt is visible.

3 Carefully add fluid, avoiding spilling it on surrounding paintwork. Use only the specified hydraulic fluid; mixing different types of fluid can cause damage to the system and/or a loss of braking effectiveness. After filling to the correct level, refit the cap securely. Wipe off any spilt fluid.

Washer fluid level

● Screenwash additives not only keep the windscreen clean during bad weather, they also prevent the washer system freezing in cold weather – which is when you are likely to need it most. Don't top-up using plain water, as the screenwash will become diluted, and will freeze in cold weather.

Warning: On no account use engine coolant antifreeze in the screen washer system – this may damage the paintwork.

1 The windscreen/tailgate washer fluid reservoir filler neck is located on the driver's side of the engine compartment, adjacent to the headlight. If topping-up is necessary, open the cap.

2 When topping-up the reservoir, a screenwash additive should be added in the quantities recommended on the bottle. Though there's no harm in filling the bottle right up, there is a FULL level mark provided.

Tyre condition and pressure

It is very important that tyres are in good condition, and at the correct pressure - having a tyre failure at any speed is highly dangerous. Tyre wear is influenced by driving style - harsh braking and acceleration, or fast cornering, will all produce more rapid tyre wear. As a general rule, the front tyres wear out faster than the rears. Interchanging the tyres from front to rear ("rotating" the tyres) may result in more even wear. However, if this is completely effective, you may have the expense of replacing all four tyres at once! Remove any nails or stones embedded in the tread before they penetrate the tyre to cause deflation. If removal of a nail does reveal that the tyre has been punctured, refit the nail so that its point of penetration is marked. Then immediately change the wheel, and have the tyre repaired by a tyre dealer.

Regularly check the tyres for damage in the form of cuts or bulges, especially in the sidewalls. Periodically remove the wheels, and clean any dirt or mud from the inside and outside surfaces. Examine the wheel rims for signs of rusting, corrosion or other damage. Light alloy wheels are easily damaged by "kerbing" whilst parking; steel wheels may also become dented or buckled. A new wheel is very often the only way to overcome severe damage.

New tyres should be balanced when they are fitted, but it may become necessary to re-balance them as they wear, or if the balance weights fitted to the wheel rim should fall off. Unbalanced tyres will wear more quickly, as will the steering and suspension components. Wheel imbalance is normally signified by vibration, particularly at a certain speed (typically around 50 mph). If this vibration is felt only through the steering, then it is likely that just the front wheels need balancing. If, however, the vibration is felt through the whole car, the rear wheels could be out of balance. Wheel balancing should be carried out by a tyre dealer or garage.

1 Tread Depth - visual check
The original tyres have tread wear safety bands (B), which will appear when the tread depth reaches approximately 1.6 mm. The band positions are indicated by a triangular mark on the tyre sidewall (A).

2 Tread Depth - manual check
Alternatively, tread wear can be monitored with a simple, inexpensive device known as a tread depth indicator gauge.

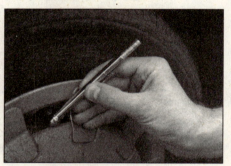

3 Tyre Pressure Check
Check the tyre pressures regularly with the tyres cold. Do not adjust the tyre pressures immediately after the vehicle has been used, or an inaccurate setting will result.

Tyre tread wear patterns

Shoulder Wear

Underinflation (wear on both sides)
Under-inflation will cause overheating of the tyre, because the tyre will flex too much, and the tread will not sit correctly on the road surface. This will cause a loss of grip and excessive wear, not to mention the danger of sudden tyre failure due to heat build-up.
Check and adjust pressures
Incorrect wheel camber (wear on one side)
Repair or renew suspension parts
Hard cornering
Reduce speed!

Centre Wear

Overinflation
Over-inflation will cause rapid wear of the centre part of the tyre tread, coupled with reduced grip, harsher ride, and the danger of shock damage occurring in the tyre casing.
Check and adjust pressures

If you sometimes have to inflate your car's tyres to the higher pressures specified for maximum load or sustained high speed, don't forget to reduce the pressures to normal afterwards.

Uneven Wear

Front tyres may wear unevenly as a result of wheel misalignment. Most tyre dealers and garages can check and adjust the wheel alignment (or "tracking") for a modest charge.
Incorrect camber or castor
Repair or renew suspension parts
Malfunctioning suspension
Repair or renew suspension parts
Unbalanced wheel
Balance tyres
Incorrect toe setting
Adjust front wheel alignment
Note: *The feathered edge of the tread which typifies toe wear is best checked by feel.*

Wiper blades

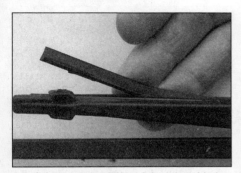
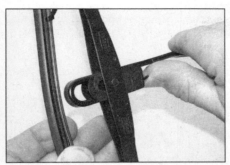
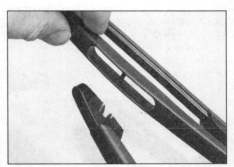

1 Check the condition of the wiper blades; if they are cracked or show any signs of deterioration, or if the glass swept area is smeared, renew them. For maximum clarity of vision, wiper blades should be renewed annually, as a matter of course.

2 To remove a windscreen wiper blade, pull the arm fully away from the screen until it locks. Swivel the blade through 90°, then depress the locking clip at the base of the mounting block, and slide the blade out of the hooked end of the arm.

3 Don't forget to check the tailgate wiper blade as well. This has a special fitting and a pattern wiper blade may not fit. A genuine one will have to be purchased, or the rubber can be renewed on its own using a universal rubber blade kit.

Battery

Caution: Before carrying out any work on the vehicle battery, read the precautions given in 'Safety first!' at the start of this manual.

✔ Make sure that the battery tray is in good condition, and that the clamp is tight. Corrosion on the tray, retaining clamp and the battery itself can be removed with a solution of water and baking soda. Thoroughly rinse all cleaned areas with water. Any metal parts damaged by corrosion should be covered with a zinc-based primer, then painted.

✔ Periodically (approximately every three months), check the charge condition of the battery as described in Chapter 5A.

✔ If the battery is flat, and you need to jump start your vehicle, see *Roadside Repairs*.

1 The battery is located on the passenger side of the engine compartment. The exterior of the battery should be inspected periodically for damage such as a cracked case or cover.

2 Check the tightness of the battery cable clamps to ensure good electrical connections. You should not be able to move them. Also check each cable for cracks and frayed conductors.

Battery corrosion can be kept to a minimum by applying a layer of petroleum jelly to the clamps and terminals after they are reconnected.

3 If corrosion (white, fluffy deposits) is evident, remove the cables from the battery terminals, clean them with a small wire brush, then refit them. Automotive stores sell a tool for cleaning the battery post . . .

4 . . . as well as the battery cable clamps.

Electrical systems

✔ Check all external lights and the horn. Refer to the appropriate Sections of Chapter 12 for details if any of the circuits are found to be inoperative.

✔ Visually check all accessible wiring connectors, harnesses and retaining clips for security, and for signs of chafing or damage.

 If you need to check your brake lights and indicators unaided, back up to a wall or garage door and operate the lights. The reflected light should show if they are working properly.

1 If a single indicator light, brake light or headlight has failed, it is likely that a bulb has blown and will need to be renewed. Refer to Chapter 12 for details. If both brake lights have failed, it is possible that the brake light switch operated by the brake pedal has failed. Refer to Chapter 9 for details.

2 If more than one indicator light or headlight has failed, it is likely that either a fuse has blown, or that there is a fault in the circuit (see Chapter 12). The main fuses are mounted behind a panel in the driver's lower storage compartment. Unclip the panel and release it from the facia.

3 To renew a blown fuse, remove it using the plastic tweezer tool provided (where applicable). Fit a new fuse of the same rating, available from car accessory shops. It is important that you find the reason that the fuse blew (see *Electrical fault finding* in Chapter 12).

Lubricants and fluids

Engine . . . . Engine oil, SAE 5W-30, to specification API SG or SH (ACEA A2)

Cooling system* . . . . Ethylene glycol-based antifreeze suitable for use in mixed-metal engines – Nissan L250 or equivalent

Manual transmission . . . . Gear oil, SAE 75W-80 or 75W-85 to specification API GL-4

Automatic transmission. . . . . Automatic transmission fluid (ATF) – Genuine Nissan ATF or equivalent (refer to Nissan dealer for correct grades of ATF if necessary)

Brake and clutch systems . . . . Hydraulic fluid to DOT 3 or DOT 4

Do not mix types of coolant with each other, nor top-up with any other type of coolant. Alternative types of coolant may only be used once the system has been drained and completely flushed, as described in Chapter 1.

Tyre pressures

Note: *Pressures given here are a guide only, and apply to original-equipment tyres – the recommended pressures may vary if any other make or type of tyre is fitted; check with the car handbook, or the tyre manufacturer or supplier for the latest recommendations. A tyre pressure label is fitted on the driver's door pillar.*

	Front	Rear
Normal load (up to 2 people)		
165/70 R 14 tyres.	2.2 bar (32 psi)	2.0 bar (29 psi)
Full load (more than 2 people)		
All tyre sizes	2.3 bar (33 psi)	2.8 bar (41 psi)
Space-saver spare tyre		
All load conditions	4.2 bar (61 psi)	4.2 bar (61 psi)

Chapter 1
Routine maintenance & servicing

Contents

Section number

Air filter element renewal 22
Automatic transmission fluid level check. 15
Automatic transmission fluid renewal. 20
Auxiliary drivebelts check and renewal 6
Brake fluid renewal 24
Charcoal canister check. 19
Clutch and brake pedal adjustment check 8
Coolant renewal and pressure cap check 25
Driveshaft gaiter check. 13
Engine oil and filter renewal 3
Exhaust system check 5
Front brake pad and disc wear check 11
General information 1

Section number

Handbrake check and adjustment. 7
Hinge and lock lubrication 10
Hose and fluid leak check 4
Manual transmission oil level check. 23
Pollen filter renewal 17
Rear brake shoe and drum wear check 18
Regular maintenance 2
Road test 16
Roadwheel nut tightness check 14
Seat belt check. 9
Spark plug renewal. 21
Steering and suspension check. 12

Degrees of difficulty

| **Easy,** suitable for novice with little experience | **Fairly easy,** suitable for beginner with some experience | **Fairly difficult,** suitable for competent DIY mechanic | **Difficult,** suitable for experienced DIY mechanic | **Very difficult,** suitable for expert DIY or professional |

Lubricants and fluids............................... Refer to *Weekly checks*

Capacities

Engine oil (including oil filter)
All models to VIN SJN***K12U2000000 .... 3.0 litres
All models from VIN SJN***K12U2000001 .... 3.4 litres

Cooling system (approximate)
All models... 4.9 litres

Manual transmission
All models... 2.6 litres

Automatic transmission
Total capacity .... 7.7 litres

Fuel tank
All models... 46.0 litres

Cooling system

Antifreeze mixture:
  50% antifreeze .... Protection down to -37°C
Note: *Refer to antifreeze manufacturer for latest recommendations.*

Auxiliary drivebelt

Drivebelt deflection*:

	Setting	Limit
Alternator:		
With air conditioning	7 to 8 mm	14 mm
Without air conditioning	10 to 11 mm	14 mm
Water pump	7 to 9 mm	12 mm

* Note: *In all cases, the drivebelt deflection is measured after applying a force of 10 kg (22 lb) as described in the text. All figures are quoted for a 'used' drivebelt – if a new belt has been fitted, the setting deflection should be decreased by 1.0 mm.*

Ignition system

Spark plugs:*
  Short reach (early models only) .... NGK BKR5E-11
  Long reach .... NGK LFR5AP-11 or Champion REC10PYC4
Electrode gap.. 1.1 mm
* Note: *The spark plugs fitted to later models have a longer threaded section into the engine (longer reach); check new plugs carefully, as the wrong ones can cause engine damage.*

Brakes

Friction material minimum thickness:
  Front brake pads .... 2.0 mm
  Rear brake shoes .... 2.0 mm

Tyre pressures

See end of *Weekly checks* on page 0•17

Torque wrench settings

	Nm	lbf ft
Automatic transmission fluid drain plug.....................	34	25
Idler pulley nut	28	21
Manual transmission drain plug	25	18
Roadwheel nuts	110	81
Seat belt mounting bolts	48	35
Spark plugs	25	18
Sump drain plug......................................	35	26

Note: *Nissan recommend that the service interval on models from VIN SJN***K12U2000001 (with the larger engine sump capacity) and all models from September 2007-on is increased to 12 000 miles or 12 months.*

The maintenance intervals in this manual are provided with the assumption that you, not the dealer, will be carrying out the work. These are the minimum maintenance intervals recommended by us for cars driven daily. If you wish to keep your car in peak condition at all times, you may wish to perform some of these procedures more often. We encourage frequent maintenance, because it enhances the efficiency, performance and resale value of your car.

When the vehicle is new, it should be serviced by a dealer service department (or other workshop recognised by the vehicle manufacturer as providing the same standard of service) in order to preserve the warranty.

The vehicle manufacturer may reject warranty claims if you are unable to prove that servicing has been carried out as and when specified, using only original equipment parts or parts certified to be of equivalent quality.

If the car is driven in dusty areas, used to tow a trailer, or driven frequently at slow speeds (idling in traffic) or on short journeys, more frequent maintenance intervals are recommended.

Every 250 miles or weekly
☐ Refer to Weekly checks

Every 4500 miles or 6 months, whichever comes first

☐ Renew the engine oil and filter (Section 3)

Note: *Nissan recommend that the engine oil and filter are changed every 9000 miles/12 months for early models or every 12 000 miles/ 12 months for later models with the increased sump capacity. However, oil and filter changes are good for the engine, and we recommend that the oil and filter are renewed more frequently, especially if the car is used mainly for short journeys.*

Every 9000 miles or 12 months, whichever comes first

☐ Check all components, pipes and hoses for fluid leaks (Section 4)
☐ Check the exhaust system (Section 5)
☐ Check the condition and tension of the auxiliary drivebelts (Section 6)
☐ Check and if necessary adjust the handbrake (Section 7)
☐ Check the clutch and brake pedal for levels and leaks (Section 8)
☐ Check the condition and operation of the seat belts (Section 9)
☐ Lubricate all hinges and locks (Section 10)
☐ Check the front brake pads and discs for wear (Section 11)
☐ Check the steering and suspension components for condition and security (Section 12)
☐ Check the condition of the driveshaft gaiters (Section 13)
☐ Check the roadwheel nuts are tightened to the specified torque (Section 14)
☐ Check the automatic transmission fluid level (Section 15)
☐ Carry out a road test (Section 16)

Every 18 000 miles or 2 years, whichever comes first

☐ Renew the pollen filter (Section 17)
☐ Check the rear brake shoes and drums for wear (Section 18)
☐ Check the charcoal canister (Section 19)
☐ Renew the automatic transmission fluid (Section 20)

Every 27 000 miles or 3 years, whichever comes first

☐ Renew the spark plugs (Section 21)
☐ Renew the air filter element (Section 22)
☐ Check the manual transmission oil level (Section 23)

Every 2 years, regardless of mileage
☐ Renew the brake fluid (Section 24)

Every 4 years, regardless of mileage
☐ Renew the coolant (Section 25)

Underbonnet view

1 Brake and clutch fluid reservoir
2 Battery negative cable
3 Oil filler cap
4 Air filter housing
5 Dipstick
6 Coolant expansion tank
7 Ignition coils
8 Air conditioning service ports
9 Engine management ECU
10 ABS modulator
11 Intelligent power distribution module (IPDM)
12 Fusible link and relay box
13 EVAP solenoid
14 Manifold absolute pressure sensor (MAP)
15 Camshaft sensor
16 Crankshaft sensor
17 Throttle body connector
18 Horn
19 Coolant temperature sensor
20 Oxygen sensor
21 Bonnet lock
22 SRS/airbag crash sensor

Front underbody view

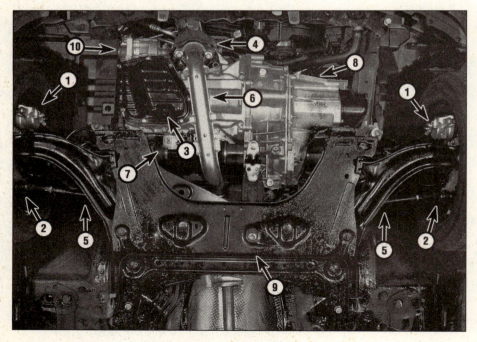

1 Brake caliper
2 Track rod end
3 Sump drain plug
4 Catalytic converter
5 Suspension track control arm
6 Exhaust front pipe
7 Oil filter
8 Gearbox filler plug
9 Front subframe
10 Air conditioning compressor

Underbody rear view

1 Shock absorbers
2 Exhaust rear silencer
3 EVAP canister
4 Rear brake flexible hoses
5 Fuel tank
6 Rear axle
7 Handbrake cables
8 Coil spring
9 Exhaust heat shield
10 Axle mounting

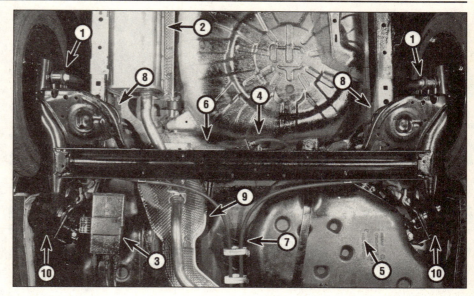

Maintenance procedures

1 General information

1 This Chapter is designed to help the home mechanic maintain his/her car for safety, economy, long life and peak performance.
2 The Chapter contains a master maintenance schedule, followed by Sections dealing specifically with each task in the schedule. Visual checks, adjustments, component renewal and other helpful items are included. Refer to the accompanying illustrations of the engine compartment and the underside of the car for the locations of the various components.
3 Servicing your car in accordance with the mileage/time maintenance schedule and the following Sections will provide a planned maintenance programme, which should result in a long and reliable service life. This is a comprehensive plan, so maintaining some items but not others at the specified service intervals, will not produce the same results.
4 As you service your car, you will discover that many of the procedures can – and should – be grouped together, because of the particular procedure being performed, or because of the proximity of two otherwise-unrelated components to one another. For example, if the car is raised for any reason, the exhaust can be inspected at the same time as the suspension and steering components.
5 The first step in this maintenance programme is to prepare yourself before the actual work begins. Read through all the Sections relevant to the work to be carried out, then make a list and gather all the parts and tools required. If a problem is encountered, seek advice from a parts specialist, or a dealer service department.
6 After all necessary maintenance work has been completed, the service interval display must be reset. Nissan technicians use a special dedicated instrument to do this, however on models equipped with a Trip Computer it is possible for the owner to reset the display as follows.
• *First, press the clock setting/oil change interval button for 3 seconds while the wrench symbol and distance to oil change are displayed. The symbol and distance display will start to flash and the current interval will be displayed. Each subsequent press of the button will increase the interval distance by 1000 km (500 miles) up to 63000 km (31500 miles) after which the display will return to zero. If zero is selected, the display will show 'Oil Good' or 'Oil Lo' and it will be necessary to repeat the previous steps in order to enter the distance setting menu.*

On models equipped with an on board computer, it is only possible to reset the interval to 9000 miles as follows:
• *Press the Menu button and select Maintenance, press OK then select Service and hold OK for approximately 20 seconds. The display will then show 'Set distance to service'. With SET NEXT highlighted select OK to reset the distance to 9000 miles (there are no other options). Press the Menu button to return to the normal screen.*

2 Regular maintenance

1 If, from the time the car is new, the routine maintenance schedule is followed closely, and frequent checks are made of fluid levels and high-wear items, as suggested throughout this manual, the engine will be kept in relatively good running condition, and the need for additional work will be minimised.
2 It is possible that there will be times when the engine is running poorly due to the lack of regular maintenance. This is even more likely if a used car, which has not received regular and frequent maintenance checks, is purchased. In such cases, additional work may need to be carried out, outside of the regular maintenance intervals.
3 If engine wear is suspected, a compression test (refer to Chapter 2A) will provide valuable information regarding the overall performance of the main internal components. Such a test can be used as a basis to decide on the extent of the work to be carried out. If, for example, a compression test indicates serious internal engine wear, conventional maintenance as described in this Chapter will not greatly improve the performance of the engine, and may prove a waste of time and money, unless extensive overhaul work is carried out first.
4 The following series of operations are those most often required to improve the performance of a generally poor-running engine:

Primary operations
a) Clean, inspect and test the battery (refer to Weekly checks).
b) Check all the engine-related fluids (refer to Weekly checks).
c) Check the condition and tension of the auxiliary drivebelt (Section 6).
d) Renew the spark plugs (Section 21).
e) Check the condition of the air filter, and renew if necessary (Section 22).
f) Check the condition of all hoses, and check for fluid leaks (Section 4).

5 If the above operations do not prove fully effective, carry out the following secondary operations:

Secondary operations
All items listed under *Primary operations*, plus the following:
a) Check the charging system (Chapter 5A).
b) Check the ignition system (Chapter 5B).
c) Check the fuel system (Chapter 4A).

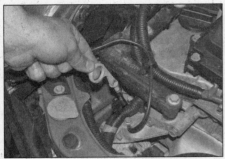
3.4a Remove the dipstick . . .

3.4b . . . and filler cap

3.5 Slacken the drain plug

Every 4500 miles or 6 months

3 Engine oil and filter renewal

1 Frequent oil and filter changes are the most important preventative maintenance procedures which can be undertaken by the home mechanic. As engine oil ages, it becomes diluted and contaminated, which leads to premature engine wear.

2 Before starting this procedure, gather together all the necessary tools and materials. Also make sure that you have plenty of clean rags and newspapers handy, to mop-up any spills. Ideally, the engine oil should be warm, as it will drain more easily, and more built-up sludge will be removed with it. Take care not to touch the exhaust or any other hot parts of the engine when working under the car. To avoid any possibility of scalding, and to protect yourself from possible skin irritants and other harmful contaminants in used engine oils, it is advisable to wear gloves when carrying out this work.

3 Firmly apply the handbrake, then jack up the front of the car and support it on axle stands (see *Jacking and vehicle support*).

4 Remove the oil filler cap, and pull out the dipstick **(see illustrations)**.

5 Using a spanner, or preferably a socket and bar, slacken the drain plug about half a turn **(see illustrations)**. Position the draining container under the drain plug, then remove the plug completely.

HAYNES HiNT *Keep the drain plug pressed into the sump while unscrewing it by hand last couple of turns. As the plug releases, move it away sharply so the stream of oil issuing from the sump runs into the container, not up your sleeve.*

6 Allow some time for the oil to drain, noting that it may be necessary to reposition the container as the oil flow slows to a trickle.

7 After all the oil has drained, wipe the drain plug with a clean rag. Remove the sealing washer and fit a new one **(see illustrations)**. Clean the area around the drain plug opening, then refit the plug and tighten it securely to the specified torque.

8 Move the container into position under the oil filter, which is located on the rear of the cylinder block **(see illustration)**. Where applicable, take care not to burn yourself on the exhaust if the engine is still hot.

9 Use an oil filter removal tool to slacken the filter initially, then unscrew it by hand the rest of the way **(see illustration)**. Empty the oil from the old filter into the container.

10 Use a clean rag to remove all oil, dirt and sludge from the filter sealing area on the engine.

11 Apply a light coating of clean engine oil to the sealing ring on the new filter, then screw the filter into position on the engine **(see illustration)**. Tighten the filter firmly by hand only – **do not** use any tools.

3.7 A fit a new washer . . .

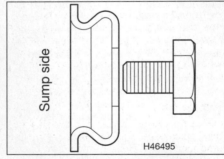
Sump side

H46495

3.7b . . . noting the correct orientation

3.7c Torque the bolt correctly

3.8 Oil filter location

3.9 Use a chain or strap wrench to slacken the filter

12 Remove the old oil and all tools from under the car, then lower the car to the ground.

13 Fill the engine through the filler hole, using the correct grade and type of oil (refer to *Weekly checks* for oil specifications) **(see illustration)**. Pour in half the specified quantity of oil first, then wait a few minutes for the oil to drain into the sump. Continue to add oil, a small quantity at a time, until the level is up to the lower mark on the dipstick. Adding approximately a further 0.5 to 1.0 litre will bring the level up to the upper mark on the dipstick.

14 Start the engine and run it for a few minutes, while checking for leaks around the oil filter seal and the sump drain plug. Note that there may be a delay of a few seconds before the oil pressure warning light goes out when the engine is first started, as the oil circulates through the new oil filter and

3.11 Lubricate the sealing ring and threads

3.13 Slowly refill with oil

the engine oil galleries before the pressure builds-up.

15 Stop the engine, and wait a few minutes for the oil to settle in the sump once more. With the new oil circulated and

the filter now completely full, recheck the level on the dipstick, and add more oil as necessary.

16 Dispose of the used engine oil safely, with reference to *General repair procedures*.

Every 9000 miles or 12 months

4 Hose and fluid leak check

Coolant

⚠️ **Warning: Refer to the safety information given in Safety first! and Chapter 3 before disturbing any of the cooling system components.**

1 Carefully check the radiator and heater coolant hoses along their entire length. Renew any hose which is cracked, swollen or which shows signs of deterioration. Cracks will show up better if the hose is squeezed. Pay close attention to the clips that secure the hoses to the cooling system components. Hose clips that have been overtightened can pinch and puncture hoses, resulting in cooling system leaks.

2 Inspect all the cooling system components (hoses, joint faces, etc) for leaks. Where any problems of this nature are found on system components, renew the component or gasket with reference to Chapter 3.

3 A leak from the cooling system will usually show up as white or antifreeze-coloured deposits, on the area surrounding the leak **(see Haynes Hint)**.

Fuel

⚠️ **Warning: Refer to the safety information given in Safety first! and Chapter 4A before disturbing any of the fuel system components.**

4 Examine each fuel hose/pipe along its length for splits or cracks.

5 Check for signs of leakage, which could be anything from a damp hose to an area of bodywork adjacent to the hose which seems especially clean (from being 'washed' by leaking fuel).

6 To identify fuel leaks between the fuel tank and the engine bay, the car should raised and securely supported on axle stands. Inspect the fuel tank and filler neck for punctures, cracks and other damage. The connection between the filler neck and tank is especially critical. Sometimes a rubber filler neck or connecting hose will leak due to loose retaining clamps or deteriorated rubber.

7 Carefully check all rubber hoses and metal fuel lines leading away from the fuel tank. Check for loose connections, deteriorated hoses, kinked lines, and other damage. Pay particular attention to the vent pipes and hoses, which often loop up around the filler neck and can become blocked or kinked, making tank filling difficult. Follow the fuel supply line to the front of the car, carefully inspecting it all the way for signs of damage or corrosion. Renew damaged sections as necessary.

Engine oil

8 Inspect the area around the camshaft cover, timing chain cover, cylinder head, oil filter and sump joint faces. Bear in mind that, over a period of time, some very slight seepage from these areas is to be expected – what you are really looking for is any indication of a serious leak caused by gasket failure.

9 Engine oil seeping from the base of the timing chain cover or the transmission bellhousing may be an indication of crankshaft or input shaft oil seal failure. Should a leak be found, renew the failed gasket or oil seal by referring to the appropriate Chapters in this manual.

Air conditioning refrigerant

⚠️ **Warning: Refer to the safety information given in Safety first! and Chapter 3, regarding the dangers of disturbing any of the air conditioning system components.**

10 The air conditioning system is filled with a liquid refrigerant, which is retained under high pressure. If the air conditioning system is opened and depressurised without the aid of specialised equipment, the refrigerant will immediately turn into gas and escape into the atmosphere.

11 If the liquid comes into contact with your skin, it can cause severe frostbite. In addition, the refrigerant contains substances which are environmentally damaging; for this reason, it should not be allowed to escape into the atmosphere. It is a criminal offence to knowingly discharge refrigerant to the atmosphere.

12 Any suspected air conditioning system leaks should be immediately referred to a Nissan dealer or air conditioning specialist. Leakage will be shown up as a steady drop in the level of refrigerant in the system.

13 Note that water may drip from the condenser drain pipe, underneath the car, immediately after the air conditioning system has been in use. This is normal, and should not be a cause for concern.

HAYNES HINT

A leak in the cooling system will usually show up as white- or antifreeze-coloured deposits on the area adjoining the leak.

4.16a Check the flexible brake hoses carefully at the front . . .

4.16b . . . and the rear

14 No service intervals are specified for the air conditioning system, however for maximum efficiency we would recommend the system is serviced every two years by a specialist. The specialist will recover the refrigerant and oil from the system and then vacuum the system to draw all the moisture out. If the applied vacuum holds – showing there are no leaks – then the correct amount of clean refrigerant and fresh oil will be draw into the system.

Brake (and clutch) fluid

 Warning: Refer to the safety information given in Safety first! and Chapter 9, regarding the dangers of handling brake fluid.

15 With reference to Chapter 9, examine the area surrounding the brake pipe unions at the master cylinder for signs of leakage. Check the area around the base of fluid reservoir, for signs of leakage caused by seal failure. Also examine the brake pipe unions at the ABS hydraulic unit, where applicable.

16 Inspect the braking system rubber hoses fitted to each front caliper, and the two hoses at the rear **(see illustrations)**. Look for perished, swollen or hardened rubber, and any signs of cracking, especially at the metal end fittings. If there's any doubt as to the condition of any hose, renew it as described in Chapter 9.

17 If fluid loss is evident, but the leak cannot be pinpointed in the engine bay, the brake calipers and underbody brake lines and should be carefully checked with the car raised and supported on axle stands. Leakage of fluid from the braking system is serious fault that must be rectified immediately.

5.2 Check the mountings

18 Refer to Chapter 6 and check for leakage around the hydraulic fluid line connections to the clutch master cylinder at the bulkhead, and to the clutch slave cylinder on the transmission.

19 Brake/clutch hydraulic fluid is a toxic substance with a watery consistency. New fluid is almost colourless, but it becomes darker with age and use.

Unidentified fluid leaks

20 If there are signs that a fluid of some description is leaking from the car, but you cannot identify the type of fluid or its exact origin, park the car overnight and slide a large piece of card underneath it. Providing that the card is positioned in roughly in the right location, even the smallest leak will show up on the card. Not only will this help you to pinpoint the exact location of the leak, it should be easier to identify the fluid from its colour. Bear in mind, though, that the leak may only be occurring when the engine is running!

Vacuum hoses

21 Although the braking system is hydraulically-operated, the brake servo unit amplifies the effort you apply at the brake pedal, by making use of the vacuum available in the inlet manifold (see Chapter 9). Vacuum is ported to the servo by means of a large-bore hose. Any leaks that develop in this hose will reduce the effectiveness of the braking system, and may affect engine running.

22 In addition, several of the underbonnet components, particularly the emission control components, are driven by vacuum via narrow-bore hoses. A leak in a vacuum hose means that air is being drawn into the hose (rather than escaping from it) and this makes leakage very difficult to detect.

23 However, if an initial examination of the hoses shows perishing and cracks (especially at the hose ends), or any signs that the hose has become hardened, renewal of that section of hose is advisable.

24 One method for detecting leaks is to use an old length of vacuum hose as a kind of stethoscope – hold one end close to (but not in) your ear and use the other end to probe the area around the suspected leak. When the end of the hose is directly over a vacuum leak, a hissing sound will be heard clearly through the

hose. Care must be taken to avoid contacting hot or moving components when testing in this manner, as the engine must be running. Renew any vacuum hoses that are found to be defective.

5 Exhaust system check

1 With the engine cold (at least an hour after the car has been driven), check the complete exhaust system from the engine to the end of the tailpipe. The exhaust system is most easily checked with the car raised on a hoist, or suitably supported on axle stands, so that the exhaust components are readily visible and accessible.

2 Check the exhaust pipes and connections for evidence of leaks, severe corrosion and damage. Make sure that all brackets and mountings are in good condition, and that all relevant nuts and bolts are tight **(see illustration)**.

3 Leakage at any of the joints or in other parts of the system will usually show up as a black sooty stain in the vicinity of the leak. To confirm the presence of a leak, with the engine running, briefly block the exhaust tailpipe with a large pad of rag – take care to avoid burning from the hot pipe or hot gases. If the system is sound, there should be a noticeable build-up of pressure – if not, the increased noise should make it possible to pinpoint the source of the leak.

4 Rattles and other noises can often be traced to the exhaust system, especially the brackets and mountings. Try to move the pipes and silencers. If the components are able to come into contact with the body or suspension parts, secure the system with new mountings. Otherwise separate the joints (if possible) and twist the pipes as necessary to provide additional clearance.

6 Auxiliary drivebelts check and renewal

General

1 Two drivebelts are fitted. One drives the water pump and the other the alternator. Adjustment is by way of an adjustable idler pulley on each belt.

Checking

2 Due to their function and material makeup, drivebelts are prone to failure after a long period of time, and should therefore be inspected regularly.

3 Remove the right-hand front wheel and for better access. Also remove the right-hand front grille and indicator lamp for a clearer view.

4 With the engine stopped, inspect the full length of the drivebelts for cracks and separation of the belt plies. It will be necessary

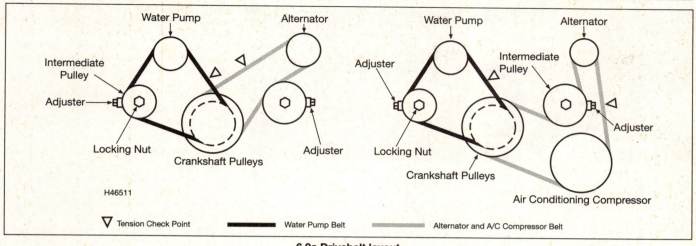

6.9a Drivebelt layout

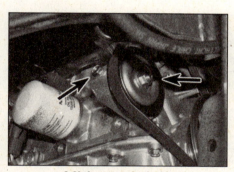

6.9b Loosen the bolts

6.10a Slacken the idler pulley bolt . . .

6.10b . . . and the adjustment bolt

to turn the engine (using a spanner or socket and bar on the crankshaft pulley bolt) in order to move the belts from the pulleys so that the belts can be inspected thoroughly. Twist the belt between the pulleys so that both sides can be viewed. Also check for fraying, and glazing which gives the belt a shiny appearance. Check the pulleys for nicks, cracks, distortion and corrosion.

5 Small cracks in the belt ribs are not usually serious, but look closely to see whether the crack has extended into the belt plies. If the belt is in any way suspect, or is known to have seen long service, renew it as described below.

6 Check the drivebelt tension by pressing on the belt at a point midway on the longest run between two pulleys. Compare the deflection noted with the figures quoted in the Specifications at the start of this Chapter. If the drivebelt appears excessively taut or slack, adjust the belt tension as described below.

7 If the belt appears not to be too slack, but has actually been slipping in service, check the belt for any sign of external contamination (eg, by oil or water). If found, cure the source of the leak before fitting a new belt as described below.

Removal

8 Jack up the right-hand front wheel, and

support the car using an axle stand (see *Jacking and vehicle support*). Remove the right hand wing liner and the quarter grille complete with the indicator lamp assembly (see Chapter 11).

9 Note the routing of the belts. Working at the rear of the engine, slacken the water pump idler pulley centre nut and undo the adjusting bolt. Push the pulley toward the engine and remove the belt (**see illustrations**).

10 Working through the front grille aperture and from below, slacken the alternator idler pulley centre nut and then slacken the side adjusting bolt (**see illustrations**). Push the idler pulley toward the engine and remove the belt.

Refitting

11 Fitting the belts is a direct reversal of removal.

12 If necessary, loosen the adjuster bolts even more to allow new (unstretched) belts to fit, and then install the belts onto the pulleys, again making sure the belts seat in the grooves.

13 Tighten the adjuster bolts to take up the slack in the belts, but do not try to set the tension at this stage.

14 Using a spanner or socket on the crankshaft pulley bolt, turn the engine through a few turns in the normal direction of travel (clockwise) to settle the belts and ensure that they are running properly in all the pulley grooves.

Tensioning

15 If not already done, loosen the two idler pulley centre nuts.

16 Adjust the belt tension by turning the adjuster bolt in the appropriate direction in small steps.

17 Check the drivebelt tension by attaching a spring balance to the belt at a point midway on the longest run between two pulleys (**see illustration**). Compare the deflection noted with the figures quoted in the specifications at the start of this Chapter. In practice it is difficult to perform this procedure due to the limited amount of space available, so as an alternative exert thumb pressure on the belt

6.17 The belt tension should be checked using this method on the longest belt run

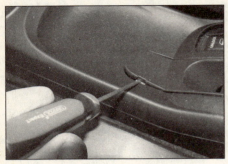

7.3a Prise the cover free . . .

7.3b . . . and remove it

and assess the deflection. Err on the side of caution. A slightly slack belt can be tightened, an overtight belt may destroy the alternator or water pump bearings.

18 To ensure accuracy, each time the belt tension is adjusted, using a spanner or socket on the crankshaft pulley bolt; turn the engine through a few turns in the normal direction of travel (clockwise) to settle the belt.

19 Repeat the procedure until the belt tension is satisfactory. On completion, tighten the idler centre nuts to the specified torque. Check that there is a gap of at least 1.0 mm between the tension adjuster bolt and the pulley. If not, obtain and fit modified pulley 11944 AX015. Lower the car to the ground, then run the engine to check for signs of slipping (noises from the belt).

20 If a new belt has been fitted, do not overtension it to allow for the belt stretching – instead, recheck the tension after (say) a month or 1000 miles. It is quite normal for a new belt to require retensioning after its initial 'running-in' period.

7 Handbrake check and adjustment

Checking

1 The handbrake should be fully applied (and capable of holding the car on a slope) after eleven to twelve clicks of the ratchet. The operating cables will stretch over time, and adjustment may be needed. However do not assume that excessive travel of the handbrake is caused by cable stretch. One of the anchor points may have failed, or more likely there is a fault with the brake shoe self-adjusting mechanism. Always check

7.4a Locate the adjusting nut . . .

the rear brakes first as described in Chapter 9 before adjusting the handbrake cable.

2 Aside from providing equal braking effort to both rear wheels, for the purposes of the MoT inspection, the handbrake lever must be securely mounted, and the ratchet mechanism should release only by means of the lever's button – if the ratchet releases (for example) when the lever is knocked sideways, the lever assembly should be removed for checking as described in Chapter 9.

Adjustment

3 Remove the trim piece below the front of the lever **(see illustrations)**.

4 Locate and then loosen the handbrake nut, so that the cable is slack **(see illustration)**.

5 Depress the footbrake firmly two to three times.

6 Jack up the rear of the car, and support it on axle stands (see *Jacking and vehicle support*).

7 With the handbrake released, turn the rear wheels, and check for signs that the handbrake may be dragging.

8 Apply the handbrake lever four or five clicks, then insert a socket and tighten the adjustment nut until the rear brake shoes are starting to drag. Release the handbrake and press the footbrake several times to centralise and settle the rear shoes. Check that the rear brakes do not drag with the handbrake released.

9 Now apply the handbrake lever eleven to twelve clicks. Wearing gloves, attempt to turn the wheel by holding the tyre and trying to rotate it. If the adjustment is right it will be impossible to turn the wheel by hand. Adjust the nut as required to achieve this position. **Note:** *Do not attempt to adjust the handbrake lever to less than eleven to twelve clicks fully-applied, as there have been*

7.4b . . . and fit a socket

instances where this has resulted in one or both leading rear brake shoes wearing excessively compared to their trailing shoes.

10 Lower the car to the ground, and check the operation of the handbrake several times before returning the car to normal service.

8 Clutch and brake pedal adjustment check

Clutch pedal

1 The Micra is equipped with a hydraulic clutch, so for the most part, wear in the clutch friction disc is automatically compensated for. If the clutch is working satisfactorily, further checking is not strictly necessary.

2 Poor clutch operation may indicate the need for bleeding the hydraulic system as described in Chapter 6. Otherwise, the pedal travel and stroke may be checked and adjusted as described in Chapter 6, Section 6.

Brake pedal

3 As with all modern cars, the braking system on the Micra is self-adjusting. Provided the brake pedal feels satisfactory (and the brakes work effectively), the chances are that the pedal does not need adjusting.

4 Excessive brake pedal travel may indicate that the brakes need bleeding as described in Chapter 9. Otherwise, if the pedal seems set too low, the free play is excessive, or if the history of the car is unknown, the brake pedal can be checked and adjusted as described in Chapter 9, Section 9.

9 Seat belt check

1 Check the seat belts for satisfactory operation and condition. Pull sharply on the belt to check that the locking mechanism engages correctly. Inspect the webbing for fraying and cuts. Check that they retract smoothly and without binding into their reels.

2 Check that the seat belt mounting bolts are tight, and if necessary tighten them to the specified torque wrench setting.

10 Hinge and lock lubrication

1 Work around the car and lubricate the hinges of the bonnet, doors and tailgate with light oil.

2 Lightly lubricate the bonnet release mechanism with a smear of grease.

3 Check carefully the security and operation of all hinges, latches and locks, adjusting them where required. Check the operation of the central locking system, where applicable.

4 Check the condition and operation of the tailgate struts, renewing them if either is leaking or no longer able to support the tailgate securely when raised.

11 Front brake pad and disc wear check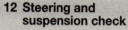

1 Apply the handbrake, then jack up the front of the car and support it securely on axle stands (see *Jacking and vehicle support*). Remove the front roadwheels.

2 The brake pad thickness, and the condition of the disc, can be assessed roughly with just the wheels removed **(see illustration)**. For a comprehensive check, the brake pads should be removed and cleaned. The operation of the caliper can then also be checked, and the condition of the brake disc itself can be fully examined on both sides. Refer to Chapter 9 for further information.

3 On completion, refit the roadwheels and lower the car to the ground.

12 Steering and suspension check

Front suspension and steering

1 Raise the front of the car, and securely support it on axle stands (see *Jacking and vehicle support*).

2 Visually inspect the balljoint dust covers and the steering rack-and-pinion gaiters for splits, chafing or deterioration. Any wear of these components will cause loss of lubricant, together with dirt and water entry, resulting in rapid deterioration of the balljoints or steering gear.

3 Grasp the roadwheel at the 12 o'clock and 6 o'clock positions, and try to rock it. Very slight free play may be felt, but if the movement is appreciable, further investigation is necessary to determine the source. Continue rocking the wheel while an assistant depresses the footbrake. If the movement is now eliminated or significantly reduced, it is likely that the hub bearings are at fault. If the free play is still evident with the footbrake depressed, then there is wear in the suspension joints or mountings.

4 Now grasp the wheel at the 9 o'clock and 3 o'clock positions, and try to rock it as before. Any movement felt now may again be caused by wear in the hub bearings or the steering track rod balljoints. If the outer balljoint is worn, the visual movement will be obvious. If the inner joint is suspect, it can be felt by placing a hand over the rack-and-pinion rubber gaiter and gripping the track rod. If the wheel is now rocked, movement will be felt at the inner joint if wear has taken place.

5 Using a large screwdriver or flat bar, check for wear in the suspension mounting bushes by levering between the relevant suspension component and its attachment point. Some movement is to be expected, as the mountings are made of rubber, but excessive wear

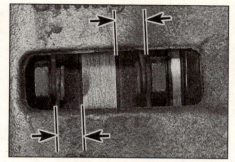

11.2 Check the thickness of the brake pads through the caliper window

should be obvious. Also check the condition of any visible rubber bushes, looking for splits, cracks or contamination of the rubber.

6 With the car standing on its wheels, have an assistant turn the steering wheel back-and-forth, about an eighth of a turn each way. There should be very little, if any, lost movement between the steering wheel and roadwheels. If this is not the case, closely observe the joints and mountings previously described. In addition, check the steering column universal joints for wear, and also check the rack-and-pinion steering gear itself.

Rear suspension

7 Chock the front wheels, then jack up the rear of the car and support securely on axle stands (see *Jacking and vehicle support*).

8 Working as described previously for the front suspension, check the rear hub bearings, the suspension bushes and the shock absorber mountings for wear.

Shock absorber

9 Check for any signs of fluid leakage around the shock absorber body, or from the rubber gaiter around the piston rod. Should any fluid be noticed, the shock absorber is defective internally, and should be renewed. **Note:** *Shock absorbers should always be renewed in pairs on the same axle.*

10 The efficiency of the shock absorber may be checked by bouncing the car at each corner. Generally speaking, the body will return to its normal position and stop after being depressed. If it rises and returns on a rebound, the shock absorber is probably

15.4 Release the dipstick

suspect. Also examine the shock absorber upper and lower mountings for any signs of wear.

13 Driveshaft gaiter check

1 With the car raised and securely supported on stands, turn the steering onto full lock, then slowly rotate the roadwheel. Inspect the condition of the outer constant velocity (CV) joint rubber gaiters while squeezing the gaiters to open out the folds. Check for signs of cracking, splits or deterioration of the rubber which may allow the grease to escape and lead to water and grit entry into the joint. Also check the security and condition of the retaining clips. Repeat these checks on the inner CV joints. If any damage or deterioration is found, the gaiters should be renewed as described in Chapter 8.

2 At the same time, check the general condition of the CV joints themselves by first holding the driveshaft and attempting to rotate the wheel. Repeat this check by holding the inner joint and attempting to rotate the driveshaft. Any appreciable movement indicates wear in the joints, wear in the driveshaft splines, or a loose driveshaft retaining nut.

14 Roadwheel nut tightness check

1 Remove the wheel trims or alloy wheel centre covers, and slacken the roadwheel nuts slightly.

2 Tighten the nuts to the specified torque, using a torque wrench.

15 Automatic transmission fluid level check

1 The level of the automatic transmission fluid should be carefully maintained. Low fluid level can lead to slipping or loss of drive, while overfilling can cause foaming, loss of fluid and transmission damage.

2 The transmission fluid level should be checked when the fluid is hot around 50 to 80°C. Allow the engine to warm up, and then drive for at least five minutes.

3 Park the car on level ground, apply the handbrake, and start the engine. With the engine idling and the brake pedal depressed, move the selector lever through all gear positions, holding the lever in each gear for about 3 seconds before moving to the next. On completion, return the lever to the P position.

4 Wait two minutes then, with the engine still idling, release the clip and remove the dipstick from its tube, which is located at the front of the transmission **(see illustration)**. Note the condition and colour of the fluid on the dipstick.

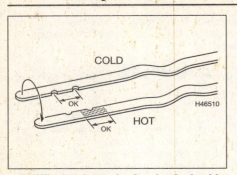

15.6 The level can also be checked cold

5 Wipe the fluid from the dipstick with a clean rag, and re-insert it into the filler tube until the cap seats.
6 Pull the dipstick out again, and note the fluid level. The level should be between the lower and upper marks, on the upper section of the dipstick (marked HOT) **(see illustration)**.
7 If the level is on the lower mark, stop the engine, and add the specified automatic transmission fluid through the dipstick tube, using a clean funnel if necessary. Cleanliness is of great importance; it is vitally important not to introduce dirt into the transmission when topping-up.
8 Add the fluid a little at a time, and keep checking the level as previously described until it is correct. The difference between the lower and upper marks on the dipstick is less than 0.5 litres. The transmission must not be overfilled – this will result in increased operating temperatures and fluid leaks. If overfilling occurs, the excess should be drained off (refer to Section 20).
9 If the car has not been driven and the engine and transmission are cold, carry out the procedures in paragraphs 3 to 6, but use the lower section of the dipstick marked COLD (or COOL).
10 The need for regular topping-up of the transmission fluid indicates a leak, which should be found and rectified without delay.
11 The condition of the fluid should also be checked along with the level. If the fluid at the end of the dipstick is black or a dark reddish-brown colour, or if it has a burned smell, the fluid should be changed. If you are in doubt about the condition of the fluid, purchase some new fluid, and compare the two for colour and smell. Fluid renewal is described in Section 20.

16 Road test

Instruments and electrical equipment

1 Check the operation of all instruments and electrical equipment.
2 Make sure that all instruments read correctly, and switch on all electrical equipment in turn, to check that it functions properly.

Steering and suspension

3 Check for any abnormalities in the steering, suspension, handling or road 'feel'.
4 Drive the car, and check that there are no unusual vibrations or noises.
5 Check that the steering feels positive, with no excessive 'sloppiness', or roughness, and check for any suspension noises when cornering and driving over bumps.

Drivetrain

6 Check the performance of the engine, clutch, transmission and driveshafts.
7 Listen for any unusual noises from the engine, clutch and transmission.
8 Make sure that the engine runs smoothly when idling, and that there is no hesitation when accelerating.
9 Check that, where applicable, the clutch action is smooth and progressive, that the drive is taken up smoothly, and that the pedal travel is not excessive. Also listen for any noises when the clutch pedal is depressed.
10 Check that all gears can be engaged smoothly without noise, and that the gear lever action is smooth and not abnormally vague or 'notchy'.
11 Listen for a metallic clicking sound from the front of the car, as the car is driven slowly in a circle with the steering on full-lock. Carry out this check in both directions. If a clicking noise is heard, this indicates wear in a driveshaft joint (see Chapter 8).

Braking system

12 Make sure that the car does not pull to one side when braking, and that the wheels do not lock when braking hard.
13 Check that there is no vibration through the steering when braking.
14 Check that the handbrake operates correctly, without excessive movement of the lever, and that it holds the car stationary on a slope.
15 Test the operation of the brake servo unit as follows. Depress the footbrake four or five times to exhaust the vacuum, then start the engine. As the engine starts, there should be a noticeable 'give' in the brake pedal as vacuum builds-up. Allow the engine to run for at least two minutes, and then switch it off. If the brake pedal is now depressed again, it should be possible to detect a hiss from the servo as the pedal is depressed. After about four or five applications, no further hissing should be heard, and the pedal should feel considerably harder.

Exhaust system

16 Listen carefully for any unusual noises from the system, which might indicate that it has started blowing, or that the mountings may be deteriorated, allowing the system to hit the underside of the car.
17 If any noises are detected, inspect the system with the car raised and supported on axle stands (see *Jacking and vehicle support*). Leaks are often accompanied by sooty stains, and are most common at the joints, and at welded sections, where pipes enter silencer boxes. Check the condition of the rubber mountings – if they are cracked or perished, fit new ones.

Every 18 000 miles or 2 years

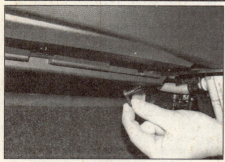

17.1a Remove the pins holding the door . . .

17.1b . . . and then unscrew and remove the sliding tray

17 Pollen filter renewal

1 Remove the glovebox and housing **(see illustrations)**.
2 Pull and compress the filter to remove it. It may seem reluctant to release because of the step in the filter **(see illustrations)**.
3 Check the condition of the element – if it is excessively dirty or otherwise contaminated, airflow into the car will be seriously reduced, and a new element should be fitted.

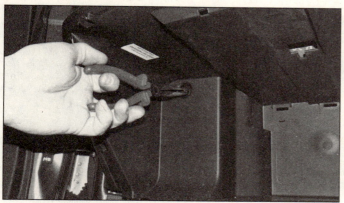

17.1c Remove the screws and release the cable clip

17.1d Remove the glovebox

4 Fit the new element (or refit the old one, as applicable), observing any markings indicating its fitted direction.

5 Refit the glovebox to complete.

18 Rear brake shoe and drum wear check

1 Remove the rear brake drums, and check the brake shoes for signs of wear or contamination. At the same time, also inspect the wheel cylinders for signs of leakage, and the brake drum for signs of wear. Refer to the relevant Sections of Chapter 9 for further information.

19 Charcoal canister check

1 The charcoal canister is mounted next to the fuel tank and collects vapours from the fuel tank for burning in the engine (rather than have them escape into the atmosphere) **(see illustration)**. The canister and its pipework should be periodically checked for damage, especially if any fuel smells have been noted. Also careful check the seal and security of the fuel filler cap.

17.2a Grasp the lower corner and . . .

20 Automatic transmission fluid renewal

1 Nissan do not specify a renewal interval for the transmission fluid. However a change of the fluid every two years will be of benefit.

2 Drive the car for a minimum of twenty minutes to warm the transmission oil

3 Raise and securely support the front of the car (see *Jacking and vehicle support*).

Caution: The transmission fluid may be very hot – protect your hands to avoid scalding.

4 Remove the drain plug at the rear of the fluid pan on the base of the transmission, and allow the contents of the transmission to drain into a suitable container **(see illustration)**. Refit the drain plug, using a new washer, and tighten it to the specified torque.

17.2b . . . then remove the filter

5 Measure the quantity of fluid recovered. This is the amount required to refill the system. Note that this will be not be the quantity detailed in the specifications. A lot of the fluid will remain trapped in the torque converter and oil galleries in the gearbox.

6 Remove the transmission dipstick. Slowly add the measured quantity of fresh automatic transmission fluid of the specified type, via the transmission dipstick tube **(see illustration)**. Use a clean funnel if necessary – it is vitally important that no foreign matter enters the transmission. Once the specified quantity of fluid has been added, allow a few minutes for the fluid level to stabilise.

7 Follow the checking procedure as described in Section 15.

8 Dispose of the old fluid safely (see *General repair procedures*).

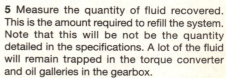

19.1 The charcoal canister location

20.4 Location of the drain plug

20.6 Slowly refill the transmission

21.5 Remove each plug in turn

21.10a Use a feeler gauge to check the gap . . .

21.10b . . . or use a wire type gauge

Every 27 000 miles or 3 years

21 Spark plug renewal

1 The correct functioning of the spark plugs is vital for the correct running and efficiency of the engine. It is essential that the plugs fitted are appropriate for the engine; suitable types are specified at the beginning of this Chapter. If the correct type is used and the engine is in good condition, the spark plugs should not need attention between scheduled renewal intervals. Spark plug cleaning should not be attempted.

2 Remove the four ignition coils as described in Chapter 5B. The Micra has a direct ignition system, featuring one ignition coil per spark plug, mounted directly over the plug, with no HT leads. This system is often called 'coil over plug' or COP.

3 The spark plugs are quite deeply recessed in the top of the engine, and a 16 mm spark plug socket and extension bar will be needed to reach them. It is not advisable to use an ordinary deep socket for this job; since the plug may tend to fall out of the socket once it has been unscrewed, and will then have to be retrieved from the recess using thin-nosed pliers (fitting the new plugs will also be a problem, of course).

4 It is advisable (if possible) to remove any dirt from the spark plug recesses using a clean brush, vacuum cleaner or compressed air before removing the plugs, to prevent dirt dropping into the cylinders. However, the deep recesses on the Micra engine make this an almost impossible task – just be aware of the danger of anything falling into the spark plug holes when the plugs are removed, and take all possible precautions.

5 Lower the socket and extension into the recesses carefully – if the socket is misaligned and forced in, the ceramic insulator may be broken off. Unscrew each plug in turn, then carefully withdraw it from the recess so that it does not fall out of the socket **(see illustration)**. As each plug is removed, examine it as follows.

6 Examination of the spark plugs will give a good indication of the condition of the engine. If the insulator nose of the spark plug is clean and white, with no deposits, this is indicative of a weak mixture or too hot a plug (a hot plug transfers heat away from the electrode slowly, a cold plug transfers heat away quickly).

7 If the tip and insulator nose are covered with hard black-looking deposits, then this is indicative that the mixture is too rich. Should the plug be black and oily, then it is likely that the engine is fairly worn, as well as the mixture being too rich.

8 If the insulator nose is covered with light tan to greyish-brown deposits, then the mixture is correct and it is likely that the engine is in good condition.

9 The spark plug electrode gap is of considerable importance as, if it is too large or too small, the size of the spark and its efficiency will be seriously impaired.

10 To check the gap (on a single earth electrode plug), measure it with a feeler blade **(see illustrations)**. If the gap is not correct, discard the plug and renew all four.

11 Before fitting the spark plugs, check that the threaded connector sleeves are tight, and that the plug exterior surfaces and threads are clean. If fitting new plugs check the gap before fitting. To set the gap, measure it with a feeler blade or spark plug gap gauge and then carefully bend the outer plug electrode until the correct gap is achieved. The centre electrode should never be bent, as this may crack the insulator and cause plug failure, if nothing worse. If using feeler blades, the gap is correct when the appropriate-size blade is a firm sliding fit. Special spark plug electrode gap adjusting tools are available from most motor accessory shops, or from some spark plug manufacturers.

12 Fit the new plug and remove the rubber/plastic hose (if used), and tighten the plug to the specified torque using the spark plug socket and a torque wrench **(see illustration)**. Refit the remaining spark plugs in the same manner.

13 Refit the ignition coils as described in Chapter 5B, and the air cleaner/inlet duct as described in Chapter 4A.

22 Air filter element renewal

1 Remove the two clips that retain the inlet ducting and rotate it through 90 degrees **(see illustrations)**. Gently pull it free from the main filter housing.

2 Prise free the two spring clips and allow the housing to drop down. The spring clips are meant to be captive, but they have a habit of falling off, so keep a close eye on them when lowering the housing. Compressing the radiator hose will help recover the filter and housing **(see illustrations)**.

21.12 Lower the plug into position with a length of hose

22.1a Prise the two clips free . . .

22.1b . . . and remove them

22.1c Rotate the inlet duct and remove it

22.2a Release the spring clips . . .

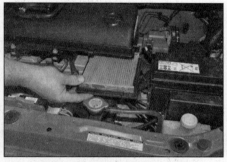

22.2b . . . and remove the filter

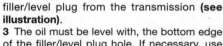
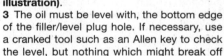
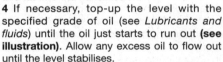

23.2 Unscrew the filler plug

23.4 Top-up if required

3 Refitting is a reversal of removal, but fit the filter to the upper body first and carefully check the two projections are firmly engaged at the rear before swinging the housing into place. Fasten the two spring clips and refit the inlet duct.

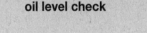

23 Manual transmission oil level check

1 Position the car over an inspection pit, on car ramps, or jack it up (see *Jacking and vehicle support*), but make sure that it is level.

2 Remove all traces of dirt, then unscrew the filler/level plug from the transmission **(see illustration)**.
3 The oil must be level with, the bottom edge of the filler/level plug hole. If necessary, use a cranked tool such as an Allen key to check the level, but nothing which might break off and fall into the transmission.
4 If necessary, top-up the level with the specified grade of oil (see *Lubricants and fluids*) until the oil just starts to run out **(see illustration)**. Allow any excess oil to flow out until the level stabilises.
5 When the level is correct, clean and refit the filler/level plug

> **HAYNES HINT** *When a transmission oil bottle is more than half-full, squeezing it will force the oil in from below – after that, the bottle will have to be manoeuvred in from above.*

6 Although not part of the manufacturer's routine maintenance schedule, it is a good idea to change the transmission oil after a high mileage has been completed, or perhaps periodically on a car which does a lot of stop-start driving. A drain plug is provided – see Chapter 7A for details.

Every 2 years, regardless of mileage

24 Brake fluid renewal

⚠️ *Warning: Brake hydraulic fluid can harm your eyes and damage painted surfaces, so use extreme caution when handling and pouring it. Do not use fluid that has been standing open for some time, as it absorbs moisture from the air. Excess moisture can cause a dangerous loss of braking effectiveness.*

1 The procedure is similar to that for bleeding the hydraulic system as described in Chapter 9, except that allowance should be made for the old fluid to be expelled when bleeding each section of the circuit.

> **HAYNES HINT** *Old hydraulic fluid is invariably much darker in colour than the new, making it easy to distinguish the two.*

2 Working as described in Chapter 9, open the first bleed screw in the sequence, and pump the brake pedal gently until the level in the reservoir is approaching the MIN mark. Top-up to the MAX level with new fluid, and continue pumping until only new fluid remains in the reservoir, and new fluid can be seen emerging from the bleed screw. Tighten the screw, and top the reservoir level up to the MAX level line.
3 Work through all the remaining bleed screws in the sequence until new fluid can be seen at all of them. Be careful to keep the master cylinder reservoir topped-up above the MIN level at all times, or air may enter the system. If this happens, further bleeding will be required, to remove the air.
4 When the operation is complete, check that all bleed screws are securely tightened, and that their dust caps are refitted. Wash off all traces of spilt fluid, and recheck the master cylinder reservoir fluid level.
5 Check the operation of the brakes before taking the car on the road.

Every 4 years, regardless of mileage

25 Coolant renewal and pressure cap check
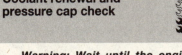

⚠️ *Warning: Wait until the engine is cold before starting this procedure. Do not allow antifreeze to come in contact with your skin, or with the painted surfaces of the car. Rinse off spills immediately with plenty of water. Never leave antifreeze lying around in an open container, or in a puddle in the driveway or on the garage floor. Children and pets are attracted by its sweet smell, but antifreeze can be fatal if ingested.*

Cooling system draining

1 With the engine completely cold, remove the expansion tank filler cap. Turn the cap anti-clockwise, wait until any pressure remaining in the system is released, then unscrew it and lift it off.

2 Position a suitable container beneath the radiator lower hose at the bottom left-hand corner of the radiator (left as seen from the driver's seat).

3 Remove the hose clip and allow the coolant to drain into the container **(see illustration)**.

4 When the flow of coolant stops, refit the hose and tighten the hose clip.

5 Remove the expansion tank. For models with air conditioning remove the two bolts and disconnect the hose. For automatics and non-air conditioned models move the relay plate to one side, and pulling towards the inner wing and upwards release the expansion tank. Disconnect the hoses and drain the reservoir.

6 If the coolant has been drained for a reason other than renewal, then provided it is clean and less than two years old, it can be re-used, though this is not recommended.

Cooling system flushing

7 If coolant renewal has been neglected, or if the antifreeze mixture has become diluted, then in time, the cooling system may gradually lose efficiency, as the coolant passages become restricted due to rust, scale deposits, and other sediment. The cooling system efficiency can be restored by flushing the system clean.

8 The radiator should be flushed independently of the engine, to avoid unnecessary contamination.

Radiator flushing

9 Disconnect the top and bottom hoses from the radiator, with reference to Chapter 3.

10 Insert a garden hose into the radiator top inlet. Direct a flow of clean water through the radiator, and continue flushing until clean water emerges from the radiator bottom outlet.

11 If after a reasonable period, the water still does not run clear, the radiator can be flushed with a good proprietary cleaning agent. It is important that their manufacturer's instructions are followed carefully. If the contamination is particularly bad, insert the hose in the radiator bottom outlet, and reverse-flush the radiator.

Engine flushing

12 Remove the thermostat as described in Chapter 3 then, if the radiator top hose has been disconnected from the engine, temporarily reconnect the hose.

13 With the top and bottom hoses disconnected from the radiator, insert a garden hose into the radiator top hose. Direct a clean flow of water through the engine, and continue flushing until clean water emerges from the radiator bottom hose.

14 On completion of flushing, refit the thermostat and reconnect the hoses with reference to Chapter 3.

15 In extreme cases, reconnect all hoses and fill the system with water and a proprietary cooling system treatment. Follow the instructions provided. This will normally require the vehicle to be driven – minus the thermostat – for a period of time. Drain and flush the system thoroughly upon completion.

Antifreeze mixture

16 The antifreeze should always be renewed at the specified intervals. This is necessary not only to maintain the antifreeze properties, but also to prevent corrosion which would otherwise occur as the corrosion inhibitors become progressively less effective.

17 Always use an ethylene-glycol based antifreeze which is suitable for use in mixed-metal cooling systems. The quantity of antifreeze and levels of protection are given in the Specifications.

18 The antifreeze recommended by Nissan at the time of writing is their premixed L250. If using an equivalent that requires diluting, do so with distilled water and not tap water.

19 Note that different types and brands of coolant should ever never be mixed with any other type.

20 Remember that a small amount of coolant will always be present in the system, even after draining. Therefore, if coolant of a different type is to be used, the engine and radiator should be thoroughly flushed with clean water as described previously in this Section.

21 Before adding antifreeze, check all hoses for condition and security.

22 After filling with antifreeze, a label should be attached to the expansion tank, stating the type and concentration of antifreeze used, and the date installed. Any subsequent topping-up should be made with the same type and concentration of antifreeze.

Caution: Do not use engine antifreeze in the windscreen/tailgate washer system, as it will cause damage to the paintwork. A screenwash additive should be added to the washer system in the quantities stated on the bottle.

Cooling system filling

23 Before attempting to fill the cooling system, make sure that all hoses and clips are in good condition, and that the clips are tight. Note that an antifreeze mixture must be used all year round, to prevent corrosion of the engine components.

24 Remove the radiator filler cap on automatic models and non-air conditioned vehicles.

25 Remove the expansion tank cap and the top heater hose from the bulkhead **(see illustration)**.

25.3 Remove the lower hose

25.25 Remove the top heater hose to bleed air from the system

26 Slowly fill the system until the level in the radiator stabilises and coolant emerges from the heater hose. Reconnect the heater hose and secure the clip. This process should take several minutes – gently squeeze the radiator hoses to help disperse any trapped air, and keep checking the level in both radiator and the expansion tank.

27 Start the engine, let it run for two minutes, then switch off. Be prepared to top-up the radiator (or expansion tank) as soon as the engine starts – the levels may drop quite quickly.

28 Leave the engine for a few minutes, then recheck the coolant levels in the radiator and/ or the expansion tank, and top-up if necessary. Fit the radiator and expansion tank caps once the levels have stabilised.

29 Start the engine once more, and run it at idle until the radiator top hose is fully warm (preferably, wait until the cooling fan cuts in). Keep an eye on the temperature display – if overheating is indicated at any time, switch the engine off immediately.

30 With the engine running gradually increase the speed to approximately 3000 rpm. Allow the engine to return to idle for 30 seconds and then repeat the process twice more. Listen carefully for noises from the heater. This is the place an air lock is most likely to form (see below). Repeat the above procedure if any noise is apparent.

31 When the engine has cooled (preferably overnight), recheck the levels once more, and top-up if necessary.

Airlocks

32 If, after draining and refilling the system, symptoms of overheating are found which did not occur previously, then the fault is almost certainly due to trapped air at some point in the system, causing an airlock and restricting the flow of coolant; usually, the air is trapped because the system was refilled too quickly.

33 If an airlock is suspected, first try gently squeezing all visible coolant hoses. A coolant hose which is full of air feels quite different to one full of coolant, when squeezed. After refilling the system, most airlocks will clear once the system has cooled, and been topped-up.

34 While the engine is running at operating temperature, switch on the heater and heater fan, and check for heat output. Provided there is sufficient coolant in the system, any lack of heat output could be due to an airlock in the system.

35 Airlocks can have more serious effects than simply reducing heater output – a severe airlock could reduce coolant flow around the engine. Check that the radiator top hose is hot when the engine is at operating temperature – a top hose which stays cold could be the result of an airlock (or a non-opening thermostat).

36 If the problem persists, stop the engine and allow it to cool down **completely**, before unscrewing the radiator and expansion tank caps, or loosening the hose clips and squeezing the hoses to bleed out the trapped air. In the worst case, the system will have to be at least partially drained (this time, the coolant can be saved for re-use) and flushed to clear the problem.

Radiator cap check

37 Clean the pressure cap, and inspect the seal inside the cap for damage or deterioration. If there is any sign of damage or deterioration to the seal, fit a new pressure cap.

Notes

Chapter 2 Part A:
Engine in-car repair procedures

Contents

	Section number			Section number
Camshafts and followers – removal, inspection and refitting	8	General engine checks		See Chapter 1
Compression test – description and interpretation	2	General information		1
Crankshaft oil seals – renewal	11	Rocker cover - removal and refitting		4
Crankshaft pulley – removal and refitting	5	Sump – removal and refitting		10
Cylinder head – removal and refitting	9	Timing chain tensioner and camshaft sprockets – removal,		
Engine oil and filter renewal	See Chapter 1	inspection and refitting		6
Engine oil level check	See Weekly checks	Top dead centre (TDC) – locating		3
Engine/transmission mountings – inspection and renewal	13	Valve clearances – checking and adjustment		7
Flywheel/driveplate – removal, inspection and refitting	12			

Degrees of difficulty

Easy, suitable for novice with little experience	**Fairly easy,** suitable for beginner with some experience	**Fairly difficult,** suitable for competent DIY mechanic	**Difficult,** suitable for experienced DIY mechanic	**Very difficult,** suitable for expert DIY or professional

Specifications

General

Designation	CR
Engine code:	
1.0 litre engine	CR10DE
1.2 litre engines	CR12DE
1.4 litre engines	CR14DE
Capacity:	
1.0 litre engines	998 cc
1.2 litre engines	1240 cc
1.4 litre engines	1386 cc
Bore:	
1.0 litre engines	71.0 mm
1.2 litre engines	71.0 mm
1.4 litre engines	73.0 mm
Stroke:	
1.0 litre engines	63.0 mm
1.2 litre engines	78.3 mm
1.4 litre engines	82.8 mm
Direction of crankshaft rotation	Clockwise (viewed from right-hand side of vehicle)
No 1 cylinder location	At timing chain end of block (right-hand end)
Firing order	1–3–4–2
Compression ratio:	
1.0 litre engines	10.2: 1
1.2 litre engines	9.9: 1
1.4 litre engines	9.9: 1
Cylinder compression pressures:	
Standard:	
1.0 litre engines	14.32 bars
1.2 litre engines	13.83 bars
1.4 litre engines	13.83 bars
Minimum:	
1.0 litre engines	12.36 bars
1.2 litre engines	11.87 bars
1.4 litre engines	11.87 bars
Maximum difference between cylinders (all engines)	0.98 bar

Valve clearances

Cold engine (only for initial start-up after overhaul):
Inlet...	0.29 to 0.37 mm
Exhaust..	0.32 to 0.40 mm

Hot engine:
Inlet...	0.31 to 0.43 mm
Exhaust..	0.34 to 0.46 mm

Camshaft and followers

Drive...	Chain
Number of bearings.................................	5
Endfloat...	0.070 to 0.143 mm

Camshaft lobe height:
Inlet...	40.359 to 40.549 mm
Exhaust...	39.743 to 39.933 mm

Bearing journal outer diameter:
No 1 bearing..	27.935 to 27.955 mm
Nos 2 to 5 bearings	23.450 to 23.470 mm

Camshaft cylinder head bearing journal internal diameter:
No 1 bearing..	28.000 to 28.021 mm
Nos 2 to 5 bearings	23.500 to 23.525 mm

Camshaft journal-to-bearing clearance:
No1 bearing	0.045 to 0.086 mm
No 2 to 5 bearings	0.030 to 0.071 mm

Available valve followers:

Thickness:	Identification mark
3.000...	00
3.020...	02
3.040...	04
3.060...	06
3.080...	08
3.100...	10
3.120...	12
3.140...	14
3.160...	16
3.180...	18
3.200...	20
3.220...	22
3.240...	24
3.260...	26
3.280...	28
3.300...	30
3.320...	32
3.340...	34
3.360...	36
3.380...	38
3.400...	40
3.420...	42
3.440...	44
3.460...	46
3.480...	48
3.500...	50
3.520...	52
3.540...	54
3.560...	56
3.580...	58
3.600...	60
3.620...	62
3.640...	64
3.660...	66
3.680...	68

Torque wrench settings

Camshaft bearing cap bolts:
	Nm	lbf ft
Stage 1: bolts 9 to 12.............................	2	1
Stage 2: bolts 1 to 8..............................	2	1
Stage 3: bolts 1 to 12.............................	6	4
Stage 4: bolts 1 to 12.............................	10	7

Torque wrench settings (continued)

	Nm	lbf ft
Camshaft sprocket access cover nuts/bolts	8	6
Camshaft sprocket retaining bolts:		
Inlet	84	62
Exhaust	84	62
Connecting rod:		
Stage 1	15	11
Stage 2	Angle tighten a further 48°	
Crankshaft pulley bolt	142	105
Crankshaft sensor	8	6
Cylinder head bolts:		
Stage 1: bolts 1 to 10	66	49
Stage 2: bolts 1 to 10	Fully slacken all the bolts in reverse order	
Stage 3: bolts 1 to 10	28	21
Stage 4: bolts 11 to 13	10	7
Stage 5: bolts 1 to 10	Angle-tighten a further 90 degrees	
Driveplate (automatic transmission)	98	72
Flywheel (manual transmission)	88	65
Front right-hand engine mounting:		
Mounting-to-engine bolts	45	33
Bracket-to-chassis bolts	65	48
Through-bolt	95	70
Steady-bar bolts	45	33
Knock sensor	18	13
Left-hand engine/transmission mounting:		
Through-bolt	65	48
Mounting-to-transmission bolts	65	48
Mounting-to-chassis bolts	48	35
Flexible mounting bolts	105	77
Main bearing cap		
Stage 1	27	20
Stage 2	Angle tighten a further 95°	
Oil pressure switch	20	15
Oil pump:		
Cover retaining bolt	8	6
Regulator valve bolt	50	37
Oil seal housing (flywheel end)	8	6
Oil strainer	8	6
Rear lower mounting bolts	80	59
Rocker cover		
M6 X 45 mm bolts	10	7
M6 X 20 mm bolts	9	7
Sump drain plug	35	26
Sump nuts and bolts	8	6
Timing chain cover	8	6
Timing chain guide bolts	18	13
Timing chain tensioner bolts	8	6

1 General information

Using this Chapter

Chapter 2 is divided into two Parts: A and B. Repair operations that can be carried out with the engine in the car are described in Part A. Part B covers the removal of the engine/transmission as a unit, and describes the engine dismantling and overhaul procedures.

Note that, while it may be possible physically to overhaul items such as the piston/connecting rod assemblies while the engine is in the car, such tasks are not normally carried out as separate operations.

Usually, several additional procedures (not to mention the cleaning of components and of oilways) have to be carried out. For this reason, all such tasks are classed as major overhaul procedures, and are described in Part B of this Chapter.

In Part A the assumption is made that the engine is installed in the car, with all ancillaries connected. If the engine has been removed for overhaul, the preliminary dismantling information, which precedes each operation, may be ignored.

Engine description

The engines are from the CR series of all-alloy Nissan engines. They are of the sixteen-valve, in-line four-cylinder, twin overhead camshaft (DOHC) chain driven type,

mounted transversely at the front of the car with the transmission attached to the left-hand end.

The crankshaft runs in five main bearings. Thrustwashers are fitted to No 3 main bearing (upper half) to control crankshaft endfloat.

The connecting rods rotate on horizontally split bearing shells at their big ends. The pistons are attached to the connecting rods by gudgeon pins, which are a press-fit in the connecting rod small-end eyes. The aluminium-alloy pistons are fitted with three piston rings – two compression rings and an oil control ring.

The inlet and exhaust valves are each closed by coil springs, and operate in guides pressed into the cylinder head; the valve seat inserts are also pressed into the cylinder head, and can be renewed separately if worn. The inlet camshaft has a hydraulically-operated variable timing sprocket, controlled by an electric solenoid. The camshaft is driven by a timing chain, and operates the sixteen valves via bucket-type followers. The followers are situated directly below the camshafts. Valve clearances are adjusted by changing the followers. The camshafts rotate directly in the cylinder head.

Lubrication is by means of an oil pump, which is driven off the right-hand end of the crankshaft. It draws oil through a strainer located in the sump, and then forces it through an externally-mounted filter into galleries in the cylinder block/crankcase. From there, the oil is distributed to the crankshaft (main bearings) and camshaft. The big-end bearings are supplied with oil via internal drillings in the crankshaft, while the camshaft bearings also receive a pressurised supply. The camshaft lobes and valves are lubricated by splash, as are all other engine components.

Liquid gasket

The CR series of engines make extensive use of 'liquid gasket' in place of traditional gasket materials. The liquid gasket acts as an adhesive as well as a sealant. This can make separating components an arduous task. Patience and gently persuasion is the order of the day. Avoid at all cost damage to the mating surfaces.

Removal of the old gasket is a thankless but essential task. Take precautions to make sure no old sealant can enter any of the oilways. A blunt scraper and an assortment of hook and pick tools will help in removing sealant from the machined groves in many of the parts that are sealed with liquid gasket.

Always use genuine liquid gasket when reassembling components. It is not the same as a traditional 'instant gasket' type product. Note that many parts may require a different diameter bead of gasket applying. This is shown in the text. As a general rule apply the sealant to the machined groves and the inner edge of bolt holes unless specified otherwise in the text. Allow a maximum open time of five minutes before installing components. Do not retighten after installation. Wipe all excess material off immediately. Wait a minimum of thirty minutes before adding oil or coolant.

Repairs with engine in car

The following work can be carried out with the engine in the car:

a) *Compression pressure – testing.*
b) *Rocker cover – removal and refitting.*
c) *Timing chain cover – removal and refitting.*
d) *Timing chain tensioner, and sprockets – removal, inspection and refitting.*
e) *Camshaft and followers – removal, inspection and refitting.*
f) *Valve clearances – adjustment.*
g) *Cylinder head – removal and refitting.*
h) *Cylinder head and pistons – decarbonising.*

i) *Sump – removal and refitting.*
j) *Crankshaft oil seals – renewal.*
k) *Engine/transmission mountings – inspection and renewal.*
l) *Flywheel/driveplate – removal, inspection and refitting.*

Note: *On automatic transmission models it is possible (though not recommended) to remove the timing chain and tensioners with the engine in situ. It is not possible on manual transmission models because the engine endplate prevents the removal of the intermediate sump pan.*

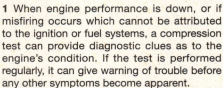

2 Compression test – description and interpretation

1 When engine performance is down, or if misfiring occurs which cannot be attributed to the ignition or fuel systems, a compression test can provide diagnostic clues as to the engine's condition. If the test is performed regularly, it can give warning of trouble before any other symptoms become apparent.
2 The engine must be fully warmed-up to normal operating temperature, the battery must be fully-charged, and the aid of an assistant will also be required.
3 Depressurise the fuel system by following one of the methods described in Chapter 4A. Start the engine, and allow it to run until it stalls. Try to start the engine at least twice more, to ensure that all residual pressure has been relieved.
4 Disable the ignition system by disconnecting the wiring connector(s) from the coils.
5 Remove the spark plugs as described in Chapter 1.
6 Fit a compression tester to the No 1 cylinder spark plug hole – the type of tester which screws into the plug thread is to be preferred.
7 Have the assistant hold the throttle wide open, and crank the engine on the starter motor; after one or two revolutions, the compression pressure should build-up to a maximum figure, and then stabilise. Record the highest reading obtained.
8 Repeat the test on the remaining cylinders, recording the pressure in each.
9 All cylinders should produce very similar pressures; any difference greater than that specified indicates the existence of a fault. Note that the compression should build-up quickly in a healthy engine; low compression on the first stroke, followed by gradually increasing pressure on successive strokes, indicates worn piston rings. A low compression reading on the first stroke, which does not build-up during successive strokes, indicates leaking valves or a blown head gasket (a cracked head could also be the cause). Deposits on the undersides of the valve heads can also cause low compression.
10 If the pressure in any cylinder is reduced to the specified minimum or less, carry out the following test to isolate the cause. Introduce

a teaspoonful of clean oil into that cylinder through its spark plug hole and repeat the test.
11 If the addition of oil temporarily improves the compression pressure, this indicates that bore or piston wear is responsible for the pressure loss. No improvement suggests that leaking or burnt valves, or a blown head gasket, may be to blame.
12 A low reading from two adjacent cylinders is almost certainly due to the head gasket having blown between them; the presence of coolant in the engine oil will confirm this.
13 If one cylinder is about 20 percent lower than the others and the engine has a slightly rough idle; a worn camshaft lobe could be the cause.
14 If the compression reading is unusually high, the combustion chambers are probably coated with carbon deposits. If this is the case, the cylinder head should be removed and decarbonised.
15 On completion of the test, refit the spark plugs and fuel pump fuse, and then reconnect the coil wiring connectors.

3 Top dead centre (TDC) – locating

1 Disconnect the battery negative terminal *(refer to Disconnecting the battery in the Reference Chapter),* then remove all the spark plugs as described in Chapter 1.
2 Apply the handbrake and ensure that the transmission is in neutral, then jack up the front of the car and support it on axle stands *(see Jacking and vehicle support).* Remove the right-hand roadwheel.
3 From underneath the front of the car, undo the retaining screws and remove the wheel arch liner from underneath the wing to gain access to the crankshaft pulley.
4 On early cars a pointer is provided on the timing chain cover and a paint mark or notch is provided on the crankshaft pulley.
5 Using a spanner (or socket and extension bar) applied to the crankshaft pulley bolt, rotate the crankshaft clockwise until the TDC notch on the crankshaft pulley rim is aligned with the pointer on the timing chain cover.
6 With the crankshaft in this position, Nos 1 and 4 cylinders are now at TDC, one of them on the compression stroke.
7 For later cars with no mark on the pulley, remover the rocker cover and rotate the engine until the two marks on the sprockets are uppermost and the lobes for the cams on No 1 cylinder are pointing outwards. This places cylinder No 1 at top dead centre on the compression stroke.
8 The precise position of TDC can also be determined with a dial gauge and extension bar through the spark plug hole. Once located this way it is recommended that permanent marks are made on the crank pulley and timing chain front cover.

4 Rocker cover – removal and refitting

Removal

1 Disconnect the battery negative terminal (refer to *Disconnecting the battery* in the Reference Chapter).

2 Remove the air filter duct and throttle housing as described in Chapters 1 and 4A.

3 Disconnect and remove the ignition coils as described in Chapter 5B and then remove the harness support bracket.

4 Remove the engine steady-bar/damper from the engine mount (**see illustrations**) and then remove the upper half of the engine mounting as described in section 13.

5 Release the retaining clip and disconnect the PCV hose from the transmission end of the cover **(see illustration)**.

6 Disconnect the wiring connector from the inlet valve timing control solenoid on the rear of the cover **(see illustration)**.

7 Working in the **reverse** of the tightening sequence, slacken and remove the cover retaining bolts **(see illustration)**.

8 Lift off the rocker cover, and recover the gasket (if fitted), and the circular seals from each of the spark plug holes. Remove the gasket from the inlet valve timing solenoid **(see illustrations)**.

9 Later engines use liquid gasket instead of a rubber seal. It may take considerable effort to break this seal.

10 Inspect the cover seals for signs of damage and deterioration, and renew as necessary.

Refitting

11 Carefully clean the cylinder head and cover mating surfaces, and remove all traces of oil.

12 Apply a 3 mm diameter bead of sealant across the joint between the cylinder head and the cylinder head endplate **(see illustration)**.

13 Fit the rubber seal to the rocker cover groove, ensuring that it is correctly located along its entire length, and install the four spark plug hole seals, ensuring that they are

4.4a Remove the steady-bar upper section . . .

4.4b . . . and the rear section

4.5 Remove the breather hose

4.6 Disconnect the solenoid plug

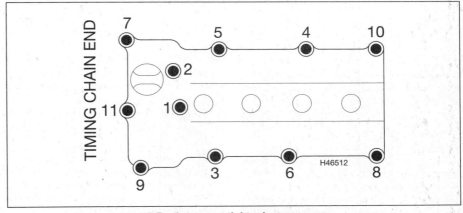

4.7 Rocker cover tightening sequence

Loosen the bolts in reverse order

4.8a Remove the cover . . .

4.8b . . . and recover the gasket

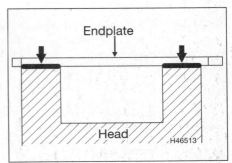

4.12 Apply liquid gasket as shown

4.13 Use a block of wood to press the seals in

the correct way round **(see illustration)** also fit a new seal to the breather if required.

14 Fit a new gasket for the inlet valve timing control solenoid.

15 For engines with a liquid gasket apply a 3 to 5 mm bead along the groves provided in the cover **(see illustration)**.

16 Carefully refit the cover to the engine, taking great care not to displace any of the rubber seals.

17 Make sure the cover is correctly seated, and then install the retaining screws and washers. Working in sequence, tighten all the cover screws to the specified torque **(see illustration 4.7)**.

18 Refit the PCV hose and secure in position with the retaining clip.

19 Reconnect the wiring connector to the inlet valve timing control solenoid.

20 Refit the ignition coils, throttle body housing and air filter, and reconnect the battery negative terminal.

5.4a Unscrew the bolt

6.3 Removing the endplate

4.15 Carefully apply sealant

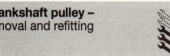

5 Crankshaft pulley – removal and refitting

Removal

1 Remove the auxiliary drivebelts as described in Chapter 1.

2 If necessary, position No 1 cylinder at TDC on its compression stroke as described in Section 3.

3 To prevent crankshaft rotation while the pulley bolt is unscrewed on manual transmission models, select top gear and have an assistant apply the brakes firmly. On automatic transmission models remove the starter motor as described in Chapter 5A and fit a locking tool to the starter ring gear. Alternatively a large old screwdriver can be used through the starter motor aperture to lock the ring gear.

5.4b . . . and remove the pulley

6.4 Mark the link with paint

4 Unscrew the pulley bolt and remove the pulley from the crankshaft. If the pulley Woodruff key is a loose fit, remove it and store it with the pulley for safekeeping **(see illustrations)**.

5 If the pulley is difficult to remove, then refit the bolt, but leave it loose. Apply penetrating oil and then use a two-legged puller on the bolt and inner section of the pulley. Do not use the outer diameter of the pulley to locate the puller, as this will damage the rubber insulator that separates the two sections of the pulley.

Refitting

6 Refit the Woodruff key (where removed).

7 Align the crankshaft pulley groove with the key, then slide the pulley onto the crankshaft, and refit the retaining bolt and washer.

8 Lock the crankshaft by the method used on removal. Oil the threads of the bolt and tighten the bolt to the specified torque.

9 Refit the auxiliary drivebelts and adjust them as described in Chapter 1.

6 Timing chain tensioner and camshaft sprockets – removal, inspection and refitting

Note: *Before the timing chain can be removed, a minimum of 3.0 bars air pressure will need to be applied to the variable valve inlet sprocket.*

Removal

1 Position No 1 cylinder at TDC on its compression stroke, as described in Section 3.

2 Remove the rocker cover and steady-bar as described in Section 4.

3 Remove the upper engine mount and remove the cylinder head endplate **(see illustration)**.

4 With No 1 cylinder set at TDC, the markings on the camshaft sprockets should be uppermost. Apply paint marks to the timing chain links, which are in line with the markings on the sprockets **(see illustration)**.

5 Measure the protrusion of the spring-loaded tensioner and compare it to the Specifications. The most accurate measurement should be taken after several rotations of the crankshaft, and at various positions on the chain.

6 Using an open-ended spanner on the hexagonal part of the inlet camshaft, hold it in position so that it does not move.

7 Apply a minimum of 3 bars air pressure to the oil passage leading to the variable valve inlet sprocket. Wear eye protection and cover the sprocket and airline with a rag **(see illustrations)**

8 While keeping the air pressure applied, slowly turn the camshaft anti-clockwise (to the rear of the vehicle). During this procedure a click (locking pin disengaging) is heard from the inlet sprocket. **Note:** *If a click has not been heard, then waggle the camshaft very slightly using the spanner, or tap the end of the camshaft with a plastic mallet.*

9 Still keeping the air pressure applied, after

6.7a Force air down the oil supply port . . .

6.7b . . . but cover with a cloth first

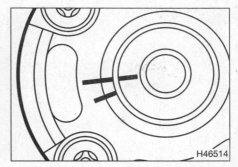

6.9 Align the inner vane mark with the upper sprocket mark

the click (locking pin disengaging) has been heard, slowly turn the inlet camshaft in the clockwise direction (to the front of the vehicle) setting it to the most advanced position. In this position the marks on the variable sprocket will be aligned (see illustration). Failure to do this correctly will damage the internal locking pin when the sprocket retaining bolt is removed.

10 Place a rag between the timing chain to stop any parts falling into the engine.

11 Retract the chain tensioner, and hold it in position by inserting a small-diameter rod or paper clip through the plate hole and into the body of the tensioner. Undo the two retaining bolts, and remove the tensioner from the end of the cylinder head. It may be difficult to retract enough to fit the pin whilst in situ, so remove it as found but take care as the spring-loaded pin may pop out.

12 Slacken the camshaft sprocket retaining bolts, whilst retaining the camshafts with a large open-ended spanner fitted to the hexagonal section of each shaft. Remove each bolt along with its washer (where applicable), disengage each sprocket from the end of its respective camshaft, and manoeuvre them out from the cylinder head (see illustrations). Place tape across the variable sprocket to maintain its position. **Note:** The timing chain cannot fall off the crankshaft sprocket, the timing chain cover prevents this.

Inspection

13 Examine the teeth on the camshaft and crankshaft sprockets for any sign of wear or damage such as chipped, hooked or missing teeth. If there is any sign of wear or damage on either sprockets or timing chain then they should be renewed as a set.

14 Inspect the links of the timing chain for signs of wear or damage on the rollers. The extent of wear can be judged by checking the amount by which the chain can be bent sideways; a new chain will have very little sideways movement. If there is an excessive amount of side play in either timing chain, it must be renewed.

15 Note that it is a sensible precaution to renew the timing chain regardless of its apparent condition, if the engine has covered a high mileage, or if it has been noted that the chain has sounded noisy when the engine

running. Although not strictly necessary, it is always worth renewing the chain and sprockets as a matched set, since it is false economy to run a new chain on worn sprockets and vice versa. If there is any doubt about the condition of the timing chain and sprockets, seek the advice of a garage or Nissan dealer service department, who will be able to advise you as to the best course of action.

16 Where visible examine the chain guides for signs of wear or damage to their chain contact faces.

17 Check the chain tensioner pad for signs of wear, and check that the plunger is free to slide freely in the tensioner body. The condition of the tensioner spring can only be judged in comparison to a new component. Renew the tensioner if its pad is worn or there is any doubt about the condition of its tensioning spring.

6.12a Remove the bolt

6.12c Undo the inlet sprocket . . .

Refitting

18 Check the crankshaft is still positioned at TDC.

19 Check the position of the camshafts.

20 If the variable inlet sprocket timing marks have moved, temporarily refit it. Only tighten the bolt sufficiently to stop air from leaking, whilst the removal procedure is repeated. There is no need to fit the chain.

21 Manoeuvre both the inlet and exhaust camshaft sprockets into position, ensuring that their timing marks are facing the position noted on removal. Engage them with the chain, aligning the inlet sprocket timing mark with the first painted link and the exhaust sprocket timing mark with the second. Check that all the timing marks are correctly aligned.

22 With the timing marks correctly positioned, install the camshaft sprocket retaining bolts

6.12b . . . and remove the exhaust sprocket

6.12d . . . and remove it

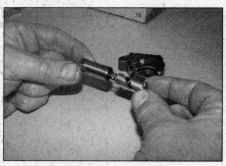

6.23a Reset the plunger by rotating and pushing the pin. Do not force it

6.23b Use a paper clip to hold it in the fully compressed position

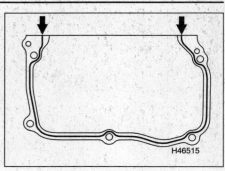

6.24 Apply liquid gasket

and washers (where applicable), and tighten them both to the specified torque.

23 Reset the chain tensioner if required **(see illustrations)** and then fit the chain tensioner to the cylinder head, and tighten its retaining bolts to the specified torque. Withdraw the rod or paper clip, and check that the tensioner pad is forced against the chain.

24 Apply a 2 to 3 mm diameter bead of liquid gasket to the cylinder head endplate and refit. Tighten the bolts securely **(see illustration)**.

25 Refit the rocker cover as described in Section 4.

7 Valve clearances –
checking and adjustment

Note: *The valve clearances must always be checked with the engine hot: Although Nissan quote valve clearances for a hot and cold engine, the valve clearances should only be checked cold prior to starting the engine after an overhaul. The valve clearances should then be checked again once the engine has been warmed-up to normal operating temperature.*
Note: *This is not a routine operation. It should only be necessary at high mileage, after overhaul, or when investigating noise or power loss which may be attributable to the valve gear.*

1 The importance of having the valve clearances correctly adjusted cannot be overstressed, as they vitally affect the performance of the engine. The clearances are checked as follows.

7.10a Followers have the size stamped on the inside face . . .

2 Draw the outline of the engine on a piece of paper, numbering the cylinders 1 to 4, with No 1 cylinder at the timing chain end of the engine. Show the position of each valve, together with the specified valve clearance. Above each valve, draw two lines for noting the actual clearance and the amount of adjustment required.

3 Warm the engine up to normal operating temperature, then switch off. Remove the rocker cover as described in Section 4.

4 Position No 1 cylinder at TDC on its compression stroke, as described in Section 3.

5 Using feeler gauges, measure the clearance between the base of the cam and the follower of the following valves, recording each clearance on the paper.

No 1 cylinder inlet and exhaust valves.
No 2 cylinder inlet valves.
No 3 cylinder exhaust valves.

6 Rotate the crankshaft through one complete turn (360°) clockwise until the TDC notch on the crankshaft pulley is realigned with the pointer, or the lobes on No 4 cylinder are pointing outwards. No 4 cylinder is now at TDC on its compression stroke.

7 Check the clearances of the following valves, and record them on the paper.

No 2 cylinder exhaust valves.
No 3 cylinder inlet valves.
No 4 cylinder inlet and exhaust valves.

8 Calculate the difference between each measured clearance and the desired value, and record it on the piece of paper. Where a valve clearance differs from the specified value, then the follower for that valve must be substituted with a thinner or thicker follower accordingly.

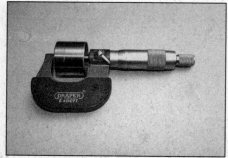

7.10b . . . but it's always best to check with a micrometer

9 The camshafts must now be removed as described in section 8.

10 The follower size is stamped on the inside face of the follower (eg, 30 indicates the shim is 3.30 mm thick), but it is advisable to use a micrometer to measure the true thickness of any shim removed, as it may have been reduced by wear **(see illustrations)**. **Note:** *Followers are available in thicknesses between 3.00 mm and 3.68 mm (see the specifications at the beginning of this Chapter).* The size of follower required is calculated as follows:

11 If the measured clearance is less than specified, subtract the measured clearance from the desired clearance, and subtract the result from the thickness of the existing follower. For example:

Sample calculation –
inlet valve clearance too small
Clearance measured = 0.26 mm
Desired clearance = 0.36 mm (0.32 to 0.40 mm)
Difference = 0.10 mm
Follower thickness fitted = 3.50 mm
Follower thickness required = 3.50 – 0.10 = 3.40 mm (marked 40)

12 If the measured clearance is greater than specified, subtract the desired clearance from the measured clearance, and add the result to the thickness of the existing follower. For example:

Sample calculation –
exhaust valve clearance too big
Clearance measured = 0.50 mm
Desired clearance = 0.40 mm (0.34 to 0.46 mm)
Difference = 0.10 mm
Follower thickness fitted = 3.76 mm
Follower thickness required = 3.76 + 0.10 = 3.86 mm (marked 86)

13 Fit the new followers as required into their respective positions and reinstall the camshafts. Rotate the engine several times by hand and then recheck the clearances.

 HAYNES HiNT *It will be helpful for future adjustment if a record is kept of the thickness of each follower fitted at each position. The followers required can be purchased in advance if the clearances and the existing follower thicknesses are known.*

8.2a Remove the cam phase sensor

8.2b Removing the double bearing cap

8.3 The bearing caps are marked

14 With all valve clearances correctly adjusted, refit the rocker cover as described in Section 4, and refit all components removed to gain access to the crankshaft pulley.

8 Camshafts and followers – removal, inspection and refitting

Removal

1 Support the engine from below with a suitable jack and block of wood to spread the load and then remove the right-hand engine steady-bar and upper engine mount bracket. Remove the right-hand headlight if required for better access as described in Chapter 12. Remove the camshaft sprockets as described in Section 6.

2 Remove the cam phase sensor from the transmission end of the cylinder head and recover the O-ring. Handle the sensor with care and avoid contact with metallic particles. At the timing chain end of the camshafts the bearing cap housing covers both of the camshafts **(see illustrations)**.

3 All other camshaft bearing caps have identification markings stamped into their top surface; the exhaust camshaft caps being marked E1 to E4 and the inlet camshaft caps being marked I1 to I4; the No 1 caps

are fitted nearest the timing chain end of the engine. Note the markings on the caps for refitting **(see illustration)**. If the caps are not marked, suitable identification marks should be made prior to removal. Using white paint or suitable marker pen, mark each cap in some way to indicate its correct fitted orientation and position. This will avoid the possibility of installing the caps in the wrong positions and/or the wrong way around on refitting.

4 Working in the **reverse** order of the tightening sequence, evenly and progressively slacken the twelve camshaft bearing cap retaining bolts by one turn at a time, to relieve the pressure of the valve springs on the bearing caps gradually and evenly **(see illustration 8.18)**. Once the valve spring pressure has been relieved, the bolts can be fully unscrewed and removed. Remove the end bearing caps first, and then remove the exhaust camshaft caps followed by the inlet camshaft caps. *Note the different coloured bolts and their fitted location.*

5 Lift the camshafts out of the cylinder head, noting their fitted position. Note the flanges on the timing chain end of the camshafts are different. The inlet cam can be identified by the pick-up ring for the camshaft sensor at the end of the camshaft **(see illustration)**.

6 Remove the followers and keep them in order. A magnet will help to remove them. Do not mix them up or you will need to check and

adjust the valve clearances all over again **(see illustration)**.

Inspection

7 Inspect the cam bearing surfaces of the head and the bearing caps. Look for score marks and deep scratches. Check the camshaft lobes for heat discoloration (blue appearance), score marks, chipped areas or flat spots.

8 Camshaft run-out can be checked by supporting each end of the camshaft on V-blocks, and measuring any run-out at the centre of the shaft using a dial gauge. Consult a Nissan dealer or engine reconditioning specialist for values.

9 Measure the height of each lobe with a micrometer, and compare the results to the figures given in the Specifications. If damage is noted or wear is excessive, new camshaft(s) must be fitted.

10 Check the cam followers and cylinder head bearing surfaces for signs of wear or damage.

11 The camshaft bearing oil clearance should now be checked by a Nissan dealer or engine reconditioning specialist.

12 If any journal is worn beyond the service limit, the cylinder head must be renewed.

Refitting

13 Liberally oil the cylinder head cam

8.5 Lift out the camshafts

8.6 Recover the followers

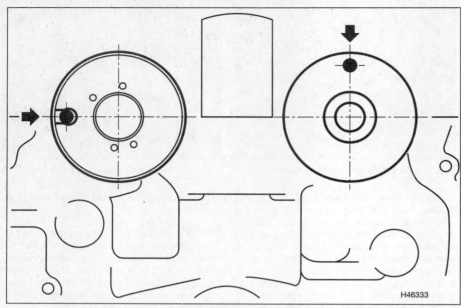

8.15 The correct alignment of the camshafts

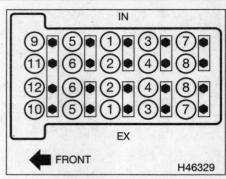

8.18 Camshaft bearing cap bolts

follower bores and the followers. Carefully refit the followers to the cylinder head; ensuring that each follower is refitted to its original bore. Some care will be required to enter the followers squarely into their bores. Liberally oil the camshaft bearing and lobe contact surfaces.

14 Lower the camshafts into their correct locations in the cylinder head.

15 Check that the crankshaft pulley TDC notch is still aligned with the pointer or mark on the timing chain cover. Position each camshaft so that its No 1 cylinder lobes are pointing away from their valves. With the shafts in this position, the sprocket locating pin in the inlet camshaft's right-hand end will be in the 9 o'clock position when viewed from the right-hand end of the engine, while that of the exhaust camshaft will be in the 12 o'clock position **(see illustration)**.

16 Ensure that the bearing cap and head mating surfaces are completely clean, unmarked and free from oil.

17 Refit the bearing caps, using the identification markings or the marks made on removal to ensure that each is installed the correct way round and in its original location. The black bolts are numbers 1 to 10. The gold bolts are fitted to the inboard side of the double bearing cap in positions 11 and 12.

18 Working in sequence, evenly and progressively tighten the camshaft bearing cap bolts by one turn at a time until the caps touch the cylinder head. Then go round again and tighten all the bolts to the specified torque setting (see Torque wrench settings for sequence). Work only as described, to impose the pressure of the valve springs gradually and evenly on the bearing caps **(see illustration)**.

19 Refit the camshaft sprockets as described in Section 6. **Note:** *If the cylinder head/*

camshafts have been overhauled, check the valve clearances 'cold' prior to refitting the rocker cover (see Section 7).

9 Cylinder head – removal and refitting

> **HAYNES HiNT** *To aid refitting, make notes on the locations of all relevant brackets and the routing of hoses and cables before removal.*

Removal

1 Disconnect the battery negative terminal (refer to *Disconnecting the battery* in the Reference Chapter).

2 Depressurise the fuel system as described in Chapter 4A.

3 Carry out the following operations as described in the relevant chapters:

a) *Remove the air cleaner assembly (Chapter 4A).*

b) *Disconnect the exhaust system front pipe from the manifold (Chapter 4A).*

c) *Disconnect the fuel pipe from the fuel*

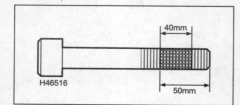

9.11 Reject any bolt with a change in diameter of more than 0.12 mm in the shaded area

rail (plug all openings, to prevent loss of fuel and entry of dirt into the fuel system). Remove the fuel rail (Chapter 4A).

d) *Disconnect the relevant electrical connectors from the throttle housing, inlet manifold and associated components.*

e) *Drain the coolant and remove the top radiator hose. Remove the heater hose and the bolt from the metal coolant pipe (Chapter 3).*

f) *Disconnect the vacuum servo unit hose and all the other relevant/breather hoses from the manifold and associated valves.*

g) *Remove the inlet manifold support brackets and inlet manifold (Chapter 4A).*

h) *Disconnect the exhaust gas sensor wiring connector.*

i) *Remove the alternator upper mounting bracket and all earth cables.*

4 Remove the timing chain tensioner and camshaft sprockets as described in Section 6.

5 Remove the camshafts as described in Section 8.

6 Slacken the retaining clip(s) and disconnect the coolant hose(s) from the cylinder head.

7 Working in the reverse of the tightening sequence, progressively slacken the ten main cylinder head bolts and the three smaller bolts, by half a turn at a time, until all bolts can be unscrewed by hand **(see illustration 9.20)**.

8 Lift out the cylinder head bolts.

9 Lift the cylinder head away with the aid of an assistant, as it is a heavy assembly. Remove the gasket from the top of the block.

10 If the cylinder head is to be dismantled for overhaul, then refer to Part B of this Chapter.

Preparation for refitting

11 Check the condition of the cylinder head bolts, and particularly their threads, whenever they are removed. Wash the bolts and wipe dry. Check each one for any sign of visible wear or damage, renewing any bolt if necessary. A micrometer can be used to check the diameter of the bolts **(see illustration)**. Although Nissan do not specify that the bolts must be renewed, it is strongly recommended that the bolts should be renewed as a complete set whenever they are disturbed. Clean and check the bolt holes in the cylinder block. The bolts must thread in easily with hand pressure only. Use a tap to clean the threads if necessary.

12 The mating faces of the cylinder head and cylinder block/crankcase must be perfectly clean before refitting the head. Use a hard plastic or wood scraper to remove all traces of gasket and carbon; also clean the piston crowns. Take particular care, as the surfaces are damaged easily. Also, make sure that the carbon is not allowed to enter the oil and water passages – this is particularly important for the lubrication system, as carbon could block the oil supply to any of the engine's components. Using adhesive tape and paper seal the water, oil and bolt holes in the cylinder block/crankcase. To prevent carbon entering the gap between the pistons and bores, smear a little grease in the gap. After cleaning each piston, use a small brush to remove all traces of grease and carbon from the gap, and then wipe away the remainder with a clean rag. Clean all the pistons in the same way.

13 Check the mating surfaces of the cylinder block/crankcase and the cylinder head for nicks, deep scratches and other damage. If slight, they may be removed carefully with a file, but if excessive, machining may be the only alternative to renewal.

14 If warpage of the cylinder head gasket surface is suspected, use a straight-edge to check it for distortion. Refer to Part B of this Chapter if necessary.

Refitting

15 Wipe clean the mating surfaces of the cylinder head and cylinder block/crankcase. Check the locating dowels are in position at each end of the cylinder block/crankcase surface.

16 Apply a 2 to 3 mm diameter bead of liquid gasket across the join between the cylinder block and timing chain cover. Fit a new gasket to the cylinder block surface, aligning it with the locating dowels.

17 With the aid of an assistant, carefully refit the cylinder head assembly to the block, aligning it with the locating dowels.

18 Apply a smear of clean oil to the threads, and to the underside of the heads, of the ten main cylinder head bolts.

19 Carefully enter each bolt into its relevant hole (do not drop them in) and screw in, by hand only, until finger-tight.

20 Working progressively and in sequence, tighten the ten main cylinder head bolts (Nos 1 to 10) to their Stage 1 torque setting, using a torque wrench and suitable socket **(see illustration)**. **Note:** *Bolts 11 to 14 in the sequence (the 6.0 mm bolts) should not be tightened now, but only after the ten main bolts have been tightened to Stage 3.*

21 Once the ten main bolts have been tightened to their Stage 1 setting, loosen them in the reverse order of the specified sequence (Stage 2).

22 Tighten the ten main bolts again by hand, then go around again in the specified sequence and tighten these ten bolts to the specified Stage 3 torque setting. Include bolts 11 to 13 this time (Stage 4).

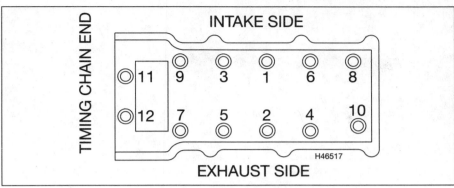

9.20 Cylinder head bolt tightening sequence

23 Finally, go around again in the specified sequence and tighten the ten main head bolts through the specified Stage 5 angle setting.

24 Refit the camshafts, sprockets and chain. If the cylinder head has been overhauled, check the valve clearances using the cold setting. Refit the rest of the components and refill the coolant system as described in Chapter 1.

25 Start the engine and warm it up to normal operating temperature, checking for oil and coolant leaks.

26 Check the valve clearances as described in Section 7.

10 Sump – removal and refitting

Removal

1 Disconnect the battery negative terminal (refer to Disconnecting the battery in the Reference Chapter).

2 Firmly apply the handbrake, and then jack up the front of the vehicle and support it securely on axle stands (see *Jacking and vehicle support*).

3 Remove the plastic wing liner from the right-hand front wing.

4 Drain the engine oil, then clean and refit the engine oil drain plug complete with a new

washer. Tighten it to the specified torque. If the engine is nearing its service interval when the oil and filter are due for renewal, it is recommended that the filter is also removed, and a new one fitted. After reassembly, the engine can then be refilled with fresh oil. Refer to Chapter 1 for further information.

5 Undo the retaining bolts in the reverse order to that shown **(see illustration)**.

6 Prise the sump off, taking care not to damage the mating surfaces.

Refitting

7 Clean all traces of sealant from the mating surfaces of the sump and upper sump.

8 Ensure that the sump and cylinder block/crankcase mating surfaces are clean and dry. Apply a continuous 3.5 to 4.5 mm diameter bead of liquid gasket to the mating surface of the sump pan. Apply the sealant to the groove in the centre of the mating surface between the holes, and around the inner edge of each bolt hole.

9 Offer it up to the sump **(see illustration)** locating it in the correct position, and refit its retaining bolts. Tighten the nuts and bolts evenly and progressively to the specified torque.

10 Wait a minimum of thirty minutes before refilling the engine with oil.

11 Refit the wing liner and roadwheel. Lower the vehicle to the ground.

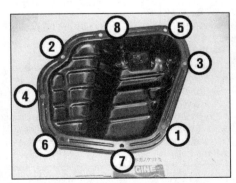

10.5 Sump bolt tightening sequence

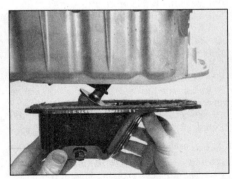

10.9 Refit the lower sump pan

11.1 Prise out the seal

11.2 Remove the spacer

11.4a Use a piece of wood to start . . .

11.4b . . . and then a suitable socket

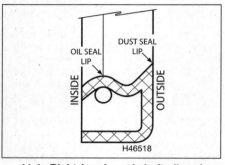

11.4c Right-hand crankshaft oil seal

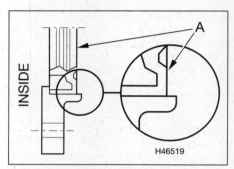

11.10 The seal (A) must not project from the carrier

11 Crankshaft oil seals – renewal

Timing chain cover oil seal

1 Remove the crankshaft pulley as described in Section 5, and the carefully lever the oil seal out of position, using a large flat-bladed screwdriver, taking care not to damage the oil pump gears or timing cover **(see illustration)**.

2 Recover the oil pump spacer from the end of the crankshaft. Note the orientation of the spacer **(see illustration)**.

3 Clean the seal housing, and polish off any burrs or raised edges, which may have caused the seal to fail in the first place.

4 Lubricate the lips of the new seal with a smear of grease and offer up the seal. Carefully ease the seal into position, taking care not to damage its sealing lip. Drive the seal into position until it seats on its locating shoulder, using a suitable tubular drift, such as a socket, which bears only on the hard outer edge of the seal **(see illustrations)**. Take care not to damage the seal lips during fitting. Note the correct orientation of the seal.

5 Wash off any traces of oil, and then refit the crankshaft pulley as described in Section 5.

Flywheel/driveplate oil seal

6 Remove the flywheel or driveplate, as described in Section 12

7 Taking care not to mark either the crankshaft or any part of the cylinder block/crankcase,

lever the seal evenly out of its housing using a large flat-bladed screwdriver.

8 Clean the seal housing, and polish off any burrs or raised edges, which may have caused the seal to fail in the first place.

9 The new seal may be supplied coated with a special grease to aid installation. Do not touch this grease. If the seal is supplied dry, grease the inner lip and outer edge.

10 A suitable drift, with an outside diameter of 102mm will be required to press the seal in place. Drive the seal in squarely until flush with the housing and then drive it just below the surface of the housing. It must not be installed flush with the housing **(see illustration)**.

11 Wash off any traces of oil, then refit the flywheel/driveplate as described in Section 14.

12 Flywheel/driveplate – removal, inspection and refitting

Removal

1 Remove the transmission as described in Chapter 7A or 7B, as applicable then, on manual transmission models, remove the clutch assembly as described in Chapter 6.

2 Prevent the flywheel/driveplate from turning by locking the ring gear teeth. Alternatively, bolt a strap between the flywheel/driveplate and the cylinder block.

3 Slacken and remove the retaining bolts, and remove the flywheel/driveplate from the end of the crankshaft. Do not drop it, as it is very heavy.

4 If necessary, on manual transmission models, remove the endplate from the cylinder block, noting which way round it is fitted. Recover the adapter plate from automatic transmission models, if fitted. If the endplate dowels are a loose fit in the block, remove them and store them for safekeeping.

Inspection

5 On manual transmission models, if the flywheel's clutch mating surface is deeply scored, cracked or otherwise damaged, the flywheel must be renewed. However, it may be possible to have it surface-ground; seek the advice of an engine reconditioning specialist.

6 If the ring gear is badly worn or has missing teeth, it must be renewed. This job is best left to a Nissan dealer or engine reconditioning specialist. The temperature to which the new ring gear must be heated for installation is critical and, if not done accurately, the hardness of the teeth will be destroyed.

Refitting

7 Install the locating dowels (where removed) and refit the endplate to the cylinder block.

8 Clean the mating surfaces of the flywheel/driveplate and crankshaft.

9 Offer up the flywheel/driveplate, and refit the retaining bolts.

10 Lock the ring gear using the method employed on dismantling, and tighten the retaining bolts to the specified torque.

11 On manual transmission models, refit the clutch as described in Chapter 6. Remove the locking tool, and refit the transmission as described in Chapter 7A or 7B.

13 Engine/transmission mountings – inspection and renewal

Inspection

1 If improved access is required, firmly apply the handbrake, and then jack up the front of the vehicle and support it securely on axle stands (see *Jacking and vehicle support*).

2 Check the mounting rubber to see if it is cracked, hardened or separated from the metal at any point; renew the mounting if any such damage or deterioration is evident **(see illustration)**.

3 Check that all the mounting's fasteners are securely tightened; use a torque wrench to check if possible.

4 Using a large screwdriver or a crowbar, check for wear in the mounting by carefully levering against it to check for free play. Where this is not possible, enlist the aid of an assistant to move the engine/transmission back-and-forth, or from side-to-side, while you watch the mounting. While some free play is to be expected even from new components, excessive wear should be obvious. If excessive free play is found, check first that the fasteners are correctly secured, and then renew any worn components as described below.

Renewal

Right-hand mounting

5 Disconnect the battery negative terminal (refer to *Disconnecting the battery* in the Reference Chapter).

6 Place a jack beneath the engine, with a block of wood on the jack head. Raise the jack until it is supporting the weight of the engine. Improved access will be gained by removing the headlight as described in Chapter 12.

7 Remove the engine stay bar (not all models) noting it's orientation. Remove the mounting bolts from the inner wing and engine support bracket. Remove the mounting as a complete unit and separate it on the bench **(see illustrations)**.

8 If necessary, undo the retaining bolts and remove the right-hand mounting bracket from the engine.

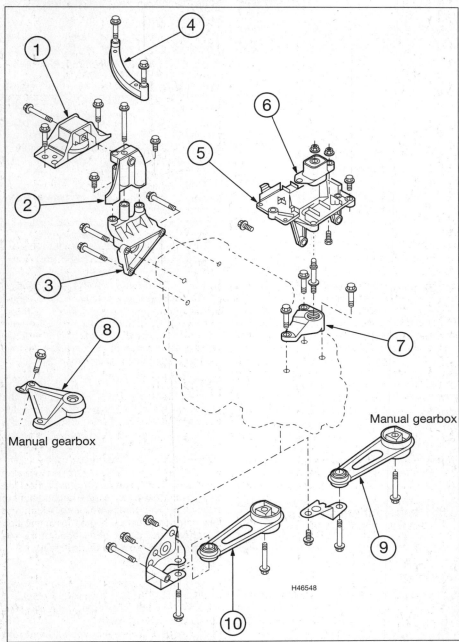

Manual gearbox

Manual gearbox

H46548

13.2 Engine/transmission mountings

1 *Right-hand insulator*	5 *Left-hand mount*	9 *Rear mount and support bracket (manual transmission)*
2 *Right-hand upper mount*	6 *Left-hand insulator*	
3 *Right-hand lower engine mount*	7 *Left-hand gearbox mount (automatic transmission)*	10 *Rear mount and support bracket (automatic transmission)*
4 *Engine mount steady-bar*	8 *Left-hand gearbox mount (manual transmission)*	

13.7a Insulator mounting bolts

13.7b Remove the rubber mounting

13.16a Insulator mounting bolts

13.16b Remove the mounting as a complete unit

9 Check carefully for signs of wear or damage on all components, and renew them where necessary.

10 On refitting, fit the mounting bracket (where removed) to the engine, and securely tighten its retaining bolts.

11 Fit the mounting to the inner wing and refit the through-bolt. Refit the engine steady-bar. Tighten the retaining bolts to the specified torque setting.

12 The jack can then be removed from underneath the engine.

13 Reconnect the battery negative terminal.

Left-hand mounting

14 Remove the battery as described in Chapter 5A and then remove the relay box.

15 Place a jack and block of wood beneath the transmission, and raise the jack to take the weight of the transmission.

16 Slacken and remove the through-bolt nut, then undo the two bolts that secure the mounting to the battery support plate. If difficulty is encountered, remove the bolts from the transmission mounting and remove the bolts that secure the battery tray to the inner wing **(see illustrations)**. Remove the rubber mounting on the bench.

17 Check carefully for signs of wear or damage on all components, and renew them where necessary.

18 On refitting, fit the transmission mounting bracket (where removed) to the gearbox and securely tighten its retaining bolts.

19 Refit the insulator to the battery mounting bracket (where applicable). Lubricate the bolt on the gearbox mounting and manoeuvre the mounting into position. Fit the bolts securing the mounting to the inner wing and tighten them to the specified torque setting.

20 Refit the nut on the through-bolt and tighten to the specified torque setting.

21 Remove the jack from underneath the engine. Refit the battery and relay box.

Rear mounting

22 If not already done, firmly apply the handbrake, and then jack up the front of the vehicle and support it securely on axle stands (see *Jacking and vehicle support*).

23 Disconnect the battery negative terminal (refer to *Disconnecting the battery* in the Reference Chapter).

24 Slacken and remove the two vertical bolts from the rear engine/transmission mounting.

25 Slacken and remove the bolts securing the support bracket to the transmission.

26 Remove the mounting.

27 Check carefully for signs of wear or damage on all components, and renew them where necessary.

28 Refit the mounting bracket and tighten its retaining bolts to the specified torque.

29 Align the rear mounting with its bracket, then insert the through-bolt and tighten its nut.

30 Lower the vehicle to the ground and reconnect the battery.

Chapter 2 Part B:
Engine removal and overhaul procedures

Contents

Section number

Crankshaft – bearing selection and refitting. 19
Crankshaft – inspection 15
Crankshaft – removal 12
Cylinder block/crankcase – cleaning and inspection. 13
Cylinder head – dismantling. 6
Cylinder head – reassembly 8
Cylinder head and valves – cleaning and inspection 7
Engine – initial start-up after overhaul 21
Engine and transmission – removal, separation, reconnection and
  refitting 4
Engine overhaul – dismantling sequence. 5

Section number

Engine overhaul – general information. 2
Engine overhaul – reassembly sequence. 17
Engine removal – methods and precautions 3
General information 1
Main and big-end bearings – inspection 16
Oil pump – removal, inspection and refitting 10
Piston rings – refitting. 18
Piston/connecting rod assembly – bearing selection and refitting . . 20
Piston/connecting rod assembly – inspection 14
Piston/connecting rod assembly – removal 11
Timing chain – removal and refitting 9

Degrees of difficulty

Easy, suitable for novice with little experience 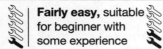	**Fairly easy,** suitable for beginner with some experience	**Fairly difficult,** suitable for competent DIY mechanic	**Difficult,** suitable for experienced DIY mechanic	**Very difficult,** suitable for expert DIY or professional

Specifications

Lubrication system

Oil pump type. . . . . Rotor-type, driven off crankshaft right-hand end
Minimum oil pressure at normal operating temperature:
  At idle . . . . 0.44 bar
  At 2000 rpm . . . . 2.65 bars
  At 6000 rpm . . . . 3.73 bars
Oil pump clearances:
  Outer rotor-to-cover clearance. . . . . 0.025 to 0.075 mm
  Inner rotor-to-cover clearance . . . . 0.025 to 0.075 mm
  Inner rotor-to-brazed portion of housing clearance . . . . 0.045 to 0.090 mm

Cylinder head

Maximum permissible surface distortion . . . . 0.1 mm

Timing chain tensioner

Maximum protrusion . . . . 10 mm

Valves

Valve head diameter:
  Inlet. . . . . 27.4 to 27.6 mm
  Exhaust. . . . . 22.4 to 22.6 mm
Valve stem diameter:
  Inlet. . . . . 5.465 to 5.480 mm
  Exhaust. . . . . 5.445 to 5.460 mm
Overall length:
  Inlet. . . . . 97.85 mm
  Exhaust. . . . . 97.92 mm
Valve stem-to-guide clearance:
  Inlet. . . . . 0.020 to 0.053 mm
  Exhaust. . . . . 0.040 to 0.073 mm

Cylinder block

Cylinder bore inner diameter:
1.0 and 1.2 litre engines:	
Grade No 1	71.000 to 71.010 mm
Grade No 2	71.010 to 71.020 mm
Grade No 3	71.020 to 71.030 mm
1.4 litre engine:	
Grade No 1	73.000 to 73.010 mm
Grade No 2	73.010 to 73.020 mm
Grade No 3	73.020 to 73.030 mm

Pistons

Piston diameter:
1.0 litre engine (measured 37.3 mm down from the top of the piston):	
Grade No 1	70.980 to 70.990 mm
Grade No 2	70.990 to 71.000 mm
Grade No 3	71.000 to 71.010 mm
1.2 litre engine (measured 34.3 mm down from the top of the piston):	
Grade No 1	70.980 to 70.990 mm
Grade No 2	70.990 to 71.000 mm
Grade No 3	71.000 to 71.010 mm
1.4 litre engine (measured 32.3 mm down from the top of the piston):	
Grade No 1	72.980 to 72.990 mm
Grade No 2	72.990 to 73.000 mm
Grade No 3	73.000 to 73.010 mm
Piston-to-bore clearance	0.010 to 0.030 mm

Piston rings

Ring-to-groove clearance:
Top compression ring	0.040 to 0.080 mm
Service limit	0.110 mm
Second compression ring	0.025 to 0.070 mm
Service limit	0.100 mm
Oil control ring	0.030 to 0.104 mm

End gaps:
Standard:	
Top compression ring	0.18 to 0.33 mm
Second compression ring	0.50 to 0.65 mm
Oil control ring	0.20 to 0.70 mm
Service limit:	
Top compression ring	0.57 mm
Second compression ring	0.85 mm
Oil control ring	0.96 mm

Crankshaft

Endfloat:
Standard	0.060 to 0.260 mm
Service limit	0.3 mm
Main bearing running clearance:	
Standard	0.018 to 0.034 mm
Service limit	0.05 mm
Big-end bearing running clearance:	
Standard	0.010 to 0.044 mm
Service limit	0.064 mm

Torque wrench settings

Refer to Chapter 2A

1 General information

Note: *After Section 5, all instructions are based on the assumption that the engine has been removed from the vehicle.*

Included in this Part of Chapter 2 are details of removing the engine/transmission from the vehicle, and general overhaul procedures for the cylinder head, cylinder block/crankcase and all other engine internal components.

The information given ranges from advice concerning preparation for an overhaul and the purchase of new parts, to detailed step-by-step procedures covering removal, inspection, renovation and refitting of engine internal components.

For information concerning in-car engine repair, as well as the removal and refitting of those external components necessary for full overhaul, refer to Part A of this Chapter and to Section 5. Ignore any preliminary dismantling operations described in Part A that are no longer relevant once the engine has been removed.

Apart from torque wrench settings, which are given at the beginning of Part A, all specifications relating to engine overhaul are at the beginning of this Part of Chapter 2.

2 Engine overhaul –
general information

It is not always easy to determine when, or if, an engine should be completely overhauled, as a number of factors must be considered.

High mileage is not necessarily an indication that an overhaul is needed, while low mileage does not preclude the need for an overhaul. Frequency of servicing is probably the most important consideration. An engine which has had regular and frequent oil and filter changes, as well as other required maintenance, should give many thousands of miles of reliable service. Conversely, a neglected engine may require an overhaul very early in its life.

Excessive oil consumption is an indication that piston rings, valve seals and/or valve guides are in need of attention. Make sure that oil leaks are not responsible before deciding that the rings and/or guides are worn. Perform a compression test, as described in Part A of this Chapter, to determine the likely cause of the problem.

Check the oil pressure with a gauge fitted in place of the oil pressure switch, and compare it with that specified. If it is extremely low, the main and big-end bearings, and/or the oil pump, are probably worn out.

Loss of power, rough running, knocking or metallic engine noises, excessive valve gear noise, and high fuel consumption may also point to the need for an overhaul, especially if they are all present at the same time. If a complete service does not remedy the situation, major mechanical work is the only solution.

An engine overhaul involves restoring all internal parts to the specification of a new engine. During an overhaul, the cylinder bores are rebored (where necessary) and the pistons and piston rings are renewed. New main and big-end bearings are generally fitted; if necessary, the crankshaft may be reground, to restore the journals. The valves are also serviced as well, since they are usually in less-than-perfect condition at this point. The end result should be an as-new engine that will give many trouble-free miles.

Note: *Critical cooling system components such as the hoses, thermostat and coolant pump should be renewed when an engine is overhauled. The radiator should be checked carefully, to ensure that it is not clogged or leaking. Also, it is a good idea to renew the oil pump whenever the engine is overhauled.*

Before beginning the engine overhaul, read through the entire procedure, to familiarise yourself with the scope and requirements of the job. Check on the availability of parts, and make sure that any necessary special tools and equipment are obtained in advance. Most work can be done with typical hand tools, although a number of precision measuring tools are required for inspecting parts to determine if they must be renewed.

The services provided by an engineering machine shop or engine reconditioning specialist will almost certainly be required, particularly if major repairs such as crankshaft regrinding or cylinder reboring are necessary. Apart from carrying out machining operations, these establishments will normally handle the inspection of parts; offer advice concerning reconditioning or renewal and supply new components such as pistons, piston rings and bearing shells. It is recommended that the establishment used is a member of the Federation of Engine Re-Manufacturers, or a similar society.

Always wait until the engine has been completely dismantled, and until all components (especially the cylinder block and the crankshaft) have been inspected, before deciding what service and repair operations must be performed by an automotive engineering works. The condition of these components will be the major factor to consider when determining whether to overhaul the original engine, or to buy a reconditioned unit. Do not, therefore, purchase parts or have overhaul work done on other components until they have been thoroughly inspected.

As a final note, to ensure maximum life and minimum trouble from a reconditioned engine, everything must be assembled with care, in a spotlessly-clean environment.

3 Engine removal –
methods and precautions

If you have decided that the engine must be removed for overhaul or major repair work, several preliminary steps should be taken.

Locating a suitable place to work is extremely important. Adequate workspace, along with storage space for the vehicle, will be needed. If a workshop or garage is not available, at the very least, a flat, level, clean work surface is required.

Cleaning the engine compartment and engine/transmission before beginning the removal procedure will help keep tools clean and organised.

An engine hoist will also be necessary. Make sure the equipment is rated in excess of the combined weight of the engine and transmission. Safety is of primary importance, considering the potential hazards involved in removing the engine/transmission from the vehicle.

The help of an assistant is essential. Apart from the safety aspects involved, there are many instances when one person cannot simultaneously perform all of the operations required during engine/transmission removal.

Plan the operation ahead of time. Before starting work, arrange for the hire of, or obtain, all of the tools and equipment you will need. Some of the equipment necessary to perform engine/transmission removal and installation safely (in addition to an engine hoist) is as follows: a heavy-duty trolley jack, complete sets of spanners and sockets as described at the rear of this manual, wooden blocks, and plenty of rags and cleaning solvent for mopping-up spilled oil, coolant and fuel. If the hoist must be hired, make sure that you arrange for it in advance, and perform all of the operations possible without it beforehand. This will save you money and time.

Plan for the vehicle to be out of use for quite a while. An engineering machine shop or engine reconditioning specialist will be required to perform some of the work, which cannot be accomplished without special equipment. These places often have a busy schedule, so it would be a good idea to consult them before removing the engine, in order to accurately estimate the amount of time required to rebuild or repair components that may need work.

During the engine/transmission removal procedure, it is advisable to make notes of the locations of all brackets, cable ties, earthing points, etc, as well as how the wiring harnesses, hoses and electrical connections are attached and routed around the engine and engine compartment. An effective way of doing this is to take a series of photographs of the various components before they are disconnected or removed. A simple inexpensive disposable or digital camera is ideal for this and the resulting photographs will prove invaluable when the engine is refitted.

Always be extremely careful when removing and refitting the engine/transmission. Serious injury can result from careless actions. Plan ahead and take your time, and a job of this nature, although major, can be accomplished successfully.

The engine and transmission can be removed either by lowering or lifting. We show removing the engine and transmission by lifting. Lowering will require removal of the radiator and something suitable to lower the unit onto that will protect the sump and allow the unit to be pulled out. A suitable sturdy trolley can easily be fabricated by the home mechanic for this task.

4 Engine and transmission
– removal, separation, reconnection and refitting

Removal

1 Depressurise the fuel system as described in Chapter 4A.

2 Disconnect the battery negative terminal (refer to *Disconnecting the battery* in the Reference Chapter).

3 Firmly apply the handbrake, then jack up the front of the vehicle and support it securely on axle stands (*see Jacking and vehicle support*). Remove both front roadwheels.

4 Undo all the retaining screws, and remove both the front wing liners.

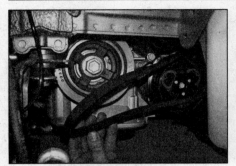
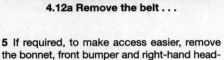

4.12a Remove the belt . . .

4.12b . . . and unbolt the compressor

4.12c Tie the compressor to the bonnet slam panel

5 If required, to make access easier, remove the bonnet, front bumper and right-hand headlight as described in Chapters 11 and 12.

6 Drain the cooling system (see Chapter 1), saving the coolant if it is fit for re-use.

7 Drain the transmission oil as described in Chapters 7A and 1. Refit the drain and filler plugs, and tighten them to their specified torque settings.

8 If the engine is to be dismantled, working as described in Chapter 1, drain the oil and if required remove the oil filter. Clean and refit the drain plug, tightening it to the specified torque.

9 Remove the upper cowl, wipers, wiper motor and support panel.

10 Carry out the following operations as described in Chapter 4A and 5B.
 a) *Remove the air cleaner assembly.*
 b) *Disconnect and remove the battery.*
 c) *Disconnect the fuel feed hose from the fuel rail (plug all openings, to prevent loss of fuel and entry of dirt into the fuel system).*
 d) *Disconnect the electrical connectors to the throttle body, EVAP solenoid and cam sensor.*
 e) *Remove the inlet manifold and support bracket.*
 f) *Disconnect the wiring to the starter motor and remove the starter motor.*
 g) *Remove the four ignition coils.*
 h) *Disconnect the vacuum servo unit hose.*
 i) *Remove the exhaust front pipe and disconnect the wiring to the alternator.*

11 Slacken the retaining clips, and disconnect the heater hoses and all other relevant cooling system hoses from the engine, noting each hose's correct fitted location. Remove the radiator if removing the engine from below (see Chapter 3).

12 On models with air conditioning, unbolt the compressor and position it clear of the engine. Support the weight of the compressor by tying it to the vehicle body, to prevent any excess strain being placed on the compressor lines whilst the engine is removed **(see illustrations)**. Do not disconnect the refrigerant lines from the compressor (see the warnings given in Chapter 3).

13 Working around the engine remove the retaining bolts, and disconnect all the relevant earth leads from the cylinder head, manifold and gearbox.

14 Working as described in Chapter 8, remove the driveshafts and rear engine support.

Manual transmission models

15 Release the gear selector cables and pull them free from the support bracket, or unbolt and remove the bracket complete with the cables.

16 Prise free the clip and remove the clutch cable. Seal the end of the pipe and tie the pipe to one side.

17 Disconnect the plugs for the reversing light switch and the crankshaft position sensor.

Automatic transmission models

18 Remove the transmission breather hose and disconnect the RPM sensor from the bellhousing.

19 Disconnect and remove the selector cable and unplug the park/neutral position switch.

20 Remove the earth cable and unplug the turbine sensor. Disconnect the control valve electrical plug.

21 Have a suitable container ready and then disconnect the oil cooler pipes at the front of the transmission. Plug and seal the pipes at both ends.

All models

22 Loosen, but *do not* remove all the bolt securing the left- and right-hand engine mounts (see chapter 2A). Make a final check round the engine and transmission, to make sure nothing (apart from the left- and right-hand mountings) remains attached or in the way which will prevent it from being lifted out.

23 Manoeuvre the engine hoist into position, and attach it to the cylinder head using suitable lifting brackets. Raise the hoist until it is supporting the weight of the engine. Place a suitable jack with a wooden block to spread the load under the gearbox.

24 Unbolt and remove the gearbox mounting. Lower the jack slowly to see if the engine crane is positioned over the centre of gravity. If the engine and gearbox tilt over, then take the weight with the jack and reposition the engine slings. A little trial and effort will be needed to find the spot where the engine and gearbox can be lifted in a near horizontal position

25 Unbolt and remove the left-hand engine mounting and then lift the engine out. The help of an assistant will prove useful to help operate the engine crane whilst you guide the power unit clear of the engine bay. Be prepared to steady the engine when it touches down, to stop it toppling over.

Separation

26 With reference to Chapters 7A and 7B, work around the bellhousing and remove the bolts. Make a note of each bolts location. They are different lengths and some are fitted form the gearbox side, others from the engine side.

Refitting

27 Refitting is a reversal of removal, noting the following additional points:
 a) *Make sure that all mating faces are clean, and use new gaskets where necessary.*
 b) *Tighten all nuts and bolts to the specified torque setting, where given.*
 c) *On manual transmission models, lightly lubricate the splines of the transmission input shaft. On completion, bleed the clutch hydraulic system as described in Chapter 6.*
 d) *Refit the automatic transmission using the information in Chapter 7B, Section 2.*
 e) *Refit the driveshafts as described in Chapter 8.*
 f) *Refit the exhaust system as described in Chapter 4B.*
 g) *Replenish the transmission oil or fluid, and check the level with reference to Chapter 7A or 1.*
 h) *Refill the cooling system as described in Chapter 1.*

**5 Engine overhaul –
 dismantling sequence**

1 It is much easier to dismantle and work on the engine if it is mounted on a portable engine stand. These stands can often be hired from a tool hire shop. Before the engine is mounted on a stand, the flywheel should be removed from the engine, so that the engine stand bolts can be tightened into the end of the cylinder block.

2 If a stand is not available, it is possible to dismantle the engine with it blocked up on a sturdy workbench or on the floor. Be extra careful not to tip or drop the engine when working without a stand.

3 If you're going to obtain a reconditioned ('recon') engine, all external components must be removed first, to be transferred to the new engine (just as they will if you are doing a complete engine overhaul yourself). **Note:** *When removing the external components from the engine, pay close attention to details that may be helpful or important during refitting. Note the fitted position of gaskets, seals, spacers, pins, washers, bolts and other small items. These external components include the following:*

a) *Alternator, air conditioning compressor, etc ('ancillaries').*
b) *Spark plugs.*
c) *Thermostat housing.*
d) *Fuel injection equipment.*
e) *Inlet and exhaust manifolds.*
f) *Oil filter.*
g) *Engine mountings and lifting brackets.*
h) *Coolant pipes and hoses.*
i) *Flywheel.*

4 If you are obtaining a 'short' motor (which, when available, consists of the engine cylinder block, crankshaft, pistons and connecting rods all assembled), then the cylinder head, sump, oil pump, and timing chain (where applicable) will have to be removed also **(see illustration)**

5 If you are planning a complete overhaul, the engine can be disassembled and the internal components removed in the following order:

a) *Engine external components (including inlet and exhaust manifolds).*
b) *Timing sprockets.*
c) *Cylinder head.*
d) *Flywheel.*
e) *Sump (and stiffener plate or lower crankcase, as applicable).*
f) *Oil pump and timing chain.*

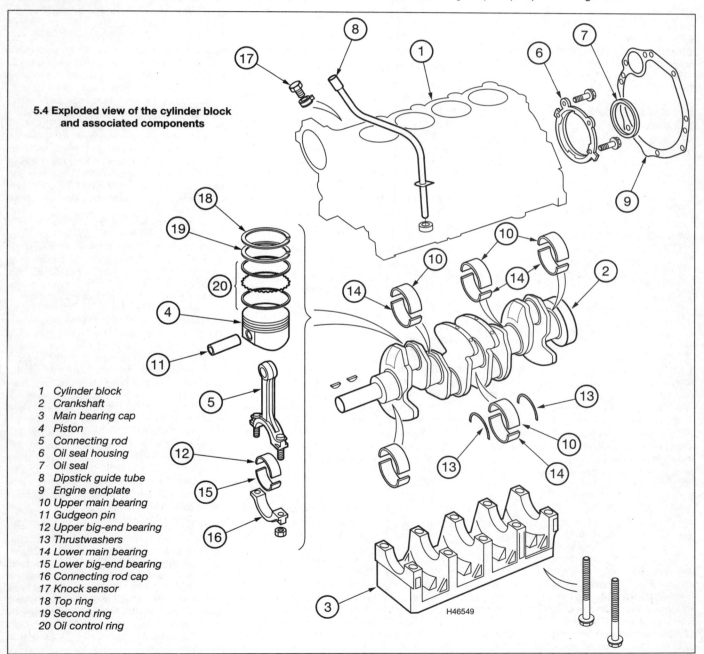

5.4 Exploded view of the cylinder block and associated components

1 Cylinder block
2 Crankshaft
3 Main bearing cap
4 Piston
5 Connecting rod
6 Oil seal housing
7 Oil seal
8 Dipstick guide tube
9 Engine endplate
10 Upper main bearing
11 Gudgeon pin
12 Upper big-end bearing
13 Thrustwashers
14 Lower main bearing
15 Lower big-end bearing
16 Connecting rod cap
17 Knock sensor
18 Top ring
19 Second ring
20 Oil control ring

H46549

6.4 Pull the oil seal free with a pair of pliers

6.5 Specialist pliers may be required to free the oil seal

6.7 Place each valve and its component parts in a labelled plastic bag

g) *Pistons and connecting rods.*
h) *Crankshaft and main bearings.*

6 Before beginning the disassembly and overhaul procedures, make sure that you have all of the correct tools necessary. Refer to the reference section at the end of this manual for further information.

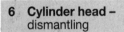

6 Cylinder head – dismantling

Note: *New and reconditioned cylinder heads are available from the manufacturer, and from engine reconditioning specialists. Some specialist tools are required for dismantling and inspection, and new components may not be readily available. It may therefore be more practical and economical to obtain a reconditioned head, rather than overhaul the original head.*

1 Remove the exhaust manifold with reference to Chapter 4A.
2 Remove the cylinder head as described in Part A of this Chapter.
3 If not already done, remove the camshaft followers as described in Part A of this Chapter.
4 Using a valve spring compressor, compress each valve spring in turn until the split collets can be removed. Release the compressor, and lift off the spring retainer, spring and spring seat. Push the valve out of the head. Using a pair of pliers, carefully extract the valve stem seal from the top of the guide **(see illustration)**.

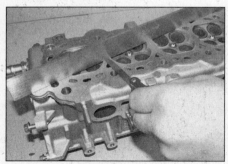

7.5 Use a straight-edge and feeler gauge to check for distortion

5 The oil seals can be difficult to extract. Soak them in penetrating fluid or try warming them with a hot air gun. Alternatively a pair of valve oil seal pliers can be purchased **(see illustration)**.
6 If, when the valve spring compressor is screwed down, the spring retainer refuses to free and expose the split collets, gently tap the top of the tool, directly over the retainer, with a light hammer. This will free the retainer.
7 It is essential that each valve is stored together with its collets, retainer, spring, and spring seat. The valves should also be kept in their correct sequence, unless they are so badly worn that they are to be renewed. If they are going to be kept and used again, place each valve assembly in a labelled polythene bag or similar small container. Note that No 1 valve is nearest to the timing chain end of the engine **(see illustration)**.

7 Cylinder head and valves – cleaning and inspection

Cleaning

1 Scrape away all traces of old gasket material from the cylinder head, but avoid using a metal scraper as it may damage the mating faces.
2 Scrape away the carbon from the combustion chambers and ports, then wash the cylinder head thoroughly with paraffin or a suitable solvent.
3 Scrape off any heavy carbon deposits

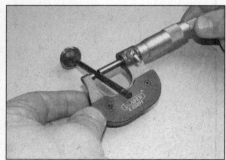

7.10 Measuring a valve stem

that may have formed on the valves, then use a power-operated wire brush to remove deposits from the valve heads and stems.

Inspection

Cylinder head

4 Inspect the head very carefully for cracks, evidence of coolant leakage, and other damage. If significant defects are found, a new cylinder head should be obtained.
5 Use a straight-edge and feeler blade to check for distortion of the cylinder head gasket surface. If the head is distorted beyond the limit given in the Specifications, seek the advice of an engine reconditioning specialist as to whether machining is possible **(see illustration)**.
6 Examine the valve seats in each of the combustion chambers. If they are severely pitted, cracked, or burned, they will need to be renewed or recut by an engine reconditioning specialist. If they are only slightly pitted, this can be removed by grinding-in the valve heads and seats with fine valve-grinding compound, as described below.
7 Check the valve guides for wear by inserting the relevant valve, and checking for side-to-side motion of the valve. A very small amount of movement is acceptable. If the movement seems excessive, remove the valve. Measure the valve stem diameter (see below), and renew the valve if it is worn. If the valve stem is not worn, the wear must be in the valve guide, and the guide must be renewed. The renewal of valve guides should be carried out by an engine reconditioning specialist, who will have the necessary tools available.
8 If renewing the valve guides, the valve seats are to be recut or reground only after the guides have been fitted.

Valves

9 Examine the head of each valve for pitting, burning, cracks, and general wear. Check the valve stem for scoring and wear ridges. Rotate the valve, and check for any obvious indication that it is bent. Look for pits and excessive wear on the tip of each valve stem. Renew any valve that shows any such signs of wear or damage.
10 If the valve appears satisfactory at this stage, measure the valve stem diameter

at several points using a micrometer. Any significant difference in the readings obtained indicates wear of the valve stem. Should any of these conditions be apparent, the valve(s) must be renewed (**see illustration**).

11 If the valves are in satisfactory condition, they should be ground (lapped) into their respective seats, to ensure a smooth, gas-tight seal. If the seat is only lightly pitted, or if it has been recut, fine grinding compound only should be used to produce the required finish. Coarse valve-grinding compound should not be used, unless a seat is badly burned or deeply pitted. If this is the case, the cylinder head and valves should be inspected by a specialist, to decide whether seat recutting, or even the renewal of the valve or seat insert (where possible) is required.

12 Valve grinding is carried out as follows, with the head supported upside-down on blocks.

13 Smear a trace of (the appropriate grade of) valve-grinding compound on the seat face, and press a suction grinding tool onto the valve head. With a semi-rotary action, grind the valve head to its seat, lifting the valve occasionally to redistribute the grinding compound (**see illustration**). A light spring placed under the valve head will greatly ease this operation.

14 If coarse grinding compound is being used, work only until a dull, matt even surface is produced on both the valve seat and the valve, then wipe off the used compound, and repeat the process with fine compound. When a smooth unbroken ring of light grey matt finish is produced on both the valve and seat, the grinding operation is complete. Do not grind-in the valves any further than absolutely necessary, or the seat will be prematurely sunk into the cylinder head.

15 When all the valves have been ground-in, carefully wash off all traces of grinding compound using paraffin or a suitable solvent, before reassembling the cylinder head.

Valve components

16 Examine the valve springs for signs of damage and discoloration. The specified Nissan procedure for checking the condition

7.13 Lapping-in a valve

of valve springs involves measuring the force necessary to compress each spring to a specified height. This is not possible without the use of the Nissan special test equipment, and therefore spring checking must be entrusted to a Nissan dealer. A rough idea of the condition of the spring can be gained by measuring the spring free length, and comparing it with a new one (**see illustration**).

17 Stand each spring on a flat surface, and position a square alongside the edge of the spring.

18 If any of the springs are damaged, distorted or have lost their tension, obtain a complete new set of springs. It is normal to renew the valve springs as a matter of course if a major overhaul is being carried out.

19 Renew the valve stem oil seals regardless of their apparent condition.

7.16 Measure the spring height and compare to a new one

8 Cylinder head – reassembly

1 Refit the spring seat then, working on the first valve, dip the new valve stem seal in fresh engine oil. Place it on the valve guide and use a suitable socket or metal tube to press the seal firmly onto the guide (**see illustrations**).

2 Lubricate the stems of the valves, and insert the valves into their original locations (**see illustration**). If new valves are being fitted, insert them into the locations to which they have been ground.

3 Locate the valve spring on top of its seat; ensuring that the spring is fitted with its closer-pitched coils at the bottom, and then refit the spring retainer (**see illustrations**).

8.1a Fit the spring seat . . .

8.1b . . . and press a new oil seal onto the valve using a suitable socket

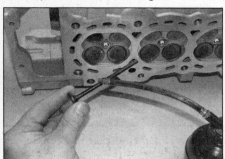
8.2 Lubricate the valve stem before fitting

8.3a Fit the vale spring . . .

8.3b . . . and spring retainer

8.4 Install the collets using grease to help locate them

4 Compress the valve spring, and locate the split collets in the recess in the valve stem **(see illustration)**. Release the compressor, then repeat the procedure on the remaining valves.

 Use a little dab of grease to hold the collets in position on the valve stem while the spring compressor is released.

5 With all the valves installed, place the cylinder head on blocks on the bench and, using a hammer and interposed block of wood, tap the end of each valve stem to settle the components.

6 The cylinder head and associated components may now be refitted as described in Part A of this Chapter, and in Chapter 4A.

---

9 Timing chain – removal and refitting

Note: *The cylinder head does **not** need to be removed to renew the timing chain.*

Removal

1 Remove the engine as described in Section 4. Remove the cylinder head endplate, camshaft sprockets and lower sump pan as described in Chapter 2A. Remove the three auxiliary bolts from the cylinder head.
2 Loosen the upper pan mounting bolts in the reverse order to that shown and then remove them **(see illustration)**. Note the position of the bolts. There are three different lengths.
3 Wearing gloves and using the cut-out provided **(see illustration)**, insert a flat-bladed screwdriver and break the seal between the upper pan and cylinder block. Take your time here and gently prise the components apart. It may be useful to run a sharp craft knife along the gap as it opens up. A selection of small wooden wedges tapped into the gap may help to separate the parts.

4 Unbolt and remove the oil strainer.
5 Set the engine to top dead centre on number one cylinder as described in Chapter 2A. The lobes of the camshaft on cylinder one will be pointing outwards. Remove the crankshaft pulley and recover the spacer with a pair of long-nosed pliers or a magnet.
6 Loosen and remove the bolts holding the chain cover. Carefully remove the cover. If the cylinder head is still in place, then take care not to damage the end of the cylinder head gasket.
7 Remove the chain and crankshaft sprockets and then unbolt the slack side guide and the tension guide, noting the special bolt that secures the tension guide in place. If the cylinder head is in place use a hot air gun to heat the two locating pins in the cylinder block. Remove them with locking pliers. This procedure is only necessary if the head is still in place. They can be left if the cylinder head has been removed, provided the cover is fitted before the cylinder head.

Refitting

8 Remove all the gasket material from the mounting surfaces. Carefully inspect the chain and sprockets for signs of wear. If you are removing the chain because the protrusion of the tensioner has exceeded the specification, then discard the chain and fit a new timing chain kit.
9 Install the chain to the crankshaft sprocket first. The crankshaft key will be in the 12 o'clock position and the blue chain link should be positioned next to the mark on the sprocket in the 7 o'clock position. Hang the top of the chain over the camshafts and install the slack side guide and the tension guide **(see illustration)**.
10 Fit the camshaft sprockets ensuring the coloured links align with the marks on the sprockets. Install the chain tensioner and remove the pin **(see illustration)**.
11 Temporarily fit the oil pump drive spacer, the crankshaft pulley and bolt. Rotate the engine several times in a clockwise direction – viewed from the right-hand side. Place the inlet camshaft in the retarded position as described in Chapter 2A. Rotate the engine again. If all is well remove the bolt, pulley and spacer.
12 Fit a new oil seal to the cover as described

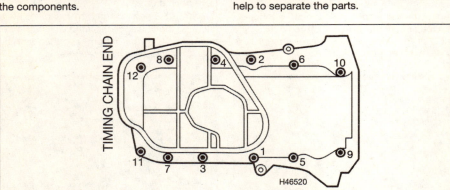

9.2 Upper oil pan bolts tightening sequence

4, 8 and 12 = 70 mm bolts
9 and 10 = 90 mm
All other bolts = 25 mm

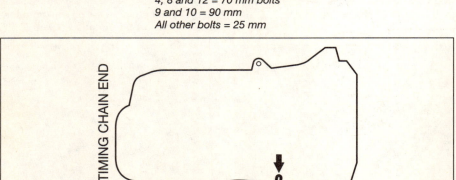

9.3 Lever apart only at the point shown

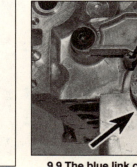

9.9 The blue link correctly positioned

in Chapter 2A and fit a new O-ring to the cylinder block. Apply a 2 to 3 mm diameter bead of sealant to the cover, and smear a very thin layer across the upper surface of the cover. The locating pins were removed to allow the cover to slide in and up to the cylinder head. It is important that the cylinder head gasket is not trapped or distorted in anyway **(see illustrations)**.

13 Loosely fit the cover bolts and the head-to-cover bolts. Using a suitable punch drive the dowel pins through the cover and into the block. There is no specific tightening sequence for the bolts, so work around the cover in a diagonal sequence to the specified torque **(see illustration)**. Refit the oil pump spacer, crankshaft pulley and bolt.

14 Refit the oil strainer and pick-up pipe.

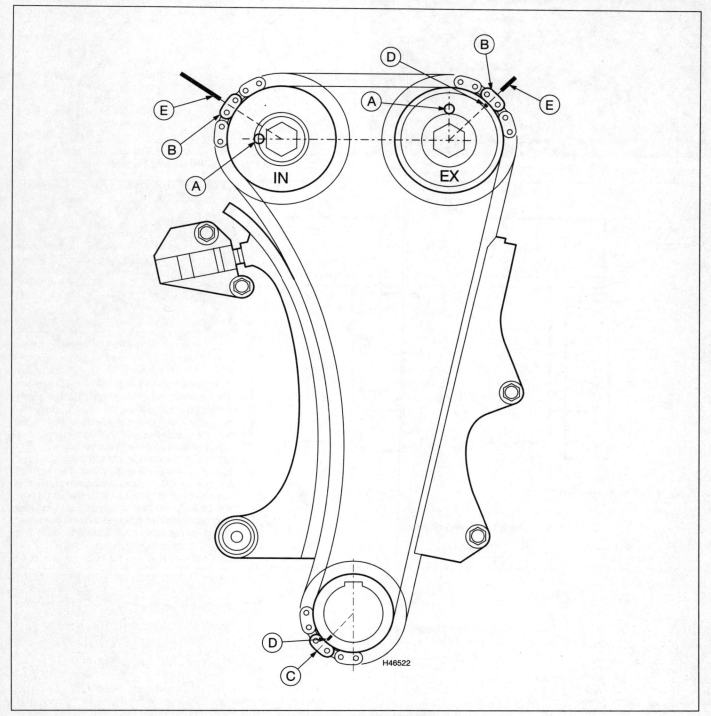

9.10 The correct chain position

A Camshaft dowel	*C Blue link*	*E Notched mark*
B Mauve or orange link	*D Stamp mark*	

9.12a Fit a new O-ring

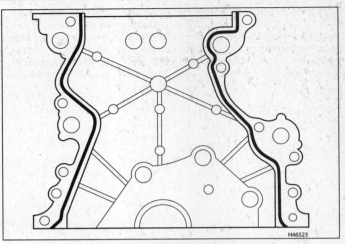

9.12b Apply the sealant correctly

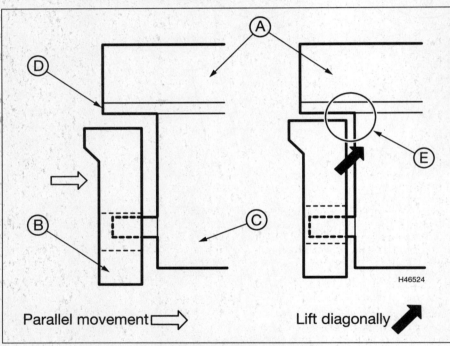

Parallel movement ⇨

Lift diagonally

9.12c Refitting the timing chain cover

A Cylinder head   C Cylinder block   E Alignment point
B Chain cover   D Head gasket

9.12d Fitting the chain cover

15 Clean all traces of sealant from the upper oil pan. Apply a bead of liquid gasket along the machined grooves in the oil pan. Apply the sealant to the outside of the three bolt holes that are located along the right-hand front edge of the block **(see illustrations)**.

16 Locate the bolts in their correct positions (they are different lengths), and then tighten the bolts in the correct sequence to the specified torque **(see illustration 9.2)**. Immediately remove all the sealant that has been squeezed from the joint. Refit the lower oil pan as described in Chapter 2A.

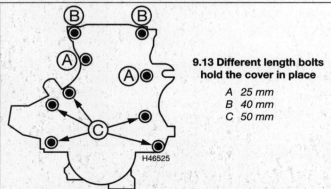

9.13 Different length bolts hold the cover in place

A 25 mm
B 40 mm
C 50 mm

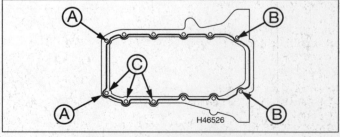

9.15a Apply liquid gasket to the sump

1 A-A and B-B = 5.5 to 6.5 mm diameter bead
2 A-B = 4.0 to 5.0 mm diameter bead
3 Apply to outside of bolt holes C

9.15b Refit the upper oil pan

10.1 Oil pump cover bolts

10. 2a Lift out the inner rotor . . .

10 Oil pump –
removal, inspection and refitting

1 The oil pump is an integral part of the timing chain cover, so remove the cover as described in Section 9, and then remove the retaining bolts from the pump on the rear of the timing chain cover **(see illustration)**.
2 Remove both the oil pump rotors from the cover, noting their fitted position **(see illustrations)**.
3 Inspect the pump rotors, regulator valve piston and the cover for obvious signs of wear or damage.
4 Fit the rotors to the cover and, using feeler blades of the appropriate thickness, measure the clearance between the outer rotor and cover, and between the tips of inner and outer rotor **(see illustration)**.
5 Using feeler gauge blades and a straight-edge placed across the top of the cover and the gears, measure the inner and outer gear endfloat.
6 If any measurement is outside the specified limits, or the rotors and cover are damaged, the complete timing chain cover assembly should be renewed.
7 Lubricate the rotors with clean engine oil, and refit them to the pump body. Ensure that the rotors are fitted in the correct position noted on removal.
8 Ensure that the mating surfaces are clean and dry, and refit the pump cover. Fit the cover retaining bolts and tighten them to the specified torque settings.

11 Piston/connecting
rod assembly – removal

Note: *Do not be tempted to remove the dipstick guide tube. It is designed to be fitted once only. If removed a new guide tube will have to be fitted.*

1 Remove the sumps, timing chain and cylinder head.
2 If there is a pronounced wear ridge at the top of any bore, it may be necessary to remove it with a scraper or ridge reamer, to

10. 2b . . . and the outer

avoid piston damage during removal. Such a ridge indicates excessive wear of the cylinder bore.
3 Each connecting rod and bearing cap should be stamped with its respective cylinder number, No 1 cylinder being at the timing chain end of the engine **(see illustration)**. If no markings are visible, using quick-drying paint or similar, mark each connecting rod and big-end bearing cap with its respective cylinder number on the flat machined surface provided.
4 Turn the crankshaft to bring pistons 1 and 4 to BDC (bottom dead centre).
5 Working through the bearing cap unscrew the nuts from No 1 piston big-end bearing cap. Take off the cap, and recover the bottom half bearing shell. If the bearing shells are to be re-used, tape the cap and the shell together.
6 Using a hammer handle, push the piston up through the bore, and remove it from the

11.3 Connecting rods should be stamped with their relevant cylinder number

10.4 Measuring the inner rotor clearance

top of the cylinder block. Recover the bearing shell, and tape it to the connecting rod for safekeeping.
7 Loosely refit the big-end cap to the connecting rod, and secure with the nuts – this will help to keep the components in their correct order.
8 Remove No 4 piston assembly in the same way.
9 Turn the crankshaft through 180° to bring pistons 2 and 3 to BDC (bottom dead centre), and remove them in the same way.

12 Crankshaft –
removal

1 Remove the sump, timing chain and flywheel.
2 Remove the pistons and connecting rods, as described in Section 11. If no work is to be done on the pistons and connecting rods, there is no need to remove the cylinder head, or to push the pistons out of the cylinder bores. The pistons should just be pushed far enough up the bores that they are positioned clear of the crankshaft journals.
3 Check the crankshaft endfloat as described in Section 15, then proceed as follows.
4 Undo the retaining bolts, and remove the oil seal housing from the left-hand (flywheel) end of the cylinder block. If the locating dowels are a loose fit, remove them and store them with the housing for safekeeping.
5 Working in the **reverse** of the tightening sequence **(see illustration 19.10a)**, slacken

12.6a Lift the main bearing cap from the crankshaft

12.6b Lifting out the crankshaft

12.6c Recover the bearing shells from the cap

12.8a Remove the upper shell from the block . . .

12.8b . . . and remove the thrustwashers

the main bearing cap retaining bolts by a turn at a time. Once all bolts are loose, unscrew and remove them from the cylinder block.

6 A gentle tap with a soft-faced hammer will release the bearing cap. Withdraw the bearing cap and recover the lower main bearing shells **(see illustrations)**. Tape each shell to its respective cap for safekeeping.

7 Carefully lift out the crankshaft, taking care not to displace the upper main bearing shells.

8 Recover the upper bearing shells from the cylinder block, and tape them to their respective caps for safekeeping. Remove the thrustwasher halves from the side of No 3 main bearing, and store them with the bearing cap **(see illustrations)**.

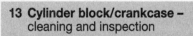

13 Cylinder block/crankcase – cleaning and inspection

Cleaning

1 Remove all external components and electrical switches/sensors from the block.

2 Scrape all traces of sealant from the cylinder block/crankcase, taking care not to damage the gasket sealing surfaces.

3 Remove all oil gallery plugs (where fitted). The plugs are usually very tight – they may have to be drilled out, and the holes retapped. Use new plugs when the engine is reassembled.

4 If any of the castings are extremely dirty, all

should be steam-cleaned, or cleaned with a suitable degreasing agent.

5 After cleaning, clean all oil holes and oil galleries one more time. Flush all internal passages with warm water until the water runs clear. Dry thoroughly, and apply a light film of oil to the cylinder bores to prevent rusting. If possible, use compressed air to speed up the drying process, and to blow out all the oil holes and galleries.

 Warning: Wear eye protection when using compressed air.

6 If the castings are not very dirty, you can do an adequate cleaning job with very hot, soapy water and a stiff brush. Take plenty of time, and do a thorough job. Regardless of the cleaning method used, be sure to clean all oil holes and galleries very thoroughly, and to dry all components well. Protect the cylinder bores as described above, to prevent rusting.

13.7 Cleaning a cylinder block thread with a suitable tap

7 All threaded holes must be clean, to ensure accurate torque readings during reassembly. To clean the threads, run the correct-size tap into each of the holes to remove rust, corrosion, thread sealant or sludge, and to restore damaged threads **(see illustration)**. If possible, use compressed air to clear the holes of debris produced by this operation.

8 Apply suitable sealant to the new oil gallery plugs, and insert them into the holes in the block. Tighten them securely.

9 If the engine is not going to be reassembled right away, cover it with a large plastic bag to keep it clean; protect all mating surfaces and the cylinder bores as described above, to prevent rusting.

Inspection

10 Visually check the casting for cracks and corrosion. Look for stripped threads in the threaded holes. If there has been any history of internal water leakage, it may be worthwhile having an engine reconditioning specialist check the cylinder block/crankcase with special equipment. If defects are found, have them repaired if possible, or obtain a new block.

11 Check each cylinder bore for scuffing and scoring. Check for signs of a wear ridge at the top of the cylinder, indicating that the bore is excessively worn.

12 Accurate measuring of the cylinder bores requires specialised equipment and experience. We recommend having the bores measured by an automotive engineering workshop, which will also be able to supply appropriate pistons should a rebore be necessary.

13 If the cylinder bores and pistons are in reasonably good condition, and not worn to the specified limits, and if the piston-to-bore clearances can be maintained properly, then it will only be necessary to renew the piston rings. If this is the case, the bores should be honed, to allow the new rings to bed-in correctly and provide the best possible seal. An engine reconditioning specialist will carry out this work at moderate cost.

14 Piston/connecting rod assembly – inspection

1 Before the inspection process can begin, the piston/connecting rod assemblies must be cleaned, and the original piston rings removed from the pistons. **Note:** *Always use new piston rings when the engine is reassembled.*
2 Carefully expand the old rings over the top of the pistons. The use of two or three old feeler blades will be helpful in preventing the rings dropping into empty grooves **(see illustration)**. Be careful not to scratch the piston with the ends of the ring. The rings are brittle, and will snap if they are spread too far. They're also very sharp – protect your hands and fingers.
3 Scrape away all traces of carbon from the top of the piston. A hand-held wire brush (or a piece of fine emery cloth) can be used, once the majority of the deposits have been scraped away.
4 Remove the carbon from the ring grooves in the piston, using an old ring. Break the ring in half to do this. Be careful to remove only the carbon deposits – do not remove any metal, and do not nick or scratch the sides of the ring grooves.
5 Once the deposits have been removed, clean the piston/connecting rod assembly with paraffin or a suitable solvent, and dry thoroughly. Make sure that the oil return holes in the ring grooves are clear.
6 If the pistons and cylinder bores are not damaged or worn excessively, and if the cylinder block does not need to be rebored, the original pistons can be refitted. Normal piston wear shows up as even vertical wear on the piston thrust surfaces, and slight looseness of the top ring in its groove. New piston rings, however, should always be used when the engine is reassembled.
7 Carefully inspect each piston for cracks around the skirt, around the gudgeon pin holes, and at the piston ring 'lands' (between the ring grooves).

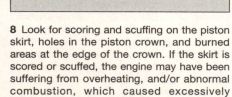

HAYNES HiNT *A good alternative to compressed air is to inject an aerosol water-dispersant lubricant into each hole, using the long tube usually supplied. Warning: Wear eye protection when cleaning out these holes in this way.*

8 Look for scoring and scuffing on the piston skirt, holes in the piston crown, and burned areas at the edge of the crown. If the skirt is scored or scuffed, the engine may have been suffering from overheating, and/or abnormal combustion, which caused excessively high operating temperatures. The cooling and lubrication systems should be checked thoroughly. Scorch marks on the sides of the

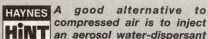

14.2 Using a feeler gauge to aid piston ring removal

pistons show that blow-by has occurred. A hole in the piston crown, or burned areas at the edge of the piston crown, indicates that abnormal combustion (pre-ignition, knocking, or detonation) has been occurring. If any of the above problems exist, the causes must be investigated and corrected, or the damage will occur again.
9 Corrosion of the piston, in the form of pitting, indicates that coolant has been leaking into the combustion chamber and/or the crankcase. Again, the cause must be corrected, or the problem may persist in the rebuilt engine.
10 Measure the piston ring-to-groove clearance by placing a new piston ring in each ring groove and measuring the clearance with a feeler blade. Check the clearance at three or four places around each groove. If the measured clearance is greater than specified, new pistons will be required.
11 Accurate measurement of the pistons requires specialised equipment and experience. We recommend having the piston measured by an automotive engineering workshop, which will also be able to supply appropriate pistons should a rebore be necessary.
12 Check the fit of the gudgeon pin by twisting the piston and connecting rod in opposite directions. Any noticeable play indicates excessive wear of the gudgeon pin, piston, or connecting rod small-end bearing.
13 The gudgeon pin is a press-fit in the piston and can only be remove with a suitable press. If the pistons are to be removed, this work is best left to a specialist.

15.2 Using a dial gauge to check the crankshaft endfloat

14 Examine each connecting rod carefully for signs of damage, such as cracks around the big-end and small-end bearings. Check that the rod is not bent or distorted. Damage is highly unlikely, unless the engine has been seized or badly overheated. Detailed checking of the connecting rod assembly and any remedial action necessary can only be carried out by an engine reconditioning specialist with the necessary equipment.

15 Crankshaft – inspection

Checking endfloat

1 If the crankshaft endfloat is to be checked, this must be done when the crankshaft is still installed in the cylinder block/crankcase, but is free to move (see Section 12).
2 Check the endfloat using a dial gauge in contact with the end of the crankshaft. Push the crankshaft fully one way, and then zero the gauge. Push the crankshaft fully the other way and check the endfloat **(see illustration)**. The result can be compared with the specified amount, and will give an indication as to whether new thrustwashers are required.
3 If a dial gauge is not available, feeler blades can be used. First push the crankshaft fully towards the flywheel/driveplate end of the engine, then use feeler blades to measure the gap between the No 4 crankpin web and No 3 main bearing thrustwasher.

Inspection

4 Clean the crankshaft using paraffin or a suitable solvent, and dry it, preferably with compressed air if available. Be sure to clean the oil holes with a pipe cleaner or similar probe, to ensure that they are not obstructed.

⚠ *Warning: Wear eye protection when using compressed air.*

5 Check the main and big-end bearing journals for uneven wear, scoring, pitting and cracking.
6 Big-end bearing wear is accompanied by distinct metallic knocking when the engine is running (particularly noticeable when the engine is pulling from low speed) and some loss of oil pressure.
7 Main bearing wear is accompanied by severe engine vibration and rumble – getting progressively worse as engine speed increases – and again by loss of oil pressure.
8 Check the bearing journal for roughness by running a finger lightly over the bearing surface. Any roughness (which will be accompanied by obvious bearing wear) indicates that the crankshaft requires regrinding (where possible) or renewal.
9 Accurate measurement of the crankshaft requires specialised equipment and experience. We recommend having the crankshaft measured by an automotive

engineering workshop, which will also be able to supply appropriate journal bearings should a regrind be necessary.

10 If the crankshaft has been reground, check for burrs around the crankshaft oil holes (the holes are usually chamfered, so burrs should not be a problem unless regrinding has been carried out carelessly). Remove any burrs with a fine file or scraper, and thoroughly clean the oil holes as described previously.

11 Nissan can supply undersized bearing shells for both the main bearings and big-end bearings. If the crankshaft journals have not already been reground, it may be possible to have the crankshaft reconditioned, and to fit the undersize shells. If the crankshaft has worn beyond the specified limits, it will have to be renewed. Consult your Nissan dealer or engine reconditioning specialist for further information on parts availability.

16 Main and big-end bearings – inspection

1 Even though the main and big-end bearings should be renewed during the engine overhaul, the old bearings should be retained for close examination, as they may reveal valuable information about the condition of the engine. The bearing shells are graded by thickness, the grade of each shell being indicated by the colour code marked on it.

2 Bearing failure can occur due to lack of lubrication, the presence of dirt or other foreign particles, overloading the engine, or corrosion. Regardless of the cause of bearing failure, the cause must be corrected (where applicable) before the engine is reassembled, to prevent it from happening again **(see illustration)**.

3 When examining the bearing shells, remove

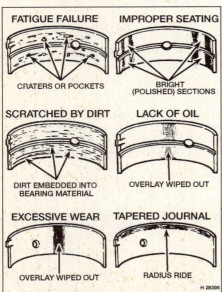

FATIGUE FAILURE

IMPROPER SEATING

CRATERS OR POCKETS

BRIGHT (POLISHED) SECTIONS

SCRATCHED BY DIRT

LACK OF OIL

DIRT EMBEDDED INTO BEARING MATERIAL

OVERLAY WIPED OUT

EXCESSIVE WEAR

TAPERED JOURNAL

OVERLAY WIPED OUT

RADIUS RIDE

H 28395

16.2 Typical bearing failure

them from the cylinder block/crankcase, the main bearing caps, the connecting rods and the connecting rod big-end bearing caps. Lay them out on a clean surface in the same general position as their location in the engine. This will enable you to match any bearing problems with the corresponding crankshaft journal. Do not touch any shell's bearing surface with your fingers while checking it, or the delicate surface may be scratched.

4 Dirt and other foreign matter get into the engine in a variety of ways. It may be left in the engine during assembly, or it may pass through filters or the crankcase ventilation system. It may get into the oil, and from there into the bearings. Metal chips from machining operations and normal engine wear are often present. Abrasives are sometimes left in engine components after reconditioning, especially when parts are not thoroughly cleaned using the proper cleaning methods. Whatever the source, these foreign objects often end up embedded in the soft bearing material, and are easily recognised. Large particles will not embed in the bearing, and will score or gouge the bearing and journal. The best prevention for this cause of bearing failure is to clean all parts thoroughly, and keep everything spotlessly clean during engine assembly. Frequent and regular engine oil and filter changes are also recommended.

5 Lack of lubrication (or lubrication breakdown) has a number of interrelated causes. Excessive heat (which thins the oil), overloading (which squeezes the oil from the bearing face) and oil leakage (from excessive bearing clearances, worn oil pump or high engine speeds) all contribute to lubrication breakdown. Blocked oil passages, which usually are the result of misaligned oil holes in a bearing shell, will also oil-starve a bearing, and destroy it. When lack of lubrication is the cause of bearing failure, the bearing material is wiped or extruded from the steel backing of the bearing. Temperatures may increase to the point where the steel backing turns blue from overheating.

6 Driving habits can have a definite effect on bearing life. Full-throttle, low-speed operation (labouring the engine) puts very high loads on bearings, tending to squeeze out the oil film. These loads cause the bearings to flex, which produces fine cracks in the bearing face (fatigue failure). Eventually, the bearing material will loosen in pieces, and tear away from the steel backing.

7 Short-distance driving leads to corrosion of bearings, because insufficient engine heat is produced to drive off the condensed water and corrosive gases. These products collect in the engine oil, forming acid and sludge. As the oil is carried to the engine bearings, the acid attacks and corrodes the bearing material.

8 Incorrect bearing installation during engine assembly will lead to bearing failure as well. Tight-fitting bearings leave insufficient bearing running clearance, and will result in oil starvation. Dirt or foreign particles trapped

behind a bearing shell result in high spots on the bearing, which lead to failure.

9 Do not touch any shell's bearing surface with your fingers during reassembly; there is a risk of scratching the delicate surface, or of depositing particles of dirt on it.

10 As mentioned at the beginning of this Section, the bearing shells should be renewed as a matter of course during engine overhaul; to do otherwise is false economy. Refer to Sections 19 and 20 for details of bearing shell selection.

17 Engine overhaul – reassembly sequence

Before reassembly begins, ensure that all new parts have been obtained, and that all necessary tools are available. Read through the entire procedure, to familiarise yourself with the work involved, and to ensure that all items necessary for reassembly of the engine are at hand. In addition to all normal tools and materials, thread-locking compound will be needed. A suitable tube of liquid sealant will also be required for the joint faces that are fitted without gaskets; it is recommended that Nissan's Genuine Liquid Gasket (available from your Nissan dealer) is used.

In order to save time and avoid problems, engine reassembly can be carried out in the following order:

a) Crankshaft (Section 19).
b) Piston/connecting rod assemblies (Section 20).
c) Timing chain and cover (Section 9).
d) Upper and lower sumps (Section 9).
e) Cylinder head (see Part A of this Chapter).
f) Flywheel/driveplate (see Part A of this Chapter).
g) Engine external components.

At this stage, all engine components should be absolutely clean and dry, with all faults repaired. The components should be laid out (or in individual containers) on a completely clean work surface.

18 Piston rings – refitting

1 Before fitting new piston rings, the ring end gaps must be checked as follows.

2 Lay out the piston/connecting rod assemblies and the new piston ring sets, so that the ring sets will be matched with the same piston and cylinder during the end gap measurement and subsequent engine reassembly.

3 Insert the top ring into the first cylinder, and push it down the bore using the top of the piston. This will ensure that the ring remains square with the cylinder walls. Push the ring down into the bore until the piston skirt is level with the block mating surface, then withdraw the piston.

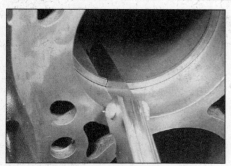

18.4 Measuring a piston ring end gap

18.9a Fit the oil control ring expander . . .

18.9b . . . then install the side rails

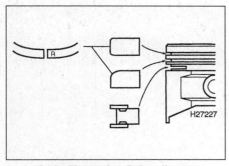

18.10a Piston ring fitting diagram

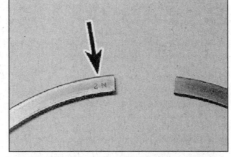

18.10b If marked, install the rings with the mark uppermost

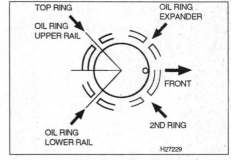

18.12 Position the ring gaps correctly

4 Measure the end gap using feeler gauges, and compare the measurements with the figures given in the Specifications **(see illustration)**.

5 If the gap is too small (unlikely if reputable parts are used), it must be enlarged, or the ring ends may contact each other during engine operation, causing serious damage. Ideally, new piston rings providing the correct end gap should be fitted. As a last resort, the end gap can be increased by filing the ring ends very carefully with a fine file. Mount the file in a vice with soft jaws, slip the ring over the file with the ends contacting the file face, and slowly move the ring to remove material from the ends. Take care, as piston rings are sharp, and are easily broken.

6 With new piston rings, it is unlikely that the end gap will be too large. If the gaps are too large, check that you have the correct rings for the engine and for the particular cylinder bore size.

7 Repeat the checking procedure for each ring in the first cylinder, and then for the rings in the remaining cylinders. Remember to keep rings, pistons and cylinders matched up.

8 Once the ring end gaps have been checked and if necessary corrected, the rings can be fitted to the pistons. **Note:** *Always follow any instructions supplied with the new piston ring sets – different manufacturers may specify different procedures. Do not mix up the top and second compression rings, as they have different cross-sections.*

9 The oil control ring (lowest on the piston) is installed first. It is composed of three separate components. Slip the expander into the groove, then install the upper side rail into

the groove between the expander and the ring land, and then install the lower side rail in the same manner **(see illustrations)**.

10 Install the second ring next. **Note:** *The second ring and top ring are different, and can be identified by their cross-sections. Making sure the ring is the correct way up, fit the ring into the middle groove on the piston, taking care not to expand the ring any more than is necessary* **(see illustrations)**.

11 Install the top ring in the same way; making sure the ring is the correct way up. Where the ring is symmetrical, fit it with its identification marking facing upwards.

12 With all the rings in position on the piston, space the ring end gaps correctly **(see illustration)**.

13 Repeat the above procedure for the remaining pistons and rings.

19 Crankshaft –
bearing selection and refitting

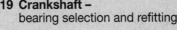

Bearing selection

1 Main bearings for the engines described in this Chapter are available in standard sizes and one undersize to suit reground crankshafts. Refer to your Nissan dealer or automotive engineering workshop for details.

Refitting

2 Clean the backs of the bearing shells and the bearing locations in both the cylinder block and the main bearing cap.

3 Press the bearing shells into their locations, ensuring that the tab on each shell engages in the notch in the cylinder block/crankcase. Take care not to touch any shell's bearing surface with your fingers. Note that all the upper bearing shells are grooved, and have oil holes in them; the lower shells are plain **(see illustration)**.

4 Wipe dry the shells with a lint-free cloth. Liberally lubricate each bearing shell in the cylinder block/crankcase with clean engine oil **(see illustration)**.

5 Using a little grease, stick the upper thrustwashers to each side of the No 3 main bearing upper location; ensure that the oilway grooves on each thrustwasher face outwards (away from the cylinder block).

6 Lower the crankshaft into position, and check the crankshaft endfloat as described in Section 15.

7 Thoroughly degrease the mating surfaces

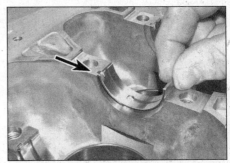

19.3 Fit the upper bearing shells and align the tab with the cut-out (arrowed)

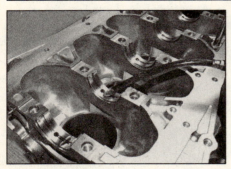

19.4 Lubricate the main bearing shells with clean engine oil

19.10a Bearing cap tightening sequence

19.10b Torque the bolts . . .

19.10c . . . and then angle tighten

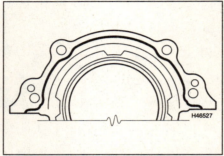
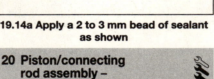

19.14a Apply a 2 to 3 mm bead of sealant as shown

19.4b Applying the liquid gasket

of the cylinder block and the main bearing caps.

8 Lubricate the lower bearing shells in the main bearing cap with clean engine oil. Make sure that the locating lugs on the shells engage with the corresponding recesses in the cap.

9 Fit the main bearing cap, with the arrow pointing to the timing chain end of the block. Insert the bolts, tightening them by hand only.

10 Working in sequence, tighten the bearing cap retaining bolts to approximately half the specified torque setting **(see illustrations)**. Then go around in the same sequence and tighten the bolts to the full specified torque setting. Check that the crankshaft rotates freely before proceeding any further.

11 Fit the piston/connecting rod assemblies as described in Section 20.

12 Ensure that the mating surfaces of the oil seal housing and cylinder block are clean and dry. Note the correct fitted depth of the oil seal then, using a large flat-bladed screwdriver, lever the seal out of the housing (See Chapter 2A).

13 Fit the new crankshaft seal to the housing, making sure that its sealing lip is facing inwards. Tap the seal squarely into the housing until it is positioned at the same depth as the original was noted prior to removal.

14 Apply a 2 to 3 mm diameter bead of liquid gasket to the oil seal housing mating surface, and make sure that the locating dowels are in position. Slide the housing over the end of the crankshaft, and into position on the cylinder block. Tighten the housing retaining bolts to the specified torque setting **(see illustrations)**.

15 Refit the flywheel, timing chain and sump.

20 Piston/connecting rod assembly – bearing selection and refitting

Bearing selection

1 Big-end bearings for the engines described in this Chapter are available in standard sizes and one undersize to suit reground crankshafts. Refer to your Nissan dealer or automotive engineering workshop for details.

Refitting

2 Clean the backs of the bearing shells, and the bearing locations in both the connecting rod and bearing cap.

3 Press the bearing shells into their locations, ensuring that the tab on each shell engages in the recess in the connecting rod and cap **(see illustration)**. Take care not to touch any shell's bearing surface with your fingers, and ensure that the shells are correctly installed so that the upper shell oil hole is correctly aligned with connecting rod oil hole.

4 Note that the following procedure assumes that the crankshaft and main bearing caps are in place (see Section 19).

5 Wipe dry the shells and connecting rods with a lint-free cloth.

6 Lubricate the cylinder bores, the pistons, and piston rings, then lay out each piston/connecting rod assembly in its respective position.

7 Start with assembly No 1. Make sure that the piston rings are still spaced as described

in Section 18, and then clamp them in position with a piston ring compressor.

8 Insert the piston/connecting rod assembly into the top of cylinder No 1. Ensure that the piston front marking (in the form of either an arrow or a dot) on the piston crown is on the timing chain side of the bore. Using a block of wood or hammer handle against the piston crown, tap the assembly into the cylinder until the piston crown is flush with the top of the cylinder **(see illustration)**.

9 Ensure that the bearing shell is still correctly installed. Liberally lubricate the crankpin and both bearing shells. Taking care not to mark the cylinder bores, tap the piston/connecting rod assembly down the bore and onto the crankpin. Refit the big-end bearing cap, tightening its retaining nuts finger-tight at first **(see illustrations)**. **Note:** *the faces with the identification marks must match (which means that the bearing shell locating tabs abut each other).*

10 Tighten the bearing cap retaining nuts to their Stage 1 torque setting, using a torque wrench and suitable socket. Then tighten them through the specified Stage 2 angle setting **(see illustrations)**.

11 Rotate the crankshaft. Check that it turns freely; some stiffness is to be expected if new components have been fitted, but there should be no signs of binding or tight spots.

12 Refit the remaining three piston/connecting rod assemblies in the same way.

13 Refit the timing chain and sump, and the install the cylinder head.

20.3 Align the shell with the cut-out (arrowed)

20.8 Tap the piston into the bore

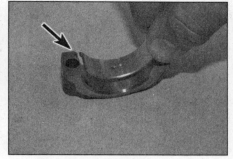

20.9a Correctly locate the bearing . . .

20.9b . . . and fit to the connecting rod

20.10a Torque the bolts . . .

20.10b . . . and then angle-tighten

21 Engine – initial start-up after overhaul

1 With the engine refitted in the vehicle, double-check the engine oil and coolant levels. Make a final check that everything has been reconnected, and that there are no tools or rags left in the engine compartment.

2 Start the engine, noting that this may take a little longer than usual, due to the fuel system components having been disturbed. Make sure that the oil pressure warning light goes out then allow the engine to idle.

3 While the engine is idling, check for fuel, water and oil leaks. Don't be alarmed if there are some odd smells and smoke from parts getting hot and burning off oil deposits.

4 Assuming all is well; keep the engine idling until hot water is felt circulating through the top hose, then switch off the engine.

5 After a few minutes, recheck the oil and coolant levels as described in *Weekly checks*, and top-up as necessary.

6 If they were tightened as described, there is no need to retighten the cylinder head bolts once the engine has first run after reassembly.

7 If new pistons, rings or crankshaft bearings have been fitted, the engine must be treated as new, and run-in for the first 500 miles. *Do not* operate the engine at full-throttle, or allow it to labour at low engine speeds in any gear. It is recommended that the oil and filter be changed at the end of this period.

Notes

Chapter 3
Cooling, heating and ventilation systems

Contents

Section number

Air conditioning system – general information and precautions 10
Air conditioning system components – removal and refitting 11
Coolant level check .... See *Weekly checks*
Coolant pump – removal, inspection and refitting 7
Coolant renewal .... See Chapter 1
Cooling system hoses – disconnection and renewal 2
Cooling temperature sensor – testing, removal and refitting 6

Section number

Electric cooling fan – testing, removal and refitting 5
General information and precautions 1
Heater/ventilation components – removal and refitting 9
Heater/ventilation system – general information 8
Radiator – removal, inspection and refitting................. 3
Thermostat – removal, testing and refitting 4

Degrees of difficulty

Easy, suitable for novice with little experience	Fairly easy, suitable for beginner with some experience	Fairly difficult, suitable for competent DIY mechanic	Difficult, suitable for experienced DIY mechanic	Very difficult, suitable for expert DIY or professional

Specifications

General

Radiator cap opening pressure	0.78 to 0.98 bars
Thermostat:	
Opening temperature	86.5 to 89.5°C
Maximum valve lift	8.0 mm or more
Electric cooling fan cut-in temperature	92°C
Engine coolant temperature sensor:	
Resistance and voltage:	

At -10°C	7.4 to 11.4 kilohms	4.4 V
At 20°C	2.1 to 2.9 kilohms	3.5 V
At 50°C	0.98 to 1.00 kilohms	2.2 V
At 90°C	0.236 to 0.260 kilohms	0.9 V
Compressor clutch clearance	0.2 to 0.5 mm	

Torque wrench settings

	Nm	lbf ft
Compressor mounting bolts...........................	20	15
Coolant pump bolts	12	9
Coolant pump pulley	8	6
Engine coolant temperature sensor	24	18
High-pressure pipe mounting bolt	4	3
Refrigerant pressure sensor	10	7
Thermostat housing securing bolts	7	5

1 General information and precautions

General information

The cooling system is of pressurised type, comprising a coolant pump driven by the auxiliary drivebelt from the crankshaft pulley, crossflow radiator, coolant expansion tank, electric cooling fan, thermostat, heater matrix, and all associated hoses and switches **(see illustration)**.

The system functions as follows. The coolant pump pumps cold coolant around the cylinder block and head passages, and through the inlet manifold, heater and throttle housing to the thermostat housing.

When the engine is cold, the coolant is returned from the thermostat housing to the coolant pump. When the coolant reaches a predetermined temperature, the thermostat opens, and the coolant passes through the top hose to the radiator. As the coolant circulates through the radiator, it is cooled by the inrush of air when the car is in forward motion. The airflow is supplemented by the action of the electric cooling fan when necessary. Upon reaching the bottom of the radiator, the coolant has now cooled, and the cycle is repeated.

When the engine is at normal operating temperature, the coolant expands, and some of it is released through the valve in the radiator pressure cap into the expansion tank. Coolant collects in the tank, and is returned to the radiator when the system cools.

A single electric cooling fan arrangement is used on all models. The fan assembly is mounted behind the radiator and controlled by the engine management electronic control unit in conjunction with the engine coolant temperature sensor. On models with air conditioning this is a two speed fan. Later models with air conditioning have an integrated radiator and condenser. The air conditioning system must be professionally evacuated and the refrigerant recovered before removal of the radiator/condenser. Automatic transmission models have an oil cooler built into the radiator.

Precautions

⚠️ *Warning: Do not attempt to remove the radiator pressure cap, or to disturb any part of the cooling system, while the engine is hot, as there is a high risk of scalding. If the radiator pressure cap must be removed before the engine and radiator have fully cooled (even though this is not recommended), the pressure in the cooling system must first be relieved. Cover the cap with a thick layer of cloth, to avoid scalding, and slowly unscrew the pressure cap until a hissing sound is heard. When the hissing has stopped, indicating that the pressure has reduced, slowly unscrew the pressure cap until it can be removed; if more hissing sounds are heard, wait until they have stopped before unscrewing the cap completely. At all times, keep your face well away from the pressure cap opening, and protect your hands.*

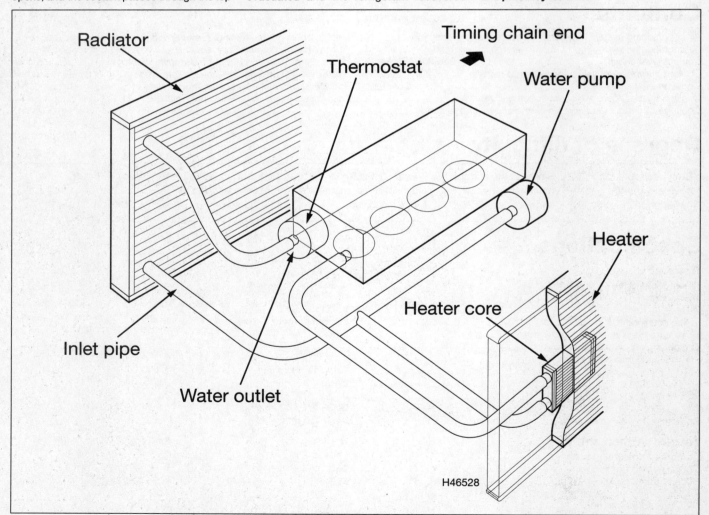

1.1 The cooling system

• *Do not allow antifreeze to come into contact with your skin, or with the painted surfaces of the vehicle. Rinse off spills immediately, with plenty of water. Never leave antifreeze lying around in an open container, or in a puddle in the driveway or on the garage floor. Children and pets are attracted by its sweet smell, but antifreeze can be fatal if ingested.*
• *If the engine is hot, the electric cooling fan may start rotating even if the engine is not running. Be careful to keep your hands, hair, and any loose clothing well clear when working in the engine compartment.*
• *Refer to Section 10 for precautions to be observed when working on models equipped with air conditioning.*

2 Cooling system hoses – disconnection and renewal

1 The number, routing and pattern of hoses will vary according to model, but the same basic procedure applies. Before commencing work, make sure that the new hoses are to hand, along with new hose clips if needed. It is good practice to renew the hose clips at the same time as the hoses.
2 Drain the cooling system, as described in Chapter 1, saving the coolant if it is fit for re-use.
3 Release the hose clips from the hose concerned. Two types of clip are used; worm-drive and spring. The worm-drive clip is released by turning its screw anti-clockwise.

The spring clip is released by squeezing its tags together with pliers, at the same time working the clip away from the hose stub.
4 Unclip any wires, cables or other hoses, which may be attached to the hose being removed. Make notes for reference when reassembling if necessary.
5 Release the hose from its stubs with a twisting motion. Be careful not to damage the stubs on delicate components such as the radiator. If the hose is stuck fast, the best course is often to cut it off using a sharp knife, but again be careful not to damage the stubs.
6 Before fitting the new hose, smear the stubs with washing-up liquid or a suitable rubber lubricant to aid fitting. Do not use oil or grease, which may attack the rubber.
7 Fit the hose clips over the ends of the hose, and then fit the hose over its stubs. Work the hose into position. When satisfied, locate and tighten the hose clips.
8 Refill the cooling system as described in Chapter 1. Run the engine, and check that there are no leaks.
9 Recheck the tightness of the hose clips on any new hoses after a few hundred miles.
10 Top-up the coolant level if necessary.

3 Radiator – removal, inspection and refitting

Note: *If leakage is the reason for removing the radiator, bear in mind that minor leaks can often be cured using a radiator sealant with the radiator in situ.*

Removal

1 Disconnect the battery negative terminal (*refer to Disconnecting the battery in the Reference Chapter*).
2 Drain the cooling system as described in Chapter 1 and remove the air filter duct. Jack up the front of the car, and support it on axle stands (*see Jacking and vehicle support*). Remove the front wheels and then remove the front wing liners, bumper and grille as described in Chapter 11.
3 Disconnect the remaining coolant hose(s) from the radiator and remove the expansion bottle **(see illustrations)**. On models with automatic transmission, fluid cooler hoses are connected to the bottom of the radiator – disconnect these and plug the pipes.
4 Some models with air conditioning have an integrated condenser. The air conditioning system must be depressurised before removal.
5 Disconnect the fan motor wiring connector(s) and release any cables or wiring harness from the fan shroud **(see illustrations)**, and then remove the plastic air guide panel from the right hand side of the radiator.
6 Using stout cord, support the radiator by tying it to the upper support panel – often called the bonnet slam panel. If air conditioning is fitted do the same with the condenser.
7 Support the lower panel with a suitable jack and then remove the panel mounting bolts. Slowly lower the jack, ensuring that the radiator is fully supported by the cord. Remove the lower panel and recover the rubber insulators. Undo the cord and lower the radiator to the floor **(see illustrations)**

3.3a Remove the lower hose . . .

3.3b . . . and the upper

3.5a Unplug the wiring to the fan speed controller where fitted . . .

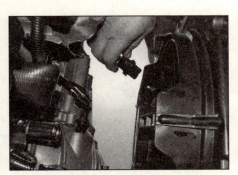

3.5b . . . and the connector to the fan

3.7a Remove the support panel . . .

3.7b . . . and recover the mountings

4.1 Thermostat location

4.4a Remove the bolts . . .

4.4b . . . and then remove the housing

Inspection

8 If the radiator has been removed due to suspected blockage, reverse-flush it as described in Chapter 1. Clean dirt and debris from the radiator fins, using an airline (in which case, wear eye protection) or a soft brush. Be careful, as the fins are sharp, and easily damaged.

9 If necessary, a radiator specialist can perform a 'flow test' on the radiator, to establish whether an internal blockage exists.

10 A leaking radiator must be referred to a specialist for permanent repair. Do not attempt to weld or solder a leaking radiator, as damage to the plastic components may result.

11 Inspect the condition of the radiator mounting rubbers, and renew them if necessary.

Refitting

12 Refitting is a reversal of removal, bearing in mind the following points:
- a) Ensure that the radiator lower lugs engage correctly with the lower mounting rubbers.
- b) On completion, refill the cooling system as described in Chapter 1.

4 Thermostat – removal, testing and refitting

Note: A new seal will be required when refitting the thermostat housing.

Removal

1 The thermostat is located in a housing bolted to the left-hand side of the cylinder head, at the transmission end of the engine **(see illustration)**.

2 Disconnect the battery negative terminal (refer to *Disconnecting the battery* in the Reference Chapter).

3 Drain the cooling system as described in Chapter 1. For improved access, also remove the air cleaner assembly as described in Chapter 4A, Section 11.

4 Remove the spring clip and pull off the hose. Unscrew the securing bolts, and remove the thermostat housing **(see illustrations)**.

5 Lift the thermostat and seal from the housing, noting the fitted position of the thermostat. The small air bleed valve in the thermostat should be in the uppermost position **(see illustration)**.

Testing

Note: *Frankly, if there is any question about the operation of the thermostat, it's best to renew it – they are not usually expensive items. Testing involves heating in, or over, an open pan of boiling water, which carries with it the risk of scalding. A thermostat which has seen more than five years' service may well be past its best already.*

6 A rough test of the thermostat may be made by suspending it with a piece of string in a container full of water. Heat the water to bring it to the boil – the thermostat must open by the time the water boils. If not, renew it.

7 If a thermometer is available, the precise opening temperature of the thermostat may be determined; compare with the figures given in the Specifications. The opening temperature is also marked on the thermostat.

8 A thermostat which fails to close as the water cools down must also be renewed.

Refitting

9 Commence refitting by thoroughly cleaning the mating faces of the cover and the housing.

10 Refit the thermostat and new seal to the housing, making sure it is fitted in the position noted on removal.

11 Fit the thermostat housing, then refit the securing bolts, and tighten to the specified torque.

12 If removed, refit the air cleaner assembly (see Chapter 4A), then reconnect the coolant hose and refill the cooling system as described in Chapter 1.

13 Reconnect the battery negative terminal.

4.5 Correct location of the bleed valve

5 Electric cooling fan – testing, removal and refitting

Testing

1 Battery voltage for operation of the cooling fan is supplied via a relay, which is energised by the ignition switch through a fuse. The circuit is completed by the engine management electronic control unit applying an earth to activate the relay.

2 If the fan does not appear to work, run the engine until normal operating temperature is reached, then allow it to idle. The fan should cut in within a few minutes (before the temperature gauge needle enters the red section). If the fan does not operate, switch the ignition off and remove the coolant temperature sensor connector from the right hand rear of the cylinder head. Connect a 150 ohm resistor across the terminals of the plug and start the engine. The fan should run.

3 Switch the ignition on and, using a voltmeter, check for battery voltage between a vehicle earth and the supply wire to the fan. If battery voltage is present, test the fan motor as described in paragraph 2. If the fan motor operates with voltage applied directly to it, the fault must be lie with either the wiring or any of the modules that command the cooling fan to run. At this point a diagnostic check would be advisable, from either a Nissan garage or suitably-equipped diagnostic specialist.

4 The fan motor itself can be tested, by disconnecting it from the wiring loom and connecting a 12 volt supply directly to it. The motor should operate – if not, the motor, or the motor wiring, is faulty.

Removal

5 Disconnect the battery negative terminal (refer to *Disconnecting the battery* in the Reference Chapter) and then jack up and support the front of the vehicle.

6 Disconnect the motor wiring connector and fan control resistor on air conditioning equipped cars.

7 Early cars have the housing secured with two bolts at the top, on later cars the housing is a simple push-fit. Remove the housing and lower it to the ground.

Refitting

8 Refitting is a reversal of removal.

6 Coolant temperature sensor – testing, removal and refitting

Testing

1 The sensor is located at the rear of the cylinder head at the transmission end.

2 The unit contains a thermistor – an electronic component whose electrical resistance decreases at a predetermined rate as its temperature rises.

3 The engine management ECU supplies the sensor with a set voltage and then, by measuring the current flowing in the sensor circuit, it determines the engine temperature. This information is then used, in conjunction with other inputs, to control the engine management system and associated components.

4 If the sensor circuit should fail to provide plausible information, the ECU back-up facility will override the sensor signal. In this event, the ECU assumes a predetermined setting which will allow the engine management system to operate, albeit at reduced efficiency. When this occurs, the engine warning light on the instrument panel will come on and the coolant fan will also run constantly.

5 The sensor itself can be tested by unplugging the connector and checking the resistance with the engine cold. Warm up the engine with the multimeter still connected and monitor the change in resistance as the sensor warms up. The resistance values are given in the Specifications. **Note:** *Do not attempt to test the circuit for resistance with the wiring connector fitted, as there is a high risk of damaging the ECU.*

6 Refer to Chapter 4A for further details of the engine management system.

Removal

7 Disconnect the battery negative terminal (refer to *Disconnecting the battery* in the Reference Chapter).

8 Partially drain the cooling system to just below the level of the sensor (see Chapter 1).

Alternatively, have ready a suitable bung to plug the aperture in the housing when the sensor is removed.

9 Disconnect the wiring connector from the sensor **(see illustration)**.

10 Carefully unscrew the sensor and recover the sealing ring. If the system has not been drained, plug the sensor aperture to prevent further coolant loss.

Refitting

11 Check the condition of the sealing ring and renew it if necessary.

12 Refitting is a reversal of removal, but refill (or top-up) the cooling system as described in Chapter 1 and *Weekly checks*.

13 On completion, start the engine and run it until it reaches normal operating temperature. Continue to run the engine until the cooling fan cuts in and out correctly.

7 Coolant pump – removal, inspection and refitting

Removal

1 Disconnect the battery negative terminal (refer to *Disconnecting the battery* in the Reference Chapter).

2 Drain the cooling system as described in Chapter 1. Jack up the front of the car, and support it on axle stands (see *Jacking and vehicle support*). Remove the front wheels and then remove the right hand front wing liner as

6.9 Disconnecting the coolant temperature sensor

described in Chapter 11. Drain the cooling system as described in Chapter 1.

3 Loosen, but do not remove, the bolts securing the coolant pump pulley and then remove the auxiliary drivebelts as described in Chapter 1.

4 Unscrew the securing bolts, and remove the coolant pump pulley. If you forgot to loosen the pulley bolts it will be necessary to counterhold the pulley in order to unscrew the bolts, and this is most easily achieved by wrapping an old drivebelt tightly around the pulley to act in a similar manner to a strap wrench.

5 Alternatively, remove the tensioner pulley and remove the pump complete with its pulley **(see illustrations)**.

6 Unscrew the coolant pump securing bolts, noting the different bolt lengths and their locations. Have a container ready to catch any coolant and then, using a block of wood and a hammer, tap the pump free **(see illustration)**.

7.5a Remove the nut and the outer washer...

7.5b ... and recover the pulley ...

7.5c ... spacer ...

7.5d ... and inner washer

7.6 Removing the pump

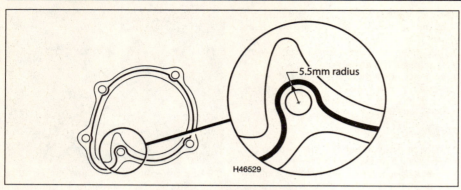

5.5mm radius

H46529

7.10 Apply liquid gasket as shown

Inspection

7 Check the pump body and impeller for signs of excessive corrosion. Turn the impeller, and check for stiffness due to corrosion, or roughness due to excessive endplay.

8 No spare parts are available for the pump, and if faulty, worn or corroded, a new pump should be fitted.

Refitting

9 Commence refitting by thoroughly cleaning all traces of gasket/sealant from the mating faces of the pump and cylinder block.

10 Apply a 2 to 3mm bead of liquid gasket to the mounting surface of the pump (**see illustration**).

11 Place the pump in position in the cylinder block, refit the bolts to their correct locations and tighten to the specified torque.

12 Refit the pump pulley, if removed, then refit the securing bolts and tighten to the specified torque. Counterhold the pulley using an old drivebelt or finally tighten when the drivebelts are installed.

13 Refit and tension the auxiliary drivebelts as described in Chapter 1, and then refit the wing liner.

14 Lower the car to the ground and refill the cooling system as described in Chapter 1.

15 Reconnect the battery negative terminal.

8 Heater/ventilation system – general information

1 The heater/ventilation system consists of a four-speed blower motor (housed behind the facia), face level vents in the centre and at each end of the facia, and air ducts to the front footwells.

2 The control unit is located in the facia, and the controls operate flap valves to deflect and mix the air flowing through the various parts of the heating/ventilation system. The flap valves are contained in the air distribution housing, which acts as a central distribution unit, passing air to the various ducts and vents.

3 Cold air enters the system through the grille at the rear of the engine compartment. It then passes through the pollen filter. If required, the airflow is boosted by the blower

fan, and then flows through the various ducts, according to the settings of the controls. Stale air is expelled through ducts at the rear of the vehicle. If warm air is required, the cold air is passed over the heater matrix, which is heated by the engine coolant.

4 All models have a recirculation switch that enables the outside air supply to be closed off, while the air inside the vehicle is recirculated. This is most useful when rapid heating, or cooling (for cars with air conditioning) is required. It can also be useful to prevent unpleasant odours entering from outside the vehicle, but should only be used briefly, as the recirculated air inside the vehicle will soon become stale.

9 Heater/ventilation components – removal and refitting

General information

Removal of the heater matrix, control flaps and air conditioning evaporator is one of the most complex operations covered in this manual. On the production line the first item fitted to the cabin is the heater control box, and consequently access can only be gained by complete removal of the dashboard. Very few component parts are accessible or removable with the dashboard in place. The blower motor resistor, heater control panel and cables are the only items accessible with the dashboard in place. All other items require

9.4a Remove the recirculation control lever

the removal of the dashboard as described in Chapter 11.

Heater blower motor resistor

1 Remove the glovebox as described in Chapter 1 for access to the pollen filter. Unplug the resistor and remove the two screws.

2 To check the fan resistor, an ohmmeter can be used to check the resistance between the terminals on the resistor. Connecting the negative wire to terminal No 1, and connect the positive end to each of the other terminals in turn:

　Terminal 2 = Approx 0.32 ohms
　Terminal 3 = Approx 1.4 ohms
　Terminal 4 = Approx 2.7 ohms

Heater control panel

Removal

3 Remove the audio unit and central air vents as described in Chapter 11.

4 Pull free the air intake lever and remove the two upper screws (**see illustrations**). Prise the cover free and disconnect the wiring to the 12 V power outlet. With the outer cover removed, unscrew the four screws that hold the panel in place. Pull the control unit forward.

5 Gently tilt the unit to expose the control cables. Prise the cables free, noting their positions. Use a felt pen to highlight the witness marks on the outer cable clamp point. This will avoid any need for adjustment later. Remove the control panel.

Refitting

6 Refitting is a reversal of removal.

Recirculation control cable

Removal

7 To gain access to the recirculation control cable remove the glovebox as described in Chapter 1 for access to the pollen filter. Unplug the connector to the blower speed controller for better a clearer view.

8 Lever the cable free, avoiding damage to the link arm.

Refitting

9 Refitting is a reversal of removal, but check the adjustment of the cable if required. Do this by moving the air control lever to

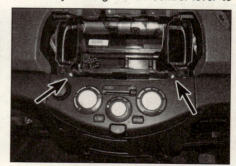

9.4b Remove the two screws

9.16 Remove the refrigerant pipes from the bulkhead on models with air conditioning

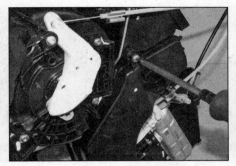

9.18a Remove the cover . . .

9.18b . . . and the cable

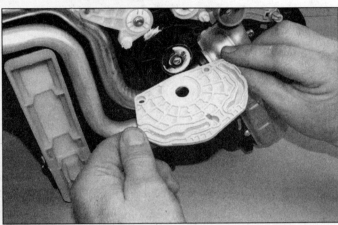

9.18c Remove the screw and lift of the link plate

9.18d Remove the three screws

'recirculation'. Hook the end of the cable onto the link arm and pull it towards the cable clamp and then push the outer cable into it's clamp. Check the cable operates smoothly.

Mode control and air mix cables

Removal

10 The mode control cable and the air mixture door control cable can be accessed by removing the lower panel stay cover as described in Chapter 11.
11 Lever the air mix outer cable free from the clamp and unhook the inner cable. The mode cable can be removed in a similar manner.

Refitting

12 To refit the air mix cable, turn the temperature control dial to the cold position and push the door control lever toward the outer cable clamp. Refit the cable inner and push the outer cable into the clamp.
13 When refitting the mode cable control, set the control switch to the ventilation position, hook the inner cable to the link arm and push down on the link. Push the outer cable into the clamp, taking care not to move the inner cable. Check the cable operates smoothly.

Heater matrix

> ⚠ **Warning: On models with air conditioning, the system must be discharged before starting this procedure. The heater assembly must**

be moved back inside the car to allow the matrix's rigid pipes to clear the bulkhead, and this means detaching the air conditioning pipes where they pass through the bulkhead as well. Discharging the air conditioning system must be carried out by a specialist.

Removal

14 Drain the cooling system as described in Chapter 1 and disconnect the battery. If air conditioning is fitted have the system professionally evacuated.
15 Remove the steering column and dashboard as described in Chapters 10 and 11.
16 Disconnect the heater hoses at the bulkhead. Using masking tape and a pen mark them 'upper' and 'lower' to aid refitting.

9.18e Removing the rear pipe cover

Disconnect the refrigerant pipes at the bulkhead on cars with air conditioning and immediately seal the pipes **(see illustration)**.
17 If not already done, remove the panel support bracket from the front right hand side of the heater unit. Pull the heater module free from the bulkhead. If you have not sealed the pipes at the bulkhead, expect some coolant to spill from the matrix. Remove the unit from the car.
18 Working on the bench, remove the cables and link plate that cover the matrix. Remove the screw that holds the pipe clip and pipe cover in place. Remove the single screw that retains the rear pipe cover. Two screws now hold the matrix in place. Undo the screws and pull the matrix free **(see illustrations)**.

9.18f Withdraw the matrix

9.20a Press the tag and rotate clockwise

9.20b Pull out the fan and motor

Refitting

19 Refitting is a reversal of removal, but a pressure test of the cooling system is recommended before the dashboard is refitted. Even new parts can be faulty.

Blower motor

20 Remove the heater unit as described above. Press the catch and rotate the motor clockwise. Pull the motor free from the housing (see illustrations).

10 Air conditioning system –
general information
and precautions

General information

1 Air conditioning is available on certain models. Higher specification models also have climate control. Both systems enable the temperature of the incoming air to be lowered. It also dehumidifies the air, which makes for rapid demisting and increased comfort.
2 The cooling side of the system works in the same way as a domestic refrigerator. Refrigerant gas is drawn into a belt-driven compressor, and passes into a condenser mounted in front of the radiator, where it loses heat and becomes liquid. The liquid passes through an expansion valve to an evaporator, where it changes from liquid under high pressure to gas under low pressure. This change is accompanied by a drop in temperature, which cools the evaporator. The refrigerant returns to the compressor, and the cycle begins again.
3 Air blown through the evaporator passes to the heater assembly, where it is mixed with hot air blown through the heater matrix, to achieve the desired temperature in the passenger compartment.
4 The heating side of the system works in the same way as on models without air conditioning (see Section 8).
5 Climate control is an enhancement of the standard manual system. Operation of the system is controlled electronically to maintain

a constant preselected cabin temperature. Using information gathered from various temperature sensors the control unit adjusts (using electric motors) the various flaps and vents in the heater module to maintain cabin temperature.

Precautions

⚠ *Warning: The air conditioning system is under high pressure. Do not loosen any fittings or remove any components until after the system has been discharged. Air conditioning refrigerant should be properly discharged at a dealer service department or an automotive air conditioning repair facility capable of handling R134a refrigerant. Always wear eye protection when disconnecting air conditioning system fittings.*

6 When an air conditioning system is fitted, it is necessary to observe the following special precautions whenever dealing with any part of the system, its associated components, and any items which necessitate disconnection of the system:

a) *While the refrigerant used – R134a – is less damaging to the environment than the previously-used R12, it is still a very dangerous substance. It must not be allowed into contact with the skin or eyes, or there is a risk of frostbite. It must also not be discharged in an enclosed space – while it is not toxic, there is a risk of suffocation. The refrigerant is heavier than air, and so must never be discharged over a pit.*

b) *The refrigerant must not be allowed to come in contact with a naked flame, otherwise a poisonous gas will be created – under certain circumstances, this can form an explosive mixture with air. For similar reasons, smoking in the presence of refrigerant is highly dangerous, particularly if the vapour is inhaled through a lighted cigarette.*

c) *Never discharge the system to the atmosphere – R134a is not an ozone-depleting ChloroFluoroCarbon (CFC) like*

R12, but is instead a hydrofluorocarbon, which causes environmental damage by contributing to the 'greenhouse effect' if released into the atmosphere.

d) *R134a refrigerant must not be mixed with R12; the system uses different seals (now green-coloured, previously black) and has different fittings requiring different tools, so that there is no chance of the two types of refrigerant becoming mixed accidentally.*

e) *If for any reason the system must be disconnected, entrust this task to your Nissan dealer or a vehicle air conditioning specialist.*

f) *It is essential that the system be professionally discharged prior to using any form of heat – welding, soldering, brazing, etc – in the vicinity of the system, before having the car oven-dried at a temperature exceeding 70°C after repainting, and before disconnecting any part of the system.*

**11 Air conditioning
system components –**
removal and refitting

⚠ *Warning: Do not attempt to open the refrigerant circuit. Refer to the precautions given in Section 10.*

1 The only operation, which can be carried out easily without discharging the refrigerant is renewal of the auxiliary (compressor) drivebelt, which is described in Chapter 1. All other operations must be referred to a Nissan dealer or an air conditioning specialist.
2 If necessary for access to other components, or engine removal the compressor can be unbolted and moved aside, without disconnecting its flexible hoses, after removing the drivebelt.
3 Working on the air conditioning system once it has been depressurised, is no different to any other system on the car. However remember:

a) *Always plug and seal all pipes and components immediately upon removal.*

11.10a Remove the cover screws . . .

11.10b . . . and remove the cover

11.11a Slide up the lower cover

This not only stops dirt entering the system, but also stops moisture from entering.
b) Always fit new seals and O-rings. Lubricate them with compressor oil before fitting.
c) Many of the air conditioning sensors are mounted on the pipe work on short 'stubs'. A flat side is provided to support the stub when removing the component. Use a suitable spanner on the flat side to avoid strain on the pipework.
d) After completion of the work the system must be pressured-tested with oxygen-free nitrogen, before filling with the correct amount of refrigerant.

11.11b Remove the sensor . . .

11.11c . . . and lift out the evaporator

Condenser

Removal

4 For models with an integrated radiator and air condioning condenser follow the instructions in Section 3.
5 For all models with a separate condenser follow the instructions in Section 3, but do not drain the radiator.
6 Remove the high-pressure hose and pipe from the right hand end of the condenser. Seal the holes in the condenser and plug the pipes. Unplug the high-pressure switch and unclip the harness from the end panel.
7 Support the radiator and condenser with cord or cable ties. Remove the radiator lower support – see Section 3 – and lower the condenser to the ground.

Refitting

8 Refitting is a reversal of removal, but use new O-rings, lubricated with compressor oil.

Evaporator

Removal

9 Follow the instructions in Section 9 and remove the heater module.

10 Working on the bench, remove the screws that hold the expansion valve cover in place. Remove the screws that secure the pipes and expansion valve and recover the foam piece **(see illustrations)**.
11 Turn the unit upside down and remove the screws that retain the lower half of the heater box. Slide up the lower cover, pull out the temperature sensor and remove the evaporator **(see illustrations)**.

Refitting

12 Refitting is a reversal of removal, but take care with the sensor wiring.

Compressor

Removal

13 Remove the drivebelt as described in Chapter 1. Better access can be gained by removing the alternator as described in Chapter 5A.
14 Remove the air inlet duct and unplug the compressor wiring. Remove the hose mounting bolts. Plug and seal the pipes and the compressor immediately.
15 The compressor is heavy, so support its weight with cord before removing the three mounting bolts.

Refitting

16 Refitting is a reversal of removal, but use new O-rings, lubricated with compressor oil.

Compressor magnetic clutch

Checking and testing

17 Specialist tools are required to dismantle the clutch. The clearance and operation can be checked with the compressor in the car though.
18 Using feeler gauges check the clearance between the clutch and pulley. Compare to the specifications at the beginning of the chapter.
19 Disconnect the electrical plug and using a fused test wire briefly apply battery voltage to terminal 1. The clutch should engage.

Expansion valve

Removal

20 Unbolt the refrigerant pipes from the bulkhead and seal the pipes. Remove the two bolts from expansion valve and remove it from the bulkhead.

Refitting

21 Refit in the reverse order of removal. Fit new O-rings. Lubricate the O-rings and fittings with compressor oil before fitting.

Chapter 4 Part A:
Fuel system

Contents

	Section number			Section number
Accelerator pedal – removal and refitting	10		Fuel pump/fuel pressure – checking	5
Air cleaner assembly – removal and refitting	11		Fuel system – depressurisation	2
Air filter element renewal	See Chapter 1		Fuel tank – removal, inspection and refitting	6
Fuel injection system – checking	8		General information and precautions	1
Fuel injection system components – removal and refitting	9		Hose and leak check	See Chapter 1
Fuel lines and fittings – general information	4		Inlet manifold – removal and refitting	12
Fuel pump/fuel gauge sender unit – removal and refitting	7		Unleaded petrol – general information and usage	3

Degrees of difficulty

Easy, suitable for novice with little experience	Fairly easy, suitable for beginner with some experience	Fairly difficult, suitable for competent DIY mechanic	Difficult, suitable for experienced DIY mechanic	Very difficult, suitable for expert DIY or professional

Specifications

General

System type	Nissan L-type sequential multi-port fuel injection
Fuel octane requirement	95 RON unleaded
Fuel tank capacity	46 litres
Fuel system pressure:	
Regulated pressure at idle	3.5 bar
Idle speed (ECU-controlled):	
Manual transmission models	650 ± 50 rpm
Automatic transmission models	700 ± 50 rpm

Torque wrench settings	Nm	lbf ft
Accelerator pedal to bracket	5	4
Air cleaner assembly (lower to upper half):		
Stage 1	2	1
Stage 2	4	3
Fuel rail mounting bolts:		
Stage 1	12	9
Stage 2	24	18
Fuel tank mounting bolts	25	18
Inlet manifold nuts/bolts	8	6
Fuel pump lock ring	70	52
Throttle body mountings	8	6

1 General information and precautions

General information

The fuel system consists of a fuel tank (mounted under the floor, beneath the rear seats), fuel hoses, an electric fuel pump mounted in the fuel tank, and a sequential electronic fuel injection system controlled by an engine management electronic control unit (ECU).

The electric fuel pump supplies fuel under pressure to the fuel rail, which distributes fuel to the injectors. A pressure regulator fitted to the pump itself controls the system pressure. With this system there is no fuel return line, which reduces evaporative emissions caused by warmer fuel returning to the fuel tank. From the fuel rail, fuel is injected into the inlet ports, just above the inlet valves, by four fuel injectors. The fuel rail is mounted to the cylinder head, just above the plastic inlet manifold.

The amount of fuel supplied by the injectors is precisely controlled by the ECU. The ECU uses the signals from the crankshaft position sensor and the camshaft position sensor to trigger each injector separately in cylinder firing order (sequential injection), with benefits in terms of better fuel economy and leaner exhaust emissions.

The ECU is the heart of the entire engine management system, controlling the fuel injection, ignition and emissions control systems. The ECU receives information from various sensors which is then computed and compared with preset values stored in its memory, to determine the required period of injection.

Information on crankshaft position and engine speed is generated by a Hall Effect crankshaft position sensor. As the crankshaft rotates, the sensor transmits a pulse to the ECU every time a tooth passes it. Similarly, the time interval between pulses is used to determine engine speed. This information is then fed to the ECU for further processing.

The camshaft position sensor is located at the transmission end of the cylinder head, and functions similarly to the crankshaft position sensor.

Engine temperature information is supplied by the coolant temperature sensor (see Chapter 3). The sensor is an NTC (Negative Temperature Coefficient) thermistor – that is, a semi-conductor whose electrical resistance decreases as its temperature increases. The sensor provides the ECU with a constantly-varying (analogue) voltage signal, corresponding to the temperature of the engine coolant. This is used to refine the calculations made by the ECU, when determining the correct amount of fuel required to achieve the ideal air/fuel mixture ratio.

Inlet air temperature and air density information for air/fuel mixture ratio calculations is provided by a Manifold absolute pressure sensor (MAP).

The throttle plate inside the throttle body is controlled by stepper type motor, and responds to demands from the accelerator position sensor. As the valve opens, the amount of air that can pass through the system increases. As the throttle valve opens further, the MAP output signal alters, and the ECU opens each injector for a longer duration, to increase the amount of fuel delivered to the inlet ports.

A throttle position sensor is mounted on the end of the throttle valve spindle, to provide the ECU with a constantly-varying (analogue) voltage signal corresponding to the throttle opening. This allows the ECU to register the driver's input when determining the amount of fuel required by the engine. Idle speed is maintained by the precise control of the throttle plate in conjunction with adjustments to the fuelling and ignition timing.

Roadspeed is calculated from the information provided by the anti-lock braking system ECU to the engine management ECU.

An oxygen sensor in the exhaust system provides the ECU with constant feedback – 'closed-loop' control – which enables it to adjust the mixture to provide the best possible operating conditions for the catalytic converter. A further sensor is fitted, downstream of the converter, to monitor the converter's operation, and this provides an even finer degree of emission control.

Both the idle speed and mixture are under the control of the ECU, and cannot be adjusted.

Precautions

⚠️ **Warning: Many of the procedures in this Chapter require the removal of fuel lines and connections, which may result in some fuel spillage. Before carrying out any operation on the fuel system, refer to the precautions given in 'Safety first!' at the beginning of this manual, and follow them implicitly. Petrol is a highly-dangerous and volatile liquid, and the precautions necessary when handling it cannot be overstressed.**

Note 1: *Residual pressure will remain in the* fuel lines long after the car was last used. When disconnecting any fuel line, first depressurise the fuel system as described in Section 2.

Note 2: *Before disconnecting any of the fuel injection system sensor wiring plugs, ensure at least that the ignition is switched off (ideally, disconnect the battery). If this is not done, it could result in a fault code being logged in the system memory, and may even cause damage to the component concerned.*

2 Fuel system – depressurisation

Note: *Refer to the warning note in Section 1 before proceeding.*

⚠️ **Warning: The following procedure will merely relieve the pressure in the fuel system – remember that fuel will still be present in the system components, and take precautions accordingly before disconnecting any of them.**

1 The fuel system referred to in this Chapter is defined as the fuel tank and tank-mounted fuel pump/fuel gauge sender unit, fuel pressure regulator, the fuel filter, the fuel injectors, and the metal pipes and flexible hoses of the fuel lines between these components. All these contain fuel, which will be under pressure while the engine is running and/or while the ignition is switched on.

2 The pressure will remain for some time after the ignition has been switched off, and must be relieved before any of these components is disturbed for servicing work.

3 The simplest depressurisation method is to disconnect the fuel pump electrical supply by removing the fuel pump fuse. This is fuse 47 in the engine compartment fusebox. Unfortunately access can only be gained by removal of the left-hand headlight. Headlight removal requires the removal of the front bumper and wing liners as described in Chapters 11 and 12. Make sure the ignition is switched off, then remove the 15 amp fuse **(see illustration)**. Alternatively remove the rear seats and disconnect the fuel pump.

4 Start the engine; allow the engine to idle until it stops through lack of fuel. Turn the engine over once or twice on the starter to ensure that all pressure is released and then switch off the ignition; do not forget to refit the fuse when work is complete.

5 Note that, once the fuel system has been depressurised and drained (even partially), it will take significantly longer to restart the engine – perhaps several seconds of cranking – before the system is refilled and pressure restored.

3 Unleaded petrol – general information and usage

All petrol models are designed to run on fuel with a minimum octane rating of 95 RON.

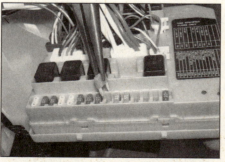

2.3 Removing the fuel pump fuse from the engine compartment fusebox

All models have a catalytic converter, and so must be run on unleaded fuel only. Under no circumstances should leaded fuel (UK '4-star' or LRP) be used, as this will damage the converter.

Super unleaded petrol (98 octane) can also be used in all models if wished, though there is no advantage in doing so.

4 Fuel lines and fittings – general information

Note: *Refer to the warning note in Section 1 before proceeding.*

Quick-release couplings

1 Quick-release couplings are employed at many of the unions in the fuel feed.
2 Before disconnecting any fuel system component, relieve the residual pressure in the system (see Section 2), and equalise tank pressure by removing the fuel filler cap.

 Warning: This procedure will merely relieve the increased pressure necessary for the engine to run – remember that fuel will still be present in the system components, and take precautions accordingly before disconnecting any of them.

3 To release the quick connectors press the square section in and pull the coupling off. If the coupling seems stuck or stiff, push and then pull the connector. Avoid excessive twisting. Where the unions are colour-coded, the pipes cannot be confused. Where both unions are the same colour, note carefully which pipe is connected to which, and ensure that they are correctly reconnected on refitting.
4 To reconnect one of these couplings, line them up, press them firmly together until it clicks. Check by trying to pull the coupling apart. Switch the ignition on and off five times to pressurise the system, and check for any sign of fuel leakage around the disturbed coupling before attempting to start the engine.

Checking fuel lines

5 Checking procedures for the fuel lines are included in Chapter 1.

Component renewal

6 If any damaged sections are to be renewed, use original-equipment hoses or pipes, constructed from exactly the same material as the section being renewed. Do not install substitutes constructed from inferior or inappropriate material; this could cause a fuel leak or a fire.
7 Before detaching or disconnecting any part of the fuel system, note the routing of all hoses and pipes, and the orientation of all clamps and clips. New sections must be installed in exactly the same manner.
8 Before disconnecting any part of the fuel system, be sure to relieve the fuel system pressure (see Section 2), and equalise tank pressure by removing the fuel filler cap. Also disconnect the battery negative (earth) lead – see Chapter 5A. Cover the fitting being disconnected with a rag, to absorb any fuel that may spray out.

5 Fuel pump/fuel pressure – checking

Note: *Refer to the warning note in Section 1 before proceeding.*

Fuel pump

1 Switch on the ignition, and listen for the fuel pump (the sound of an electric motor running, audible from beneath the rear seats). Assuming there is sufficient fuel in the tank, the pump should start and run for approximately one or two seconds, then stop, each time the ignition is switched on.
2 If the pump does not run at all, check the fuse, relay and wiring (refer to the wiring diagrams in Chapter 12).

Fuel pressure

3 A fuel pressure gauge will be required for this check, and should be connected in the fuel line at the fuel inlet connection at the rear of the engine compartment, in accordance with the gauge maker's instructions.
4 Start the engine and allow it to idle. Note the gauge reading as soon as the pressure stabilises, and compare it with the regulated fuel pressure figure listed in the Specifications.
   a) If the pressure is high, renew the fuel pressure regulator.
   b) If the pressure is low, this also suggests a fuel pressure regulator problem. However, low voltage to the fuel pump, a faulty fuel pump, or a blocked fuel pump filter (or other blockage in the fuel line) could be the cause.
5 Switch off the engine. Verify that a significant pressure remains for five minutes after the engine is turned off.
6 Carefully disconnect the fuel pressure gauge, depressurising the system first as described in Section 2. Be sure to cover the fitting with a rag before slackening it. Mop-up any spilt petrol.
7 Run the engine, and check that there are no fuel leaks.

6 Fuel tank – removal, inspection and refitting

Note: *Refer to the warning note in Section 1 before proceeding.*

Removal

1 Run the fuel level as low as possible prior to removing the tank. There is no drain plug fitted (and syphoning may prove difficult) but it may be possible to drain the tank by removing the fuel filler pipe from the base of the tank, and letting the fuel drain into a suitable container.
2 Relieve the residual pressure in the fuel system (see Section 2), and equalise tank pressure by removing the fuel filler cap.
3 Disconnect the battery negative (earth) lead (see *Disconnecting the battery*).
4 Referring to Section 7 disconnect the wiring plug and pipes from the top of the fuel pump/gauge sender unit.
5 Chock the front wheels, then jack up the rear of the car and support it on axle stands (see *Jacking and vehicle support*). Remove the right hand roadwheel.
6 Remove the middle and rear exhaust boxes as described in Chapter 4B. Then remove the heat shield.
7 Release the handbrake cable and move the cable away from the fuel tank and remove the two cable securing clips.
8 Disconnect the vent pipe at the front of the tank. Press in the square section and then push slightly before pulling off the hose. Place the end in a plastic bag and secure with tape or an elastic band.
9 Working in the wheel arch remove plastic liner and then the fuel filler hose connection at the tank end **(see illustration)**. Remove the vent hose adjacent to the filler hose.
10 Have either an assistant or a trolley jack with a block of wood support the tank, then remove the two tank support straps. When the tank is free, lower it to the ground (keeping it level, to reduce the chance of fuel spillage) and remove it from under the car.

Inspection

11 Whilst removed, the fuel tank can be inspected for damage or deterioration. Removal of the fuel pump/fuel gauge sender unit (see Section 7) will allow a partial inspection of the interior. If the tank is contaminated with sediment or water, swill it out with clean fuel. Do not under any circumstances undertake any repairs on a leaking or damaged fuel tank; this work must be carried out by a professional who has experience in this critical and potentially-dangerous work.
12 Whilst the fuel tank is removed from the

6.9 Loosen the hose clamp

7.4 Removing the cover plate

7.5 Unplug the electrical connector

7.6 Releasing the fuel line

car, it should be placed in a safe area where sparks or open flames cannot ignite the fumes coming out of the tank. Be especially careful inside garages where a natural-gas type appliance is located, because the pilot light could cause an explosion.

13 Check the condition of the filler pipe and renew it if necessary.

Refitting

14 Refitting is a reversal of the removal procedure, noting the following points:

a) *Ensure that all pipe and wiring connections are securely fitted.*

b) *Tighten the tank retaining bolts to the specified torque.*

c) *The filler hose must insert 35 mm into the tank.*

d) *Tighten the retaining clamp on the filler neck securely.*

e) *If evidence of contamination was found,*

do not return any previously-drained fuel to the tank unless it is carefully filtered first.

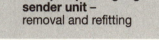

7 Fuel pump/fuel gauge sender unit – removal and refitting

Note: *Refer to the warning note in Section 1 before proceeding.*
Note: *Check the fuel level before proceeding. Never remove the fuel pump if the gauge shows more than a quarter full.*

Removal

1 A combined fuel pump, pressure regulator, filter and fuel gauge sender unit is located in the top face of the fuel tank. An access cover is provided below the rear seat, meaning that the tank does not have to be removed.
2 Disconnect the battery negative (earth) lead (see *Disconnecting the battery*).

3 Remove the rear seat as described in Chapter 11.
4 Lift up the carpet, and undo the three turnbuckle screws that secure the access cover **(see illustration)**.
5 Disconnect the wiring plug from the top of the pump/sender unit, using a small screwdriver to release the clip **(see illustration)**.
6 Depress the square part of the connector, and disconnect the fuel supply pipe from the top of the unit **(see illustration)**. Anticipate a small amount of fuel spillage as this is done. Tape over the open union on top of the unit, and place a plastic bag, secured with tape over the disconnected supply pipe, to prevent dirt getting in. Do not plug the supply pipe. Damage to the internal O-ring may happen if the pipe is plugged.
7 A simple tool will have to be fabricated to remove the locking ring. It may also be possible to remove the ring with a strap wrench. Highlight the alignment marks and then unscrew the locking ring and remove it **(see illustrations)**.
8 Lift out the fuel pump/sender unit, taking care not to damage the pump filter, nor to bend the sender unit float arm (which can get caught up on the tank lip as the unit is removed). Allow any remaining fuel to drain into the tank before finally lifting it clear. Drain the remaining fuel into a suitable container. Recover the sealing ring from the top of the tank **(see illustrations)**.
9 With the unit removed temporarily refit the locking ring to the tank. Once released the ring and/or the threads on the fuel tank can distort slightly making refitting problematic. Refitting the retainer while the fuel pump is out will help prevent this.

Fuel pump

10 The fuel pump, filter and pressure regulator are a combined unit. No separate parts are available. Any fault requires renewal of the entire unit.

Sender unit

11 The fuel gauge sender can be removed by releasing the securing clip with a small screwdriver and sliding the sender unit to the side **(see illustration)**.
12 The working of the sender can be checked

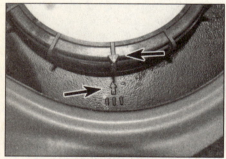

7.7a Note the alignment marks . . .

7.7b . . . remove the locking ring . . .

7.8a . . . lift out the pump and fuel gauge sender unit . . .

7.8b . . . and recover the sealing ring

7.11 Release the tank fuel level sender with a screwdriver

7.12 Checking the resistance

7.13 Align the pump with the cut-out in the tank

with a multimeter set to ohms. A digital multimeter with a bar graph scale is ideal for this, as it highlights the change in resistance clearly (see illustration).

Refitting

13 Refitting the pump/sender unit is a reversal of removal, noting the following points:
a) Refit the fuel gauge sender unit first.
b) Renew the O-ring.
c) Align the unit with the cut-out in the tank (see illustration).
d) Tighten the lock ring securely.
e) Once the unit has been refitted and the pipes connected, reconnect the battery and switch on the ignition. Check for correct pump operation and for any sign of leaks from the supply pipe before refitting the access cover.

8 Fuel injection system – checking

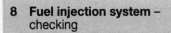

Note: Refer to the warning note in Section 1 before proceeding.

1 If a fault appears in the fuel injection system, first ensure that all the system wiring connectors are securely connected and free of corrosion – also refer to paragraphs 6 to 9 below. Then ensure that the fault is not due to poor maintenance; ie, check that the air cleaner filter element is clean, the spark plugs are in good condition and correctly gapped, the cylinder compression pressures are correct, the ignition system wiring is in good condition and securely connected, and the engine breather hoses are clear and undamaged, referring to Chapters 1, 2A and 5B.

2 If these checks fail to reveal the cause of the problem, the car should be taken to a suitably-equipped Nissan dealer or garage for testing. A diagnostic socket, often referred to as the 'data link connector' (DLC), is fitted below the interior fusebox, into which dedicated electronic test equipment can be plugged. The test equipment is capable of 'interrogating' the engine management system ECU and other systems electronically.

3 Fault codes can only be extracted from the ECU using a dedicated fault code reader. A Nissan dealer will obviously have such a

reader, but they are also available from other suppliers. It is unlikely to be cost-effective for the private owner to purchase a fault code reader, but a well-equipped local garage or auto-electrical specialist will have one.

4 Using this equipment, faults codes can be retrieved and acted upon. However it is important to understand that just because a fault for a particular component has been logged it does not necessarily mean that component is faulty. There may be a fault with the wiring to the component, or more confusingly the component may be a symptom and not the cause of the problem.

5 Experienced home mechanics equipped with digital multimeter should be able to check the supply voltage to many of the engines sensors – usually 5 V – and measure the sensor's output. Neither the air/fuel mixture (exhaust gas CO content) nor the engine idle speed is adjustable.

Limited Operation Strategy

6 Certain faults, such as failure of one of the engine management system sensors, will cause the system to revert to a backup (or 'limp-home') mode, often referred to as 'Limited Operation Strategy' (LOS), or 'fail safe mode'. This is intended to be a 'get-you-home' facility only – the engine management warning light will come on when this mode is in operation.

7 In this mode, the signal from the defective sensor is substituted with a fixed value (it would normally vary), which may lead to loss of power, poor idling, and generally-poor running, especially when the engine is cold.

9.1a Disconnecting the MAP sensor

8 However, the engine may in fact run quite well in this situation, and the only clue (other than the warning light) will be the radiator cooling fan running constantly and the maximum engine rpm limited to 2500 rpm.

9 Bear in mind that, even if the defective sensor is correctly identified and renewed, the engine will not return to normal running until the fault code is erased, taking the system out of LOS. This also applies even if the cause of the fault was a loose connection or damaged piece of wire – until the fault code is erased, the system will continue in LOS. Fault codes can be erased by disconnecting the battery negative lead. Alternatively the completion of several drive cycles after a successful repair will also extinguish the warning light.

9 Fuel injection system components – removal and refitting

Note: Refer to the precautions in Section 1 before proceeding.

Manifold absolute pressure sensor

1 The manifold absolute pressure sensor (MAP) is easy to access. It is located on the air cleaner assembly, secured by one bolt. Disconnect the wiring plug, remove the bolt and recover the sensor (see illustrations).

2 The sensor supply voltage can be checked. With the sensor disconnected, turn the ignition on. Check with a multimeter for 5 V (the sensor supply voltage) at pin 2 of the connector.

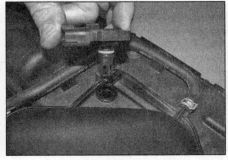

9.1b Removing the sensor

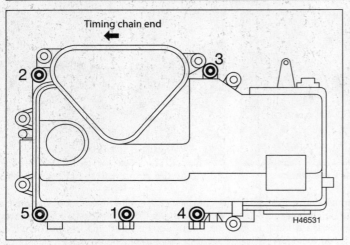

9.5a Remove the bolts in the reverse order

9.5b Separating the throttle body from the housing

9.5c Remove the connector O-ring . . .

9.5d . . . and the throttle O-ring

3 Refitting is a reversal of removal, but fit a new O-ring. **Note:** *The MAP sensor also incorporates the air temperature sensor.*

Throttle body

4 Remove the air cleaner assembly as described in section 11.

5 Loosen the bolts in the **reverse** order to that shown and separate the two halves of the air cleaner assembly. Recover the gasket, and then remove the securing bolts from the throttle body. Remove the throttle body and recover the O-rings **(see illustrations)**.

6 With the throttle body on the bench, and using a soft brush, clean the throttle plate with a proprietary throttle/carburettor cleaner.

9.16 Disconnect the fuel injectors

Under no circumstances should sharp tools be used.

7 Refitting is a reversal of removal, but use new throttle body O-rings and tighten in the order shown **(see illustration 9.5a)**.

8 On completion it will be necessary to 'teach' the ECU the closed throttle position and the idle air volume.

9 The closed throttle position is learnt by switching the ignition on for more than 10 seconds, and then turning off for a minimum of 10 seconds. During the 'off' 10 seconds the throttle valve will operate. You should be able to hear it operate.

10 To learn the idle air volume the car must be at its normal operating temperature, with all

9.17 Unscrew the hose clip

electrical loads off. The steering wheel should be in the straight-ahead position and battery voltage must be above 12.9 volts.

11 First perform an accelerator position learning procedure as described in Section 10 and then follow the idle learn procedure as described above.

12 Next turn the ignition on and wait 3 seconds. Now fully depress and release the accelerator pedal 5 times in quick succession. Wait 7 seconds and then fully depress the pedal for approximately 20 seconds, until the malfunction indicator lamp (MIL) in the instrument cluster stops flashing. The MIL light will be on at this point.

13 Fully release the pedal within 3 seconds of the MIL light coming on, and then start the engine and allow it to idle. Wait 20 seconds and then rev the engine 2 or 3 times.

Fuel rail and injectors

14 Relieve the residual pressure in the fuel system (see Section 2), and equalise tank pressure by removing the fuel filler cap.

⚠️ *Warning: This procedure will merely relieve the increased pressure necessary for the engine to run – remember that fuel will still be present in the system components, and take precautions accordingly before disconnecting any of them.*

15 Disconnect the battery negative (earth) lead (see *Disconnecting the battery*).

16 Remove the air cleaner assembly as described in Section 11 and the inlet manifold support as described in Section 12. Next remove the inlet manifold as described in Section 12 and then remove the electrical connectors from each fuel injector **(see illustration)**.

17 Remove the hose spring clip, or worm-drive clip from the fuel supply hose. Cover the hose and pipe with an absorbent cloth and pull the hose free. Expect some fuel spillage. Seal both the hose and the injector rail **(see illustration)**.

18 Remove the two bolts on the fuel rail and

gently pull the rail – complete with the injectors – from the cylinder head. This may prove difficult as the seals will have hardened with age. Apply penetrating fluid and leave to soak. Alternatively wrap each injector in turn with a rag and lever them free with a pair of long-nose pliers. Create a pivot point for the pliers with a block of wood on the cylinder head. Do not attempt to pull them free completely, just lift each in turn a few millimetres and then pull them free using the injector supply rail. Take care not to damage the injectors.

19 Working with the fuel rail and injectors on the bench, remove the clip that secures the injector to the fuel rail. Pull each injector from the fuel rail. Label the injectors to keep them in the correct order (see illustrations).

20 Refitting is the reverse of the removal procedure, noting the following points:

 a) Fit new injector O-rings, and lubricate them with clean engine oil to aid refitting. The black O-ring is fitted to the fuel supply side and the brown O-ring to the nozzle side

 b) Ensure that the hoses and wiring are routed correctly, and secured on reconnection by any clips or ties provided.

 c) On completion, switch the ignition on to activate the fuel pump and pressurise the system, without cranking the engine. Check for signs of fuel leaks around all disturbed unions and joints before attempting to start the engine.

Fuel pressure regulator

21 The pressure regulator is combined with the fuel pump, which is fitted to the fuel tank. Refer to Section 7.

ECU

Note: The ECU is fragile. Take care not to drop it, or subject it to any other kind of impact. Do not subject it to extremes of temperature, or allow it to get wet.

22 Disconnect the battery negative lead, and place the lead away from the terminal (see Disconnecting the battery). It is essential that the battery is disconnected before separating the ECU wiring plug, or the ECU itself could be damaged.

9.19a Remove the clip . . .

9.19b . . . and pull the injector from the rail

23 The engine management ECU is located on the front left inner wing, next to the suspension tower.

24 Pull back the locking pins on the ECU terminal connector and remove the plug. Take care not to touch or damage the terminal pins (see illustration).

25 Remove the bolts and recover the ECU. Refitting is a reversal of removal.

Crankshaft position sensor

26 The sensor is located in the gearbox bellhousing at the front of the engine (see illustration).

27 With the ignition switched off, disconnect the sensor wiring plug, then unscrew the mounting bolt and withdraw the sensor.

28 Inspect the sensor end for physical damage. With a multimeter the resistance can be checked between the terminals. Expect continuity or an open circuit between the terminals. Any other figure would indicate a fault. With the sensor disconnected, check for battery voltage at the terminal plug. The ignition must be on, and a fault code will be logged by the ECU. The engine management light may also be on when the car is started.

29 Refitting is a reversal of removal. Ensure that the sensor is clean when refitting, and tighten the bolt securely.

Camshaft position sensor

30 The sensor is located at the transmission end of the cylinder head. Access to the sensor is straightforward. Unscrew the bolt and remove the sensor (see illustration).

31 Inspect the sensor end for physical

damage. With a multimeter the resistance can be checked between the terminals. Expect continuity or an open circuit between the terminals. Any other figure would indicate a fault. With the sensor disconnected, check for battery voltage at the terminal plug. The ignition must be on, and a fault code will be logged by the ECU. The engine management light may also be on when the car is started.

32 Refitting is a reversal of removal, but replace the O-ring.

Coolant temperature sensor

33 See Chapter 3.

Throttle position sensor

34 The sensor is located on the throttle body. It is in fact two potentiometers working back to back. One sensor has a high output at the wide open throttle position, the other returns a low voltage to the ECU in this position. According to Nissan, the sensor is not available separately from the throttle body, and is not intended to be removed.

Oxygen sensor

35 Refer to Chapter 4B.

Knock sensor

36 Refer to Chapter 5B.

---

10 Accelerator pedal –
 removal and refitting

1 The Micra uses a 'fly by wire' throttle control. There is no accelerator cable; instead

9.24 Pull back the locking pin and release the multiplug connector

9.26 The crankshaft position sensor

9.30 Removing the camshaft position sensor

10.2 Accelerator pedal locating bolt and connector (arrowed)

11.3b Removing the spring clip from the brake servo hose

11.5 Fitting the inlet manifold seals

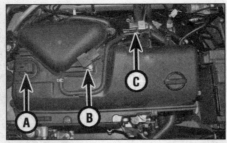

11.2 Remove the electrical connectors

A   *Throttle body*   C   *EVAP solenoid*
B   *MAP sensor*

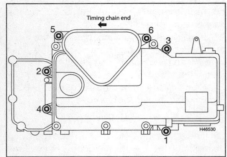

11.4 Air cleaner assembly bolt tightening sequence

12.4 Lifting the gasket from the inlet manifold

11.3a Removing the EVAP hose

a variable resistor is used to supply the ECU with the correct pedal position information. This information is processed by the ECU to calculate the required position of the throttle plate for any given pedal position.

Removal

2 The pedal and sensor are a combined unit, held in place by one bolt. Disconnect the electrical connector and remove the bolt **(see illustration)**. If necessary, unscrew the 3 bolts and remove the pedal assembly from the bracket.

Refitting

3 Refit in the reverse order of removal. On completion, check the action of the pedal to ensure that it has full unrestricted movement, and fully returns when released.
4 The ECU also needs to relearn the idle

position of the pedal. This is achieved by a simple ignition on/ignition off procedure:
a) *Fully release the pedal.*
b) *Turn the ignition ON and wait 5 seconds.*
c) *Turn the ignition OFF and wait 20 seconds.*
d) *Turn the ignition ON and wait 5 seconds.*
e) *Turn the ignition OFF and wait 20 seconds.*

11 Air cleaner assembly –
removal and refitting

Removal

1 Remove the air filter as described in Chapter 1.
2 Disconnect the wiring at the MAP sensor,

EVAP solenoid and throttle body. Label each connector if required **(see illustration)**.
3 Release the spring clip and remove the brake servo vacuum hose. Pull free the upper hose on the EVAP solenoid and plug the pipe **(see illustrations)**. On automatic transmission models, disconnect the transmission breather hose from the bracket on the air cleaner cover.
4 Remove the bolts (in the **reverse** order to that shown), that secure the assembly to the camshaft cover and inlet manifold. Lift the assembly free, taking care not to damage the inlet manifold **(see illustration)**.

Refitting

5 Refitting is a reversal of removal, but ensure the inlet manifold seals are correctly located and the PCV seal is in position **(see illustration)**. Tighten in the bolts in the order shown.

12 Inlet manifold –
removal and refitting

Note: *Refer to the warning note in Section 1 before proceeding. Note that the inlet manifold is made of plastic – do not strike it, nor use any great force when removing it.*

Removal

1 Remove the air cleaner assembly as described in Section 11 and then remove the PCV hose.
2 Remove the support bracket from the right hand end of the manifold.
3 Progressively loosen and then remove the manifold securing bolts).
4 Remove the manifold and recover the gasket **(see illustration)**.

Refitting

5 Refitting is a reversal of removal, noting the following points:
a) *Ensure that the mating faces are clean, and use a new manifold gasket.*
b) *Tighten the inlet manifold nuts and bolts to the specified torque. Note that the centre bolt is the start and finish bolt. It is in effect tightened twice.*

Chapter 4 Part B:
Emission control and exhaust systems

Contents

Section number

Catalytic converter – general information and precautions 7
Crankcase emission system – general information 3
Evaporative loss emission control system – information and
   component renewal 2

Section number

Exhaust manifold – removal and refitting 5
Exhaust system – component renewal. 6
General information 1
Oxygen sensors – removal and refitting. 4

Degrees of difficulty

| **Easy,** suitable for novice with little experience | **Fairly easy,** suitable for beginner with some experience | **Fairly difficult,** suitable for competent DIY mechanic | **Difficult,** suitable for experienced DIY mechanic | **Very difficult,** suitable for expert DIY or professional |

Specifications

General

Oxygen sensor heater resistance at 25°C:
Pre-catalytic converter	3.4 to 4.4 ohms
Post-catalytic converter	8.0 to 10.0 ohms

Torque wrench settings

	Nm	lbf ft
Catalytic converter to exhaust manifold.	32	24
Exhaust centre section to downpipe	48	35
Exhaust centre section-to-rear silencer bolts	35	26
Exhaust downpipe to catalytic converter.	48	35
Exhaust manifold nuts	27	20
Heat shield bolts.	7	5
Oxygen (lambda) sensors.	50	38

1 General information

Emission control systems

All models are designed to use unleaded petrol, and are controlled by engine management systems that are programmed to give the best compromise between driveability, fuel consumption and exhaust emission production. In addition, a number of systems are fitted that help to minimise other harmful emissions. A crankcase emission control system is fitted, which reduces the release of pollutants from the engine's lubrication system, and a catalytic converter is fitted which reduces exhaust gas pollutant. An evaporative loss emission control system is fitted which reduces the release of gaseous hydrocarbons from the fuel tank.

Crankcase emission control

To reduce the emission of unburned hydrocarbons from the crankcase into the atmosphere, the engine is sealed and the blow-by gases and oil vapour are drawn from inside the crankcase into the inlet tract to be burned by the engine during normal combustion.

Under conditions of high manifold depression, the gases will be sucked positively out of the crankcase. Under conditions of low manifold depression, the gases are forced out of the crankcase by the (relatively) higher crankcase pressure. If the engine is worn, the raised crankcase pressure (due to increased blow-by) will cause some of the flow to return under all manifold conditions.

Exhaust emission control

To minimise the amount of pollutants which escape into the atmosphere, all models are fitted with a three-way catalytic converter in the exhaust system. The fuelling system is of the closed-loop type, in which an oxygen (lambda) sensor in the exhaust system provides the engine management system ECU with constant feedback, enabling the ECU to adjust the air/fuel mixture to optimise combustion.

All models have two oxygen sensors – one before the catalytic converter and one after. This enables more efficient monitoring of the exhaust gas, allowing a faster response time. The overall efficiency of the converters can also be checked.

The oxygen sensor has a built-in heating element, controlled by the ECU through the oxygen sensor relay, to quickly bring the sensor's tip to its optimum operating temperature. The sensor's tip is sensitive to oxygen, and sends a voltage signal to the ECU that varies according on the amount of oxygen in the exhaust gas. If the inlet air/fuel mixture is too rich, the exhaust gases are low in oxygen so the sensor sends a low-voltage signal, the voltage rising as the mixture weakens and the amount of oxygen rises in the exhaust gases. Peak conversion efficiency of all major pollutants occurs if the inlet air/fuel mixture is maintained at the chemically-correct ratio for the complete combustion of petrol of 14.7 parts (by weight) of air to 1 part of fuel (the stoichiometric ratio). The sensor output voltage alters in a large step at this point, the ECU using the signal change as a reference point and correcting the inlet air/fuel mixture accordingly by altering the fuel injector pulse width.

Evaporative emission control

To minimise the escape of unburned hydrocarbons into the atmosphere, an evaporative loss emission control system is fitted to all models. The fuel tank filler cap is

2.3 Removing the wiring plug from the purge valve

sealed, and a charcoal canister is mounted adjacent to the fuel tank to collect the petrol vapours released from the fuel contained in the fuel tank. It stores them until they can be drawn from the canister (under the control of the engine management ECU) via the purge valve into the throttle body, where they are then burned by the engine during normal combustion.

To ensure that the engine runs correctly when it is cold and/or idling, and to protect the catalytic converter from the effects of an over-rich mixture, the purge control valve is not opened by the ECU until the engine has warmed up, and the engine is under load; the valve solenoid is then modulated on and off to allow the stored vapour to pass into the throttle body.

Exhaust systems

The exhaust system comprises the exhaust manifold, centre section (including the

2.9 The charcoal canister next to the fuel tank

downpipe, catalytic converter, oxygen sensors and centre silencer), and the rear silencer.

The system is supported by various metal brackets screwed to the vehicle floor, with rubber vibration dampers fitted to suppress noise.

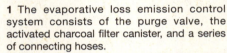

2 Evaporative loss emission control system – information and component renewal

1 The evaporative loss emission control system consists of the purge valve, the activated charcoal filter canister, and a series of connecting hoses.
2 The purge valve is bolted to the side of the air cleaner assembly, while the canister is mounted adjacent to the fuel tank at the rear.

Purge valve

3 Ensure that the ignition is switched off, then

unplug the wiring harness from the purge valve at the connector **(see illustration)**.
4 Pull the hoses off the purge valve ports. Make a note of their orientation, or preferably mark them to aid refitting later. The lower port hose is connected to the air cleaner assembly.
5 Remove the bolt and recover the purge valve.
6 Using a length of screen washer tube connected to one of the ports, blow through the valve. There should be no airflow with the valve disconnected.
7 Refitting is a reversal of removal.

Charcoal canister

8 Jack up the rear of the car, and support it on axle stands (see *Jacking and vehicle support*).
9 Disconnect the quick-release hoses by pushing the square section in, from the end of the canister, noting their locations for refitting. The third hose is a simple push-fit **(see illustration)**.
10 Unbolt the support bracket and remove the canister.
11 Refitting is a reversal of removal.

Fuel filler cap

12 The fuel filler cap is an integral part of the evaporative emissions control system. It contains both a pressure relief valve and a vacuum relief valve.
13 Remove the cap and check the condition of the seal. Always renew the cap with a genuine Nissan one; temporary or emergency filler caps are not a permanent solution.

3 Crankcase emission system – general information

1 The crankcase emission control system consists of a series of hoses that connect the crankcase vent to the cylinder head cover vent and the throttle body.
2 The system requires no attention other than to check at regular intervals that the hose(s) are free of blockages and undamaged.

4 Oxygen sensors – removal and refitting

Note: *The oxygen sensors are delicate and will not work if dropped or knocked, if their power supply is disrupted, or if any cleaning materials are used on them. Note also that when replacing a Bosch oxygen sensor with the NGK sensor introduced in May 2007, it is necessary to have the new sensor reprogrammed by a Nissan dealer.*

Removal

1 Jack up the front of the car, and support it on axle stands (see *Jacking and vehicle support*).
2 Trace the wiring back from the oxygen sensor to the connector and disconnect the wiring **(see illustrations)**.
3 Unscrew and remove the sensor from its location – an open-ended spanner or special

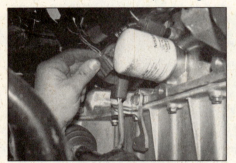

4.2a Unplug the wiring to the rear oxygen sensor

4.2b Removing the rear oxygen sensor wiring, complete with support bracket

4.2c Remove the support bracket for the front oxygen sensor . . .

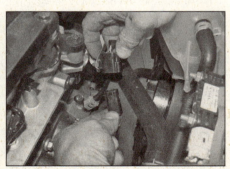

4.2d . . . and unplug the connector

4.2e Remove the heat shield to access the front oxygen sensor (arrowed)

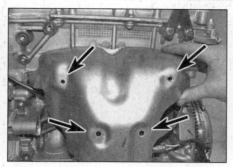

5.5a The upper heat shield bolt locations

5.5b Remove the upper shield . . .

oxygen sensor socket will be needed, as the sensor wiring means a normal socket cannot be fitted. The front sensor is difficult to access. Depending on the tools available it may be more convenient to remove the exhaust manifold and catalytic converter to remove the oxygen sensor.

4 From Build Date 16/05/2005 (VIN SJNFCAK12U2000001) the front oxygen sensor has been changed from Bosch to NGK manufacture. When replacing a Bosch sensor with a NGK sensor, the engine management ECU must be re-programmed to the new sensor parameters by a Nissan dealer.

Refitting

5 Refitting is a reversal of removal, noting the following points:

a) *Clean the threads of the sensor and the threads in the exhaust manifold.*

b) *Ideally, the sensor should be tightened to the specified torque. However, unless a slotted socket is available, this will not be possible – use the figure quoted as a guide to hand-tightening using a spanner.*

c) *Reconnect the wiring, making sure that it is in no danger of contacting the exhaust or other moving parts.*

5.5c . . . and the lower shield

5 Remove the upper and lower heat shields **(see illustrations)**.

6 Trace the oxygen sensor wiring up to the connector plug, and disconnect it.

7 Remove the two bolts securing the catalytic converter to the exhaust downpipe, and recover the springs. Lower the front part of the exhaust down (unhook the rubber mountings as necessary), and support the exhaust on an

5.7a Removing the exhaust front mounting

axle stand. Recover the gasket from the joint – a new one should be used when refitting **(see illustrations)**.

8 Unbolt and remove the catalytic converter support bracket **(see illustration)**.

9 Unscrew and remove the five nuts (in the **reverse** order to that shown) used to secure the manifold to the cylinder head **(see illustration)**. Use a wire brush and plenty of

---

5 Exhaust manifold –
removed and refitting

⚠ *Warning: Allow ample time for the exhaust system to cool before starting work.*

Removal

1 Jack up the front of the car, and support it on axle stands (see *Jacking and vehicle support*). Disconnect the battery negative lead, and position the lead away from the battery (also see *Disconnecting the battery*).

2 Remove the air intake ducting as described in Chapter 4A and then remove the right hand front wheel. Remove the wing liner.

3 Remove the drivebelts as described in Chapter 1. Disconnect the wiring from the alternator and move the alternator to one side as described in Chapter 5A.

4 If air conditioning is fitted unbolt the compressor and move it to one side. Secure it with cord to the front panel or inner wing.

5.7b Remove the bolts and springs

5.8 The catalytic converter support bracket

5.7c Recover the gasket

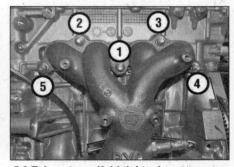

5.9 Exhaust manifold tightening sequence

5.10 Remove the inlet manifold complete with the catalytic converter from below

5.11 Recover the exhaust manifold gasket

penetrating oil first if they appear to be rusty. If the studs come free with the nuts, separate them on the bench, noting that the shorter thread side fits into the cylinder head.

> **HAYNES HiNT**
> *If a nut appears to be sticking, do not try to force it; tighten the nut back half a turn, apply some more penetrating oil to the stud threads, wait several seconds for it to soak in, then gradually unscrew the nut by one turn. Repeat this process until the nut is free.*

10 Carefully withdraw the manifold complete with the catalytic converter from the cylinder head studs **(see illustration)**.

11 Recover the manifold gasket – a new one must be used when refitting **(see illustration)**. Examine the condition of the manifold mounting studs/nuts and bolts, and obtain new ones for refitting if necessary.

Refitting

12 Refitting is a reversal of the removal procedure, noting the following points:
a) *Always fit new gaskets to the manifold-to-downpipe and manifold-to-head joints.*
b) *It is recommended that new nuts are used as a matter of course – even if the old ones came off without difficulty, they may not stand being retightened. New components will be much easier to remove in future, should this be necessary.*

6.5 The exhaust centre silencer front mounting

c) *If the old studs and bolts are re-used, clean the threads thoroughly to remove all traces of rust.*
d) *Tighten all fittings to the specified torque, in the correct sequence (see illustration 5.9).*

6 Exhaust system – component renewal

> ⚠ **Warning: Allow ample time for the exhaust system to cool before starting work. In particular, note that the catalytic converter runs at very high temperatures. If there is any chance that the system may still be hot, wear suitable gloves. When removing the exhaust centre section, take care not to damage the oxygen sensors if they are not removed from their locations.**

Removal

1 The original Nissan system fitted in the factory is in three sections. The downpipe section includes the post- catalytic converter oxygen sensor. This is joined to the centre silencer by a flexible connection. This in turn is connected to the rear silencer with a rigid fitting complete with a gasket. The rear silencer can be removed and renewed separately.

2 To remove part of the system, first jack up the front or rear of the car and support it on axle stands (see *Jacking and vehicle support*). Alternatively, position the car over an inspection pit or on car ramps.

6.7 The rear exhaust mounting flange

Downpipe

3 Trace the wiring back from the oxygen sensor, and disconnect the wiring connector. Unclip the wiring from any clips or brackets, noting how it is routed for refitting.

4 Separate the flexible coupling at the front as described in Section 5. Recover the springs and gasket. An earth wire may also be fitted to some models at this point.

5 Do the same at the rear coupling and then either twist the pipe free from the mounting rubber or unbolt the mounting from the front subframe **(see illustration)**.

Centre section

6 Remove the two bolts at the front securing the centre silencer to the downpipe, and recover the springs. Lower the front part of the exhaust down, and support the exhaust on an axle stand. Recover the gasket from the joint – a new one should be used when refitting.

7 Similarly, at the rear, remove the two bolts securing the centre section rear flange to the rear silencer **(see illustration)**. Tap the flange if necessary to separate it. Recover the gasket from the joint – a new one should be used when refitting.

8 The centre section is now only supported by one rubber insulator at the rear. Unhook the mounting and lower the section to the floor.

Rear silencer

9 Remove the two bolts (and springs) securing the centre section rear flange to the rear silencer. Tap the flange if necessary to separate it. Recover the gasket from the joint – a new one should be used when refitting.

10 Unhook the rear silencer from the rubber mountings at the front and rear, and remove it from under the car.

Refitting

11 Each section is refitted by a reversal of the removal sequence, noting the following points:
a) *Ensure that all traces of corrosion have been removed from the flanges or pipe ends, and renew all necessary gaskets.*
b) *If the flange bolts and springs are in poor condition, obtain new ones for refitting. Exhaust 'fitting kits' are now widely available from car accessory shops, which contain all the necessary parts (often including new gaskets).*
c) *Inspect the rubber mountings for signs of damage or deterioration, and renew as necessary.*
d) *If using exhaust assembly paste, make sure this is only applied to joints downstream of the catalyst.*
e) *Ensure that all rubber mountings are correctly located, and that there is adequate clearance between the exhaust system and vehicle underbody. Providing good-quality parts are fitted, the bolted flange joints should mean the exhaust alignment is preserved.*

7 Catalytic converter – general information and precautions

General information

1 The catalytic converter reduces harmful exhaust emissions by chemically converting the more poisonous gases to ones which (in theory at least) are less harmful. The catalytic converter is a three-way type; oxides of nitrogen are converted to oxygen and nitrogen, hydrocarbons become carbon dioxide and water, and carbon monoxide becomes carbon dioxide.

2 Inside the converter is a honeycomb structure, made of ceramic material and coated with the precious metals palladium, platinum and rhodium (the 'catalyst' which promotes the chemical reaction). The chemical reaction only occurs at very high temperatures (400°C) and to achieve these temperatures quickly, manufacturers have moved the converter as close as possible to the combustion chambers. Indeed many are now incorporated in the exhaust manifold and are often called 'manifold catalytic converters' or more commonly 'mani-cats'. The Micra has the converter mounted directly below the exhaust manifold.

3 The ceramic structure contained within the converter is understandably fragile, and will not withstand rough treatment. Since the converter runs at a high temperature, driving through deep standing water (in flood conditions, for example) is to be avoided, since the thermal stresses imposed when plunging the hot converter into cold water may well cause the ceramic internals to fracture, resulting in a 'blocked' converter – a common cause of failure. A converter which has been damaged in this way can be checked by shaking it (do not strike it) – if a rattling noise is heard, this indicates probable failure.

4 The converter is best removed with the exhaust manifold. It can then be separated on the bench if required.

Precautions

5 The catalytic converter is a reliable and simple device which needs no maintenance in itself, but there are some facts of which an owner should be aware if the converter is to function properly for its full service life:

a) DO NOT use leaded petrol (or lead-replacement petrol, LRP) in a car equipped with a catalytic converter – the lead (or other additives) will coat the precious metals, reducing their converting efficiency and will eventually destroy the converter.

b) Always keep the ignition and fuel systems well-maintained in accordance with the manufacturer's schedule (see Chapter 1).

c) If the engine develops a misfire, do not drive the car at all (or at least as little as possible) until the fault is cured.

d) DO NOT push- or tow-start the car – this will soak the catalytic converter in unburned fuel, causing it to overheat when the engine does start.

e) DO NOT switch off the ignition at high engine speeds – ie, do not 'blip' the throttle immediately before switching off the engine.

f) DO NOT use fuel or engine oil additives – these may contain substances harmful to the catalytic converter.

g) DO NOT continue to use the car if the engine burns oil to the extent of leaving a visible trail of blue smoke.

h) Remember that the catalytic converter operates at very high temperatures. DO NOT, therefore, park the car in dry undergrowth, over long grass or piles of dead leaves after a long run.

i) As mentioned above, driving through deep water should be avoided if possible. The sudden cooling effect may fracture the ceramic honeycomb, damaging it beyond repair.

j) Remember that the catalytic converter is FRAGILE – do not strike it with tools during servicing work, and take care handling it when removing it from the car for any reason.

k) In some cases, a sulphurous smell (like that of rotten eggs) may be noticed from the exhaust. This is common to many catalytic converter-equipped cars, and has more to do with the sulphur content of the brand of fuel being used than the converter itself.

l) If a substantial loss of power is experienced, remember that this could be due to the converter being blocked. This can occur simply as a result of high mileage, but may be due to the ceramic element having fractured and collapsed internally (see paragraph 3). A new converter is the only cure in this instance.

m) The catalytic converter, used on a well-maintained and well-driven car, should last at least 100 000 miles – if the converter is no longer effective, it must be renewed.

Notes

Chapter 5 Part A:
Starting and charging systems

Contents

	Section number		Section number
Alternator – removal and refitting	7	Electrical fault finding – general information	2
Alternator – testing and overhaul	8	Electrical system check	See Weekly checks
Alternator drivebelt – removal, refitting and tensioning	6	General information, precautions and battery disconnection	1
Battery – removal and refitting	4	Ignition switch – removal and refitting	See Chapter 12
Battery – testing and charging	3	Starter motor – removal and refitting	10
Battery check	See Weekly checks	Starter motor – testing and overhaul	11
Charging system – testing	5	Starting system – testing	9

Degrees of difficulty

Easy, suitable for novice with little experience 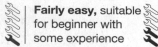	**Fairly easy,** suitable for beginner with some experience 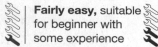	**Fairly difficult,** suitable for competent DIY mechanic 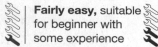	**Difficult,** suitable for experienced DIY mechanic 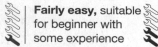	**Very difficult,** suitable for expert DIY or professional

Specifications

System type . . . .   12 volt, negative earth

Battery
Type . . . .   Lead-acid, 'maintenance-free'
Charge condition:
  Poor . . . .   11.5 volts
  Normal . . . .   12.0 volts
  Good . . . .   12.5 volts

Alternator
Nominal rating . . . .   77 amps
Regulated voltage . . . .   14.55 volts

Starter motor
No-load rating:
  Mitsubishi reduction gear type . . . .   Less than 90 amps
  Bosch non reduction type . . . .   Less than 48 amps
Brush length (minimum):
  Bosch . . . .   3.5 mm
  Mitsubishi . . . .   5.5 mm
Minimum commutator diameter
  Bosch . . . .   33.5 mm
  Mitsubishi . . . .   28.8 mm

Torque wrench settings

	Nm	lbf ft
Alternator mounting bolt	38	28
Alternator upper bracket bolt	38	28
Battery mounting bolt	14	10
Engine stay	45	33
Idler pulley bracket	20	15
Idler pulley nut	28	21
Starter motor mounting bolts	44	32

1 General information, precautions and battery disconnection

General information

The engine electrical system consists mainly of the charging and starting systems. Because of their engine-related functions, these components are covered separately from the body electrical devices such as the lights, instruments, etc (which are covered in Chapter 12). Information on the ignition system is covered in Part B of this Chapter.

The electrical system is of 12 volt negative earth type.

The battery is of the 'maintenance-free' (sealed for life) type and is charged by the alternator, which is belt-driven from the crankshaft pulley.

The starter motor is of the pre-engaged type incorporating an integral solenoid. On starting, the solenoid moves the drive pinion into engagement with the flywheel ring gear before the starter motor is energised. Once the engine has started, a one-way clutch prevents the motor armature being driven by the engine until the pinion disengages from the flywheel.

Precautions

It is necessary to take extra care when working on the electrical system to avoid damage to semi-conductor devices (diodes and transistors), and to avoid the risk of personal injury. In addition to the precautions given in *Safety first!* at the beginning of this manual, observe the following when working on the system:

• *Always remove rings, watches, etc, before working on the electrical system*. Even with the battery disconnected, capacitive discharge could occur if a component's live terminal is earthed through a metal object. This could cause a shock or nasty burn.

• *Do not reverse the battery connections*. Components such as the alternator, electronic control units, or any other components having semi-conductor circuitry could be irreparably damaged.

• If the engine is being started using jump leads and a slave battery, connect the batteries *positive-to-positive* and *negative-to-negative* (see *Jump starting*). This also applies when connecting a battery charger.

• Never disconnect the battery terminals, the alternator, any electrical wiring or any test instruments when the engine is running.

• Do not allow the engine to turn the alternator when the alternator is not connected.

• Never 'test' for alternator output by 'flashing' the output lead to earth.

• Never use an ohmmeter of the type incorporating a hand-cranked generator for circuit or continuity testing.

• Always ensure that the battery negative lead is disconnected when working on the electrical system.

• Before using electric-arc welding equipment on the car, disconnect the battery, alternator and components such as the fuel injection/ignition electronic control unit to protect them from the risk of damage.

Battery disconnection

Refer to the precautions listed in *Disconnecting the battery*, in the Reference section of this manual.

2 Electrical fault finding – general information

Refer to Chapter 12.

3 Battery – testing and charging

Testing

1 Where a 'sealed for life' maintenance-free battery is fitted, topping-up and testing of the electrolyte in each cell is not possible. The original battery is provided with a status indicator. This should always be green. The condition of the battery can therefore only be tested using a load tester, digital battery tester or a voltmeter.

2 If testing the battery using a voltmeter, connect the voltmeter across the battery and compare the result with those given in the Specifications under 'charge condition'. The test is only accurate if the battery has not been subjected to any kind of charge for the previous six hours. If this is not the case, switch on the headlights for 30 seconds, then wait four to five minutes before testing the battery after switching off the headlights. All other electrical circuits must be switched off, so check that the doors and tailgate are fully shut when making the test.

3 If the voltage reading is less than 12.0 volts, then the battery is discharged.

4 If the battery is to be charged, remove it from the car (Section 4) and charge it as described later in this Section.

Charging

Note: *The following is intended as a guide only. Always refer to the manufacturer's recommendations (often printed on a label attached to the battery), and always disconnect both terminal leads before charging a battery.*

5 A maintenance-free battery takes considerably longer to fully recharge than the standard type, the time taken being dependent on the extent of discharge, but it can take anything up to three days.

6 A constant voltage type charger is required, to be set, when connected, to 13.9 to 14.9 volts with a charger current below 25 amps. Using this method, the battery should be usable within three hours, giving a voltage reading of 12.5 volts, but this is for a partially-discharged battery and, as mentioned, full charging can take considerably longer.

7 If the battery is to be charged from a fully-discharged state (condition reading less than 12.2 volts), have it recharged by your Nissan dealer or local automotive electrician, as the charge rate is higher and constant supervision during charging is necessary.

4 Battery – removal and refitting

Note: *Refer to the warnings given in 'Safety first!' and in Section 1 of this Chapter before starting work.*

Battery

Removal

1 The battery is located on the left-hand side of the engine compartment, on a platform above the transmission.

2 Loosen the clamp nut, then detach the earth lead from the battery negative (earth) terminal post. This is the terminal to disconnect before working on, or disconnecting, any electrical component on the car. Position the lead away from the battery.

3 Pivot up the plastic cover from the positive terminal, then loosen the positive lead clamp nut. Detach the positive lead from the terminal, and position it away from the battery **(see illustration)**.

4 Remove the insulation from the battery and then using a socket on an extension bar remove the clamp that holds the battery in

4.3 Remove the positive cable

4.4a Removing the foam insulator

4.4b Remove the bolt . . .

4.4c . . . and recover the clamp

4.5 Lifting out the battery

place. Moving the relay plate to one side may help see the bolt **(see illustrations)**.

5 Lift out the battery, keeping it as level as possible. Take care, as the battery is heavy. If required, the plastic tray under the battery can also be removed **(see illustration)**.

Refitting

6 Refitting is a reversal of removal. Reconnect the battery negative lead last. Make sure the battery terminals and clamps are clean before refitting, and that the clamp nuts are tightened securely.

Battery tray

7 The battery tray is part of the left-hand front transmission mounting. It can be removed as described in Chapter 2A.

5 Charging system – testing

Note: *Refer to the warnings given in 'Safety first!' and in Section 1 of this Chapter before starting work.*

1 If the charge warning light fails to illuminate when the ignition is switched on, first check the alternator wiring connections for security. If the light still fails to illuminate, check the continuity of the warning light feed wire from the alternator to the instrument panel. If all is satisfactory, the alternator is at fault and should be renewed or taken to an auto-electrician for testing and repair.

2 If the ignition warning light illuminates when

the engine is running, stop the engine and check that the drivebelt is intact and correctly tensioned (see Chapter 1) and that the alternator connections are secure. If all is so far satisfactory, have the alternator checked by an auto-electrician for testing and repair.

3 If the alternator output is suspect even though the warning light functions correctly, the regulated voltage may be checked as follows.

4 Connect a voltmeter across the battery terminals and start the engine.

5 Increase the engine speed until the voltmeter reading remains steady; the reading should be approximately 12 to 13 volts, and no more than 14.7 volts.

6 Switch on as many electrical accessories (eg, the headlights, heated rear window and heater blower) as possible, and check that the alternator maintains the regulated voltage at around 13 to 14 volts.

7 If the regulated voltage is not as stated, the fault may be due to worn brushes, weak brush springs, a faulty voltage regulator, a faulty diode, a severed phase winding or worn or damaged slip-rings. The alternator should be renewed or taken to an auto-electrician for testing and repair.

6 Alternator drivebelt – removal, refitting and tensioning

Refer to the procedure given for the auxiliary drivebelts in Chapter 1.

7 Alternator – removal and refitting

Note: *Refer to the warnings given in 'Safety first!' and in Section 1 of this Chapter before starting work.*

1 Loosen the clamp nut, then detach the earth lead from the battery negative (earth) terminal post. Position the lead well away from the battery.

Removal

2 If not already done, jack up the front of the car, and support it on axle stands (see *Jacking and vehicle support*).

3 Better access will be gained if the right-hand front grille and indicator lamp are removed as described in Chapters 11 and 12. Access will be further improved if the air inlet duct and front bumper are also removed. Some models have another plastic panel next to the radiator. Prise the clips free and remove this if fitted.

4 Remove the auxiliary drivebelt as described in Chapter 1, and then remove the idler pulley.

5 Disconnect the wiring plug, then lift up the cover and undo the nut securing the battery supply cable. Recover any washers fitted, then lift off the supply cable and place it to one side **(see illustrations)**.

6 Remove the engine mounting stay as described in Chapter 1 and then remove the earth cable. Remove the alternator upper support bracket next **(see illustrations)**.

7.5a Disconnect the small electrical terminal . . .

7.5b . . . and then remove the main cable

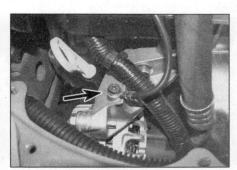

7.6a The earth cable on the upper mounting

7.6b Removing the upper mounting

7.7 The bolt is not completely removed

7.8 Withdraw the alternator from the front

7 Loosen the lower mounting bolt and rotate the alternator forwards. Unscrew the bolt until the cut-out provided in the front cover allows the alternator to be pulled free **(see illustration)**.

8 Manoeuvre the alternator out of the engine compartment through the grille opening **(see illustration)**.

Refitting

9 Refitting is a reversal of removal, noting the following points:
  a) Only fit the pivot and lockbolts hand-tight to begin with.
  b) Ensure that the wiring is reconnected correctly, and that the retaining nuts are tight.
  c) Refit and tension the auxiliary drivebelt as described in Chapter 1.

8.3a Remove the cover . . .

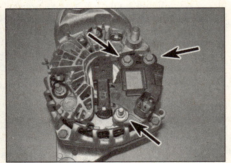

8.3b . . . and then remove the brush pack bolts (arrowed)

8.4a Push back the brushes with a small drill (arrowed)

8.4b The drill bit in position as the brush pack is refitted

8 Alternator – testing and overhaul

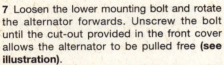

1 If the alternator is thought to be suspect, it should be removed from the car and taken to an auto-electrician for testing. Most auto-electricians will be able to supply and fit brushes at a reasonable cost. However, check on the cost of repairs before proceeding, as it may prove more economical to obtain a new or exchange alternator.

2 Before condemning the alternator it may be worth examining the condition of the brushes. Compare the length of the brushes and condition of the slip-ring. The brushes have a wear indicator marked on the side; this will give a good idea of the overall condition of the alternator.

3 Remove the alternator rear cover and the then remove the brush holder bolts. Check that the brushes are still serviceable and that they slide freely in their guides **(see illustrations)**.

4 Refitting is a reversal of removal, but a small hole will need to be drilled in the rear of the brush holder to enable the carbon brushes to be pushed back to allow them past the slip-ring **(see illustrations)**.

9 Starting system – testing

Note: Refer to the warnings given in 'Safety first!' and in Section 1 of this Chapter before starting work.

1 If the starter motor fails to operate when the ignition key is turned to the appropriate position, the following possible causes may be to blame:
  a) The battery is faulty.
  b) The electrical connections between the switch, solenoid, battery and starter motor are somewhere failing to pass the necessary current from the battery through the starter to earth.
  c) The solenoid is faulty.
  d) The starter motor is mechanically or electrically defective.

2 To check the battery, switch on the headlights. If they dim after a few seconds, this indicates that the battery is discharged – recharge (see Section 3) or renew the battery. If the headlights glow brightly, operate the ignition switch and observe the lights. If they dim, then this indicates that current is reaching the starter motor, therefore the fault must lie in the starter motor. If the lights continue to glow brightly (and no clicking sound can be heard from the starter motor solenoid), this indicates that there is a fault in the circuit or solenoid – see following paragraphs. If the starter motor turns slowly when operated, but the battery is in good condition, then this indicates that either the starter motor is faulty, or there is considerable resistance somewhere in the circuit.

3 If a fault in the circuit is suspected, disconnect the battery leads (including the earth connection to the body), the starter/

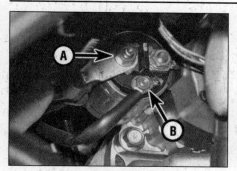

10.3 The starter motor electrical connections

A Main supply cable from the battery
B Ignition-controlled supply to the solenoid

10.4a The starter motor mounting bolts (arrowed)

10.4b Withdraw the starter motor

solenoid wiring and the engine/transmission earth strap. Thoroughly clean the connections, and reconnect the leads and wiring, then use a voltmeter or test light to check that full battery voltage is available at the battery positive lead connection to the solenoid, and that the earth is sound. Smear petroleum jelly around the battery terminals to prevent corrosion – corroded connections are amongst the most frequent causes of electrical system faults.

4 If the battery and all connections are in good condition, check the circuit by disconnecting the wire from the solenoid terminal. Connect a voltmeter or test light between the wire end and a good earth (such as the battery negative terminal), and check that the wire is live when the ignition switch is turned to the 'start' position. If it is, then the circuit is sound – if not, the circuit wiring can be checked as described in Chapter 12.

5 The solenoid contacts can be checked by connecting a voltmeter or test light between the battery positive feed connection on the starter side of the solenoid, and earth. When the ignition switch is turned to the 'start' position, there should be a reading or lighted

bulb, as applicable. If there is no reading or lighted bulb, the solenoid is faulty and should be renewed.

6 If the circuit and solenoid are proved sound, the fault must lie in the starter motor. In this event, it may be possible to have the starter motor overhauled by a specialist, but check on the cost of spares before proceeding, as it may prove more economical to obtain a new or exchange motor.

10 Starter motor – removal and refitting

Note: *Refer to the warnings given in 'Safety first!' and in Section 1 of this Chapter before starting work.*

Removal

1 Loosen the clamp nut, and then detach the earth lead from the battery negative (earth) terminal. Position the lead away from the battery.

2 Apply the handbrake, then jack up the front of the car and support on axle stands (see *Jacking and vehicle support*). Alternatively remove the wiper motor and support panel

as described in Chapter 12 and remove the starter from above.

3 Working beneath the rear of the engine, or from the top, unscrew the top nut and disconnect the wiring assembly from the starter motor. Also disconnect the lower wiring plug **(see illustrations)**.

4 Support the starter motor, then unscrew and remove the two starter mounting bolts from the transmission bellhousing, and withdraw the motor **(see illustrations)**.

Refitting

5 Refitting is a reversal of removal, but tighten the mounting bolts to the specified torque.

11 Starter motor – testing and overhaul

If the starter motor is thought to be suspect, it should be removed from the car and taken to an auto-electrician for testing. Most auto-electricians will be able to supply and fit brushes at a reasonable cost. However, check on the cost of repairs before proceeding as it may prove more economical to obtain a new or exchange motor.

Chapter 5 Part B:
Ignition system

Contents

Section number

General information and precautions. 1
Ignition coils – removal, testing and refitting 3
Ignition system – testing. 2

Section number

Ignition system sensors – removal and refitting. 4
Ignition timing – checking and adjustment. 5
Spark plug renewal. . . . . See Chapter 1

Degrees of difficulty

| Easy, suitable for novice with little experience | | Fairly easy, suitable for beginner with some experience | | Fairly difficult, suitable for competent DIY mechanic | | Difficult, suitable for experienced DIY mechanic | | Very difficult, suitable for expert DIY or professional | |

Specifications

General

System type.	Coil over plug system, (COP) with one ignition coil per cylinder, controlled by the engine ECU
Firing order.	1-3-4-2
Location of No 1 cylinder.	Timing chain end
Ignition timing (ECU-controlled).	8 to 12° BTDC @ idle

Ignition system data

Ignition timing.	Controlled by the engine ECU

Torque wrench settings

	Nm	lbf ft
Ignition coil mounting bolts	4	3
Knock sensor	18	15
Spark plugs.	25	18

1 General information and precautions

General information

The ignition system is integrated with the fuel injection system to form a combined engine management system under the control of the engine ECU (see Chapter 4A for further information). The main ignition system components include the ignition switch, the battery, the crankshaft speed/position sensor, the camshaft position sensor, the knock sensor, the four ignition coils, and the spark plugs.

A Coil Over Plug (COP) system is fitted where the main functions of a conventional distributor are performed by a computerised module within the engine ECU. Based on the inputs from the crankshaft and camshaft position sensors (besides all the input on engine load, temperature, etc, from the fuel system sensors), the engine ECU is able to calculate precisely the best ignition timing for any given situation. The ECU sends out the trigger to each coil in the firing order, and the coils, which are fitted directly to their individual spark plugs, ignite the fuel/air mixture in the cylinders. Having one coil per cylinder gives an even greater control refinement, as the timing can be altered rapidly to suit changing conditions. Unlike the distributorless ignition systems seen on many modern cars, there is no 'wasted spark' with the coil-on-plug direct system, which theoretically means extended spark plug life. Greater potential reliability is also derived from having no ignition HT leads.

The information contained in this Chapter concentrates on the ignition-related components of the engine management system. Information covering the fuel, exhaust and emission control components can be found in the applicable Parts of Chapter 4.

Precautions

The following precautions must be observed, to prevent damage to the ignition system components and to reduce risk of personal injury:

a) Do not keep the ignition on for more than 10 seconds if the engine will not start.
b) Ensure that the ignition is switched off before disconnecting any of the ignition wiring.
c) Ensure that the ignition is switched off before connecting or disconnecting any ignition test equipment, such as a timing light.
d) Do not earth the coil primary or secondary circuits.

⚠ **Warning: Voltages produced by an electronic ignition system are considerably higher than those produced by conventional ignition systems. Extreme care must be taken when working on the system with the ignition switched on. Persons with surgically-implanted cardiac pacemaker devices should keep well clear of the ignition circuits, components and test equipment.**

3.3a The ignition coils and cylinder order

3.3b Removing the wiring plug

3.4 Twist and pull the coil free

2 Ignition system – testing

Note: *Don't overlook the possibility of a problem with the immobiliser system on a non-starting engine (see Chapter 12). Genuine Nissan keys will contain the necessary transponder chip, but ones supplied from other sources may not.*

1 If the engine either will not turn over at all, or only turns very slowly, check the battery and starter motor as described in Chapter 5A.

2 Check each coil's resistances as described in Section 3; renew the coil if faulty, but be careful to check carefully the wiring connections themselves before doing so, to ensure that the fault is not due to dirty or poorly-fastened connectors.

3 If the engine runs but has an irregular misfire, check the wiring plugs on the ignition coils, ensuring that all connections are clean and securely fastened. Also ensure that there is no damage to the wiring harness leading to each coil. It's not unknown for a coil to break down under load, especially in hot conditions. Check the spark plugs (by substitution, if necessary).

4 The most likely cause of total failure would be a problem with the crankshaft sensor (the camshaft sensor would perhaps be a close second). Check the condition of the wiring, and that the wiring plugs are clean and secure, as a first step. These components are

both relatively easy to renew, but first weigh up their cost compared with having the car checked by a Nissan dealer or other specialist – the fault may lie elsewhere.

5 If simple checks fail to reveal the cause of the problem, the car should be taken to a Nissan dealer or suitably-equipped garage for diagnostic testing. A wiring connector is incorporated in the engine management circuit (under the steering column) into which a special electronic diagnostic tester can be plugged. The tester, in the hands of an experienced technician will locate the probable fault, alleviating the need to test all the system components individually which is a time-consuming operation that carries a high risk of damaging the ECU. If necessary, the system wiring and wiring connectors can be checked as described in Chapter 12.

3 Ignition coils – removal, testing and refitting

Removal

1 Make sure the ignition is switched off (take out the key).

2 Remove the air filter duct and air cleaner assembly as described in Chapter 4A.

3 Disconnect the wiring plug from the first coil to be removed. Though it seems unlikely that the wiring plugs could be mixed up, it might be safest to disconnect and remove one coil at a time. If all the coils are to be removed, mark them and their respective wiring plugs with labels or tape to indicate their fitted positions **(see illustrations)**.

4 Remove the coil mounting bolt, then pull upwards to remove the coil from its spark plug **(see illustration)**.

Testing

5 Using an ohmmeter, measure the resistances of the ignition coil. Disconnect the coils in

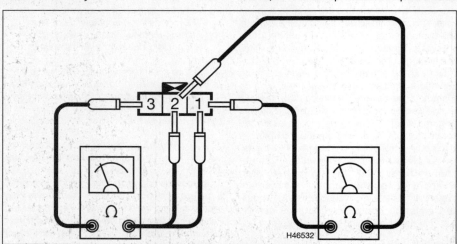

3.5 Test procedure for the coils

turn. First measure between terminals 2 and 3. Depending on which way round the ohmmeter is connected, it should indicate continuity (zero resistance) or open-circuit (infinite resistance). Either reading is possible because the coil contains a power transistor which is polarity-sensitive. Reverse the meter probes and check that the reading changes. Next measure between terminals 1 and 2 – the meter should indicate continuity. Finally check the resistance between terminals 1 and 3. Continuity should exist. Confirm your findings with a Nissan dealer before renewing the coil (see illustration).

6 Disconnect the coils in turn and check for battery voltage at the positive terminal of the coil wiring plug, with the ignition temporarily switched on. The coils are supplied from fuse 52 (20 amp) in the underbonnet fusebox.

7 Nissan state that a spark test can be carried out. Disconnect the plugs for the fuel injectors before proceeding. Remove the coil and the reconnect the wiring plug. Fit a new or known good spark plug to the coil. Arrange the coil so that the spark plug is earthed against the cylinder head (use a jumper wire if necessary). Avoid holding the coil as very high voltages will be present. Have an assistant crank the engine whilst checking the plug for a spark. It is perfectly acceptable to swap the coils around. If a faulty coil has been identified, before condemning it, try fitting it to another cylinder. This procedure should only be attempted by the experienced home mechanic, as there is a risk the spark could ignite fuel/air mixture rising from the open plug hole, and also a risk of damaging the car's ECU.

Refitting

8 Refitting is a reversal of removal. Repeat for the other coils as necessary.

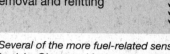

4 Ignition system sensors – removal and refitting

Note: *Several of the more fuel-related sensors described in Chapter 4A may also have a bearing on the ignition system. Those listed below are simply the most likely to give rise to an ignition system fault.*

Crankshaft position sensor

1 Refer to Chapter 4A, Section 9.

Camshaft position sensor

2 Refer to Chapter 4A, Section 9.

Knock sensor

3 The sensor is used to detect the onset of pinking (pre-ignition or detonation, usually noticed in hot conditions, or when running on sub-standard or low-octane fuel). It is screwed into the engine block, and works by detecting the specific vibrations produced by pinking. When signalled by the knock sensor, the ECU retards the ignition timing until the pinking stops, then advances it slowly until it just recurs, thus maintaining maximum engine efficiency while avoiding the risk of engine damage.

4 To gain access to remove the sensor, first remove the throttle body and inlet manifold as described in Chapter 4A. The experienced home mechanic may be able to reach around to the rear of the inlet manifold without any other work.

5 Disconnect the wiring plug from the sensor, then unscrew and remove it from the engine (see illustration).

6 Refitting is a reversal of removal, but the wiring connector must be parallel with the

4.5 The location of the knock sensor (inlet manifold removed)

head gasket and pointing toward the engine timing chain end. It is essential that the sensor is tightened to the specified torque, as failure to do so may prevent it from working properly.

5 Ignition timing – checking and adjustment

Due to the nature of the ignition system, the ignition timing is constantly being monitored and adjusted by the engine management ECU, and nominal values cannot be given. Therefore, it is not possible for the home mechanic to check the ignition timing.

The only way in which the ignition timing can be checked is using special electronic test equipment, connected to the engine management system diagnostic connector (refer to Chapter 4A). No adjustment of the ignition timing is possible. Should the ignition timing be incorrect, then a fault must be present in the engine management system.

Notes

Chapter 6
Clutch

Contents

Section number

Clutch – general check. . . . . See Chapter 1
Clutch assembly – removal, inspection and refitting 7
Clutch hydraulic pipes/hoses – removal and refitting 4
Clutch hydraulic system – bleeding 5

Section number

Clutch master cylinder – removal and refitting. 2
Clutch pedal – removal, refitting and checking 6
Clutch slave cylinder/release bearing – removal and refitting 3
General information 1

Degrees of difficulty

Easy, suitable for novice with little experience	Fairly easy, suitable for beginner with some experience	Fairly difficult, suitable for competent DIY mechanic	Difficult, suitable for experienced DIY mechanic	Very difficult, suitable for expert DIY or professional

Specifications

General

Clutch type . . . . Single dry plate, diaphragm spring, hydraulically-operated release mechanism

Friction disc

Rivet head depth (minimum) . . . . 0.3 mm
Disc run-out (maximum) . . . . 1.0 mm

Clutch pedal

Pedal height from floor . . . . 164.0 to 170.0 mm
Pedal free play . . . . 0.5 mm
'Bite' point . . . . 25.0 mm (minimum) from floor

Torque wrench settings

	Nm	lbf ft
Clutch pedal nuts	14	10
Pressure plate-to-flywheel bolts:		
Stage 1	15	12
Stage 2	25	19
Slave cylinder mounting bolts	21	15

1 General information

The clutch consists of a friction disc, a pressure plate assembly and a slave cylinder/release bearing, sandwiched between the engine and the transmission. The clutch is operated hydraulically, with a master cylinder mounted on the bulkhead, attached to the pedal, and a concentric slave cylinder mounted in the gearbox. The slave cylinder operates directly on the clutch and incorporates the release bearing. The clutch fluid reservoir is shared with the brake fluid reservoir on the top of the brake master cylinder.

The clutch friction disc is fitted between the engine flywheel and the clutch pressure plate, and is allowed to slide on the transmission input shaft splines.

The pressure plate assembly is bolted to the engine flywheel. When the engine is running, drive is transmitted from the crankshaft, via the flywheel, to the friction disc (these components being clamped securely together by the pressure plate assembly) and from the friction disc to the transmission input shaft.

To interrupt the drive, the spring pressure must be relaxed by the hydraulically-operated release mechanism. Depressing the clutch pedal operates the master cylinder, which in turn operates the concentric slave cylinder. This causes the springs to deform and releases the clamping force on the pressure plate.

When the pedal is released, the diaphragm spring forces the pressure plate into contact with the friction linings on the friction disc. The disc is now firmly sandwiched between the pressure plate and the flywheel, thus transmitting engine power to the transmission.

Wear of the friction material on the friction disc is automatically compensated for by the operation of the hydraulic system. As the friction material on the disc wears, the pressure plate moves towards the flywheel, causing the clutch diaphragm spring inner fingers to move outwards. When the clutch pedal is released, excess fluid is expelled through the master cylinder into the fluid reservoir.

 Warning: Brake (and clutch) fluid is poisonous. Take care to keep it off bare skin, and in particular not to get splashes in your eyes. The fluid also attacks paintwork and plastics – wash off spillages immediately with cold water. Finally, the fluid is highly inflammable, and should be handled with the same care as petrol. The brake and clutch systems share the same fluid – any work on the clutch system which involves a great loss of fluid may mean that the braking system will have to be checked and bled on completion.

2.3 Release the pushrod

3.2 Removing the combined slave cylinder and release bearing

4 If the slave cylinder is faulty, it must be renewed.

Refitting

5 Refitting is a reversal of removal, noting the following points:
 a) *Tighten the mounting bolts and fluid pipe union to the specified torque, where given.*
 b) *Bleed the clutch on completion, as described in Section 5.*

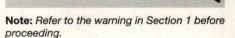

4 Clutch hydraulic pipes/hoses – removal and refitting

Note: *Refer to the warning in Section 1 before proceeding.*

Removal

Low-pressure supply hose

1 Because the clutch supply hose is located low down on the brake fluid reservoir, removing the hose will result in the loss of almost the entire contents. However because the clutch supply hose is fitted above the minimum brake fluid level air will not enter the brake system.

2 To remove the supply hose, first remove the filler cap from the brake master cylinder and cover the master cylinder with a plastic bag or latex glove. Refit the cap next. This will help create a partial vacuum in the master cylinder and help minimise the loss of fluid.

3 Have a new hose with new clips to hand, and then remove the hose from the master cylinder. Fit the hose to the brake master cylinder, keeping the end above the level of the fluid in the master cylinder. Next remove the hose from the clutch master cylinder. Immediately fit the new hose to the clutch master cylinder, but do not push it fully home yet.

4 Remove the plastic bag from the master cylinder and place a rag under the clutch master cylinder supply hose. Pull the hose back slightly until fluid emerges, and then push the hose fully home. Finally fit the new spring or worm-drive hose clips. This method will minimise the amount of air entering the system. If you are lucky the clutch may not require bleeding.

Pressure pipe

5 To remove the pressure pipe, first wipe all traces of dirt from the master cylinder and slave cylinder connections. Prise the clip free from the master cylinder at the bulkhead and then remove the pipe. Plug the end of the pipe and the outlet from the master cylinder.

6 Prise the spring clip free from the slave cylinder and remove the pipe. Seal the pipe and the outlet at the slave cylinder. Taking care not to cut or damage the plastic pressure pipe prise it free from the support clip on the gearbox, and then work along the bulkhead releasing the pipe from the assorted clips **(see illustration).**

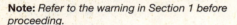

2 Clutch master cylinder – removal and refitting

Note: *Refer to the warning in Section 1 before proceeding.*

Removal

1 At the top of the master cylinder, release the spring clip on the supply hose, and pull off the hose. Either clamp the master cylinder fluid supply hose from the reservoir, or have ready a plug of some kind to fit to the hose end once the hose is disconnected. Plug or tape over the master cylinder pipe stub to prevent fluid loss or dirt entry.

2 Pull out the clip from the slave cylinder supply pipe union at the side of the master cylinder. There will be some loss of fluid as the pipe is removed – wipe up any spillage, and rinse any painted surfaces with water (avoid getting water inside the master cylinder or the disconnected pipe, however).

3 Inside the car, move the driver's seat fully to the rear, and remove the steering column lower trim panel. Using a pair of needle-nosed pliers or two screwdrivers, unhook and remove the master cylinder pushrod from the clutch pedal **(see illustration).**

4 Next rotate the master cylinder clockwise and remove it from the car.

5 If the master cylinder is faulty, it must be renewed. Parts are not available to repair the cylinder.

Refitting

6 Refitting is a reversal of removal, noting the following points:
 a) *Tighten the mounting nuts and fluid pipe union securely.*
 b) *Ensure that the fluid hose connection is clean and securely made (if the spring clip is no longer effective, use a Jubilee clip).*
 c) *Bleed the clutch on completion, as described in Section 5.*

3 Clutch slave cylinder/ release bearing – removal and refitting

Note: *Refer to the warning in Section 1 before proceeding.*

Removal

1 Because the slave cylinder is fitted inside the bellhousing of the gearbox, the transmission must be removed as described in Chapter 7A. Do not operate the clutch without the slave cylinder compressed against the clutch, because the piston will be forced out of the cylinder and destroyed.

2 With the transmission on the bench, unscrew and remove the two slave cylinder mounting bolts, and withdraw the cylinder from the input shaft **(see illustration).**

3 If required remove the clip from the cylinder and remove the elbow-shaped hydraulic pipe that contains the bleed nipple. New cylinders are normally supplied complete with this pipe and bleed nipple.

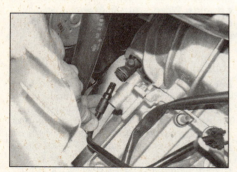

4.6a Pull up the clip and release the clutch hose . . .

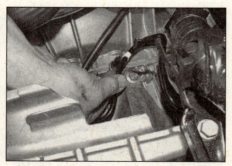

4.6b . . . and pull it free from the clip

Refitting

7 Refitting is a reversal of removal, noting the following points:

a) *Ensure that the fluid hose connections are clean, and securely made*
b) *Bleed the clutch on completion, as described in Section 5.*

5 Clutch hydraulic system – bleeding

Note: *Refer to the warning in Section 1 before proceeding.*

1 The correct operation of any hydraulic system is only possible after removing all air from the components and circuit; this is achieved by bleeding the system.

2 During the bleeding procedure, add only clean, unused hydraulic fluid of the recommended type; never re-use fluid that has already been bled from the system. Ensure that sufficient fluid is available before starting work.

3 If there is any possibility of incorrect fluid being already in the system, the hydraulic circuit must be flushed completely with correct, uncontaminated fluid.

4 If hydraulic fluid has been lost from the system, or air has entered because of a leak, ensure that the fault is cured before continuing further.

5 The bleed screw is screw is part of the slave cylinder. It is located next to the supply pipe.

6 First check that all the hydraulic hoses are securely fitted to the master and slave cylinders. Clean any dirt from around the bleed screw.

7 Unscrew the brake master cylinder fluid reservoir cap, and top-up the fluid level to the upper (MAX) level line; refit the cap loosely, and remember to maintain the fluid level at least above the lower (MIN) level line throughout the procedure, or there is a risk of further air entering the system.

Bleeding

8 Connect a brake bleeding kit, or suitable length of clear tubing, to the bleed nipple. The end of the tube should be immersed in a container part filled with brake fluid.

9 Slide the locking pin, next to the nipple up one step. Do not remove it completely.

10 Have an assistant press and release the clutch pedal slowly 15 times. The last pedal stroke must be held down. There is a possibility that the supply pipe at the slave cylinder may be dislodged during this process. It must therefore be held in position during the bleeding operation.

11 With the clutch pedal still down slowly slide the supply pipe backwards 5 mm. Prepare for some fluid loss from the pipe. Do not pull the pipe back more than 5 mm or air will enter the system.

12 Slide the supply tube back into position and push the securing pin fully home. Close

the bleed nipple and release the clutch pedal. This process may have to be repeated several times.

13 When bleeding is complete, and correct pedal feel is restored, check that the bleed screw is securely tightened and wash off any spilt fluid. Refit the dust cap to the bleed screw.

14 Check the hydraulic fluid level in the reservoir, and top-up if necessary.

15 Discard any hydraulic fluid that has been bled from the system; it will not be fit for re-use.

16 If the clutch is not operating correctly after carrying out the bleeding procedure, the master cylinder or slave cylinder may be faulty.

17 If the clutch system is being bled following a significant loss of fluid, check and if necessary bleed the braking system also, as described in Chapter 9.

6 Clutch pedal – removal, refitting and checking

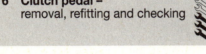

Removal

1 Inside the car, move the driver's seat fully to the rear, and remove the steering column lower trim panel. Using a pair of needle-nosed pliers or two screwdrivers, unhook and remove the master cylinder pushrod from the clutch pedal.

2 Unplug the connector for the clutch position switch.

3 Remove the three securing bolts and withdraw the pedal (see illustration).

Refitting

4 Refitting is a reversal of removal. Check the operation of the clutch thoroughly before taking the car out on the road. Check the pedal height and bite point if necessary, as described below.

Checking

5 For maximum accuracy, the clutch should be bled as described in Section 5 before carrying out any checks.

6 With the pedal released, measure the distance from the floor (directly below the pedal) to the top of the rubber pad (pedal height). Do not lift the pedal when making the measurement.

7 Check the pedal free play by depressing the pedal until resistance is felt, and measure the distance from the fully-released position to this point. It may be easier, therefore, to press the pedal by hand for this check.

8 If the first two measurements are correct, the final check is that the clutch pedal 'bite point' (the point where the clutch begins to engage) should be at least the distance specified from the pedal to the floor.

9 No adjustment facility is provided. If a fault exists the pedal assembly must be renewed as a complete unit.

6.3 The clutch pedal bolts

7 Clutch assembly – removal, inspection and refitting

⚠ *Warning: Dust created by clutch wear and deposited on the clutch components may contain asbestos, which is a health hazard. DO NOT blow it out with compressed air, or inhale any of it. DO NOT use petrol or petroleum-based solvents to clean off the dust. Brake system cleaner or methylated spirit should be used to flush the dust into a suitable receptacle. After the clutch components are wiped clean with rags, dispose of the contaminated rags and cleaner in a sealed, marked container.*
Note: *Although some friction materials may no longer contain asbestos, it is safest to assume that they do, and to take precautions accordingly.*

Removal

1 Unless the complete engine/transmission unit has to be removed from the car (see Chapter 2B), the clutch can be reached by removing the transmission as described in Chapter 7A.

2 Unless a new clutch is being fitted, use chalk or a marker pen to mark the relationship of the pressure plate assembly to the flywheel.

3 Hold the flywheel stationary using a suitable tool engaged with the starter ring gear teeth – a piece of metal can be tightened to one of the bolt holes, or alternatively an assistant can use a wide-bladed screwdriver engaged with the teeth. We fabricated a simple tool to lock the flywheel (see illustration).

7.3 Lock the flywheel with a suitable tool

7.5 Removing the clutch assembly

7.15a Centralise the disc first with this type of tool

4 Working in a diagonal sequence, slacken the pressure plate bolts by half a turn at a time, until spring pressure is released and the bolts can be unscrewed by hand. Discard the bolts – new ones should be used when refitting.

5 Prise the pressure plate assembly off its locating dowels, and collect the friction disc, noting which way round the disc is fitted **(see illustration)**.

6 Remove the bolts from the concentric slave cylinder and remove it from the input shaft.

Inspection

Note: *Due to the amount of work necessary to remove and refit clutch components, it is usually considered good practice to renew the clutch friction disc, pressure plate assembly and release bearing/slave cylinder as a matched set, even if only one of these is actually worn enough to require renewal. It is also worth considering the renewal of the clutch components on a preventative basis if the engine and/or transmission have been removed for some other reason.*

7 When cleaning clutch components, read first the warning at the beginning of this Section; remove the dust using a clean, dry cloth, and working in a well-ventilated atmosphere.

8 Check the friction disc linings for signs of wear, damage or oil contamination. If the friction material is cracked, burnt, scored or damaged, or if it is contaminated with oil or grease (shown by shiny black patches), the friction disc must be renewed. Check the depth of the rivets below the friction material surface. If any are at or near the surface of the friction material, then the friction disc must be renewed.

9 If the friction material is still serviceable, check that the centre boss splines are unworn, that the torsion springs are in good condition and securely fastened, and that all the rivets are tight. If any wear or damage is found, the friction disc must be renewed.

10 If the friction material is fouled with oil, this must be due to an oil leak from the crankshaft oil seal, or from the transmission input shaft. Renew the seal as described in the appropriate part of Chapter 2 or 7, before installing the new friction disc.

11 Check the pressure plate assembly for obvious signs of wear or damage; shake it to check for loose rivets or worn or damaged fulcrum rings, and check that the drive straps securing the pressure plate to the cover do not show signs of overheating (such as a deep yellow or blue discoloration). If the diaphragm spring is worn or damaged, or if its pressure is in any way suspect, then the pressure plate assembly should be renewed.

12 Examine the machined bearing surfaces of the pressure plate and of the flywheel; they should be clean, completely flat, and free from scratches or scoring. If either is discoloured from excessive heat, or shows signs of cracks, it should be renewed – although minor damage of this nature can sometimes be polished away using emery paper.

13 Check that the release bearing contact surface rotates smoothly and easily, with no sign of noise or roughness. Also check that the surface itself is smooth and unworn, with no signs of cracks, pitting or scoring. Nissan recommend that the slave cylinder/release bearing is renewed every time the transmission is removed.

Refitting

14 On reassembly, ensure that the disc contact surfaces of the flywheel and pressure plate are completely clean, smooth, and free from oil or grease. Use solvent to remove any protective grease from new components.

15 Fit the friction disc so that its spring hub assembly faces away from the flywheel; there may also be a marking showing which way round the plate is to be refitted. Depending on the type of centralising tool being used, the friction disc may be held in position at this stage **(see illustrations)**.

16 Refit the pressure plate assembly, aligning the marks made on dismantling (if the original pressure plate is re-used), and locating the pressure plate on its locating dowels. Fit the pressure plate bolts, but tighten them only finger-tight, so that the friction disc can still be moved.

17 The friction disc must now be centralised, so that when the transmission is refitted, its input shaft will pass through the splines at the centre of the friction disc.

18 Centralisation can be achieved by passing a screwdriver or other long bar through the friction disc and into the hole in the crankshaft;

7.15b Refitting the clutch assembly

7.15c The clutch and tool in position

the friction disc can then be moved around until it is centred on the crankshaft hole. Alternatively, a clutch-aligning tool can be used to eliminate the guesswork; these can be obtained from most accessory shops. The normal type consists of a spigot bar with several different adapters, but a more recent type consists of a tool which clamps the friction disc to the pressure plate before locating the two items on the flywheel. A home-made aligning tool can be fabricated from a length of metal rod or wooden dowel which fits closely inside the crankshaft hole, and has insulating tape wound around it to match the diameter of the friction disc splined hole.

19 When the friction disc is centralised, tighten the pressure plate bolts evenly in two stages to the specified torque **(see illustration)**.

20 Apply a thin smear of molybdenum disulphide grease to the splines of the friction

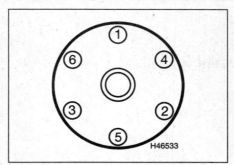

7.19 Clutch assembly bolt tightening sequence

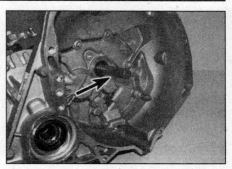

7.20 Lightly lubricate the input shaft

disc and the transmission input shaft **(see illustration)**.

Caution: Do not apply too much grease, as there is a risk that it will contaminate the friction disc material.

21 Fit a new concentric slave cylinder to the gearbox.

22 Refit the transmission as described in Chapter 7A.

Chapter 7 Part A:
Manual transmission

Contents

	Section number		Section number
Gear lever and gearchange cables – removal and refitting	3	Transmission oil level check	See Chapter 1
General information	1	Transmission oil renewal	2
Oil seals – renewal	6	Transmission overhaul – general information	8
Reversing light switch – removal and refitting	5	Vehicle speed sensor – removal and refitting	4
Transmission – removal and refitting	7		

Degrees of difficulty

Easy, suitable for novice with little experience	**Fairly easy,** suitable for beginner with some experience	**Fairly difficult,** suitable for competent DIY mechanic	**Difficult,** suitable for experienced DIY mechanic	**Very difficult,** suitable for expert DIY or professional

Specifications

General

Transmission type	Five forward speeds, one reverse. Synchromesh on all forward gears. Gearchange linkage operated by twin cables
Transmission code	JH3
Transmission oil type	See end of *Weekly checks*
Transmission oil capacity	See Chapter 1 Specifications

Gear ratios

1st	4.100:1
2nd	2.050:1
3rd	1.390:1
4th	1.030:1
5th	0.820:1
Reverse	3.550:1
Final drive	4.070:1

Torque wrench settings

	Nm	lbf ft
Crankshaft sensor bolt	9	7
Engine/transmission mountings:		
Left-hand mounting bolts (battery tray to body)	48	35
Left-hand mounting bolts (mounting to gearbox)	50	37
Rear mounting support bracket bolts	80	59
Gear lever assembly mounting bolts	12	9
Oil filler/level and drain plugs	25	18
Reversing light switch	25	18
Shift/selector cable bracket bolts to body	7	5
Shift/selector lever assembly bracket to gearbox	35	26
Starter motor mounting bolts	39	29
Transmission-to-engine bolts	48	35

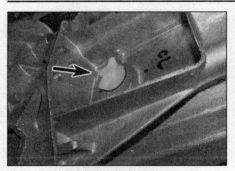

2.3 The oil filler plug

1 General information

This Part of Chapter 7 contains information on the manual transmission. Service procedures for the automatic transmission system are contained in Part B.

The transmission is contained in a cast-aluminium alloy casing bolted to the engine's left-hand end, and consists of the gearbox and final drive differential – often called a transaxle. One of two different units may be fitted, depending on engine size – for the purposes of this manual, the two units differ only in detail.

The 5-speed transmissions fitted to the Micra have a cable-actuated gearchange linkage, with gear selection via a floor-mounted lever and two cables.

2.4a The oil drain plug

2.4c . . . and drain the oil

Drive is transmitted from the crankshaft via the clutch to the input shaft, which has a splined extension to accept the clutch friction disc. From the input shaft, drive is transmitted to the output shaft, from where the drive is transmitted to the differential crownwheel, which rotates with the differential and planetary gears, thus driving the sun gears and driveshafts. The rotation of the planetary gears on their shaft allows the inner roadwheel to rotate at a slower speed than the outer roadwheel when the car is cornering.

The transmission selector mechanism causes the appropriate selector fork to move its respective synchro-sleeve along the output shaft, to lock the gear pinion to the synchro-hub. Since the synchro-hubs are splined to the output shaft, this locks the pinion to the shaft, so that drive can be transmitted. To ensure that gearchanging can be made quickly and quietly, a synchromesh system is fitted to all forward gears, consisting of baulk rings and spring-loaded fingers, as well as the gear pinions and synchro-hubs. The synchromesh cones are formed on the mating faces of the baulk rings and gear pinions.

2 Transmission oil renewal

1 This operation is much quicker and more efficient if the car is first taken on a journey of sufficient length to warm the engine/transmission up to normal operating temperature. Always take care to avoid burning yourself on the hot exhaust manifold/downpipe when working underneath the car.
2 Park the car on level ground, switch off the ignition and apply the handbrake firmly. For improved access, jack up the front of the car and support it securely on axle stands (see *Jacking and vehicle support*). Note that the car can be raised at the front only for oil draining, but for level checking the car must be level (which can be achieved either by lowering the front or raising the back of the car).
3 Remove all traces of dirt, then unscrew the filler/level plug from the front face of the transmission **(see illustration)**. A new washer should be fitted to the filler/level plug when refitting.
4 Wipe clean the area around the drain plug, which is situated on the base of the transmission, next to the rear engine steady-bar. Position a suitable container under the drain plug, and unscrew the plug – this will also probably be tight, and will need a new washer when refitting **(see illustration)**.
5 Allow the oil to drain completely into the container. If the oil is hot, take precautions against scalding. Clean the drain plug, being especially careful to wipe any metallic particles off the magnetic insert. Discard the sealing washer; it should be renewed whenever it is disturbed **(see illustration)**.
6 When the oil has finished draining, clean the drain plug threads and those of the transmission casing, fit a new sealing washer and refit the drain plug, tightening it to the specified torque wrench setting.
7 Refilling the transmission is an awkward operation. Above all, allow plenty of time for the oil level to settle properly before checking it. Note that the car must be parked on flat level ground (or if it is raised, it must be level) when checking the oil level.
8 Fill the transmission with the specified grade of oil (see *Lubricants and fluids*) until the oil just starts to run out. Allow any excess oil to flow out until the level stabilises.
9 When the level is correct, clean and refit the filler/level plug (with a new washer), then tighten it by hand.
10 Although not strictly necessary, to ensure maximum accuracy, take the car on a short journey so that the new oil is distributed fully around the transmission components, then check the level again on your return.

2.4b Remove the plug . . .

2.5 Fit a new sealing washer

3 Gear lever and gearchange cables – removal and refitting

Removal

1 Remove the centre console as described in Chapter 11.
2 Remove the battery as described in Chapter 5A and air filter inlet ducting. More working space is available if the entire air filter and throttle body assembly are removed as described in Chapter 4A.

3.3a Remove the cable ends

3.3b A pair of long nosed-pliers are useful

3 Prise free the cables at the transmission and release them from the retaining bracket. It is also possible to work round the cables and remove them complete with the support bracket **(see illustrations)**.

4 Jack up the front of the car, and support it on axle stands (see *Jacking and vehicle support*).

5 Remove the exhaust centre silencer as described in Chapter 4B, and then remove the heat shield from the transmission tunnel. Next remove the two support brackets from either side of the transmission tunnel.

6 Working inside the car, remove the four bolts securing the gear lever unit to the floor, then lower it from the car. Take care not to kink or bend the cables during removal.

7 If the gearbox is to be removed, now is an ideal time to remove the cable support bracket from the top of the gearbox. Whilst not strictly necessary it will allow more room to manoeuvre the gearbox out of the vehicle.

8 With the gearchange assembly removed from the vehicle it may be worth removing the lower plate from the gearchange to examine the cable fixing point and plastic link plate for wear. Early models did suffer from premature wear at this point. The gearchange assembly is a complete unit. No individual parts are available. In the event of a fault the entire assembly must be renewed.

Refitting

9 Refitting is a reversal of removal. Check that all gears can be selected before taking the car out on the road.

4 Vehicle speed sensor – removal and refitting

There is no speed sensor fitted to the gearbox. Roadspeed information is collected by the ABS control unit and passed to the engine control unit (ECU). See Chapter 9 for further details.

5 Reversing light switch – removal and refitting

Removal

1 The switch is located on the rear of the transmission, next to the gearbox end cover **(see illustration)**. It is a combined reversing light switch and neutral position switch. With the transmission fitted, the switch is obscured by the wing liner.

2 Unplug the wiring from the switch.

3 This is a good time to test the switch. With the ignition on, battery voltage should be available at pin number 2 of the connecter. The supply for the switch is provide by fuse 50 in the underbonnet fusebox.

4 Turn the ignition off and select reverse gear. Using a multimeter set to ohms check for continuity across the switch terminals one and two. Place the gear lever into neutral and check that the switch is now open circuit. Next

3.3c Removing the outer cable from the support bracket

5.1 The reversing light switch and earth cable

7.6 Remove the crankshaft sensor

7.10a Removing the earth cable . . .

7.10b . . . and remove the reversing light switch cable clip

7.13 The rear engine steady-bar/support bracket

test the neutral position function by testing at terminals two and three. Continuity should exist with the car in neutral.

5 Have a suitable clean container ready and then unscrew and remove the switch from the transmission. Allow any oil to drain out into the container, or alternatively immediately plug the hole.

Refitting

6 Refitting is a reversal of removal. Use a thread-locking compound on the switch and tighten the switch securely. Check the oil level as described in Chapter 1.

6 Oil seals – renewal

1 Oil leaks frequently occur due to wear or deterioration of the driveshaft oil seals. Renewal of these seals is relatively easy, since the repairs can be performed without removing the transmission from the car.

Driveshaft oil seals

2 The driveshaft oil seals are located at the sides of the transmission, where the driveshafts enter the transmission. If leakage at the seal is suspected, raise the car and support it securely on axle stands. If the seal is leaking, oil will be found on the side of the transmission below the driveshaft.

3 Refer to Chapter 8 and remove the appropriate driveshaft.

4 Using a large screwdriver or lever, carefully prise the oil seal out of the transmission casing, taking care not to damage the transmission casing.

5 Wipe clean the oil seal seating in the transmission casing.

6 Dip the new oil seal in clean oil, then press it a little way into the casing by hand, making sure that it is square to its seating.

7 Using suitable tubing or a large socket, carefully drive the oil seal fully into the casing until it contacts the seating.

8 Refit the driveshaft with reference to Chapter 8.

7 Transmission – removal and refitting

Note: *Read through this procedure before starting work to see what is involved, particularly in terms of lifting equipment. Depending on the facilities available, the home mechanic may prefer to remove the engine and transmission together, then separate them on the bench, as described in Chapter 2B. The help of an assistant is highly recommended if the transmission is to be removed (and later refitted) on its own.*

Removal

1 Remove the air cleaner and ducting as described in Chapter 4A.

2 Remove the battery as described in Chapter 5A. Also working from the information in

Chapter 5A, remove the starter motor and the support bracket for the wiring loom.

3 Remove the gear selection cables as described in Section 3. Move the cables clear of the transmission, taking care not to kink or bend them.

4 Remove the cable support bracket from the transmission housing.

5 Remove and seal the clutch hydraulic supply pipe as described in Chapter 6. Take care not to kink the hose and tie it up to the bulkhead or inlet manifold.

6 Remove the breather pipe from the top of the gearbox and then remove the crankshaft position sensor **(see illustration)**.

7 Remove the two uppermost transmission-to-engine bolts – access to these is hampered by the coolant hoses and wiring at the end of the cylinder head, but should still be possible.

8 Jack up the front of the car, and support it on axle stands (see *Jacking and vehicle support*). The car must be raised sufficiently that the transmission can be lowered out and removed underneath. Consideration should also be given to the need to support the engine, once the rear and left-hand mountings are disconnected.

9 Remove the wing liners and front bumper as described in Chapter 11.

10 Unbolt and remove the earth strap from the left-hand end of the transmission. Next disconnect the reversing light switch and free the wiring from the cable clip. Free the loom from the cable clips and then working from above remove the wiring loom from the top of the gearbox. Tie the loom out of the way **(see illustrations)**.

11 Remove both driveshafts as described in Chapter 8.

12 Just loosen ('crack') the two front transmission-to-engine bolts, but leave them in place for now – this avoids using any substantial force to remove the bolts when the transmission is only supported on a jack.

13 Remove the exhaust downpipe as described in Chapter 4B, and then remove the engine steady-bar/mounting support bracket from the rear of the transmission **(see illustration)**

14 Using a substantial hydraulic ('trolley') jack with a block of wood, raise the transmission slightly, to take the weight off its mountings.

15 Before the engine left-hand mounting is disconnected, the engine must be supported, preferably from above, using either an engine crane or support bar. We constructed a simple support bar **(see illustrations)**.

16 With the engine securely supported, remove the left-hand front engine mounting as described in Chapter 2A. Removing the battery tray and mounting complete is a better option than attempting to separate the mounting *in situ*.

17 Check that the transmission is securely supported (preferably with the help of an assistant), then remove all the bolts from the bellhousing except two **(see illustration)**.

18 Make a final check from below and above

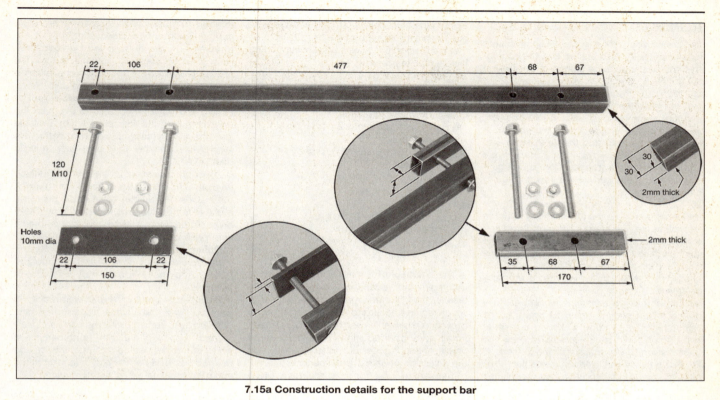

7.15a Construction details for the support bar

that there is nothing left attached to the transmission, nor anything in the way which would prevent the unit from being lowered out.

19 Carefully lower the transmission, checking all the time that nothing is getting caught or stretched. Also take care that the engine right-hand mounting is not being too distorted, or placed under excess strain.
20 Once the transmission is low enough to clear the inner wing, adjust the fabricated support bar to take the weight of the engine. Remove the jack and the slowly remove the two remaining transmission-to-engine front bolts. As this is done, be prepared for the unit to start separating – have your assistant support it. If the transmission does not separate, prise it gently apart – it is located on dowels, and they may stick.
21 As the transmission is withdrawn from the engine, make sure its weight is supported at all times – the transmission input shaft (or the clutch) may otherwise be damaged as it is withdrawn through the clutch assembly bolted to the engine flywheel
22 Once the transmission is clear of the engine, keep the transmission steady on the

jack head or trolley, and carefully lower it down. With the help of your assistant, remove it from under the car (**see illustrations**).
23 The clutch components can now be inspected with reference to Chapter 6,

and renewed if necessary. Unless they are virtually new, it is worth renewing the clutch components as a matter of course, even if the transmission has been removed for some other reason.

7.15b The support bar in position. Note the wooden blocks

7.17 The gearbox supported from above with an engine crane

7.22a The gearbox lowered using an engine crane

7.22b Alternatively, a transmission jack can be used

Refitting

24 If removed, refit the clutch components (see Chapter 6). Also ensure that the engine-to-transmission adapter plate is in position on the engine.

25 With the transmission secured to the trolley jack (depending on the removal method) as on removal, raise it into position, and then carefully slide it onto the engine, at the same time engaging the input shaft with the clutch friction disc splines. If marks were made between the transmission and engine on removal, these can be used as a guide to correct alignment.

26 Do not use excessive force to refit the transmission – if the input shaft does not slide into place easily, readjust the angle of the transmission so that it is level, and/or turn the input shaft so that the splines engage properly with the disc. If problems are still experienced, check that the clutch friction disc is correctly centralised (Chapter 6).

27 Once the transmission is successfully mated to the engine, insert as many of the transmission-to-engine bolts as possible, and tighten them progressively, to draw the transmission fully onto the locating dowels.

28 Raise the transmission into position, then refit the engine left-hand and rear mountings.

Tighten the bolts hand-tight only at this stage, but sufficiently to support the transmission so that the support bar, engine hoist or supporting jack can be removed.

29 Tighten the engine mounting bolts to the specified torque.

30 Further refitting is a reversal of removal, noting the following points:

a) Refit the starter motor as described in Chapter 5A.

b) Refit the driveshafts as described in Chapter 8.

c) Refill the transmission with oil as described in Section 2.

8 Transmission overhaul – general information

The overhaul of a manual transmission is a complex (and often expensive) engineering task for the DIY home mechanic to undertake, which requires access to specialist equipment. It involves dismantling and reassembly of many small components, measuring clearances precisely and if necessary, adjusting them by the selection of shims and spacers. Internal transmission components are also often difficult to obtain and in many instances, extremely expensive. Because of this, if the transmission develops a fault or becomes noisy, the best course of action is to have the unit overhauled by a specialist repairer or to obtain an exchange reconditioned unit.

Nevertheless, it is not impossible for the more experienced mechanic to overhaul the transmission, if the special tools are available and the job is carried out in a deliberate step-by-step manner, to ensure that nothing is overlooked.

The tools necessary for an overhaul include internal and external circlip pliers, bearing pullers, a slide hammer, a set of pin punches, a dial test indicator, and possibly, a hydraulic press. In addition, a large, sturdy workbench and a vice will be required.

During dismantling of the transmission, make careful notes of how each component is fitted to make reassembly easier and accurate.

Before dismantling the transmission, it will help if you have some idea of where the problem lies. Certain problems can be closely related to specific areas in the transmission which can make component examination and renewal easier. Refer to Fault diagnosis at the end of this manual for more information.

Chapter 7 Part B:
Automatic transmission

Contents

	Section number
Automatic transmission – removal and refitting	9
Automatic transmission overhaul – general information	8
Fault codes – retrieval and description	2
Fluid level check/renewal	See Chapter 1
General information	1
Oil pan – removal and refitting	7
Oil seals – renewal	6
Selector lever and cable – removal, refitting and adjustment	3
Shift lock system – component renewal	4
Transmission switches/sensors – removal and refitting	5

Degrees of difficulty

| **Easy,** suitable for novice with little experience | | **Fairly easy,** suitable for beginner with some experience | | **Fairly difficult,** suitable for competent DIY mechanic | | **Difficult,** suitable for experienced DIY mechanic | | **Very difficult,** suitable for expert DIY or professional | |

Specifications

General
Transmission type number	3CX1E or 3CX3A
Application	Option on 1.2 and 1.4 litre models
Description	Electro-hydraulically controlled planetary gearbox providing four forward speeds and one reverse speed. Shift lock system
Automatic transmission fluid type	See *Lubricants and fluids*
Automatic transmission fluid capacity	See Chapter 1 Specifications

Torque converter
Fitted depth	16.2 mm

Ratios
1st	2.861:1
2nd	1.562:1
3rd	1.000:1
4th	0.697:1
Reverse	2.310:1
Final drive	4.072:1

Torque wrench settings
	Nm	lbf ft
Engine mounting	65	48
Engine steady-bar	80	59
Fluid drain plug	35	26
Oil pan bolts	8	6
Park/Neutral position switch mounting bolts	3	2
Revolution sensor bolt	6	4
Selector cable mounting bolt	15	11
Starter motor mounting bolts	34	25
Torque converter-to-driveplate bolts	51	38
Transmission selector lever nut	12	9
Transmission-to-engine bolts	48	35
Turbine revolution sensor	6	4

1 General information

The Nissan 3CX automatic transmission has four forward speeds (and one reverse). The automatic gear changes are electronically-controlled, rather than hydraulically as with previous conventional types. The transmission control functions are managed by a separate transmission control module (TCM). The advantage of electronic management is to provide a faster and smoother gearchange response combined with maximum fuel economy. A kickdown facility is also provided, to enable a faster acceleration response when required.

The transmission consists of three main assemblies, these being the torque converter, which is directly coupled to the engine's driveplate; the final drive unit, which incorporates the differential unit; and the planetary gearbox, with its multidisc clutches and brake bands. The transmission is lubricated by automatic transmission fluid (ATF).

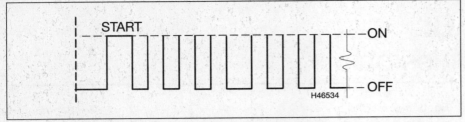

2.15 Faults are shown as a longer flash of the overdrive off warning light

The torque converter incorporates an automatic lock-up feature, which eliminates any possibility of converter slip in the top two gears; this aids performance and economy. The 'overdrive' 4th gear can be deselected manually, using a button on the selector lever – in this mode, only the first three ratios are used. The control circuit uses inputs from all the engine management sensors, and can adapt the transmission functions as required – for example, under full-throttle acceleration, upshifts are delayed longer, to make full use of engine power. For maximum economy the overdrive should be 'on' at higher speeds. A dashboard light illuminates when the overdrive is 'off'.

Another feature of this transmission is the shift lock system, a safety feature to avoid incorrect operation. Besides the conventional selector lever lock button (to inhibit shifting into R, P, 2 and 1 positions), the shift lock system prevents the lever being moved from P until the ignition is on and the brake pedal is depressed. Correct functioning of the brake stop-light switch is therefore vital for this system to work correctly – see Chapter 9. A further feature of this system is that the ignition key cannot be removed unless the selector lever is in the P position. In the event of a flat battery the lever will not move from the park position, even with the brake pedal depressed. An override control is provided at the rear of the selector lever console to enable the lever to be moved to the neutral position. Apply the handbrake and footbrake. Press the shift lock release button and the selector lever will now move freely to the neutral position.

The TCM incorporates a fault diagnosis system. Fault codes can be retrieved with suitable diagnostic equipment. A limited number of faults can be displayed via the overdrive warning light (see Section 2). Fault

3.3 Selector cable removal points

codes that are considered emissions related are not stored in the TCM. These are stored in the main engine control module (ECM). It is important that any transmission fault be identified and rectified at the earliest possible opportunity. Delay in doing so will only cause further problems. Consult a Nissan dealer or automatic transmission specialist. The fault diagnosis is carried out with the gearbox in the car, so consult your chosen specialist before removing the gearbox.

The TCM also has an electronic fail-safe mode. In the event of a major electrical input/output failure the transmission will default to running in third gear, regardless of the selector lever position. The vehicle will lack acceleration and may fell sluggish when running in fail-safe mode.

2 Fault codes – retrieval and description

Retrieval

1 Park on a flat surface, move the selector to the P position, turn the ignition off and apply the handbrake.

2 Turn the ignition off and wait at least five seconds.

3 Turn the ignition on. The overdrive off indicator lamp will be on for two seconds.

4 Turn the ignition off and wait at least five seconds.

5 Press the shift lock release button and move the selector from P to D.

6 Turn the ignition on. Do not start the car.

7 Press and hold the overdrive control switch. The warning light will be on.

8 Keep pressing the overdrive switch and move the lever to position 2. The warning light will be on.

9 Release the overdrive switch. The warning light is still on.

10 Mover the lever to the 1 position. The warning light will be on.

11 Press and hold the overdrive control switch. The warning light is off.

12 Depress the accelerator pedal fully while pressing the overdrive switch.

13 Any recorded faults will now be shown as series of flashes from the overdrive off warning light.

14 End the sequence by turning the ignition off for at least five seconds.

Description

15 The start of the sequence is always a two second 'on' period followed by a series of twelve one-second 'on' and one-second 'off' flashes from the warning light (**see illustration**), except a low voltage fault which is indicated by four flashes per second.

16 A fault is indicated by a longer flash at some point in the sequence. Count its position in the sequence and check the description.

Position of longest flash	Fault definition
All equal	System good
1	Vehicle speed sensor (gearbox)
2	Vehicle speed sensor (engine)
3	Accelerator position sensor
4	Shift solenoid valve A
5	Shift solenoid valve B
6	Overrun clutch solenoid
7	Torque converter clutch solenoid valve
8	Fluid temperature sensor
9	Engine speed signal
10	Turbine revolution sensor
11	Line pressure solenoid valve
12	CAN communication line

17 If a fault is indicated by the warning lamp, do not condemn the component with out further testing. A through check of all wiring, connectors and earth points on the faulty components circuit should be checked first. Where possible the faulty component should also be tested. Specialist equipment, such as an oscilloscope may be needed to correctly test the component.

18 The TCM is capable of recording more faults than indicated by the warning lamp, but these can only be accessed with specialist diagnostic equipment. If no faults are found in the TCM memory, but you have a car with apparent gearbox problems then seek the help of an automatic gearbox specialist or your local Nissan dealer.

3 Selector lever and cable – removal, refitting and adjustment

Selector cable

Removal

1 Remove the battery and air cleaner assembly as described in Chapters 5A and 4A. Jack up and support the vehicle.

2 Remove the front bumper as described in Chapter 11.

3 With the handbrake on and the selector lever in neutral, disconnect the cable at the gearbox end (**see illustration**). Pull out the upper clip and either undo the bolt, or preferably remove the split pin and washer from the rear.

4 Remove the exhaust downpipe, centre box and heat shields as described in Chapter 4B. Remove the bolts securing the cable to the transmission tunnel. Next remove the cover plate to gain access to the cable housing and remove the cable lockplate (**see illustration**).

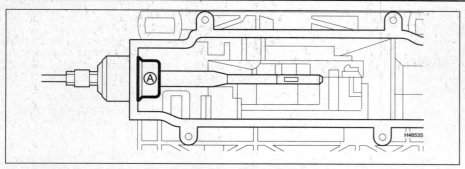

3.4 Location of the cable lockplate (A)

3.13 Preloading the selector cable

Unhook the cable. Unbolt the support bracket and remove the cable.

Refitting

5 Refitting is a reversal of removal, but make sure the ribbed section of the cable eye is pointing down when reconnected to the selector lever. Check and if necessary adjust the cable as described below.

Checking

6 Place the selector in the P position and turn the ignition ON. Do not start the car.

7 Press the brake pedal and move the lever through all the settings. Check for noise or rattles whilst doing so. Confirm that the actual position matches that shown on the position indicator.

8 Confirm that the reversing lights only come on in the R position. Check that the lights are not on in any other position.

9 Check that the engine can only be started in the park or neutral positions. Keep the brake pedal depressed at all times while trying to start the car in all the other positions.

10 With the car on firm and level ground, select the park position and release the handbrake. The transmission should be locked. Try to push the car to confirm this.

Adjustment

11 Place the selector lever in the P position.

12 Remove the locknut and control cable from the manual shaft, and place the manual shaft in the P position.

13 Refit the cable and locknut loosely and then push and pull the end of the cable two or three times. Apply a force of 1 kg to the cable and tighten the locknut **(see illustration)**. Do not apply any force to the manual shaft after the locknut has been tightened.

14 Check the operation of the selector lever as described above, and refit the air cleaner assembly.

Selector lever

Removal

15 Remove the centre console as described in Chapter 11 and disconnect the wiring at the shift lock solenoid and the position warning lamp. Remove the key interlock cable by squeezing the locking tabs and unhooking the cable.

16 Follow the cable removal procedure in this

Section and then remove the four main fixing bolts of the lever assembly.

17 Working from inside the car release the

two centre locating tangs. Next push the two outer tangs inward and lower the assembly down and out of the car **(see illustration)**.

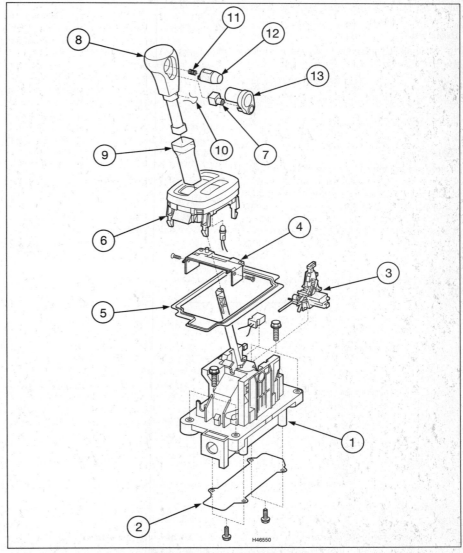

3.17 The shift control assembly

1	*Control assembly*	4	*Bracket*
2	*Cover plate*	5	*Gasket*
3	*Shift lock*	6	*Position indicator*
	solenoid		*plate*

7	*Overdrive switch*	11	*Spring*
8	*Lever knob*	12	*Selector*
9	*Cover*		*button*
10	*Locking pin*	13	*Cover*

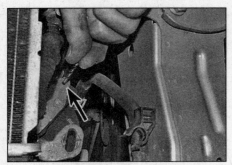

5.8 Insert a 4 mm drill bit as shown

18 If required the lever knob may also be removed. Place the lever in the neutral position and push down the cover. Remove the locking pin, and remove the knob and cover as a complete assembly.

Refitting

19 Refitting is a reversal of removal, but follow the checking procedure described above.

4 Shift lock system – component renewal

Removal

1 Remove the centre console as described in Chapter 11 and the selector end of the cable.
2 Remove the steering column cover and the instrument side panel as described in Chapter 11.
3 Working under the steering wheel remove the holder from the key cylinder and then remove the interlock cable. Detach the support cable from the instrument support panel and remove the cable.

Refitting

4 Refitting is a reversal of removal, noting the following points:
 a) *Turn the key to the lock position and the selector lever to the P position.*
 b) *Move the slider at the lever end to the locked position.*

5 Transmission switches/ sensors – removal and refitting

Description

1 With the gearbox *in situ*, it is possible to remove and refit the park/neutral switch, the turbine speed sensor and the revolution sensor. The turbine sensor measures the input shaft speed. The revolution sensor measures the gearbox output speed. These two figures are used by the transmission control module (TCM) to calculate the optimum gear shift points for smooth running and maximum economy. If required, the TCM can also be removed.
2 Before starting any work on the electrical components disconnect the battery. See the Reference section at the rear of this manual.

Park/neutral position switch

Removal

3 Remove the selector cable at the gearbox, as described in Section 3.
4 Unplug the cable from the switch, and mark the position of the switch in relation to the selector shaft and gearbox.
5 Remove the three bolts that hold the switch in position and set the manual shaft to the P position. The switch can now be removed.

Refitting

6 Refitting is a reversal of removal, but the position of the switch should be checked if there was any concern with its operation.

Adjustment

7 Loosen the three retaining bolts,
8 Insert a 4 mm drill into the manual shaft adjustment hole and rotate the switch so the drill bit can also pass through the hole in the switch **(see illustration)**.
9 Tighten the securing bolts to the specified torque, and refit the cable. Check and adjust the cable as described in Section 3.

Checking

10 With the switch disconnected check for continuity with a multimeter or test bulb **(see illustration)**. The ignition must be off and you will have to override the key interlock with the switch at the rear of the centre console to move the selector lever.
11 If this test is not conclusive, recheck with the selector cable disconnected.

Revolution sensor

Removal

12 Remove the air cleaner assembly as described in Chapter 4A, then disconnect the wiring harness on the top of the gearbox, prise free the cable clip and remove the cable retaining bolt.
13 Remove the fixing bolt at the sensor and gently work the sensor free. Apply penetrating fluid if required.

Refitting

14 Refitting is a reversal of removal, but tighten the bolt to the specified torque.

Turbine revolution sensor

Removal

15 Remove the selector cable and support bracket with reference to Section 3. Disconnect the wiring and remove the bolt. Gently free the sensor and recover the O-ring.

Refitting

16 Refitting is a reversal of removal, but fit a

8	7	2	1	3
6	9	5	4	

1,(3)   2,(4,5,6,7,8,9)

Ω

H46532

5.10 Check for continuity at the switch

Selector lever position	Continuity at terminals
P	1 to 2, 3 to 7
R	3 to 8
N	1 to 2, 3 to 9
D	3 to 6
2	3 to 5
1	3 to 4

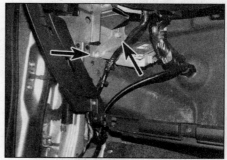

5.17 The TCM fixing bolts

new O-ring. Lubricate the O-ring and sensor housing with small amount of transmission fluid before refitting. Tighten the bolt to the specified torque.

Transmission control module

Removal

17 The TCM is fitted to the left-hand front kick panel. Access requires the removal of the glovebox as described in Chapter 1, Section 17 **(see illustration)**.
18 Disconnect the two harness plugs.
19 Remove the two bolts and withdraw the TCM.

Refitting

20 Refitting is a reversal of removal.

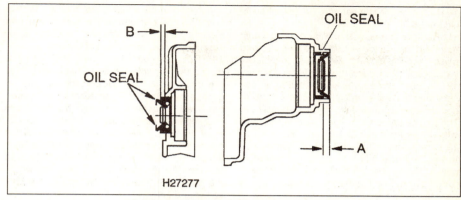

6.4 Correct fitted position of the oil seals

Right-hand seal (A) = 1.1 mm   Left-hand seal (B) = 0.0 mm

| 6 | Oil seals –
removal and refitting | |

Removal

1 Drain the oil from the transmission as described in Chapter 1 and then remove the driveshafts as described in Chapter 8.
2 With a large flat-bladed screwdriver or dedicated oil seal removing tool, lever the oil seal out of the housing. Take care not to damage the housing or the gearbox casing.

Refitting

3 Obtain new seals and lubricate them with transmission fluid. You will need a large socket or length of pipe to drive the new seals home. It is important that the inner lip of the new seal is not damaged or stressed in any way, so chose a socket that sits on the outer edge of the seal only.
4 Drive the seals in evenly and check that they protrude the correct distance from the differential casing **(see illustration)**.
5 Install the driveshafts and refill the gearbox with ATF.

| 7 | Oil pan –
removal and refitting | |

Note: *This procedure should only be required if you suspect a serious mechanical failure of the gearbox. There are no serviceable parts accessible with the cover removed, however the cover plate does have a magnet fitted to catch any metallic debris from the gearbox.*

Removal

1 Drain the oil from the transmission as described in Chapter 1.
2 Slacken off all the plate retaining bolts. More fluid will escape so have a suitable container ready to catch the fluid.
3 Remove the plate and check the magnet.

Refitting

4 Refitting is a reversal of removal, but new

bolts and a gasket must be fitted. The bolts are self sealing and can not be re used. Tighten the bolts to the specified torque.

| 8 | Automatic transmission overhaul –
general information | |

In the event of a fault occurring, it will be necessary to establish whether the fault is electrical, mechanical or hydraulic in nature, before repair work can be contemplated. Diagnosis requires detailed knowledge of the transmission's operation and construction, as well as access to specialised test equipment, and so is deemed to be beyond the scope of this manual. It is therefore essential that problems with the automatic transmission are referred to a Nissan dealer or automatic gearbox specialist for assessment.

Note that a faulty transmission should not be removed before the car has been assessed by a dealer, as fault diagnosis is carried out with the transmission in situ.

| 9 | Automatic transmission –
removal and refitting | 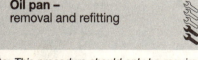 |

Note: *Read through this procedure before starting work to see what is involved, particularly in terms of lifting equipment. Depending on the facilities available, the home mechanic may prefer to remove the engine and transmission together, then separate them on the bench, as described in Chapter 2B. The help of an assistant is highly recommended if the transmission is to be removed (and later refitted) on its own.*

Removal

1 Remove the air cleaner as described in Chapter 4A.
2 Remove the battery as described in Chapter 5A.
3 Jack up the front of the car, and support it on axle stands (see *Jacking and vehicle support*). The car must be raised sufficiently

so that the transmission can be lowered out and removed from underneath.
4 Remove the front wing liners and bumper as described in Chapter 11.
5 Remove the control cable. Remove the nut securing the end of the cable or pull out the retaining clip from the rear. Disconnect the Park/Neutral position switch and free the wiring harness. Remove the support bracket and pull the cable free.
6 Noting their positions for refitting, disconnect the wiring plugs from the following components on and around the transmission
  a) Turbine rpm sensor (by the Park/Neutral position switch).
  b) The earth cable.
  c) The terminal cord assembly harness (directly behind the Park/Neutral position switch).
  d) Rpm sensor (on top).
7 Remove the starter motor as described in Chapter 5A.
8 Working underneath gain access to the torque converter bolts **(see illustration)**. Turn the engine clockwise **only** to access the bolts in turn. Lock the engine, if required with a suitable tool placed in the starter motor aperture. Alternatively a socket can be used on the crankshaft pulley bolt.
9 Drain the gearbox fluid, as described in Chapter 1, and then disconnect the oil cooler hoses at the front of the gearbox. Expect some fluid spillage. Plug and seal the pipes and hose immediately.

9.8 Remove the access plate to reach the torque converter bolts

10 Remove the driveshafts as described in Chapter 8.

11 Remove the heat shield from the exhaust manifold as described in Chapter 4B and disconnect the exhaust. Remove it completely if you intend to support the engine from below.

12 Support the engine with a suitable jack from below or alternatively a simple support can be fabricated as described in Chapter 7A. The engine can also be supported from above with an engine crane or support bar.

13 Just loosen ('crack') the transmission-to-engine bolts, but leave them in place for now – this avoids using any substantial force to remove the bolts when the transmission is only supported on a jack.

14 Unclip and remove the radiator cooling fan. Whilst not strictly necessary this will allow much more room to manoeuvre the gearbox out of the engine bay.

15 Remove the rear engine steady-bar. Note the direction mark on the bracket; this should point to the front of the engine.

16 Support the gearbox with a suitable jack. Take care not to damage the transmission drain plug. Raise the jack to take the weight of the gearbox.

> **HAYNES HINT** *Before removing the transmission from the engine, it is helpful for refitting to paint or scratch an alignment mark or two across the engine/ transmission, so that the transmission can be offered up in approximately the right alignment to engage the dowels.*

17 Remove the left-hand engine mounting bolt and lower the transmission to clear the battery tray. Alternatively remove the battery tray and mounting as a complete unit. This will allow more clearance for removal of the gearbox.

18 Now remove all but two of the engine to gearbox mounting bolts. Check again that the gearbox is fully supported and that all pipes, mounts and connectors have been removed. Loosen the remaining two bolts and separate the transmission slightly. Check again that you have enough room to pull the gearbox backwards and that it is still securely supported. Remove the remaining bolts and pull the gearbox back. Now lower it slowly to the ground. An assistant will make this task easier and safer.

19 Once the transmission is clear of the engine, keep the transmission steady on the jack head, and carefully lower it down. With the help of your assistant, remove it from under the car. Keep the torque converter pressed into place, otherwise it may fall out. If the unit is to be transported anywhere, bolt a strip of metal across the transmission mating face, and wedge a piece of wood behind to hold the converter.

Refitting

20 Before refitting the transmission check the fitted depth of the torque converter, as follows. Place a straight-edge horizontally across the mating face of the transmission, and measure directly back from it to one of the converter mounting bolt bosses **(see illustration)**. If the dimension is not as specified, the converter has become dislodged (or incorrectly refitted) and should be pressed carefully back into place.

21 With the transmission secured to the trolley jack as on removal, raise it into position, and then carefully slide it onto the engine, at the same time engaging the input shaft with the torque converter. If marks were made between the transmission and engine on removal, these can be used as a guide to correct alignment.

22 Do not use excessive force to refit the transmission – if the input shaft does not slide into place easily, readjust the angle of the transmission so that it is level, and/or turn the input shaft. If problems are still experienced, check that the torque converter is correctly installed (see paragraph 20).

23 Once the transmission is successfully mated to the engine, insert in their correct locations as many of the transmission-to-engine bolts as possible, and tighten them progressively, to draw the transmission fully onto the locating dowels **(see illustration)**.

24 Raise the transmission into position, and then refit the engine left-hand and rear mountings. Tighten the bolts hand-tight only at this stage, but sufficiently to support the transmission so that the support bar, engine hoist or supporting jack can be removed.

25 Tighten the engine mounting bolts and gearbox bolts to the specified torque.

26 Further refitting is a reversal of removal, noting the following points:

a) *Refit the starter motor as described in Chapter 5A.*

c) *Refit the driveshafts as described in Chapter 8.*

d) *Refit the exhaust as described in Chapter 4B.*

e) *Refill the transmission with fluid as described in Chapter 1.*

f) *Check the tightness of the crankshaft pulley bolt if it was used to lock the engine at any point.*

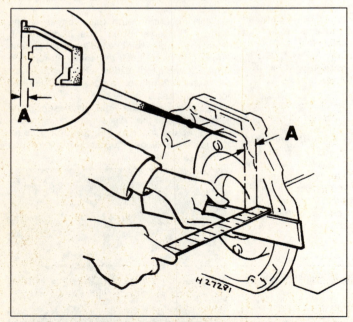

9.20 Prior to refitting, check the fitting of the torque converter

Dimension A should be 16.2 mm or more

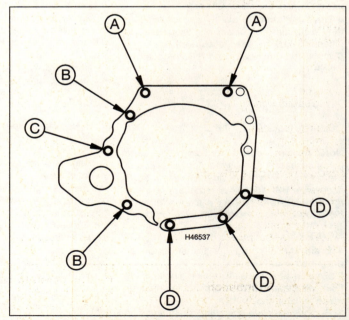

9.23 Locate the bolts correctly

A = 40 mm   B = 44 mm   C = 69 mm   D = 49 mm

Chapter 8
Driveshafts

Contents

Driveshaft gaiter check. . . . . .See Chapter 1
Driveshaft inner joint gaiter – renewal 3
Driveshaft outer joint gaiter – renewal 4

Section number

Driveshafts – inspection and joint renewal. 5
Driveshafts – removal and refitting. 2
General information 1

Section number

Degrees of difficulty

| **Easy,** suitable for novice with little experience | 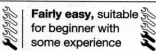 | **Fairly easy,** suitable for beginner with some experience | | **Fairly difficult,** suitable for competent DIY mechanic | | **Difficult,** suitable for experienced DIY mechanic | | **Very difficult,** suitable for expert DIY or professional | |

Specifications

General

Driveshaft type	Solid steel shafts with inner and outer constant velocity (CV) joints. Outer joints of the ball-and-cage (Rzeppa) type, inner joints of the spider-and-yoke (tripod) type. Dynamic damper fitted to right-hand driveshaft
Lubricant:	
Type/specification.	Special grease supplied in sachets with gaiter kits – inner and outer joints use different grease types
Quantity (per joint):	
Inner joint	100g
Outer joint	50g

Torque wrench settings

	Nm	lbf ft
Driveshaft (hub) nut*	238 to 322	176 to 234
Lower arm balljoint nut.	60	44
Roadwheel nuts	103	76
Track rod end nut*	35	26
Swivel hub-to-strut bolts	110	80

* Use new nut

1 General information

Drive is transmitted from the differential to the front wheels by means of two, unequal-length driveshafts.

Each driveshaft is fitted with an inner and outer constant velocity (CV) joint. Each outer joint is splined to engage with the wheel hub, and is threaded so that it can be fastened to the hub by a large nut. The inner joint is also splined to engage with the differential sunwheel gears.

Approximately halfway along the right-hand driveshaft, a dynamic (vibration) damper weight is attached by two clips.

2.5a Use a Torx-type key to stop the balljoint from rotating . . .

2 Driveshafts – removal and refitting

Removal

1 Remove the relevant wheel trim, or the wheel centre cover (alloy wheels) for access to the driveshaft nut.

2 Ensure that the handbrake is applied (ideally, have an assistant apply the footbrake), then slacken the driveshaft nut using a suitable socket and extension bar. Loosen the driveshaft nut almost to the end of its threads, but do not remove it at this stage.

⚠ **Warning: The driveshaft nut is done up extremely tight, and considerable effort will be required to loosen it. Do not use poor-quality, badly-fitting tools for this task, due to the risk of personal injury.**

2.9 Removing the front hub-to-strut bolts

2.12a Prise free the inner joint

2.5b . . . and then use a balljoint separator to split the track rod end

3 Slacken the relevant front wheel nuts, then jack up the front of the car, and support securely on axle stands (see *Jacking and vehicle support*). Remove the roadwheel.

4 Drain the transmission oil or fluid as described in Chapter 7A or 1, as applicable. If this is not done, be prepared for considerable loss of oil or fluid when the driveshafts are removed from the transmission.

5 Unscrew the nut until the threads on the track rod end are below the head of the nut, and then use a balljoint splitter to separate the track rod from the swivel hub **(see illustrations)**. Take care not to damage the balljoint rubber during the separation procedure. Once the swivel is free remove the nut. A new nut should be used when refitting.

6 Using a soft-faced hammer, drive the shaft back through the swivel hub. If an ordinary hammer is used, place a small piece of wood

2.11 Pull the shaft free from the hub

2.12b Access to the left-hand shaft is difficult

over the end of the driveshaft – in addition to the loosened driveshaft nut, this will protect the threads from damage.

7 It's likely that the splines will be very tight (corrosion may even be a factor, if the driveshaft has not been disturbed for some time), and considerable force may be needed to push the driveshaft out. Do not attempt to push the driveshaft all the way out, just free it off.

8 Remove the brake caliper and ABS sensor as described in Chapter 9 and tie it securely to the coil spring.

9 Remove the nuts from the two bolts used to secure the swivel hub to the base of the suspension strut. Note which way the bolts are fitted and then tap the bolts out. Separate the hub from the base of the strut **(see illustrations)**.

10 Once the splines have been released, remove the driveshaft nut and discard it – the nut is only intended to be used once.

11 Pull the hub outwards, and push the driveshaft inwards, to separate the splined end from the hub **(see illustration)**. It is helpful to have an assistant on hand, to pull either the hub or the shaft. Do not bend the driveshaft excessively at any stage, or the joints may be damaged – the inner and outer joints should not be bent through more than 18° and 45° respectively. Do not let the driveshaft hang down under its own weight – tie it up level if necessary.

12 The driveshafts are held into the transmission by a spring circlip, which can take some effort to release. Using a suitable drift on the shoulder of the driveshaft inner joint, tap the joint out of the transmission. Alternatively, use a pry bar with a block of wood behind to prise the inner joint out **(see illustrations)**. Take care not to damage the driveshaft boot or the securing clips. Be prepared for a small amount of oil/fluid loss when the driveshaft releases (or a large amount, if the transmission was not drained).

13 Manoeuvre the driveshaft out of position, ensuring that the constant velocity joints are not placed under excessive strain, and remove the driveshaft from underneath the car.

14 Whilst the driveshaft is removed, plug the differential aperture with a clean, lint-free cloth to prevent dirt getting in.

15 Extract the circlip from the groove on the inner end of the driveshaft, and obtain a new one.

16 Check the condition of the differential oil seals, and if necessary renew them as described in Chapter 7A or 7B.

Caution: If the car is lowered back onto its wheels while the driveshafts are removed, this could cause damage to the wheel bearings.

Refitting

17 Locate the new circlip in the groove on the inner end of the driveshaft, and turn the clip so its open side is facing downwards.

3.3a Cut through the large clip with a hacksaw . . .

3.3b . . . and prise free the small clip

3.3c Slide back the boot

18 Lubricate the driveshaft inner splines with transmission oil/fluid. Carefully refit the driveshaft into the transmission, taking care not to damage the oil seal. Turn the driveshaft until it engages the splines on the differential gears.

19 Push the driveshaft fully home, so that the circlip engages. Try pulling the shaft out, to make sure the circlip is fully engaged.

20 Apply a little molybdenum disulphide grease to the driveshaft outer splines. Pull the hub outwards, and insert the outer end of the driveshaft. Turn the driveshaft to engage the splines in the hub, and fully push on the hub.

21 Screw on the new driveshaft nut, and use it to draw the driveshaft fully through the hub. Delay fully tightening the nut until the wheel is back on, and the car has been lowered to the ground.

22 Locate the hub onto the base of the suspension strut, and secure with the two bolts, inserted from the front. Tap the bolts through if necessary. Tighten the nuts to the specified torque.

23 Locate the track rod end balljoint into the swivel hub. Tighten the new nut to the specified torque.

24 Fill the transmission, and check the level as described in Chapter 1.

25 Refit the wheel, and lower the car to the ground. Tighten the wheel nuts to the specified torque.

26 Fully tighten the driveshaft nut to the specified torque. Finally, refit the wheel trim (or centre cover).

3 Driveshaft inner joint gaiter – renewal

1 Remove the driveshaft from the car, as described in Section 2.

2 If required, mount the driveshaft in a vice.

3 Note the fitted location of both of the inner joint gaiter retaining clips, then release the clips from the gaiter, and slide the gaiter back along the driveshaft a little way **(see illustrations)**.

4 Mark the driveshaft in relation to the joint housing, to ensure correct refitting.

5 Remove the inner joint housing from the tripod.

6 Extract the circlip retaining the tripod on the driveshaft **(see illustration)**.

7 Check that the inner end of the driveshaft is marked in relation to the splined tripod hub. If not, use dabs of paint on the driveshaft and one end of the tripod.

8 Using a soft-metal or wooden drift on the tripod centre hub (not on the outer rollers), tap off the tripod from the end of the driveshaft **(see illustration)**.

9 Finally, slide off the inner gaiter.

10 Clean the driveshaft, and obtain a new joint retaining circlip. The gaiter retaining clips must also be renewed.

11 Tape the end of the shaft to prevent damage to the gaiter and then slide the new gaiter onto the driveshaft, together with new clips **(see illustration)**.

12 Refit the tripod on the driveshaft splines,

3.6 Remove the circlip

3.11 Cover the splines with tape to prevent damage to the boot

if necessary using a soft-faced mallet and a suitable socket to drive it fully onto the splines. It must be fitted with the previously-made marks aligned. Secure it in position using a new circlip. Ensure that the circlip is fully engaged in its groove.

13 Scoop out all of the old grease from the joint housing, and then pack the joint and gaiter with new grease (see Specifications at the beginning of this Chapter). Guide the joint housing onto the tripod joint, making sure that the previously-made marks are aligned **(see illustration)**.

14 Slide the gaiter along the driveshaft, and locate it on the tripod joint housing. The small-diameter end of the gaiter must be located in the groove on the driveshaft, while the larger end of the gaiter should also locate in a groove on the housing.

15 Ensure that the gaiter is not twisted or distorted, and then insert a small screwdriver

3.8 Drive off the tripod

3.13 Fill the joint with new grease

3.16a Slide on a new clip . . .

3.16b . . . and tighten

4.2 Pull back the gaiter

4.4 Fill with fresh grease

4.7a Crimp the large clip . . .

4.7b . . . and the smaller one

under the lip of the gaiter at the housing end. This will allow trapped air to escape.

16 Remove the screwdriver, then fit the retaining clips and tighten them **(see illustrations)**.

4 Driveshaft outer joint gaiter – renewal

1 If required, mount the driveshaft in a vice.
2 Note the fitted locations of both of the outer joint gaiter retaining clips, then release the clips from the gaiter, and slide the gaiter back along the driveshaft **(see illustration)**.
3 With the shaft secured in a suitable vice, strike the inner section of the joint with brass drift or similar. It may take several hard blows to force the joint off the shaft. Recover the circlip from the end of the shaft.
4 Scoop out all of the old grease, and then pack the joint with new grease (see Specifications at the beginning of this Chapter). Take care that the fresh grease does not become contaminated with dirt or grit as it is being applied **(see illustration)**.
5 Fit the inner clip and gaiter to the driveshaft, and with a soft-faced hammer drive the outer joint over the new circlip and onto the shaft. The small-diameter end of the gaiter must be located in the groove on the driveshaft.
6 Ensure that the gaiter is not twisted or distorted, then insert a small screwdriver under the lip of the gaiter at the housing end, to allow any trapped air to escape.

7 Remove the screwdriver, fit the new retaining clips in the previously-noted positions, and tighten them **(see illustrations)**.

5 Driveshafts – inspection and joint renewal

1 If any of the checks described in the relevant part of Chapter 1 reveal apparent excessive wear or play in any driveshaft joint, first remove the wheel trim (or centre cover), and check the condition of the driveshaft nut. Check that it is tightened to the specified torque. Repeat this check on the other side of the car.
2 Road test the car, and listen for a metallic clicking from the front as the car is driven slowly in a circle on full-lock. If a clicking noise is heard, this indicates wear in the outer constant velocity joint, which means that the joint must be renewed; reconditioning is not possible.
3 The outer CV joint is available as a separate assembly, alternatively renew the entire shaft.
4 If vibration, consistent with roadspeed, is felt through the car when accelerating, there is a possibility of wear in the inner joints.
5 Check the condition and security of the damper fitted to the right-hand driveshaft **(see illustration)**.

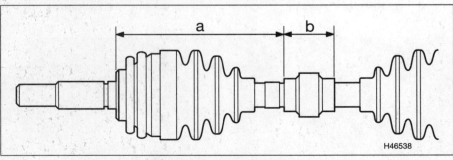

H46538

5.5 Correct location of the damper

a = 434 to 440 mm   b = 58 mm

Chapter 9
Braking system

Contents

Section number

ABS hydraulic unit – removal and refitting. 15
ABS wheel sensors – testing, removal and refitting. 16
Anti-lock braking system (ABS) – general information. 14
Brake fluid level check . . . . See *Weekly checks*
Brake fluid renewal. . . . . See Chapter 1
Brake pedal – removal, refitting and checking. 9
Braking system check . . . . See Chapter 1
Front brake caliper – removal, overhaul and refitting. 3
Front brake disc – inspection, removal and refitting 4
Front brake pads – renewal 2
General information 1
Handbrake cables – removal and refitting 20
Handbrake lever – removal and refitting. 19

Section number

Handbrake warning light switch – removal and refitting 21
Hydraulic pipes and hoses – inspection, removal and refitting 10
Hydraulic system – bleeding 11
Master cylinder – removal and refitting 8
Rear brake drum – removal, inspection and refitting 5
Rear brake shoes – renewal 6
Rear wheel cylinder – removal, overhaul and refitting 7
Steering angle and yaw sensors - removal and refitting 17
Stop-light switch – removal and refitting 18
Vacuum servo unit – testing, removal and refitting 12
Vacuum servo unit vacuum hose and non-return valve – removal,
    testing and refitting. 13

Degrees of difficulty

| **Easy,** suitable for novice with little experience | | **Fairly easy,** suitable for beginner with some experience | | **Fairly difficult,** suitable for competent DIY mechanic | | **Difficult,** suitable for experienced DIY mechanic | | **Very difficult,** suitable for expert DIY or professional |

Specifications

Brake pedal

Pedal height (from floor):
    Manual transmission. . . . . 156 to 166 mm
    Automatic transmission . . . . 166 to 176 mm
Depressed pedal height (engine running with 50 kg force applied):
    Manual transmission. . . . . 80 mm or more
    Automatic transmission . . . . 85 mm or more
Pedal free play . . . . 3 to 11 mm
Stop-light switch clearance (between stop rubber and switch thread) . 0.74 to 1.96 mm

Front brakes

Type . . . . Ventilated disc, with single sliding-piston caliper
Disc diameter . . . . 260.0 mm
Disc thickness:
    New . . . . 22.0 mm
    Minimum. . . . . 20.0 mm
Maximum disc thickness variation . . . . 0.03 mm
Maximum disc/hub run-out (installed) . . . . 0.058 mm
Caliper piston diameter . . . . 53.59 mm
Brake pad thickness (minimum) . . . . 2.0 mm

Rear drum brakes

Type . . . . Leading and trailing shoes, with automatic adjusters
Drum internal diameter:
    New . . . . 202.0 mm
    Maximum . . . . 203.2 mm
Brake shoe thickness (minimum) . . . . 1.5 mm

Torque wrench settings

	Nm	lbf ft
ABS hydraulic unit to body.	13	10
ABS rear wheel sensor securing bolt (front wheel sensor is push-fit) . .	22	16
ABS wiring bracket bolt	29	21
Brake pedal mounting bracket nuts	21	15
Brake pipe unions	15	11
Caliper guide pin bolts	35	26
Caliper hose union (banjo bolt).	18	13
Caliper mounting bracket (carrier) bolts.	105	77
Hand brake mounting bolts	21	15
Master cylinder-to-servo mounting nuts	12	9
Rear hub nut.	175	129
Rear wheel cylinder mounting bolt.	9	7
Roadwheel nuts	103	76
Stub axle bolts	55	41
Yaw rate sensor	5	4

1 General information

The braking system is of diagonally-split, dual-circuit design, with ventilated discs at the front, and drum brakes at the rear. An anti-lock braking system (ABS) is fitted as standard. The front calipers are of single sliding-piston design, using asbestos-free pads. The rear drum brakes are of the leading and trailing shoe type, and are self-adjusting.

The vacuum servo unit uses inlet manifold depression (generated only when the engine is running) to boost the effort applied by the driver at the brake pedal and transmits this increased effort to the master cylinder pistons.

All models are also equipped with Electronic Brake force Distribution (EBD). Simply, this is an electronically-managed version of a rear brake regulator valve commonly fitted to non-ABS cars. To prevent rear wheel lock-up, the ABS unit software limits the brake fluid pressure supplied to the rear wheels. A further refinement fitted to some models is an 'electronic stability programme' (ESP), featuring a 'traction control system' (TCS). Using information supplied by the steering sensor, the yaw sensor (part of the SRS system), and others, ESP controls the brake and engine power to the wheels. TCS controls the wheel spin of the driven wheels via the ABS sensors and limits the throttle opening position to achieve this. All of these systems

are fail-safe. A malfunction will illuminate the dashboard warning light, and the system will operate with standard conventional braking until the fault is repaired.

The handbrake is cable-operated, and acts on the rear brakes. The cables operate on the rear trailing brake shoe operating levers.

Precautions

The car's braking system is one of its most important safety features. When working on the brakes, there are a number of points to be aware of, to ensure that your health (or even your life) is not being put at risk.

• When servicing any part of the system, work carefully and methodically – do not take short-cuts; also observe scrupulous cleanliness when overhauling any part of the hydraulic system.

• Always renew components in axle sets, where applicable – this means renewing brake pads, shoes, etc, on BOTH sides, even if only one set of pads is worn, or one wheel cylinder is leaking (for example). In the instance of uneven brake wear, the cause should be investigated and fixed (on front brakes, sticking caliper pistons is a likely problem).

• Use only genuine Nissan parts, or at least those of known good quality.

• Although genuine Nissan brake pads and shoes are asbestos-free, the dust created by wear of non-genuine parts may contain asbestos, which is a health hazard. Never blow it out with compressed air, and don't inhale any of it.

• DO NOT use petroleum-based solvents

to clean brake parts; use brake cleaner or methylated spirit only.

• DO NOT allow any brake fluid, oil or grease to contact the brake pads/shoes or discs/drums.

⚠ **Warning: Brake fluid is poisonous. Take care to keep it off bare skin, and in particular not to get splashes in your eyes. The fluid also attacks paintwork and plastics – wash off spillages immediately with cold water. Finally, brake fluid is highly inflammable, and should be handled with the same care as petrol.**

2 Front brake pads – renewal

Note: *Refer to the precautions in Section 1 before proceeding.*

1 Apply the handbrake. Loosen the front wheel nuts, then jack up the front of the car and support it on axle stands (see *Jacking and vehicle support*). Remove the front wheels. Work on one brake assembly at a time, using the assembled brake for reference if necessary. Remove the master cylinder filler cap.

2 Slacken and remove the lower caliper guide pin bolt, using a slim open-ended spanner to prevent the guide pin itself from rotating **(see illustrations)**.

3 With the lower guide pin bolt removed, pivot the caliper upwards **(see illustration)** and tie it to the front strut if required.

2.2a A thin spanner will be required to hold the guide pin

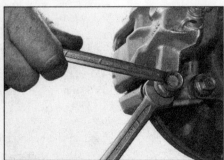

2.2b Removing the guide pin bolt

2.3 Swing the caliper upwards

2.5 Withdraw the pads

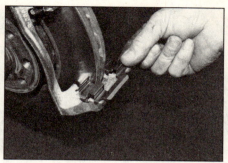

2.6 Remove the pad retaining plate

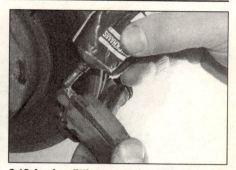

2.13 Apply a little copper-based greased to the pad-to-bracket surface

4 Make a note of how the pad upper and lower support plates are fitted, as they are liable to fall out when the pads are removed.

5 Withdraw the two brake pads from the caliper mounting bracket **(see illustration)**.

6 Recover the pad retaining plates **(see illustration)**.

7 First measure the thickness of each brake pad's friction material (not including the backing plate). If either pad is worn at any point to the specified minimum thickness or less, all four pads must be renewed. Also, the pads should be renewed if any are fouled with oil or grease; there is no satisfactory way of degreasing friction material, once contaminated. If any of the brake pads are worn unevenly, or are fouled with oil or grease, trace and rectify the cause before reassembly.

8 If the brake pads are still serviceable, carefully clean them using a clean, fine wire brush or similar, paying particular attention to the sides and back of the metal backing. If the pads are 'glazed' (have a shiny appearance) it may be helpful to roughen the surface of the friction material in order to restore the pads' braking effectiveness. Clean out the grooves in the friction material (where applicable), and pick out any large embedded particles of dirt or debris. Carefully clean the pad locations in the caliper body/mounting bracket.

9 Prior to fitting the pads, check that the spacers are free to slide easily in the caliper body bushes, and are a reasonably tight fit. Brush the dust and dirt from the caliper and piston, but *do not* inhale it, as it may contain asbestos, which is a health hazard. Inspect the dust seal around the piston for damage, and the piston for evidence of fluid leaks, corrosion or damage. If attention to any of these components is necessary, refer to Section 3.

10 The caliper piston must be pushed back into the caliper to make room for the new pads – this may require considerable effort. Either use a G-clamp, sliding-jaw (water pump) pliers, or suitable pieces of wood as levers.

Caution: Pushing back the piston causes a reverse-flow of brake fluid, which has been known to 'flip' the master cylinder rubber seals, resulting in a total loss of braking. To avoid this, clamp the caliper flexible hose and open the bleed screw – as the piston is pushed back, the fluid can be directed into a suitable container using a hose attached to the bleed screw. Close the screw just before the piston is pushed fully back, to ensure no air enters the system.

11 If the recommended method of opening a bleed screw before pushing back the piston is not used, the fluid level in the reservoir will rise, and possibly overflow. Make sure that there is sufficient space in the brake fluid reservoir to accept the displaced fluid, and if necessary, syphon some off first. Any brake fluid spilt on paintwork should be washed off with clean water without delay – brake fluid is also a highly-effective paint-stripper.

12 Where applicable, refit the pad upper and lower support plates to the mounting bracket.

13 Although not essential, it is useful to apply a little copper brake grease to the edges of the pads, in the areas which will slide in the mounting bracket (such as the end lugs, or 'ears') **(see illustration)**. Though anti-squeal shims are fitted, there is no harm in applying a little brake grease to the backs of the pads, where they will contact the caliper piston. Ensure that no grease ends up on the pad friction material, or on the disc.

14 Install the pads and anti-squeal shims, ensuring that the friction material of each pad is against the brake disc. On genuine Nissan pads, the inner pad may have a wear indicator pin, often referred to as 'screech pin' – if so, this should be facing upwards.

15 Pivot the caliper down into position. Install the guide pin bolt, tightening it to the specified torque setting while retaining the guide pin with an open-ended spanner.

16 On completion, firmly depress the brake pedal a few times, to bring the pads to their normal working position. Check the level of the brake fluid in the reservoir, and top-up if necessary. Refit the filler cap.

17 Give the car a short road test, to make sure that the brakes are functioning correctly, and to bed-in the new linings to the contours of the disc. New linings will not provide maximum braking efficiency until they have bedded-in; avoid heavy braking as far as possible for the first hundred miles or so.

3 Front brake caliper –
removal, overhaul and refitting

Note: *Refer to the precautions in Section 1 before proceeding.*

Removal

1 Apply the handbrake. Loosen the front wheel nuts, then jack up the front of the car and support it on axle stands (see *Jacking and vehicle support*). Remove the appropriate front wheel.

2 If the caliper is to be completely removed (as opposed to simply being unbolted and moved aside for other servicing work to be carried out) fit a brake hose clamp to the flexible hose leading to the caliper. This will minimise brake fluid loss during subsequent operations. Loosen the union on the caliper end of the flexible brake hose. Once loosened, do not try to unscrew the hose at this stage.

3 Holding the upper guide pin using one spanner, unscrew and remove the upper guide pin bolt.

4 The caliper can now be removed from the mounting bracket **(see illustration)**. If it is simply to be unbolted and moved aside, support it from a convenient point under the wheel arch, using a piece of wire, string, or a cable-tie. Do not allow the caliper to hang unsupported on its flexible hose.

5 Remove the brake pads as described in Section 2.

6 To remove the caliper completely, support

3.4 Removing the front caliper

3.7a The caliper mounting bolts (arrowed)

3.7b Removing the caliper

it in one hand and remove the banjo bolt, not forgetting the copper washers from each side of the banjo connection on the hose. Once the caliper is detached, plug the open hydraulic unions in the caliper and hose, to keep out dust and dirt.

7 If required (for instance, when renewing the discs), the caliper carrier bracket can be unbolted from the hub carrier **(see illustrations)**.

Overhaul

Note: *Before starting work, check on the availability of parts (caliper overhaul kit/seals).*

8 With the caliper on the bench, brush away all traces of dust and dirt, but take care not to inhale any dust, as it may be harmful to your health.

9 Pull the dust cover rubber seal from the end of the piston.

10 Apply low air pressure to the fluid inlet union, to eject the piston. Only low air pressure is required for this, such as is produced by a foot-operated tyre pump **(see illustration)**.

Caution: The piston may be ejected with some force. Position a thin piece of wood between the piston and the caliper body, to prevent damage to the end face of the piston in the event of it being ejected suddenly.

11 Using a suitable blunt instrument, prise the piston seal from the groove in the cylinder bore. Take care not to scratch the surface of the bore **(see illustration)**.

12 Clean the piston and caliper body with methylated spirit, and allow to dry. Examine the surfaces of the piston and cylinder bore for wear, damage and corrosion. If the piston alone is unserviceable, a new piston must be obtained, along with seals. If the cylinder bore is unserviceable, the complete caliper must be renewed. The seals must be renewed, regardless of the condition of the other components.

13 Coat the piston and seals with clean brake fluid, then manipulate the piston seal into the groove in the cylinder bore.

14 Push the piston squarely into its bore, taking care not to damage the seal.

15 Fit the dust cover rubber seal onto the piston and caliper, then depress the piston fully.

Refitting

16 Refit the caliper by reversing the removal operations. Make sure that the flexible brake hose is not twisted. Tighten the mounting bolts and wheel nuts to the specified torque.

17 Bleed the brake circuit according to the procedure given in Section 11, remembering to remove the brake hose clamp from the flexible hose. Make sure there are no leaks

from the hose connections. Test the brakes carefully before returning the car to normal service.

4   Front brake disc – inspection, removal and refitting

Note: *Refer to the precautions in Section 1 before proceeding.*

Inspection

1 Apply the handbrake. Loosen the relevant wheel nuts, jack up the front of the car and support it on axle stands. Remove the appropriate front wheel.

2 Remove the front brake caliper from the disc with reference to Section 3, and undo the two caliper bracket securing bolts. Do not disconnect the flexible hose. Support the caliper on an axle stand, or suspend it out of the way with a piece of wire, taking care to avoid straining the flexible hose.

3 Temporarily refit two of the wheel nuts to diagonally-opposite studs, with the flat sides of the nuts against the disc. Tighten the nuts progressively, to hold the disc firmly.

4 Scrape any corrosion from the disc. Rotate the disc, and examine it for deep scoring, grooving or cracks. Using a micrometer, measure the thickness of the disc in several places. The minimum thickness is stamped on the disc hub. Light wear and scoring is normal, but if excessive, the disc should be removed, and either reground by a specialist, or renewed. If regrinding is undertaken, the minimum thickness must be maintained. Obviously, if the disc is cracked, it must be renewed.

5 Using a dial gauge or a flat metal block and feeler gauges, check that the disc run-out 10 mm from the outer edge does not exceed the limit given in the Specifications. To do this, fix the measuring equipment, and rotate the disc, noting the variation in measurement as the disc is rotated. The difference between

3.10 Use low pressure air to force the piston from the caliper

3.11 Extract the seal with a blunt instrument

the minimum and maximum measurements recorded is the disc run-out.

6 If the run-out is greater than the specified amount, check for variations of the disc thickness as follows. Mark the disc at eight positions 45° apart then, using a micrometer, measure the disc thickness at the eight positions, 15 mm in from the outer edge. If the variation between the minimum and maximum readings is greater than the specified amount, the disc should be renewed.

7 The hub face run-out can also be checked in a similar way. First remove the disc as described later in this Section, fix the measuring equipment, then slowly rotate the hub, and check that the run-out does not exceed the amount given in the Specifications. If the hub face run-out is excessive, this should be corrected (by renewing the hub bearings – see Chapter 10) before rechecking the disc run-out.

Removal

8 With the wheel and caliper removed, remove the wheel nuts which were temporarily refitted in paragraph 3.

9 Mark the disc in relation to the hub, if it is to be refitted.

10 Remove the Torx-type disc retaining screw, and remove the disk **(see illustrations)**. The disc may be reluctant to come free so apply penetrating fluid first. If the disk is to be renewed it can be hammered free. If the disc is to be re-used then a puller tool may have to be employed.

Refitting

11 Make sure that the disc and hub mating surfaces are clean, then locate the disc on the wheel studs. Align the previously-made marks if the original disc is being refitted.

12 Refit the disc retaining screw.

13 Refit the brake caliper and carrier bracket with reference to Section 3.

14 Refit the wheel, and lower the car to the ground. Tighten wheel nuts to their specified torque.

15 Test the brakes carefully before returning the car to normal service.

---

5 Rear brake drum –
removal, inspection and refitting

Note: *Refer to the precautions in Section 1 before proceeding.*

Removal

1 Chock the front wheels, release the hand-brake and engage 1st gear. Loosen the relevant wheel nuts, jack up the rear of the car and support it on axle stands (see *Jacking and vehicle support*). Remove the appropriate rear wheel.

2 Prise free the hub cap from the drum and undo the hub nut. Pull the drum and bearing free from the stub axle. Do not use

4.10a Remove the screw . . .

4.10b . . . and recover the disc

too much force in removing the drum, or the shoe components could be damaged **(see illustrations)**.

3 If difficulty is encountered, a large three-legged puller will be required. This is however a last resort as damage will occur to the brake parts and possibly the bearing.

4 With the brake drum removed, clean the dust from the drum, brake shoes, wheel cylinder and backplate, using brake cleaner or methylated spirit. Take care not to inhale the dust, as it may contain asbestos.

Inspection

5 Clean the inside surfaces of the brake drum, then examine the internal friction surface for signs of scoring or cracks. If the drum was difficult to remove, this may have been due to a wear lip on the outer edge. If it is cracked, deeply scored, or has worn to a diameter greater than the maximum given in

the Specifications, then it should be renewed, together with the drum on the other side.

6 Regrinding of the brake drum is not recommended, however the lip at the edge of the drum should be ground away to allow easy removal in the future.

7 Check the wheel cylinder for signs of fluid leakage. A clue to a cylinder which may have just started leaking is a build-up of black brake dust around the cylinder rubber boots. Carefully lift their rubber boots with a small screwdriver, and look for dampness. Renew if necessary, as described in Section 7.

> **HAYNES HINT** *If one wheel cylinder is found to be leaking, the one on the opposite side should also be at least checked. With safety in mind, it may be advisable to renew the other one as a matter of course – the likelihood is, it too will fail soon.*

5.2a Tap the hub cap free with a blunt chisel

5.2b Remove the hub nut with a socket . . .

5.2c . . . and recover the hub nut

5.2d Removing the drum

6.2 The rear right-hand brake components before removal

6.4a Use pliers to release the spring clip

6.4b Recover the clip . . .

6.4c . . . and the pin

6.5a Lever the shoe free from the stop

6.5b Free the shoes from the other stop and wheel cylinder

6.6a Rotate to access the handbrake cable fixing

6.6b Unhook the cable

Refitting

8 Refitting is a reversal of removal, noting the following points:
   a) *Secure the drum using a new nut and tighten to the specified torque.*
   b) *Fit a new hub cap.*
   c) *With the wheel refitted and the car lowered to the ground, apply the footbrake and handbrake fully several times, to centre up the shoes and to set the automatic adjuster.*
   d) *Test the brakes carefully before returning the car to normal service.*

6 Rear brake shoes – renewal

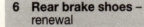

Note: *Refer to the precautions in Section 1 before proceeding.*
1 Chock the front wheels, release the handbrake and engage 1st gear. Loosen the relevant wheel nuts, jack up the rear of the car and support it on axle stands (see *Jacking and vehicle support*). Remove the rear wheels.

HAYNES HiNT
Work on one brake assembly at a time, using the assembled brake for reference if necessary.

2 Before going any further, note the fitted position of the springs and the brake shoes (if possible, take a digital picture) **(see illustration)**.
3 Clean the components with brake cleaner, and allow to dry. Position a tray beneath the backplate, to catch the fluid and residue.
4 Remove the two shoe hold-down springs, use a pair of pliers to depress and twist the cups so that they can be withdrawn off the pins. Remove the hold-down pins from the backplate **(see illustrations)**.
5 Release the shoe from the lower stop and unhook and pull both shoes free **(see illustrations)**.

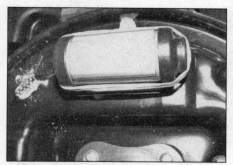

6.7 Secure the piston with an elastic band

6.8a Remove the lower spring . . .

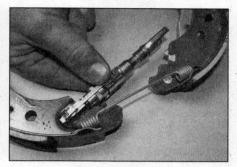

6.8b . . . adjuster . . .

6 Rotate the rear shoes to access the handbrake cable, and then use thin-nosed pliers to unhook the handbrake cable end fitting from the operating lever **(see illustrations)**.

7 To prevent the wheel cylinder pistons from being accidentally ejected, fit a suitable elastic band or wire lengthways over the cylinder/pistons **(see illustration)**. DO NOT press the brake pedal while the shoes are removed.

8 Working on a clean bench, remove the lower spring. Remove the adjuster and the upper spring. Wind the adjuster back to the starting position, noting that the left-hand adjuster has a **left-hand thread (see illustrations)**.

9 If the wheel cylinder shows signs of fluid leakage, or if there is any reason to suspect it of being defective, inspect it now, as described in the next Section.

10 Clean the backplate, and apply small amounts of high melting-point brake grease to the brake shoe contact points. Be careful not to get grease on any friction surfaces.

11 Lubricate the sliding components of the brake shoe adjuster with a little high melting-point brake grease. Oil the threads of the adjuster.

12 Fit the new brake shoes using a reversal of the removal procedure, but cover the new shoes' friction surface with masking tape to avoid contamination.

13 Carry out the renewal procedures on the remaining rear brake. Remove the masking tape.

14 Before refitting the drum, check its condition as described in Section 5.

15 With the drum in position, refit the wheel.

16 Lower the car to the ground, and tighten the wheel nuts to the specified torque.

17 Depress the brake pedal several times, in order to operate the self-adjusting mechanism and set the shoes at their normal operating position.

18 Make several forward and reverse stops, and operate the handbrake fully two or three times (adjust the handbrake as required – see Section 19). Give the car a road test, to make sure that the brakes are functioning correctly, and to bed-in the new shoes to the contours of the drum. Remember that the new shoes will not give full braking efficiency until they have bedded-in.

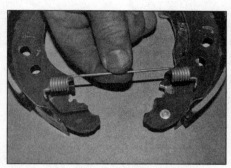

6.8c . . . and upper spring

6.8d Wind back the automatic adjuster

7 Rear wheel cylinder – removal, overhaul and refitting

Note: *Refer to the precautions in Section 1 before proceeding. Also bear in mind that if the brake shoes have been contaminated by fluid leaking from the wheel cylinder, they must be renewed. The shoes on BOTH sides of the car must be renewed, even if they are only contaminated on one side.*

Removal

1 Remove the brake drum as described in Section 6. If the wheel cylinders have been leaking there will probably be a significant build-up of brake dust on the failed seals (the dust sticks to the leaking fluid). A leak can be confirmed by carefully prising up the outer lip of the seal – any wetness means a new cylinder will be needed.

2 In recent years, the availability of wheel cylinder repair kits has greatly decreased, but it may still be worth asking. Wheel cylinders do not have to be fitted in pairs (providing they are the same size), but if one is leaking, it's reasonable to assume the other one soon will be too. If the leak has been going on for some time, it may be serious enough to have contaminated the brake shoes, in which case new shoes should be fitted on BOTH sides.

3 Minimise fluid loss either by removing the master cylinder reservoir cap, and then tightening it down onto a piece of polythene to obtain an airtight seal, or by using a brake hose

clamp, a G-clamp, or similar tool, to clamp the flexible hose at the nearest convenient point to the wheel cylinder.

4 Pull the brake shoes apart at their top ends, so that they are just clear of the wheel cylinder. The automatic adjuster will hold the shoes in this position, so that the cylinder can be withdrawn.

5 Wipe away all traces of dirt around the hydraulic union at the rear of the wheel cylinder, then undo the union nut. This nut may well be very tight – it pays to apply penetrating oil (or WD-40) in advance, and to use a proper brake spanner when loosening it.

6 Unscrew the bolts securing the wheel cylinder to the backplate **(see illustration)**.

7 Withdraw the wheel cylinder from the backplate so that it is clear of the brake shoes. Plug the open hydraulic unions, to prevent the entry of dirt, and to minimise further fluid loss whilst the cylinder is detached.

7.6 The wheel cylinder bolts (arrowed), brake pipe fitting and bleed nipple

8.5 The master cylinder bolts

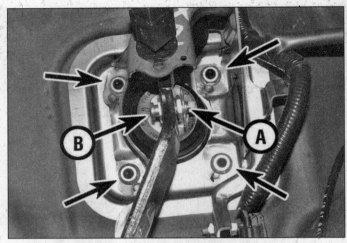

9.5 The brake pedal assembly mounting bolts (arrowed),
split pin (A), and pivot bolt (B)

Overhaul

8 No overhaul procedures or parts were available at the time of writing – check availability of spares before dismantling. Renewing a wheel cylinder as a unit is recommended.

Refitting

9 Wipe clean the backplate and remove the plug from the end of the hydraulic pipe. Fit the cylinder onto the backplate and screw in the hydraulic union nut by hand, being careful not to cross-thread it.

10 Tighten the mounting bolt, then fully tighten the hydraulic union nut.

11 Retract the automatic brake adjuster mechanism, so that the brake shoes engage with the pistons of the wheel cylinder. To do this, prise the shoes apart slightly, turn the automatic adjuster to its minimum position, and release the shoes.

12 Remove the clamp from the flexible brake hose, or the polythene from the master cylinder (as applicable).

13 Refit the brake drum with reference to Section 6.

14 Bleed the hydraulic system as described in Section 11. Providing suitable precautions were taken to minimise loss of fluid, it should only be necessary to bleed the relevant rear brake.

15 Test the brakes carefully before returning the car to normal service.

8 Master cylinder – removal and refitting

Note: *Refer to the precautions in Section 1 before proceeding.*

Removal

1 Disconnect the wiring plug for the fluid level warning sensor from the side of the reservoir.

2 Draw off the hydraulic fluid from the reservoir, using an old battery hydrometer or similar. Alternatively, raise the car, remove the wheels, then slacken the front bleed nipples and drain the fluid from the reservoir.

3 Disconnect the clutch master cylinder supply hose from the reservoir. Plug or cap the hose, to prevent fluid loss or dirt entry.

4 Identify the locations of the brake pipes on the master cylinder, then unscrew the union nuts and disconnect the pipes. These nuts may well be very tight – it pays to apply penetrating oil (or WD-40) in advance, and to use a proper brake spanner when loosening them.

5 Undo the master cylinder securing nuts, then withdraw the master cylinder from the studs on the servo unit **(see illustration)**. Recover the O-ring – a new one will be needed when refitting.

6 If required, the reservoir can be removed from the cylinder, by extracting the mounting pin and lifting the reservoir off. Recover the two reservoir seals, and fit new ones when reassembling.

7 If the master cylinder is faulty, it must be renewed. At the time of writing, no overhaul kits were available.

Refitting

8 Refitting is a reversal of the removal procedure, noting the following points:

a) *Clean the contact surfaces of the master cylinder and servo, and locate a new O-ring on the back of the master cylinder.*

b) *Refit and tighten the nuts to the specified torque.*

c) *Carefully insert the brake pipes in the apertures in the master cylinder, then tighten the union nuts. Make sure that the nuts enter their threads correctly.*

d) *Fill the reservoir with fresh brake fluid.*

e) *Bleed the brake hydraulic system as described in Section 11. Depending on the amount of fluid lost, it may also be necessary to bleed the clutch as described in Chapter 6.*

f) *Test the brakes carefully before returning the car to normal service.*

9 Brake pedal – removal, refitting and checking

Note: *Refer to the precautions in Section 1 before proceeding.*

Removal

1 Working inside the car, move the driver's seat fully to the rear (or remove it completely as described in Chapter 11) to allow maximum working area. Remove the lower trim panel below the steering column as described in Chapter 11.

2 Disconnect the wiring plug to the accelerator pedal and brake light switch.

3 Remove the brake light switch by rotating it 45°.

4 Using long-nosed pliers, pull out the spring clip used to secure the servo pushrod clevis pin. Pull out the clevis pin and detach the pushrod from the pedal.

5 Remove the bolts that hold the pedal assembly in place **(see illustration)**.

Refitting

6 Prior to refitting the pedal, apply a little grease to the pivot shaft, pedal bushes and actuator rods.

7 Refitting is a reversal of the removal procedure, but make sure that the clevis pin and servo operating rod are correctly located.

8 Test the brakes and operation of the servo unit before using on the road.

Checking

Note: *For maximum accuracy, the brakes should be bled as described in Section 11 before checking the pedal.*

9 With the pedal released, measure the distance from the floor and compare with the specified dimension **(see illustration)**.

10 Have an assistant on hand to check the operation of the brake lights. Push the brake pedal in by hand, approximately 5 to 10 mm.

With the pedal in this position, adjust the stop-light switch so that the brake lights are just going out.

11 Release the pedal, then slowly press it by hand, and check that the brake lights are on before the pedal has travelled 15 mm. The stop-light can also be adjusted by measuring the clearance between the switch plunger and the top of the pedal, and comparing with that specified.

12 Now press the pedal repeatedly using your foot, until the vacuum in the servo is dissipated and the pedal has a firm feel.

13 Check the pedal free play by depressing the pedal with your hand until resistance is felt – this should be no more than a very few millimetres. Incorrect free play suggests a problem elsewhere in the braking system.

14 Other than checking the pedal as stated, no adjustments are possible. If a fault exists with the pedal the complete assembly must be renewed.

15 On completion, test the brakes carefully before returning the car to normal service.

10 Hydraulic pipes and hoses – inspection, removal and refitting

Note: *Refer to the precautions in Section 1 before proceeding.*

Inspection

1 Jack up the front and rear of the car, and support on axle stands. Make sure the car is safely supported on a level surface.

2 Check for signs of leakage at the pipe unions, then examine the flexible hoses for signs of cracking, chafing and fraying.

3 The brake pipes should be examined carefully for signs of dents, corrosion or other damage. Corrosion should be scraped off, and if the depth of pitting is significant, the pipes renewed. This is particularly likely in those areas underneath the car body where the pipes are exposed and unprotected.

4 Renew any defective brake pipes and/or hoses.

Removal

5 If a section of pipe or hose is to be removed, loss of brake fluid can be reduced by unscrewing the filler cap, and completely sealing the top of the reservoir with cling film or adhesive tape. Alternatively, the reservoir can be emptied (see Section 8).

6 To remove a section of pipe, hold the adjoining hose union nut with a spanner to prevent it from turning, then unscrew the union nut at the end of the pipe, and release it. Repeat the procedure at the other end of the pipe, then release the pipe by pulling out the clips attaching it to the body.

7 Where the union nuts are exposed to the full force of the weather, they can sometimes be quite tight. If an open-ended spanner is used, burring of the flats on the nuts is not

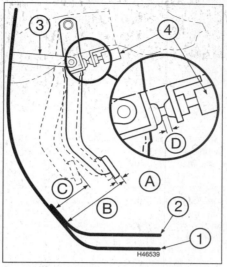

9.9 Brake pedal height checking points

A	Pedal free play	1	Floor
B	Pedal free height	2	Front
C	Depressed pedal		sidemember
	height	3	Servo pushrod
D	Stop-light switch	4	Stop-light
	clearance		switch

uncommon, and for this reason, it is preferable to use a split ring (brake) spanner, which will engage all the flats. If such a spanner is not available, self-locking grips may be used as a last resort; these may well damage the nuts, but if the pipe is to be renewed, this does not matter.

8 To further minimise the loss of fluid when disconnecting a flexible brake line from a rigid pipe, clamp the hose as near as possible to the pipe to be detached, using a brake hose clamp or a pair of self-locking grips with protected jaws.

9 To remove a flexible hose, first clean the ends of the hose and the surrounding area, then unscrew the union nuts from the hose ends. Remove the spring clip, and withdraw the hose from the support bracket **(see illustration)**. Where applicable, unscrew the hose from the caliper.

10 Brake pipes supplied with flared ends and union nuts can be obtained individually or in sets from Nissan dealers or accessory

10.9 Brake hose and spring clip on the front strut

shops. The pipe is then bent to shape, using the old pipe as a guide, and is ready for fitting. Be careful not to kink or crimp the pipe when bending it; ideally, a proper pipe-bending tool should be used.

Refitting

11 Refitting of the pipes and hoses is a reversal of removal. Make sure that all brake pipes are securely supported in their clips, and ensure that the hoses are not kinked. Check also that the hoses are clear of all suspension components and underbody fittings, and will remain clear during movement of the suspension and steering.

12 On completion, bleed the hydraulic system as described in Section 11.

11 Hydraulic system – bleeding

Note: *Refer to the precautions in Section 1 before proceeding.*

1 If the master cylinder has been disconnected and reconnected, then the complete system (all circuits) must be bled of air. If a component of one circuit has been disturbed, then only that particular circuit need be bled.

2 Before starting, disconnect the electrical plug at the ABS modulator. Bleeding should start with the furthest bleed nipple from the master cylinder, followed by the next one until the bleed nipple nearest the master cylinder is bled last.

3 There are a variety of do-it-yourself 'one-man' brake bleeding kits available from motor accessory shops, and it is recommended that one of these kits be used wherever possible, as they greatly simplify the brake bleeding operation. Follow the kit manufacturer's instructions in conjunction with the following procedure. If a pressure-bleeding kit is obtained, then it will not be necessary to depress the brake pedal in the following procedure.

4 During the bleeding operation, do not allow the brake fluid level in the reservoir to drop below the minimum mark. If the level is allowed to fall so far that air is drawn in, the whole procedure will have to be started again from scratch. Only use new fluid for topping-up, preferably from a freshly-opened container. Never re-use fluid bled from the system.

5 Before starting, check that all rigid pipes and flexible hoses are in good condition, and that all hydraulic unions are tight. Take great care not to allow hydraulic fluid to come into contact with the car paintwork, otherwise the finish will be seriously damaged. Wash off any spilt fluid immediately with cold water.

Bleeding

Basic (two-man) method

6 Collect together a clean glass jar of reasonable size, a suitable length of plastic or rubber tubing which is a tight fit over the bleed

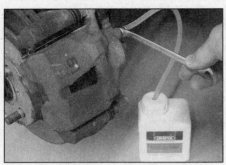

11.15 Using a one-man bleeding kit

screw, and a ring spanner to fit the screw. The help of an assistant will also be required.

7 Remove the dust cap from the first screw in the sequence. Fit the spanner and tube to the screw, place the other end of the tube in the jar, and pour in sufficient fluid to cover the end of the tube.

8 Ensure that the master cylinder reservoir fluid level is maintained at least above the MIN level line throughout the procedure.

9 Have the assistant fully depress the brake pedal several times to build-up pressure, then maintain it on the final downstroke.

10 While pedal pressure is maintained, unscrew the bleed screw (approximately one turn) and allow the compressed fluid and air to flow into the jar. The assistant should maintain pedal pressure, following it down to the floor if necessary, and should not release it until instructed to do so. When the flow stops, tighten the bleed screw again, have the assistant release the pedal slowly, and recheck the reservoir fluid level.

11 Repeat the steps given in paragraphs 9 and 10 until the fluid emerging from the bleed screw is free from air bubbles. If the master cylinder has been drained and refilled, and air is being bled from the first screw in the sequence, allow approximately five seconds between cycles for the master cylinder passages to refill.

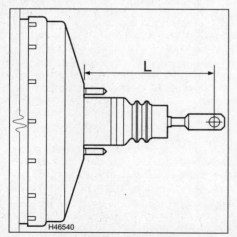

12.11 Check the length of the pushrod

L = 115.35 mm

12 When no more air bubbles appear, tighten the bleed screw securely, remove the tube and spanner, and refit the dust cap. Do not overtighten the bleed screw.

13 Repeat the procedure on the remaining screws in the sequence, until all air is removed from the system and the brake pedal feels firm again.

Using a one-way valve kit

14 As their name implies, these kits consist of a length of tubing with a one-way valve fitted, to prevent expelled air and fluid being drawn back into the system; some kits include a translucent container, which can be positioned so that the air bubbles can be more easily seen flowing from the end of the tube.

15 The kit is connected to the bleed screw, which is then opened (**see illustration**). The user returns to the driver's seat, depresses the brake pedal with a smooth, steady stroke, and slowly releases it; this is repeated until the expelled fluid is clear of air bubbles.

16 Note that these kits simplify work so much that it is easy to forget the master cylinder reservoir fluid level; ensure that this is maintained at least above the MIN level line at all times.

Using a pressure-bleeding kit

17 These kits are usually operated by the reservoir of pressurised air contained in the spare tyre. However, note that it will probably be necessary to reduce the pressure to a lower level than normal; refer to the instructions supplied with the kit.

18 By connecting a pressurised, fluid-filled container to the master cylinder reservoir, bleeding can be carried out simply by opening each screw in turn (in the specified sequence), and allowing the fluid to flow out until no more air bubbles can be seen in the expelled fluid.

19 This method has the advantage that the large reservoir of fluid provides an additional safeguard against air being drawn into the system during bleeding.

20 Pressure-bleeding is particularly effective when bleeding 'difficult' systems, or when bleeding the complete system at the time of routine fluid renewal.

All methods

21 When bleeding is complete, and firm pedal feel is restored, wash off any spilt fluid, tighten the bleed screws securely, and refit their dust caps.

22 Check the hydraulic fluid level in the master cylinder reservoir, and top-up if necessary (see *Weekly checks*).

23 Discard any hydraulic fluid that has been bled from the system; it will not be fit for re-use.

24 Check the feel of the brake pedal. If it feels at all spongy, air must still be present in the system, and further bleeding is required. Failure to bleed satisfactorily after a reasonable repetition of the bleeding procedure may be due to worn master cylinder seals.

25 Check the clutch operation on completion;

it may be necessary to bleed the clutch hydraulic system with reference to Chapter 6.

12 Vacuum servo unit – testing, removal and refitting

Note: *Refer to the precautions in Section 1 before proceeding.*

Testing

1 To test the operation of the servo unit, depress the footbrake four or five times to dissipate the vacuum, then start the engine while keeping the footbrake depressed. As the engine starts, there should be a noticeable give in the brake pedal as vacuum builds-up. Allow the engine to run for at least two minutes, and then switch it off. If the brake pedal is now depressed again, it should be possible to hear a hiss from the servo when the pedal is depressed. After four or five applications, no further hissing should be heard, and the pedal should feel harder.

2 Before assuming that a problem exists in the servo unit itself, inspect the non-return valve as described in the next Section.

Removal

3 Refer to Section 8 and remove the master cylinder.

4 Release the spring clip, then pull off the vacuum hose from the connection on the front of the servo unit.

5 Remove the wiper motor and linkage as described in Chapter 12.

6 Working inside the car move the driver's seat fully to the rear, to allow maximum working area.

7 Remove the lower dash trim panel and unplug the electrical connectors to the brake light switch and accelerator pedal position switch.

8 Using long-nosed pliers, pull out the spring clip used to secure the servo pushrod clevis pin. Pull out the clevis pin and detach the pushrod from the pedal.

9 Have an assistant support the servo unit under the bonnet, then unscrew and remove the four nuts from the brake pedal mounting bracket. Remove the pedal assembly.

10 Have your assistant carefully withdraw the servo unit into the engine compartment. Recover the servo mounting gasket – a new one should be used when refitting.

11 Check the free length of the servo pushrod before reinstalling (**see illustration**).

Refitting

12 Refitting is a reversal of the removal procedure, noting the following points:
  a) Make sure the new gasket is correctly positioned on the servo.
  b) Refit the master cylinder as described in Section 8.
  c) Test the brakes carefully before returning the car to normal service.

13 Vacuum servo unit vacuum hose and non-return valve – removal, testing and refitting

Note: *Refer to the precautions in Section 1 before proceeding.*

Removal

1 With the engine switched off, depress the brake pedal four or five times, to dissipate any remaining vacuum from the servo unit.
2 Release the spring clip and disconnect the vacuum hose at the servo unit
3 Remove the non-return valve by pulling it free from the rubber grommet. If it is reluctant to move, prise it free, using a screwdriver with its blade inserted under the flange.
4 Detach the vacuum hose from the inlet manifold connection.
5 If the hose or the fixings are damaged or in poor condition, they must be renewed.

Testing

6 Examine the non-return valve for damage and signs of deterioration, and renew it if necessary. The valve may be tested by blowing through its connecting hoses in both directions. It should only be possible to blow from the servo end towards the inlet manifold.

Refitting

7 Refitting is a reversal of the removal procedure. If fitting a new non-return valve, ensure that it is fitted the correct way round.

14 Anti-lock braking system (ABS) – general information

ABS is fitted to Micra models as standard. The system comprises a hydraulic regulator unit and the four roadwheel sensors. The regulator unit contains the electronic control unit (ECU), the hydraulic solenoid valves and the electrically-driven return pump. The purpose of the system is to prevent the wheel(s) locking during heavy braking. This is achieved by automatic release of the brake on the relevant wheel, followed by re-application of the brake.

The solenoid valves are controlled by the ECU, which itself receives signals from the four wheel sensors fitted to the wheel hubs, which monitor the speed of rotation of each wheel. By comparing these signals, the ECU can determine the speed at which the vehicle is travelling – this information is used instead of a vehicle speed sensor signal on some models. It can use this speed to determine when a wheel is decelerating at an abnormal rate, compared to the speed of the car, and therefore predicts when a wheel is about to lock. During normal operation, the system functions in the same way as a non-ABS braking system.

If the ECU senses that a wheel is about to lock, it closes the relevant outlet solenoid valves in the hydraulic unit, which then isolates the relevant brake(s) on the wheel(s) which is/ are about to lock from the master cylinder, effectively sealing-in the hydraulic pressure.

If the speed of rotation of the wheel continues to decrease at an abnormal rate, the ECU opens the inlet solenoid valves on the relevant brake(s), and operates the electrically-driven return pump which pumps the hydraulic fluid back into the master cylinder, releasing the brake. Once the speed of rotation of the wheel returns to an acceptable rate, the pump stops; the solenoid valves switch again, allowing the hydraulic master cylinder pressure to return to the caliper, which then re-applies the brake. This cycle can be carried out many times a second.

The action of the solenoid valves and return pump creates pulses in the hydraulic circuit. When the ABS system is functioning, these pulses can be felt through the brake pedal.

The operation of the ABS system is entirely dependent on electrical signals. To prevent the system responding to any inaccurate signals, a built-in safety circuit monitors all signals received by the ECU. If an inaccurate signal or low battery voltage is detected, the ABS system is automatically shut-down, and the warning light on the instrument panel is illuminated, to inform the driver that the ABS system is not operational. Normal braking should still be available, however.

Most models are also equipped with an additional safety feature called EBD (Electronic Brake force Distribution), which automatically apportions braking effort between the front and rear wheels. The EBD function is built into the system's software, and the intention is to limit braking effort (fluid pressure) to the rear wheels, to further prevent them locking up under heavy braking.

Traction control (TCS) and electronic stability (ESP) also feature on many models. Both are further developments of the ABS system, that utilise information from the steering angle sensor – in the steering column – and the yaw rate/lateral acceleration (or G-) sensor – on top

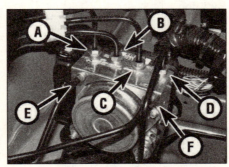

15.3 The ABS control unit

A *Right-hand front caliper*
B *Left-hand rear wheel cylinder*
C *Right-hand rear wheel cylinder*
D *Left-hand front brake caliper*
E *Master cylinder secondary supply*
F *Master cylinder primary supply*

of the airbag control unit beneath the centre console, to further refine braking control. TCS limits the amount of torque available to the front wheels when slippage is detected by the wheel sensors. ESP improves stability by monitoring braking effort and steering angle by controlling the braking and engine power to all four wheels.

If a fault does develop in the any of these systems, the vehicle must be taken to a Nissan dealer or suitably-equipped specialist for fault diagnosis and repair.

15 ABS hydraulic unit – removal and refitting

Note: *Refer to the precautions in Section 1 before proceeding.*

Removal

1 The ABS unit is accessible at the rear of the engine compartment on the passenger's side. Access may be improved by unbolting the windscreen scuttle panel, as described in the windscreen wiper motor removal procedure in Chapter 12.
2 Disconnect the wiring multiplug from the ABS unit.
3 Taking precautions against the spillage of brake fluid, and noting their positions for refitting, unscrew the six brake pipe unions on the top and side of the unit, and disconnect the pipes **(see illustration)**. Use a proper brake spanner on the unions, to avoid rounding them off if they are tight.
4 Unbolt the mounting bracket from the inner wing and cross member. Remove the hydraulic unit from the engine compartment, together with its mounting bracket.
5 If required, the hydraulic unit can be separated from its mounting bracket, after removing the nut.

Refitting

6 Refitting is a reversal of removal. Ensure that the multiplug is securely connected, and that the brake pipe unions are tightened to the specified torque. On completion, bleed the hydraulic system as described in Section 11.

16 ABS wheel sensors – testing, removal and refitting

Note: *Refer to the precautions in Section 1 before proceeding.*

Testing

1 The Micra is fitted with 'active' wheel speed sensors. Unlike conventional wheel speed sensors they require a power supply and are capable of measuring wheel speed down to zero.
2 Checking of the sensors is done before removal, connecting a voltmeter to the disconnected sensor multiplug. Using an

16.8 Removing the front ABS wheel speed sensor

analogue (moving coil) meter is not practical, since the meter does not respond quickly enough. A digital meter should be used to check that the sensor is operating correctly.

3 To do this, raise the relevant wheel then disconnect the wiring to the ABS. With the ignition on, check battery voltage at one of the terminals of the supply connector.

4 Reconnect the sensor and backprobe the signal wire. Take care not to damage the wiring and ideally use a wire piercing probe. Spin the wheel and check that the output voltage is between 0.9 and 1.65 volts. This is dependant on wheel position and not the speed of the wheel.

5 Alternatively, an oscilloscope may be used to check the output of the sensor – a digital square wave will be traced on the screen.

6 The output signal for the front sensors is generated by the magnet in the wheel bearing passing in front of the sensor. Renewal also requires renewal of the wheel bearing, as described in Chapter 10, as this contains the magnetic ring that induces the sensors output. The rear pick-up ring is a press-fit on the rear hub. Do not remove it unless necessary.

Removal

Front wheel sensor

7 Apply the handbrake and loosen the relevant front wheel nuts. Jack up the front of the car and support it on axle stands. Remove the wheel.

8 The sensor is a simple push-fit on the pick-up ring **(see illustration)**

9 Trace the wiring and detach it from the strut

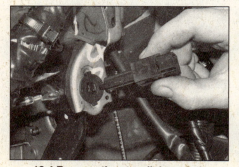

18.4 Remove the stop-light switch

16.10 The rear sensor mounting bolt

leg. Remove the support clips and unplug the sensor.

Rear wheel sensor

10 The rear wheel sensor is bolted to the drum brake backplate. Unbolt it and remove, and then trace the wiring to the connector on the rear axle on the left-hand side, and adjacent to the rear crossmember on the right **(see illustration)**.

Refitting

11 Refitting is a reversal of the removal procedure.

17 Steering angle and yaw sensors - removal and refitting

Note: *Refer to the precautions in Section 1 before proceeding.*

Steering angle sensor

Removal

1 The steering angle sensor is located beneath the steering column switch and airbag clockspring assembly. First remove the assembly as described in Chapter 12.

2 Undo the three screws and remove the sensor from the bottom of the clockspring assembly.

Refitting

3 Refitting is a reversal of removal. Note if the ABS hydraulic unit is renewed, it will be necessary to have the steering angle sensor neutral position adjusted by a Nissan dealer.

19.4 The electrical connector for the handbrake on warning lamp

Yaw rate sensor

Caution: *The yaw rate sensor has delicate internal components and must not be dropped or struck.*

Removal

4 The yaw rate sensor is located on top of the airbag control unit beneath the centre console. First remove the centre console as described in Chapter 11.

5 Note which way round the sensor is fitted, then disconnect the wiring and unscrew the retaining nuts to remove the sensor.

Refitting

6 Refitting is a reversal of removal, but make sure it is fitted the correct way round and tighten the nuts to the specified torque.

18 Stop-light switch – removal and refitting

Note: *Refer to the precautions in Section 1 before proceeding.*

Removal

1 Working inside the car move the driver's seat fully to the rear, to allow maximum working area.

2 Remove the trim panel below the steering wheel.

3 Disconnect the wiring plug from the stop-light switch at the top of the brake pedal bracket.

4 Rotate the switch through 45° and withdraw the switch from the bracket **(see illustration)**.

Refitting

5 Refitting is a reversal of removal. Once the switch has been fitted and reconnected, check the operation of the switch as described in Section 9.

19 Handbrake lever – removal and refitting

Note: *Refer to the precautions in Section 1 before proceeding.*

Removal

1 Chock the front wheels, and engage 1st gear.

2 Though not essential, access to the handbrake lever is greatly improved by removing one of the front seats, as described in Chapter 11.

3 Remove the centre console as described in Chapter 11.

4 Disconnect the electrical connector from the handbrake warning light switch **(see illustration)**.

5 Remove the two bolts securing the lever assembly to the floor, and remove it from the car.

19.6 Remove the cables

6 Work the cables free from the connector plate (see illustration).

Refitting

7 Refitting is a reversal of removal.
8 When refitting the lever, it will be necessary to reset and adjust the mechanism, as described in Chapter 1. If new cables have been fitted, recheck the adjustment after (say) one month or 1000 miles.

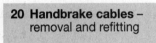

20 Handbrake cables –
removal and refitting

Note: *Refer to the precautions in Section 1 before proceeding.*
Caution: Since the cables are routed close to the exhaust system in several places, this procedure should only be attempted when the engine and exhaust system are completely cool. The engine should have been switched off for at least a few hours (preferably, after it has been left overnight).

20.3c . . . and then remove the cable

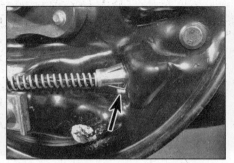

20.3a The tangs must be compressed to free the cable

Removal

1 Chock the front wheels, and engage 1st gear. Loosen the wheel nuts on the relevant rear wheel, then jack up the rear of the car and support it on axle stands (see *Jacking and vehicle support*). Fully release the handbrake lever.
2 Remove the brake drum and brake shoes as described in Sections 5 and 6.
3 Work the cable free from the brake backplate (see illustrations).
4 Remove the exhaust centre box as described in Chapter 4B and then remove the heat shields.
5 Unbolt the support brackets from the body.
6 Remove the centre console as described in Chapter 11.
7 Unhook the cables free from the connector plate and using a suitable spanner compress the locating tangs on the cable and push it out of the transmission tunnel (see illustration).
8 If one cable is being renewed due to wear or other problems, consider renewing them both as a pair, to ensure even operation.

Refitting

9 Refitting is a reversal of the removal procedure, noting the following points:
  a) Make sure that the cable end fittings are

20.7 Compressing the locating tangs with a spanner

20.3b Use a suitable ring spanner to compress them . . .

correctly located, and that the cables are routed as before, without any kinks or sharp bends.
  b) Adjust the handbrake as described in Chapter 1.

21 Handbrake warning light switch –
removal and refitting

Note: *Although not absolutely necessary, access to the handbrake switch is greatly improved if the driver's seat is removed as described in Chapter 11.*

Removal

1 Remove the centre console as described in Chapter 11.
2 Disconnect the wiring to the switch.
3 Using a Torx-type tool remove the switch (see illustration).

Refitting

4 Refitting is a reversal of removal, but check that the switch works after two clicks of the handbrake. If necessary, check the handbrake adjustment as described in Chapter 1.

21.3 Remove the securing screw

Chapter 10
Suspension and steering

Contents

Section number

Front hub bearings – renewal 3
Front suspension anti-roll bar – removal and refitting 5
Front suspension lower arm – removal and refitting 6
Front suspension lower arm balljoint – renewal 7
Front suspension strut – removal, overhaul and refitting 4
Front suspension subframe – removal and refitting 8
Front swivel hub – removal and refitting 2
General information 1
Rear axle assembly – removal and refitting 12
Rear hub and bearings – inspection and renewal 9

Section number

Rear shock absorber – removal and refitting 10
Rear spring – removal and refitting 11
Roadwheel nut tightness check ....See Chapter 1
Steering and suspension check ....See Chapter 1
Steering column and power steering – removal and refitting 14
Steering rack – removal and refitting 16
Steering rack rubber gaiters – renewal 15
Steering wheel – removal and refitting 13
Track rod end – removal and refitting 17
Wheel alignment and steering angles – general information 18

Degrees of difficulty

Easy, suitable for novice with little experience 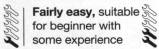	Fairly easy, suitable for beginner with some experience	Fairly difficult, suitable for competent DIY mechanic	Difficult, suitable for experienced DIY mechanic	Very difficult, suitable for expert DIY or professional

Specifications

Wheel alignment and steering angles

Front wheel toe-setting	0 ± 2 mm
Front wheel camber	-0° 51' to -0° 39'
Front wheel castor	3° 42' to 5° 12'
Kingpin offset	9° 03' to 10° 33'
Rear wheel camber	-1° 56' to -0° 26'
Rear wheel toe-in	0 to 8 mm

Torque wrench settings

	Nm	lbf ft
Front suspension		
Anti-roll bar bracket bolts	30	22
Anti-roll bar drop link nuts	45	33
Brake caliper mounting bracket (carrier) bolts	105	77
Driveshaft (hub) nut	238 to 322	176 to 238
Lower arm balljoint pinch-bolt	60	44
Lower arm front pivot bolt	100	74
Lower arm rear mounting bolt	110	81
Subframe mounting bolts:		
Front bolts (to link arm);		
Manual transmission	100	74
Automatic transmission	150	111
Rear bolts	110	81
Support plate bolts	45	33
Subframe support arm-to-chassis bolts	65	48
Suspension strut piston rod nut	68	50
Suspension strut top mounting nuts	18	13
Swivel hub-to-suspension strut pinch-bolt/nut	110	81

Torque wrench settings (continued)

	Nm	lbf ft
Rear suspension		
Rear axle beam pivot nut/bolt	100	74
Rear axle beam mounting bracket	50	37
Rear hub nut...	141 to 209	104 to 154
Shock absorber lower mounting nut	100	74
Shock absorber upper mounting top nut......................	20	15
Stub axle bolts	55	41
Steering		
Steering column intermediate shaft pinch-bolts	30	22
Steering column mounting nuts	17	13
Steering rack securing nuts/bolts	95	70
Steering wheel securing bolt	35	26
Track rod end balljoint nut	35	26
Roadwheels		
Roadwheel nuts	103	76

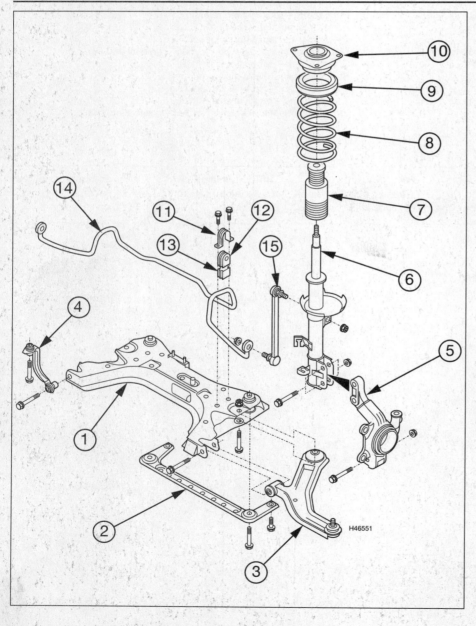

H46551

1 General information

The front suspension is of independent type, with a subframe, MacPherson struts, lower arms, and an anti-roll bar. The struts, which incorporate coil springs and integral shock absorbers, are attached at their upper ends to the reinforced strut mountings on the body shell. The lower end of each strut is bolted to the top of a cast swivel hub, which carries the hub, and the brake disc and caliper. The hubs run within non-adjustable bearings in the swivel hubs. The lower end of each swivel hub is attached, via a balljoint, to a lower arm assembly. The balljoints are integral with the lower arms. Each lower arm is attached at its inboard end to the subframe, via flexible rubber bushes, and controls both lateral and fore-and-aft movement of the front wheels. An anti-roll bar is fitted to all models. The anti-roll bar is mounted on the subframe, and is connected to the suspension struts via vertical drop links **(see illustration)**.

The rear suspension is semi-rigid beam axle with a U-section beam welded between pressed-steel trailing arms. This U-section beam allows a limited torsional flexibility, giving each rear wheel a certain degree of independent movement, whilst maintaining optimum track and wheel camber control. This type of arrangement is called a 'twist beam' rear axle. The axle is attached to the

1.1 The front suspension components

1	Subframe	9	Strut bearing
2	Support panel	10	Upper mount
3	Track control arm	11	Anti-roll bar clamp
4	Subframe support arm	12	Upper rubber bush
5	Swivel hub	13	Lower rubber bush
6	Strut	14	Anti-roll bar
7	Dust seal and bump stop	15	Anti-roll bar drop link
8	Coil spring		

body with pivot bolts and rubber bushes. The rear suspension is separate springs and shock absorbers. The compact springs are mounted under the car, so only the shock absorber housings encroach on the boot area, resulting in more boot space. The shock absorbers are bolted to the trailing arm section of the rear axle at the base, and to the body housings at the top. The rear hubs are integral with the brake drums. They are fitted to removable stub axles, which are bolted to the trailing arms **(see illustration)**.

The steering is of conventional rack-and-pinion type, incorporating a collapsible safety column. The steering rack is mounted on the front suspension subframe. The steering rack track rods are attached via the track rod ends to the steering arms on the swivel hubs.

All Micra models are equipped with electric power steering. The motor, reduction gear and electronics are all mounted on the steering column, below the dashboard. Using information from the steering angle sensor and wheel speed sensors the power assistance can be varied as conditions demand. The column, motor and electronic control hardware are a complete sub-assembly. No individual parts are available.

2 Front swivel hub –
removal and refitting

Removal

1 Remove the relevant wheel trim, or the wheel centre cover (alloy wheels) for access to the driveshaft nut.

2 Ensure that the handbrake is applied (ideally, have an assistant apply the footbrake), then slacken the driveshaft nut using a suitable socket and extension bar **(see illustration)**. Loosen the driveshaft nut almost to the end of its threads, but do not remove it at this stage. Push or drive the shaft into the hub, to check that it is free as described in Chapter 8.

⚠️ *Warning: The driveshaft nut is done up extremely tight, and considerable effort will be required to loosen it. Do not use poor-quality, badly-fitting tools for this task, due to the risk of personal injury.*

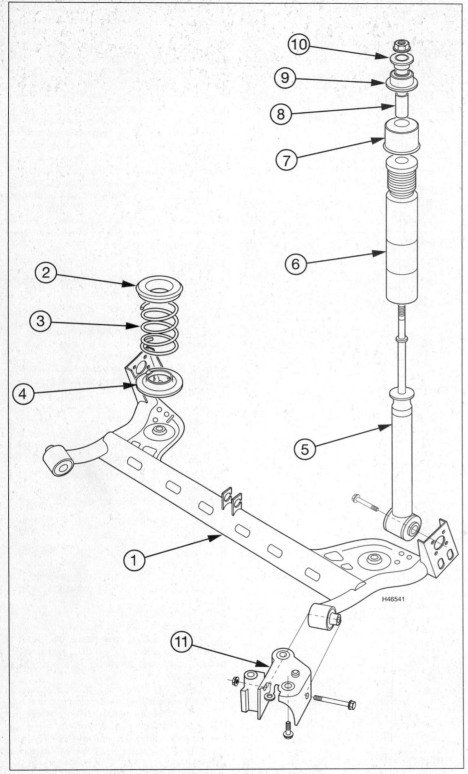

1.2 The rear suspension components

1	Rear axle	5	Shock absorber	8 Spacer
2	Rubber spring seat	6	Bump stop and dust	9 Lower bush
3	Coil spring		seal	10 Upper bush
4	Rubber spring seat	7	Cover	11 Body mounting

2.2 An alternative method of loosening the front hub nut

2.4 Pull the clip free

2.9 Using a balljoint separator to remove the track rod end

2.10a Using a large lever and support to separate the balljoint

2.10b Recover the plastic washer

3 Apply the handbrake, slacken the relevant front wheel nuts, then jack up the front of the car and support securely on axle stands (see *Jacking and vehicle support*). Remove the appropriate roadwheel.

4 Pull the spring retainer free from the flexible brake hose from where it locates on the strut **(see illustration)**.

5 Unscrew the bolts securing the brake caliper mounting bracket to the swivel hub, then slide the caliper/bracket assembly from the swivel hub and brake disc (there is no need to remove the brake pads). Suspend the caliper/bracket assembly from the strut coil spring using wire or string – do not allow the caliper to hang on the brake hose.

6 Mark the brake disc in relation to the hub (assuming it is to be refitted), then remove the disc holding screw. Withdraw it from the hub.

7 Remove the ABS sensor from the pick-up ring.

8 Slacken the track rod end balljoint nut, and unscrew it as far as the ends of the threads. A Torx key can be used to stop the swivel rotating while the nut is unscrewed.

9 Disconnect the track rod end balljoint from the swivel hub using a balljoint separator tool (leave the nut fitted to protect the threads); taking care not to damage the balljoint rubber seal **(see illustration)**. Once the balljoint has been released, remove the balljoint nut and discard it.

10 Slacken the lower arm balljoint pinch-bolt and remove it. A hammer and punch may be required. Discard the nut. Push the end of the lower arm down to free the balljoint from the swivel hub, and recover the plastic washer. If the balljoint is very tight, it may be necessary to lever down using a large screwdriver, or similar tool, but take care not to damage the balljoint rubber seal **(see illustrations)**.

11 Remove the nuts from the two bolts used to secure the swivel hub to the base of the suspension strut. Note which way the bolts are fitted (this should be from the front), then support the hub and tap the bolts out

12 The splined end of the driveshaft now has to be released from its location in the hub.

13 Once the splines have been released, remove the driveshaft nut.

14 Pull the hub outwards, and push the driveshaft inwards, to separate the splined end from the hub. It is helpful to have an assistant on hand, to pull either the hub or the shaft. Do not bend the driveshaft excessively at any stage, or the joints may be damaged – the inner and outer joints should not be bent through more than 18° and 45° respectively. Do not let the driveshaft hang down under its own weight – tie it up level if necessary. Pull off the hub, and remove it.

Refitting

15 Refitting is a reversal of removal, bearing in mind the following points:
- a) *Fit the swivel hub-to-strut bolts in from the front. Use new nuts.*
- b) *Fit a new nut to the track rod end.*
- c) *Do not fully tighten the driveshaft nut until the car is resting on its wheels.*
- d) *Tighten all fixings to the specified torque.*
- e) *Have the front wheel alignment checked on completion.*

3 Front hub bearings – renewal

Note: *A press, a suitable puller, or similar improvised tools will be required for this operation. Obtain a bearing overhaul kit before proceeding.*

1 With the swivel hub removed as described in Section 2, proceed as follows.

2 The bearing removal process involves three stages – removing the hub flange (where the wheel mounts), tapping off the inner race from the hub flange, then driving out the bearing itself from the hub.

3 The hub flange must first be removed from the bearing/swivel hub assembly. It is preferable to use a press to do this, but it is possible to drive out the hub using a metal tube of suitable diameter. Alternatively, a suitable puller can be used.

4 Have an assistant hold the hub assembly over a work surface, then using a metal bar, tube, or socket of suitable diameter, drive the hub flange through the bearing and remove it **(see illustrations)**. This process will destroy the bearing, as the inner race will separate with the flange.

5 The bearing inner race left on the hub flange must now be removed, which is most easily done using a puller. Otherwise, grip the edge of the flange in a vice, and tap the race off with a chisel, taking care not to damage the flange's bearing surface **(see illustrations)**.

3.4a Drive out the hub flange . . .

3.4b . . . and remove it

3.5a Preparing to remove the bearing race

3.5b Pulling the bearing race free

3.6a Prise out the circlip and discard it

3.6b Bearing kits may contain a different style circlip

3.7 Drive out the old bearing with a suitable tube or old socket

3.8 Remove the pick-up ring

Tap the race at the top and both sides (even turn the flange over in the vice) to stop it jamming as it comes off.

6 Now the bearing itself must be removed. First, remove the large bearing retaining circlip, using a pair of circlip pliers or small screwdriver **(see illustrations)**.

7 After applying a generous amount of spray lubricant, we were able to drive the bearing out, using a large socket **(see illustration)**. Avoid damaging the pick-up ring for the wheel speed sensor. Mount the swivel hub across two large blocks of wood (or even bricks) – putting it across the open jaws of a vice might result in damage to the vice, owing to the amount of force which will be necessary.

8 Remove the pick-up ring for the wheel speed sensor **(see illustration)** and then using emery paper, clean off any burrs or raised

edges from the hub flange and hub carrier, which might stop the components going back together.

9 Apply a light coat of lubricant to the inside of the hub carrier, and to the outside of the new bearing. Refit the pick-up ring **(Note:** *Nissan recommend that the ring should be renewed with the wheel bearing, although it is not part of the wheel bearing kit)*. Start fitting the bearing by offering it squarely into the carrier, then give it a few light taps with a soft-faced hammer all round to locate it – keep the bearing square as this is done, or it will jam.

10 The new bearing contains the magnetic ring for the wheel speed sensor. Do not drop it or subject it to the influence of strong magnetic fields. The magnet side of the bearing must be inboard when fitted. The correct side will be

marked on the packaging, but not necessarily on the bearing, so take all precautions to ensure the bearing is fitted the correct way round **(see illustration)**.

11 Fitting the bearing by tapping it in all the way with a hammer will likely damage it. We used a length of threaded bar (available from motor factors, DIY stores, etc), with two nuts, some large washers and two drilled plates on the outside and inside of the hub carrier **(see illustrations)**.

12 The hub carrier bearing housing has a flange, so the bearing can be pressed in until fully home. Just before the bearing is finally in place locate the wheel speed sensor pick-up ring in the correct position **(see illustration)**. When the bearing is in place, refit the bearing retaining circlip.

13 The hub flange can be pressed into the

3.10 The new bearing is clearly marked

3.11a Ready to pull the bearing into the hub

3.11b Slowly pull the bearing home. Check that it always remains square to the housing

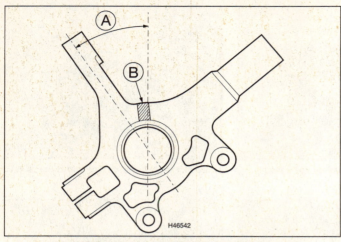

3.12 Correct location of the pick-up ring

A 33° to 37°   B Paint mark

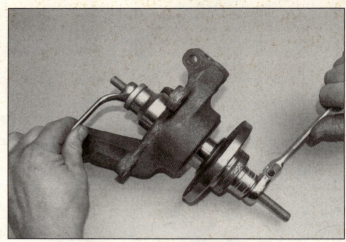

3.13 Pull the flange into the bearing

new bearing using a very similar method to the one just used, but substitute the plates with old sockets **(see illustration)**.

14 On completion, refit the swivel hub as described in Section 2.

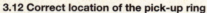

4 Front suspension strut –
removal, overhaul and refitting

Removal

1 Disconnect the battery negative lead, and

4.2 Precisely mark the position of the bolts

4.11 The spring compressors correctly located

position the lead away from the battery (also see *Disconnecting the battery*), and then remove the wiper and front cowl as described in Chapter 12.

2 Mark the position of the bolts on the strut tower. There is considerable play in the front strut when the bolts are loosened. Marking their position precisely will avoid having to have the camber adjusted after completing any necessary work **(see illustration)**.

3 Loosen, but do not remove the bolts,

4 Apply the handbrake; slacken the relevant front wheel nuts, then jack up the front of the car and support securely on axle stands (see

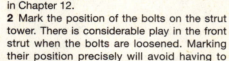

4.7 Removing the anti-roll bar link arm

4.12 Removing the strut securing nut

Jacking and vehicle support). Remove the roadwheel.

5 Disconnect the wiring to the wheel speed sensor and prise it free from the bracket on the strut tower.

6 Remove the retaining clip securing the brake flexible hose. Release the hose and wiring from the strut.

7 Unbolt the ant-roll bar link arm from the strut. A Torx fitting is provided in the balljoint to prevent it from rotating while the nut is unscrewed **(see illustration)**.

8 Remove the nuts from the two bolts used to secure the swivel hub to the base of the suspension strut. Note which way the bolts are fitted (this should be from the front). Tap the bolts out, then separate the strut base from the hub.

9 All that's holding the strut in place now are the three top mounting bolts on top of the inner wing.

10 Support the strut from under the wheel arch then, working in the engine compartment, unscrew the three suspension strut top mounting nuts. Lower the strut out, and remove it from under the wheel arch.

Overhaul

Note: *A spring compressor tool will be required for this operation.*

11 With the suspension strut resting on a bench, or clamped in a vice, fit a spring compressor tool, and compress the coil spring to relieve the pressure on the spring seats. Ensure that the compressor tool is securely located on the spring, in accordance with the tool manufacturer's instructions **(see illustration)**.

12 Using a suitable ring spanner and hex key, loosen and remove the strut top nut **(see illustration)**. Discard the nut, and obtain a new one for refitting.

13 Remove the top mounting plate, bearing, dust boot and the spring (with compressor tool still fitted) **(see illustrations)**.

14 With the strut assembly now completely dismantled, examine all the components for wear, damage or deformation, and check the thrust bearing for smoothness of operation. Renew any of the components as necessary.

15 Examine the strut for signs of fluid leakage. Check the strut piston for signs of pitting along its entire length, and check the strut body for signs of damage. While holding it in an upright position, test the operation of the strut by moving the piston through a full stroke, and then through short strokes of 50 to 100 mm. In both cases, the resistance felt should be smooth and continuous. If the resistance is jerky or uneven or if there is any visible sign of wear or damage to the strut, renewal is necessary.

16 If any doubt exists as to the condition of the coil spring, carefully remove the spring compressors and check the spring for distortion and signs of cracking. Renew the spring if it is damaged or distorted, or if there is any doubt as to its condition.

17 Inspect all other components for damage or deterioration, and renew any that are suspect.

18 If the spring compressor tool has been removed from the spring, refit it and compress the spring sufficiently to enable it to be refitted to the strut.

19 Slide the spring over the strut, and position it so that the lower end of the spring is resting against the stop on the lower seat. The narrower coils fit toward the strut. A mark may also be present one coil up from the bottom. This is the bottom of the coil and must seat on the strut.

20 Slide the dust boot into position, and fit the upper bearing separately or with the top mounting.

21 Refit the upper spring seat, and rotate it as necessary to position the stop against the upper end of the spring – in this position, the RH (or LH) marking on top should point to the front of the vehicle.

22 Fit a new piston rod nut, and tighten to the specified torque. Prevent the upper spring seat from turning using a hex key as for loosening.

23 Slowly slacken the spring compressor tool to relieve the tension in the spring. Check that the ends of the spring locate correctly against the stops on the spring seats. If necessary, turn the spring and the upper seat so that the components locate correctly before the compressor tool is removed. Remove the compressor tool when the spring is fully seated.

Refitting

24 Refitting is a reversal of removal, bearing in mind the following points:
a) Fit the swivel hub-to-strut bolts in from the front.
b) Tighten all fixings to the specified torque.
c) Have the front wheel alignment checked on completion.

4.13a Remove the top mount and bearing . . .

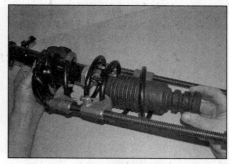

4.13b . . . and then the boot and combined bump stop

5 Front suspension anti-roll bar – removal and refitting

Note: *If it is wished to renew just the anti-roll bar drop links and/or bushes, this can be accomplished with much less additional dismantling than described below for removing the bar itself.*

Removal

1 Apply the handbrake, loosen the front wheel nuts, then jack up the front of the car and support it on axle stands (see *Jacking and vehicle support*). Remove both front wheels and the engine lower covers.

2 Unscrew and remove the track rod balljoint nuts. Using a balljoint separator tool if necessary, detach the track rods from the swivel hubs.

3 Remove the anti-roll bar drop links as described in Section 4 and then remove the subframe vertical supports.

4 Referring to Chapter 4B if necessary, unbolt the exhaust downpipe and remove the mounting from the subframe.

5 Unbolt and remove the rear engine steady-bar.

6 Remove the nuts and bolts securing the steering rack in position.

7 Using a block of wood on a trolley jack support the subframe. Make sure the jack does not obscure the subframe mounting bolts. Remove the bolts and then lower the subframe just enough to gain access to the bolts holding the anti-roll bar brackets in place.

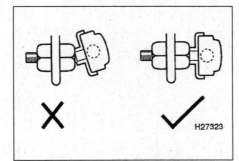

5.10 Correct alignment of the link arm

8 On automatic models remove the two bolts securing each clamp to the subframe, then lift the clamp from the anti-roll bar. Manual transmission models only have one bolt per clamp. The other leg of the clamp locks into the subframe. The rubber bushes are split, and can be removed once the clamps are taken off. Note that automatic models have a two-piece bush fitted.

9 Manoeuvre the anti-roll bar out between the subframe, suspension arms, exhaust system, and the underside of the car.

Refitting

10 Refitting is a reversal of removal, bearing in mind the following points:
a) Tighten all fixings to the specified torque.
b) Use new nuts on the drop links and align them correctly **(see illustration)**.
c) Have the front wheel alignment checked on completion.

6 Front suspension lower arm – removal and refitting

Removal

1 Slacken the front wheel nuts on the side concerned, then apply the handbrake, jack up the front of the car, and support securely on axle stands (see *Jacking and vehicle support*). Remove the roadwheel.

2 Undo the nut and remove the pinch-bolt from the balljoint. Push the end of the lower arm down to free the balljoint from the swivel hub. If the balljoint is very tight, it may be necessary to lever it down using a large screwdriver, or similar tool, but take care not to damage the balljoint rubber seal **(see illustration 2.10a)**.

3 Remove the lower arm front pivot bolt, then unscrew the rear mounting bolt and remove the lower arm from under the car.

Overhaul

4 Examine the rubber bushes and the suspension lower balljoint for wear and damage. At the time of writing, the balljoint and rubber bushes could not be renewed on the lower arm. Renew the complete lower arm if there is any wear or damage.

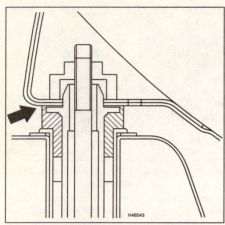

8.16 Use a feeler gauge to check the subframe bush. There should be no clearance between the bush and the body

Refitting

5 Refitting is a reversal of removal, bearing in mind the following points:
a) Tighten all fixings to the specified torque.
b) The lower arm front pivot bolt and rear mounting bolt should be tightened firmly by hand initially. When the wheels are refitted and the car is lowered so the weight is fully on the suspension, tighten both bolts to their specified torques.
c) Use a new nut on the lower arm balljoint nut.
d) Have the front wheel alignment checked on completion.

7 Front suspension lower arm balljoint – renewal

If the lower arm balljoint is worn, or the rubber seal is damaged, the complete lower arm must be renewed as described in Section 6. At the time of writing, the balljoint could not be renewed separately from the lower arm, as it is pressed and possibly bonded in place during manufacture.

8 Front suspension subframe – removal and refitting

Removal

1 Make sure the front wheels (and steering wheel) are in the straight-ahead position. If possible, lock the steering in this position using the steering column lock.
2 Removal of the subframe is a similar procedure to removal of the anti-roll bar as described in section 5.
3 Slacken the front wheel nuts. Apply the handbrake, then jack up the front of the car, and support securely on axle stands (see *Jacking and vehicle support*). For obvious reasons, do not support the car under the

subframe, nor in such a way as to hinder lowering the subframe out. Remove the roadwheels.
4 Slacken the track rod end balljoint nut, and unscrew it as far as the ends of the threads.
5 Disconnect the track rod end balljoints from the swivel hubs using a balljoint separator tool (leave the nuts fitted to protect the threads), taking care not to damage the balljoint rubber seals. Once the balljoints have been released, remove the balljoint nuts.
6 Remove nut and pinch-bolt from the lower arm balljoint. Push the ends of the lower arms down to free the balljoints from the swivel hubs. If a balljoint is very tight, it may be necessary to lever down using a large screwdriver, or similar tool, but take care not to damage the balljoint rubber seal.
7 Referring to Chapter 4B if necessary, unbolt and remove the exhaust downpipe. Remove the exhaust mounting and rear engine steady-bar.
8 Unbolt and remove the subframe support bars fitted to the subframe front.
9 Unbolt and remove the steering rack bolts. Using rope or strong cord tie up and support the steering rack.
10 Support the subframe from below, using at least two substantial jacks (one either side).
11 With the subframe securely supported, progressively loosen the four mounting bolts.
12 Undo and remove the bolts securing the subframe support panel and then remove it.
13 When all the bolts have been removed, check once more that nothing is still attached to the subframe, and that nothing is still fitted which would hinder it from being lowered. With the help of an assistant, lower the subframe and remove it from under the car.
14 Check the fixing bolts for damage to the threads. Renew them if any damage is found.

Refitting

15 With the help of an assistant, position the subframe on the jacks, then raise the jack to lift the subframe into position under the car. Line up the mounting holes as the subframe is raised into position.
16 The remainder of refitting is a reversal of removal, noting the following points:
a) Tighten the two long bolts first, and then the two short bolts.

9.6 Removing the pick-up ring for the wheel speed sensor

b) Use a feeler gauge to check the contact position of the mounting bush **(see illustration)**.
c) Tighten all fixings to the specified torque.
d) Have the front wheel alignment checked on completion.

9 Rear hub and bearings – inspection and renewal

Note: *The rear hub and bearing are a complete unit. If the rear bearings are worn, a new bearing must be fitted to the drum. There is no separate hub. The ABS rear wheel sensor is fitted to the hub, and while it can be removed and refitted, Nissan recommend a new one should always be fitted.*

Inspection

1 The rear hub bearings are non-adjustable.
2 To check the bearings for excessive wear, chock the front wheels, then jack up the rear of the vehicle and support it on axle stands. Fully release the handbrake.
3 Grip the rear wheel at the top and bottom, and attempt to rock it. If excessive movement is noted, or if there is any roughness or vibration felt when the wheel is spun, it is indicative that the hub bearings are worn.

Removal

4 Loosen the rear wheel nuts, then chock the front wheels (or engage a gear). Jack up the rear of the car, and support it on axle stands (see *Jacking and vehicle support*). Remove the rear wheel.
5 Remove the brake drum as described in Chapter 9. While the drum is removed, it would make sense to inspect the rear brake components for wear, and the wheel cylinder for signs of fluid leakage.
6 Using a pair of water-pump pliers, gently work the ABS rotor free from the drum and hub assembly **(see illustration)**.
7 Remove the circlip next. Use circlip pliers or a small screwdriver **(see illustrations)**.
8 Using a length of threaded bar and a combination of old sockets and a drilled metal plate, withdraw the bearing from the drum **(see illustrations)**.

9.7a Locate the circlip eyes

9.7b Use circlip pliers . . .

9.7c . . . to remove it

9.8a A suitable socket is fitted to the inside . . .

Refitting

9 Refitting is a reversal of removal, noting the following points:
  a) *Arrange the threaded bar such that the socket only pulls on the outer edge of the bearing (see illustrations).*
  b) *Always fit a new circlip and bearing.*
  c) *Use a block of wood to press fit the ABS rotor.*
  d) *Refit the brake drum as described in Chapter 9.*

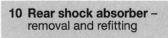

10 Rear shock absorber – removal and refitting

Removal

1 Working in the boot, remove the boot side trim to gain access to the shock absorber top nut as described in Chapter 11.

2 Using a spanner to hold the flat section of the shock absorber piston rod loosen the nut. Leave the nut fitted just by a few threads, until the lower mounting has been removed and the shock absorber is ready to be lowered out.

3 Slacken the relevant rear wheel nuts. Chock the front wheels, select 1st gear, then jack up the rear of the car, and support securely on axle stands (see *Jacking and vehicle support*). Remove the rear roadwheel.

4 Support the 'trailing arm' section of the beam axle using a trolley jack, then unscrew

9.8b . . . and a short length of box section pipe is fitted to the outside

9.8d . . . and then use two wheel bolts to space the metal plate away from the drum

the shock absorber lower mounting bolt (see illustration).

5 Lower the trailing arm on the jack. Support the shock absorber, then remove the upper

9.8c Fit nuts and draw the bearing out until it is flush with the housing . . .

9.8e Continue to tighten until the bearing comes free

mounting nut, and remove the unit from under the wheel arch. Recover the shock absorber top washer and rubber bush from the mounting inside the boot.

9.9a Arrange a suitable socket on the inside . . .

9.9b . . . and then fit the plate to the outside to draw the bearing in

9.9c Exchange the plate for a socket when the bearing is flush with housing to complete the installation

10.4 Support the trailing arm and remove the bolt

Refitting

6 Ensure that the shock absorber is fully reassembled before offering it into position – check that the upper mounting(s) have been refitted (or transferred to the new unit, where applicable).

7 Fit the lower mounting nut first, and tighten it by hand only at this stage.

8 Raise the trailing arm using the jack, and fit the top mounting through the hole under the wheel arch. Fit the upper mounting and washer, then fit and tighten the nut so that top rubber insulator is slightly compressed.

9 Refit the wheel, then lower the car to the ground, and tighten the wheel nuts to the specified torque.

10 Bounce the rear of the car a couple of times to settle the rear suspension, then tighten the shock absorber lower mounting nut to the specified torque. Finally tighten the upper mounting to the specified torque and refit the trim.

11 Rear spring – removal and refitting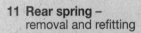

Removal

1 Slacken the rear wheel nuts. Chock the front wheels, select 1st gear, then jack up the rear of the car, and support securely on axle stands (see *Jacking and vehicle support*). Remove both rear roadwheels.

2 Support the 'trailing arm' section of the beam axle using a trolley jack, then unscrew the shock absorber lower mounting bolt.

13.3 Remove the electrical connector

12.2 Remove the two rear brake flexible hoses

3 Slowly lower the trailing arms on the jack, until the spring tension is released, and the springs can be pulled out of their location. We found it was best to remove the jack, and then press down the trailing arm to remove the spring – make sure, however, that no excess strain is placed on the brake hoses.

4 Recover the spring upper and lower mounting rubbers, noting how they are fitted. If they are in poor condition, fit new ones.

Refitting

5 Refitting is a reversal of removal, noting the following points:
  a) Make sure the spring is properly engaged in the upper and lower mounts.
  b) Delay fully tightening the shock absorber lower mounting nut to its specified torque until the car is resting on its wheels.

12 Rear axle assembly – removal and refitting

Removal

1 Slacken the rear wheel nuts. Chock the front wheels, select 1st gear, then jack up the rear of the car, and support securely on axle stands (see *Jacking and vehicle support*). Remove the rear roadwheels.

2 Disconnect the rear brake flexible hoses from the rear axle. Anticipate some fluid spillage – if possible, clamp the hoses before disconnecting them. Slide out the metal clip used to secure the hose each side and move the hoses clear of the axle **(see illustration)**.

13.5 Loosen the securing bolt

3 Unbolt the brackets for the handbrake cable, and the ABS sensor from the rear axle. Move the cables and wiring clear as far as possible, so that it does not get caught up when the axle is lowered.

4 Remove the rear hubs, brake shoes and handbrake cables as described in Chapter 9.

5 Remove the rear springs as described in Section 11.

6 Support the rear axle using two substantial jacks, one at each end. Having an assistant will also be useful – the axle is a heavy and awkward assembly to remove without help.

7 Make a final check that nothing is still attached to the axle which would hamper its removal.

8 With the axle securely supported, unscrew and remove the pivot bolt each side. Lower the axle on the jacks, making sure that nothing gets caught, until it can be withdrawn from under the car.

Refitting

9 Refitting of the axle assembly is a reversal of removal, bearing in mind the following points:
  a) Do not fully tighten the axle mounting bolts, or the shock absorber lower mounting nuts, until the weight of the car is resting on its wheels.
  b) Tighten all fixings to the specified torque.
  c) Refit the springs and rear hubs as described in Sections 11 and 9 respectively.
  d) Bleed the brakes as described in Chapter 9.

13 Steering wheel – removal and refitting

Removal

1 Disconnect the battery negative lead, and position the lead away from the battery (also see *Disconnecting the battery*). Wait at least five minutes before proceeding. If this waiting period is not observed, there is a danger of accidentally activating the airbag(s).

2 Remove the airbag unit from the steering wheel as described in Chapter 12.

3 Unplug the wiring connector at the steering wheel **(see illustration)**.

4 Ensure that the front wheels are pointing in the straight-ahead position, and if possible, engage the steering lock in this position.

5 Prevent the steering wheel turning by grasping the rim firmly, then unscrew but do not remove the steering wheel securing bolt **(see illustration)**. Do not rely on the steering column lock to prevent the wheel turning, as this may damage the lock.

> **HAYNES HINT** *Don't unscrew the bolt all the way – leave it in by a thread or two. This way, if excess effort is needed to pull the wheel off its splines, the wheel won't suddenly fly off and cause injury.*

6 Grip the steering wheel on each side (or top and bottom), then pull and withdraw it from the splines on the end of the column. The wheel may prove difficult to remove from its splines. Nissan have provided two M8 threaded holes in the wheel hub, for use with a puller. If a puller is not available, a home-made alternative can be made.

7 Once the wheel has released, remove the securing bolt completely, and withdraw the wheel, taking care to feed the cable for the airbag through the wheel (see illustration).

Refitting

8 Make sure that the front wheels are pointing in the straight-ahead position, then fit the steering wheel to the column.

9 Refit the steering wheel securing bolt, and tighten to the specified torque – again, do not rely on the steering column lock to hold the wheel as the bolt is tightened. Double-check that the steering wheel is fully engaged with the splines by gripping it and gently rocking while pressing down firmly, then tighten the bolt again to the specified torque.

10 The remainder of the refitting procedure is a reversal of removal. Refit the airbag unit as described in Chapter 12.

14 Steering column and power steering – removal and refitting

Removal

1 Disconnect the battery negative lead, and position the lead away from the battery

13.7 Removing the steering wheel

(also see *Disconnecting the battery*). Wait at least five minutes before proceeding. If this waiting period is not observed, there is a danger of accidentally activating the airbag(s).

2 Remove the airbag unit from the steering wheel as described in Chapter 12.

3 Move the driver's seat fully to the rear, to allow maximum working area. Alternatively remove the seat completely as described in Chapter 11.

4 Remove the three screws securing the steering column lower shroud, and lower it out (see illustrations).

5 Remove the airbag clockspring and steering column switches as described in Chapter 12.

6 On models with automatic transmission, disconnect the shift lock cable from the ignition switch as described in Chapter 7B, and unclip the cable from the steering column as necessary.

7 Remove the plastic tray panel from under the instrument panel and then remove the

dashboard upper panel as described in Chapter 11.

8 Disconnect the wiring connectors from the ignition switch, noting their fitted positions and then working from above disconnect the wiring to the power steering motor and control unit. Access is extremely tight here, so consider partly removing the column and shaft to gain room to remove the electrical plugs. Work the cable free from the cable clips.

9 Remove the column lower mounting bolt and then loosen, but do not remove the two upper bolts that secure the column and motor to the support beam (see illustration).

10 The motor and column are heavy items and an assistant will be required to manoeuvre the assembly out from under the dashboard. If forced to work on your own, then consider supporting the assembly with a rope tied to the crossmember.

11 Remove the bolts from the upper mounting, and carefully withdraw the column from the car (see illustration).

12 Do not at any point allow the shaft to rotate more than 360°. If this should happen the steering angle sensor will have to be recalibrated by a Nissan dealer using diagnostic equipment.

13 If the intermediate shaft upper pinch-bolt is removed it must be refitted in the correct position (see illustration).

Refitting

14 Refitting is a reversal of removal, bearing in mind the following points:
a) Tighten all fixings to the specified torque.
b) Refit the driver's airbag and the clockspring unit as described in Chapter 12.

14.4a The shroud locating screws

14.4b Remove the lower shroud . . .

14.4c . . . and the upper

14.9 Remove the lower pinch-bolt

14.11 Manoeuvring the column and power steering assembly from the dashboard

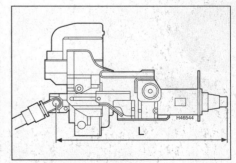

14.13 Set the pinch-bolt so that the dimension L = 429 mm

15.2a Remove the outer spring clip . . .

15.2b . . . and cut off the inner plastic tie

15.2c Pull the boot from the rack

16.5 The steering rack mounting bolts

15 Steering rack rubber gaiters – renewal

1 Remove the relevant track rod end as described in Section 17.

2 Remove the inboard and outboard securing clips, then slide the gaiter off the end of the track rod **(see illustrations)**.
3 Thoroughly clean the track rod, then slide the new gaiter into position.
4 Fit the gaiter securing clips, using new clips if necessary, making sure that the gaiter is not twisted.

17.2 Measure the exposed threads

17.3a Use a Torx key to stop the swivel from rotating

17.3b Just loosen the locknut

17.5a Unscrew the track rod end . . .

5 Refit the track rod end as described in Section 17.

16 Steering rack – removal and refitting

Removal

1 Working inside the car remove the steering column lower pinch-bolt as described in Section 14. If not already done so make sure the steering wheel lock is engaged.
2 Jack up the front of the car, and support it on axle stands (see *Jacking and vehicle support*), and remove the wheels.
3 Using a balljoint spliter remove the track rod ends from the swivel hub as described in Section 17.
4 Remove the exhaust downpipe as described in Chapter 4B.
5 Unbolt and remove the nuts and bolts that secure the rack to the subframe **(see illustration)**.
6 Withdraw the steering rack towards the right-hand side of the car.

Refitting

7 Refitting is a reversal of removal, noting the following points:
  a) *Tighten all fixings to the specified torque.*
  b) *Fit new nuts to the rack bolt, track rod ends and column pinch-bolt.*

17 Track rod end – removal and refitting

Note: *A balljoint separator tool will be required for this operation.*

Removal

1 Slacken the relevant front wheel nuts. Apply the handbrake, then jack up the front of the car, and support securely on axle stands (see *Jacking and vehicle support*). Remove the roadwheel.
2 Measure the exposed number of threads on the track rod, as a guide to refitting **(see illustration)**.
3 Slacken the track rod end balljoint nut, and unscrew it as far as the ends of the threads. With the joint still in position slacken the locknut on the track rod **(see illustrations)**.
4 Disconnect the track rod end balljoint from the swivel hub using a balljoint separator tool (leave the nut fitted to protect the threads), taking care not to damage the balljoint rubber seal. Once the balljoint has been released, remove the balljoint nut.
5 If the same track rod is to be refitted, mark its position relative to the steering track rod. Slacken the track rod end locknut, and then unscrew the track rod end from the track rod **(see illustrations)**.

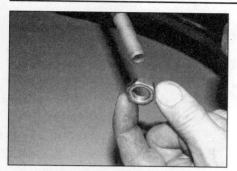

17.5b . . . and remove the locknut

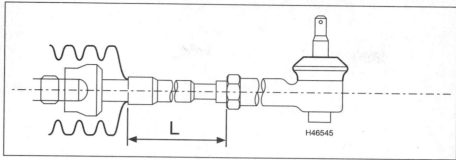

H46545

17.6 Initial setting position for the track rod end

L = 62.6 mm

Refitting

6 Screw the track rod end onto the track rod until it is exactly in the same position, noted before removal. If a new track rod end has been fitted (and it is not exactly the same as the original), screw it in place until it is in the position indicated in the illustration **(see illustration)**. This is the initial setting position. The tracking must be checked and adjusted if required.

7 Engage the track rod end balljoint pin with the swivel hub, then fit the new nut.

8 Refit the roadwheel, then lower the car to the ground, and tighten the wheel nuts.

9 Check the front wheel alignment at the earliest opportunity.

18 Wheel alignment and steering angles – general information

Front wheel alignment

1 Accurate front wheel alignment is essential to precise steering and for even tyre wear. Before considering the steering angles, check that the tyres are correctly inflated, that the front wheels are not buckled, the hub bearings are not worn, and that the steering linkage and front suspension are in good order, without slackness or wear at the joints.

2 Wheel alignment consists of four factors:

Camber, is the angle at which the roadwheels are set from the vertical when viewed from the front or rear of the car. Positive camber is the angle (in degrees) that the wheels are tilted outwards at the top from the vertical. The camber angle is given for reference only, and cannot be adjusted.

Castor, is the angle between the steering axis and a vertical line when viewed from each side of the car. Positive castor is indicated when the steering axis is inclined towards the rear of the car at its upper end. This angle is not adjustable.

Steering axis inclination (kingpin inclination), is the angle, when viewed from the front or rear of the car, between the vertical and an imaginary line drawn between the upper and lower front suspension strut mountings. This angle is not adjustable.

Toe, is the amount by which the distance between the front inside edges of the roadwheel rim differs from that between the rear inside edges. If the distance between the front edges is less than that at the rear, the wheels are said to toe-in. If the distance between the front inside edges is greater than that at the rear, the wheels toe-out.

3 Owing to the need for precision gauges to measure the small angles of the steering and suspension settings, it is preferable that checking of camber and castor is left to a service station having the necessary equipment. Camber and castor is set during production of the car, and any deviation from the specified angle will be due to accident damage or gross wear in the suspension mountings.

4 To check the front wheel alignment, first make sure that the lengths of both track rods are equal when the steering is in the straight-ahead position. The track rod lengths can be adjusted if necessary by releasing the locknuts from the track rod ends and rotating the track rods. If necessary, self-locking grips can be used to rotate the track rods.

5 Obtain a tracking gauge. These are available in various forms from accessory stores, or one can be fabricated from a length of steel tubing suitably cranked to clear the sump and transmission, and having a setscrew and locknut at one end.

6 With the gauge, measure the distances between the two wheel inner rims (at hub height) at the rear of the wheel. Push the car forward to rotate the wheel through 180° (half a turn) and measure the distance between the wheel inner rims, again at hub height, at the front of the wheel. This last measurement should differ from the first by the appropriate toe-in which is given in the Specifications. The car must be on level ground.

7 If the toe-in is found to be incorrect, release the track rod end locknuts and turn both track rods equally. Only turn them a quarter-of-a-turn at a time before rechecking the alignment. If necessary use self-locking grips to turn the track rods – **do not** grip the threaded part of the track rod during adjustment. It is important not to allow the track rods to become unequal in length during adjustment, otherwise the alignment of the steering wheel will become incorrect and tyre scrubbing will occur on turns.

8 On completion tighten the locknuts without disturbing the setting. Check that the track rod end balljoint is at the centre of its arc of travel (ie, not twisted to the front or rear).

Rear wheel alignment

9 Figures are provided in the Specifications for rear wheel camber and toe-setting are for reference only. No adjustment is possible, so any significant deviation from the quoted figures is likely to be due to accident damage, or possibly to poor reassembly. Refer to paragraph 2 for a description of the settings.

Notes

Chapter 11
Bodywork and fittings

Contents

	Section number
Body exterior fittings – removal and refitting	20
Bonnet – removal, refitting and adjustment	7
Bonnet lock – removal and refitting	9
Bonnet release cable – removal and refitting	8
Bumpers – removal and refitting	6
Central locking system components – general information	16
Centre console – removal and refitting	24
Door handles and locks – removal and refitting	12
Door inner trim panel – removal and refitting	11
Door window glass and regulator – removal and refitting	13
Doors – removal and refitting	10
Electric window components – removal and refitting	17
Exterior mirrors and associated components – removal and refitting	18
Facia assembly – removal and refitting	25

	Section number
General information	1
Hinge and lock lubrication	See Chapter 1
Interior trim and fittings – removal and refitting	23
Maintenance – bodywork and underframe	2
Maintenance – upholstery and carpets	3
Major body damage – repair	5
Minor body damage – repair	4
Seat belt check	See Chapter 1
Seat belt components – removal and refitting	23
Seats – removal and refitting	21
Tailgate and support struts – removal, refitting and adjustment	14
Tailgate lock components – removal and refitting	15
Windscreen, side and tailgate glass – general information	19

Degrees of difficulty

| **Easy,** suitable for novice with little experience | 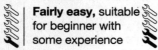 | **Fairly easy,** suitable for beginner with some experience | | **Fairly difficult,** suitable for competent DIY mechanic | | **Difficult,** suitable for experienced DIY mechanic | | **Very difficult,** suitable for expert DIY or professional | |

Specifications

Torque wrench settings	Nm	lbf ft
Bonnet hinge bolts	11	8
Bumper mountings	13	10
Door check strap bolts	30	22
Front seat mounting bolts	25	18
Hinge bolts:		
Front doors	43	32
Rear doors	25	18
Tailgate	11	8
Lock striker:		
Doors	23	17
Tailgate	11	8
Rear seat hinge bolts	37	27
Seat belt mounting bolts	48	38

1 General information

The bodyshell is of three- and five-door Hatchback configurations, and is made of pressed-steel sections. Most components are welded together, but some use is made of structural adhesives. The front wings are bolted on.

The bonnet, doors and some other vulnerable panels are made of zinc-coated metal, and are further protected by being coated with an anti-chip primer prior to being sprayed.

Extensive use is made of plastic materials, mainly in the interior, but also in exterior components. The front and rear bumpers are injection-moulded from a synthetic material which is very strong, and yet light. Plastic components such as wheel arch liners are fitted to the underside of the car, to improve the body's resistance to corrosion.

2 Maintenance – bodywork and underframe

The general condition of a car's bodywork is the one thing that significantly affects its value. Maintenance is easy, but needs to be regular. Neglect, particularly after minor damage, can lead quickly to further deterioration and costly repair bills. It is important also to keep watch on those parts of the car not immediately visible, for instance the underside, inside all the wheelarches, and the lower part of the engine compartment.

The basic maintenance routine for the bodywork is washing – preferably with a lot of water, from a hose. This will remove all the loose solids which may have stuck to the car. It is important to flush these off in such a way as to prevent grit from scratching the finish. The wheelarches and underframe need washing in the same way, to remove any accumulated mud which will retain moisture and tend to encourage rust. Paradoxically enough, the best time to clean the underframe and wheel arches is in wet weather, when the mud is thoroughly wet and soft. In very wet weather, the underframe is usually cleaned of large accumulations automatically, and this is a good time for inspection.

Periodically, except on models with a wax-based underbody protective coating, it is a good idea to have the whole of the underframe of the car steam-cleaned, engine compartment included, so that a thorough inspection can be carried out to see what minor repairs and renovations are necessary. Steam-cleaning is available at many garages, and is necessary for the removal of the accumulation of oily grime, which sometimes is allowed to become thick in certain areas. If steam-cleaning facilities are not available, there are one or two excellent grease solvents available, which can be brush-applied; the dirt can then be simply hosed off. Note that these methods should not be used on cars with wax-based underbody protective coating, or the coating will be removed. Such cars should be inspected annually, preferably just prior to Winter, when the underbody should be washed down, and any damage to the wax coating repaired. Ideally, a completely fresh coat should be applied. It would also be worth considering the use of such wax-based protection for injection into door panels, sills, box sections, etc, as an additional safeguard against rust damage, where such protection is not provided by the manufacturer.

After washing paintwork, wipe off with a chamois leather to give an unspotted clear finish. A coat of clear protective wax polish will give added protection against chemical pollutants in the air. If the paintwork sheen has dulled or oxidised, use a cleaner/polisher combination to restore the brilliance of the shine. This requires a little effort, but such dulling is usually caused because regular washing has been neglected. Care needs to be taken with metallic paintwork, as special non-abrasive cleaner/polisher is required to avoid damage to the finish. Always check that the door and ventilator opening drain holes and pipes are completely clear, so that water can be drained out. Brightwork should be treated in the same way as paintwork. Windscreens and windows can be kept clear of the smeary film which often appears, by the use of proprietary glass cleaner. Never use any form of wax, or other body or chromium polish, on glass.

3 Maintenance – upholstery and carpets

Mats and carpets should be brushed or vacuum-cleaned regularly, to keep them free of grit. If they are badly stained, remove them from the car for scrubbing or sponging, and make quite sure they are dry before refitting. Seats and interior trim panels can be kept clean by wiping with a damp cloth. If they do become stained (which can be more apparent on light-coloured upholstery), use a little liquid detergent and a soft nail brush to scour the grime out of the grain of the material. Do not forget to keep the headlining clean in the same way as the upholstery. When using liquid cleaners inside the car, do not over-wet the surfaces being cleaned. Excessive damp could get into the seams and padded interior, causing stains, offensive odours or even rot. If the inside of the car gets wet accidentally, it is worthwhile taking some trouble to dry it out properly, particularly where carpets are involved. *Do not leave oil or electric heaters inside the car for this purpose.*

4 Minor body damage – repair

Repairs of minor scratches

If the scratch is very superficial, and does not penetrate to the metal of the bodywork, repair is very simple. Lightly rub the area of the scratch with a paintwork renovator, or a very fine cutting paste, to remove loose paint from the scratch, and to clear the surrounding bodywork of wax polish. Rinse the area with clean water.

In the case of metallic paint (and some solid colours), the most commonly-found scratches are not in the basecoat paint, but in the lacquer top coat, and appear white. If care is taken, these can sometimes be rendered less obvious by very careful use of paintwork renovator (which would otherwise not be used on metallic paintwork); otherwise, repair of these scratches can be achieved by applying lacquer with a fine brush.

Apply touch-up paint to the scratch using a fine paint brush; continue to apply fine layers of paint until the surface of the paint in the scratch is level with the surrounding paintwork. Allow the new paint at least two weeks to harden, then blend it into the surrounding paintwork by rubbing the scratch area with a paintwork renovator or a very fine cutting paste. Finally, apply wax polish.

Where the scratch has penetrated right through to the metal of the bodywork, causing the metal to rust, a different repair technique is required. Remove any loose rust from the bottom of the scratch with a penknife, then apply rust-inhibiting paint, to prevent the formation of rust in the future. Using a rubber or nylon applicator, fill the scratch with bodystopper paste. If required, this paste can be mixed with cellulose thinners, to provide a very thin paste which is ideal for filling narrow scratches. Before the stopper-paste in the scratch hardens, wrap a piece of smooth cotton rag around the top of a finger. Dip the finger in cellulose thinners, and quickly sweep it across the surface of the stopper-paste in the scratch; this will ensure that the surface of the stopper-paste is slightly hollowed. The scratch can now be painted over as described earlier in this Section.

Repairs of dents

When deep denting of the bodywork has taken place, the first task is to pull the dent out, until the affected bodywork almost attains its original shape. There is little point in trying to restore the original shape completely, as the metal in the damaged area will have stretched on impact, and cannot be reshaped fully to its original contour. It is better to bring the level of the dent up to a point which is about 3 mm below the level of the surrounding bodywork. In cases where the dent is very shallow anyway, it is not worth trying to pull it out at all. If the underside of the dent is accessible, it can be hammered out gently from behind, using a mallet with a wooden or plastic head. Whilst doing this, hold a suitable block of wood firmly against the outside of the panel, to absorb the impact from the hammer blows and thus prevent a large area of the bodywork from being 'belled-out'.

Should the dent be in a section of the bodywork which has a double skin, or some other factor making it inaccessible from behind, a different technique is called for. Drill several small holes through the metal inside the area – particularly in the deeper section. Then screw long self-tapping screws into the holes, just sufficiently for them to gain a good purchase in the metal. Now the dent can be pulled out by pulling on the protruding heads of the screws with a pair of pliers.

The next stage of the repair is the removal of the paint from the damaged area, and from an inch or so of the surrounding 'sound' bodywork. This is accomplished most easily by using a wire brush or abrasive pad on a power drill, although it can be done just as effectively by hand, using sheets of abrasive paper. To complete the preparation for filling, score the surface of the bare metal with a screwdriver or the tang of a file, or alternatively, drill small holes in the affected area. This will provide a really good 'key' for the filler paste.

To complete the repair, see the Section on filling and respraying.

Repairs of rust holes or gashes

Remove all paint from the affected area, and from an inch or so of the surrounding 'sound' bodywork, using an abrasive pad or a wire brush on a power drill. If these are not available, a few sheets of abrasive paper will do the job most effectively. With the paint removed, you will be able to judge the severity of the corrosion, and therefore decide whether to renew the whole panel (if this is possible) or to repair the affected area. New body panels are not as expensive as most people think, and it is often quicker and more satisfactory to fit a new panel than to attempt to repair large areas of corrosion.

Remove all fittings from the affected area, except those which will act as a guide to the original shape of the damaged bodywork (eg body side mouldings etc). Then, using tin snips or a hacksaw blade, remove all loose metal and any other metal badly affected by corrosion. Hammer the edges of the hole inwards, in order to create a slight depression for the filler paste.

Wire-brush the affected area to remove the powdery rust from the surface of the remaining metal. Paint the affected area with rust-inhibiting paint; if the back of the rusted area is accessible, treat this also.

Before filling can take place, it will be necessary to block the hole in some way. This can be achieved by the use of aluminium or plastic mesh, or aluminium tape.

Aluminium or plastic mesh, or glass-fibre matting, is probably the best material to use for a large hole. Cut a piece to the approximate size and shape of the hole to be filled, then position it in the hole so that its edges are below the level of the surrounding bodywork. It can be retained in position by several blobs of filler paste around its periphery.

Aluminium tape should be used for small or very narrow holes. Pull a piece off the roll, trim it to the approximate size and shape required, then pull off the backing paper (if used) and stick the tape over the hole; it can be overlapped if the thickness of one piece is insufficient. Burnish down the edges of the tape with the handle of a screwdriver or similar, to ensure that the tape is securely attached to the metal underneath.

Filling and respraying

Before using this Section, see the Sections on dent, deep scratch, rust holes and gash repairs.

Many types of bodyfiller are available, but generally speaking, those proprietary kits which contain a tin of filler paste and a tube of resin hardener are best for this type of repair. A wide, flexible plastic or nylon applicator will be found invaluable for imparting a smooth and well-contoured finish to the surface of the filler.

Mix up a little filler on a clean piece of card or board – measure the hardener carefully (follow the maker's instructions on the pack), otherwise the filler will set too rapidly or too slowly. Using the applicator, apply the filler paste to the prepared area; draw the applicator across the surface of the filler to achieve the correct contour and to level the surface. As soon as a contour that approximates to the correct one is achieved, stop working the paste – if you carry on too long, the paste will become sticky and begin to 'pick-up' on the applicator. Continue to add thin layers of filler paste at 20-minute intervals, until the level of the filler is just proud of the surrounding bodywork.

Once the filler has hardened, the excess can be removed using a metal plane or file. From then on, progressively-finer grades of abrasive paper should be used, starting with a 40-grade production paper, and finishing with a 400-grade wet-and-dry paper. Always wrap the abrasive paper around a flat rubber, cork, or wooden block – otherwise the surface of the filler will not be completely flat. During the smoothing of the filler surface, the wet-and-dry paper should be periodically rinsed in water. This will ensure that a very smooth finish is imparted to the filler at the final stage.

At this stage, the 'dent' should be surrounded by a ring of bare metal, which in turn should be encircled by the finely 'feathered' edge of the good paintwork. Rinse the repair area with clean water, until all of the dust produced by the rubbing-down operation has gone.

Spray the whole area with a light coat of primer – this will show up any imperfections in the surface of the filler. Repair these imperfections with fresh filler paste or bodystopper, and once more smooth the surface with abrasive paper. If bodystopper is used, it can be mixed with cellulose thinners, to form a really thin paste which is ideal for filling small holes. Repeat this spray-and-repair procedure until you are satisfied that the surface of the filler, and the feathered edge of the paintwork, are perfect. Clean the repair area with clean water, and allow to dry fully.

The repair area is now ready for final spraying. Paint spraying must be carried out in a warm, dry, windless and dust-free atmosphere. This condition can be created artificially if you have access to a large indoor working area, but if you are forced to work in the open, you will have to pick your day very carefully. If you are working indoors, dousing the floor in the work area with water will help to settle the dust which would otherwise be in the atmosphere. If the repair area is confined to one body panel, mask off the surrounding panels; this will help to minimise the effects of a slight mis-match in paint colours. Bodywork fittings (eg chrome strips, door handles etc) will also need to be masked off. Use genuine masking tape, and several thicknesses of newspaper, for the masking operations.

Before commencing to spray, agitate the aerosol can thoroughly, then spray a test area (an old tin, or similar) until the technique is mastered. Cover the repair area with a thick coat of primer; the thickness should be built up using several thin layers of paint, rather than one thick one. Using 400 grade wet-and-dry paper, rub down the surface of the primer until it is really smooth. While doing this, the work area should be thoroughly doused with water, and the wet-and-dry paper periodically rinsed in water. Allow to dry before spraying on more paint.

Spray on the top coat, again building up the thickness by using several thin layers of paint. Start spraying at the top of the repair area, and then, using a side-to-side motion, work downwards until the whole repair area and about two inches of the surrounding original paintwork is covered. Remove all masking material 10 to 15 minutes after spraying on the final coat of paint.

Allow the new paint at least two weeks to harden, then, using a paintwork renovator or a very fine cutting paste, blend the edges of the paint into the existing paintwork. Finally, apply wax polish.

Plastic components

With the use of more and more plastic body components by the car manufacturers (eg bumpers, spoilers, and in some cases, major body panels), rectification of more serious damage to such items has become a matter of either entrusting repair work to a specialist in this field, or renewing complete components. Repair of such damage by the DIY owner is not really feasible, owing to the cost of the equipment and materials required for effecting such repairs. The basic technique involves making a groove along the line of the

6.1 Note the locating tabs

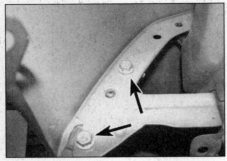

6.3 The front bumper bolts

crack in the plastic, using a rotary burr in a power drill. The damaged part is then welded back together, using a hot air gun to heat up and fuse a plastic filler rod into the groove. Any excess plastic is then removed, and the area rubbed down to a smooth finish. It is important that a filler rod of the correct plastic is used, as body components can be made of a variety of different types (eg polycarbonate, ABS, polypropylene).

Damage of a less serious nature (abrasions, minor cracks etc) can be repaired by the DIY owner using a two-part epoxy filler repair. Once mixed in equal, this is used in similar fashion to the bodywork filler used on metal panels. The filler is usually cured in twenty to thirty minutes, ready for sanding and painting.

If the owner is renewing a complete component himself, or if he has repaired it with epoxy filler, he will be left with the problem of finding a suitable paint for finishing which is compatible with the type of plastic used. At one time, the use of a universal paint was not possible, owing to the complex range of plastics encountered in body component applications. Standard paints, generally speaking, will not bond to plastic or rubber satisfactorily, but suitable paints to match any plastic or rubber finish, can be obtained from dealers. However, it is now possible to obtain a plastic body parts finishing kit which consists of a pre-primer treatment, a primer and coloured top coat. Full instructions are normally supplied with a kit, but basically, the method of use is to first apply the pre-primer to the component concerned, and allow it to dry for up to 30 minutes. Then the primer is applied, and left to dry for about an hour before finally applying the special-coloured

top coat. The result is a correctly-coloured component, where the paint will flex with the plastic or rubber, a property that standard paint does not normally posses.

5 Major body damage – repair

Where serious damage has occurred, or large areas need renewal due to neglect, it means that complete new panels will need welding-in, and this is best left to professionals. If the damage is due to impact, it will also be necessary to check completely the alignment of the bodyshell, and this can only be carried out accurately by a Nissan dealer using special jigs. If the body is left misaligned, it is primarily dangerous, as the car will not handle properly, and secondly, uneven stresses will be imposed on the steering, suspension and possibly transmission, causing abnormal wear, or complete failure, particularly to such items as the tyres.

6 Bumpers – removal and refitting

Front bumper
Removal

1 Open the bonnet, and remove the two grilles that hold the front indicator lamps. Prise free the retainer from the centre and then reach round the back of the unit and release the tangs at the rear **(see illustration)**. Remove the grille and unplug the wiring to the indicator lamps. Repeat the operation on the other side.

Temporarily refit the plastic fasteners. These will be removed last.

2 Jack up the front of the car, and support it on axle stands (see *Jacking and vehicle support*).

3 Remove the front wing liners and the bolts that hold the bumper in place **(see illustration)**. **Note:** *On later models the positions of the stud and bolt may be reversed to that shown.* There is no need to remove the complete liner, just remove the front plastic fittings and bend the liner enough to access the bolts.

4 Working along the front lower edge of the bumper, remove the plastic trim clips and two bolts along the lower edge.

5 Next remove the front foglight wiring connectors and the washer tube for the headlights. These items are only fitted to higher specification models.

6 Prise free the retaining clip just below the headlight and then prise free the clips at the junction with the front wing **(see illustrations)**. The bumper should now only be held in place by the two clips that were refitted when the grilles were removed. Remove the clips and recover the bumper.

7 Remove the polystyrene energy absorber next – it just pulls off, and then unbolt the reinforcement panel.

8 If required the bumper reinforcement mountings can be removed next. Three bolts hold each one in place. Remove the mounting, noting that the studs for mounting the bumper reinforcement are at the bottom of the mounting.

Refitting

9 Refitting is a reversal of removal. Have an assistant available to help align the bumper, and tighten the mountings securely.

10 Check the alignment of the bumper when finished. There should be little or no clearance between the bumper and front wing. The gap between the bumper and bonnet – measured at the centre – should be 5 to 7 mm. Clearance around the headlight should be between 3 and 7 mm.

Rear bumper
Removal

11 Jack up the rear of the car, and support it on axle stands (see *Jacking and vehicle support*).

12 Open the tailgate and remove the rear lamps as described in Chapter 12.

13 Working along the lower edge of the bumper

6.6a Locate the fixing . . .

6.6b . . . and remove it

6.6c Pull the bumper free from the front wing

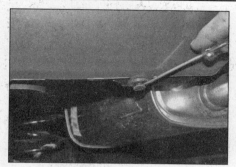

6.13 Remove the lower trim clips

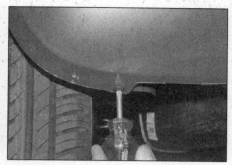

6.14a Remove the lower corner screw . . .

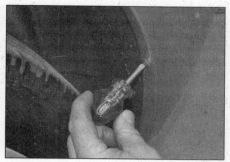

6.14b . . . and the screw in the wheel arch

6.14c If the liner is flexible there is just enough room to access the bolt

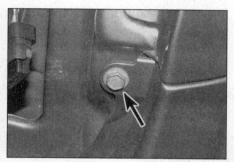

6.16 Rear bumper mounting screws are located beneath the rear light clusters

prise free the plastic trim clips. Pull out the centre peg first to remove these **(see illustration)**.

14 Next remove the rear wing liners. If you are working in a warm environment the panel should be flexible enough to just remove the rear clips and then bend the liner just sufficient to gain access to the single bolt at each side. Remove the bolts **(see illustrations)**.

15 The bumper is held in position below the rear wing by a tang that slots into the support panel. Pull the bumper away from the wing. It should pop off, if not use a small screwdriver to release the pawl.

16 The bumper is now only held in place by two screws below the rear lamp housing **(see illustration)**. Remove these and pull the bumper forward enough to disconnect the wiring to the number plate lamp and then remove the bumper. Where fitted, also disconnect the wiring from the parking aid sensors.

17 If required, remove the polystyrene shock absorbers and then remove the lower support panel.

Refitting

18 Refitting is a reversal of removal, but take care to slot the lower edge of the bumper correctly into the lower panel.

19 On completion check the alignment and make adjustments as required. There should be a clearance of between 6 and 10 mm between the tailgate and the bumper. The clearance between the rear lamp and bumper should be between 1 and 3 mm.

7 Bonnet –
removal, refitting and adjustment

Removal

1 Open the bonnet, and support it on its stay.
2 Using a marker pen or paint, mark around the hinge positions on the bonnet.
3 Disconnect the windscreen washer fluid hose from the connector on the driver's side

– there will be a small amount of washer fluid spillage when this is done **(see illustration)**.
4 With the aid of an assistant, support the bonnet, and unscrew the four bolts securing the bonnet to the hinges **(see illustration)**.
5 Lift off the bonnet.

Refitting

6 Align the marks made on the bonnet before removal, with the hinges, then refit and tighten the bonnet securing bolts.
7 Reconnect the washer hose, ensuring that it is pushed firmly onto the connector.
8 Check the bonnet adjustment as follows.

Adjustment

9 Close the bonnet, and check that there is an equal gap at each side, between the bonnet and the wing panels. Check also that the bonnet sits flush in relation to the surrounding body panels.
10 The bonnet should close smoothly and positively without excessive pressure. If this is not the case, adjustment will be required.
11 To adjust the bonnet alignment, slacken the bonnet securing bolts, and move the bonnet on the bolts as required (the bolt holes in the hinges are elongated). To adjust the bonnet closure, adjustable bump stops are fitted to the body front panel. These may be raised or lowered by screwing in or out as necessary. If desired, the bonnet lock can be adjusted as described in Section 9.

8 Bonnet release cable –
removal and refitting

Note: *If the cable has broken, use the information in this Section to establish which end of the cable has failed – if the break is inside the car, it may be possible to remove the release lever as described below, and operate the remains of the cable to get the bonnet open. If the break is under the bonnet, there are two ways the bonnet may be opened – through the radiator grille aperture, or from underneath. Even with the bonnet shut, it may still be possible to operate the lock through the grille with minimal damage, though access to the cable will be poor. From underneath, with the car jacked up and supported on axle stands, access to the bonnet lock operating lever may be a little better.*

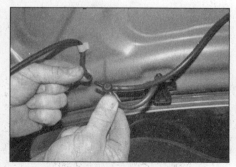

7.3 Remove the screen washer tube

7.4 The bonnet hinge nuts

8.3a Prise the outer cable free . . .

8.3b . . . remove the spring . . .

8.3c . . . and unhook the inner cable

Removal

1 The bonnet release lever is located on the lower facia panel, to the right of the steering wheel.

2 Push the driver's seat all the way back and pull up the release lever. Remove the securing screw and pull out the lever and cable.

3 Under the bonnet remove the three lock securing bolts and disconnect the cable **(see illustrations)**.

4 Release the cable from the clip from the radiator upper support. This is difficult to access. If it proves impossible to release consider unbolting the upper radiator panel.

5 Jack up the front of the car, and support it on axle stands (see *Jacking and vehicle support*).

6 Remove the roadwheel and wing liner and free the cable from the support clips along the inner wing. Pull the cable through into the wheel arch.

7 Working under the dash locate the cable grommet and pull the grommet and cable into the passenger compartment.

Refitting

8 Refitting is a reversal of removal, but apply a suitable sealant to the grommet hole before fitting.

9 Bonnet lock –
removal and refitting

Removal

1 Open the bonnet and mark the position

9.1 The lock position clearly marked

of the lock. There is an adjustment facility in the lock; marking its position will save having to re-align and adjust the lock when refitted. Unscrew the three securing bolts, and remove the lock assembly **(see illustration)**.

2 Prise out the outer cable end fitting from its slot in the bonnet lock, then unhook the inner cable from the lock operating lever.

3 If required the lock support bracket can also be removed. The front bumper will need to be removed first as described in Section 6.

Refitting

4 Refitting is a reversal of removal. If necessary, the position of the lock can be altered to adjust the lock operation, by moving the lock within the elongated holes.

10 Doors –
removal and refitting

Front door

Removal

1 Open the door and remove the door trim panel as described in Section 11.

2 Remove the power window motor and door glass as described in Chapter 12 and Section 13 of this Chapter.

3 Unplug the wiring loom from the support clips and pull the loom out from the door.

4 Unbolt the check strap from the door pillar.

5 Ensure that the door is adequately supported, with the aid of an assistant, or using wooden blocks or similar under the

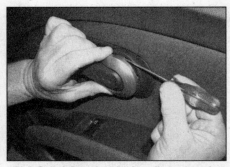

11.1 Carefully prise the handle cover trim free

bottom edge of the door (take care not to damage the paintwork).

6 Mark the position of the hinges on the body or on the door, then unscrew the bolts and remove the door from the car.

Refitting

7 Refitting is a reversal of removal, but check the alignment. There should be a gap of approximately 5 mm between the door and front wing, likewise the gap between the door and rear wing, (or door) should also be approximately 5 mm.

Rear door

Removal

8 Open the door and remove the door trim panel as described in Section 11.

9 Remove the window glass as described in Section 13.

10 Unplug the wiring loom from the support clips and pull the loom out from the door.

11 Unbolt the door check strap and then support the door.

12 Mark the position of the hinges on the body or on the door, then unscrew the bolts and remove the door from the car.

Refitting

13 Refitting is a reversal of removal, but check the alignment. There should be a gap of approximately 5 mm between the rear door and front door, likewise the gap between the door and rear wing should also be approximately 5 mm.

11 Door inner trim panel –
removal and refitting

Front door

Removal

1 Fully open the door and first remove the C-shaped door handle escutcheon. Pull the handle up to access the upper and lower locating tabs. Work the tangs free with a small screwdriver. This component is very fragile so take time and care when removing it **(see illustration)**.

2 Slide the handle cover backwards and pull up from the bottom to remove it,

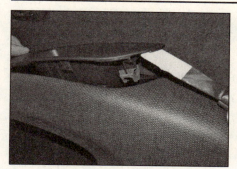

11.3a Use a broad blade to free the switch panel

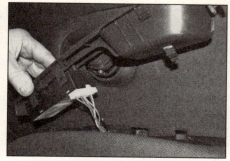

11.3b Free the switch panel . . .

11.3c . . . and unplug the connector

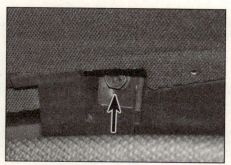

11.4a Locate the screw . . .

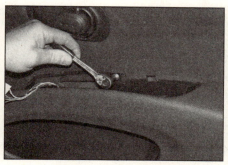

11.4b . . . and remove it

11.5 Remove the door panel

3 Using a suitable tool, and working from the rear of the switch assembly, prise the assembly free. Disconnect the wiring plug **(see illustrations)**.

4 Behind the switch assembly there is a screw. Remove the screw **(see illustrations)**.

5 The door trim panel is now secured by a number of plastic clips, all round the sides and base. Start at one of the bottom corners, and prise the panel with a wide-bladed tool to release the first few clips. Work along the base of the panel, then up the sides, releasing the clips as you go. Finally, the panel should be lifted to unhook the top edge from the door glass channel, and over the door lock button **(see illustration)**.

6 To access the door inner components, it will usually be necessary to remove the plastic membrane from the door. Use a sharp knife to slice along the bead of mastic, and carefully peel back the plastic without tearing it **(see illustration)**.

Refitting

7 Refitting is a reversal of removal. Before starting, check to see whether any trim clips have been left on the door, and transfer them to the trim panel.

11.6 Use a sharp blade to cut through the door membrane sealant

Rear door

Removal

8 Open the door fully and remove the window winder handle with a suitable tool **(see illustrations)**.

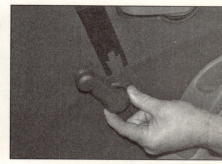

11.8a Use the correct tool . . .

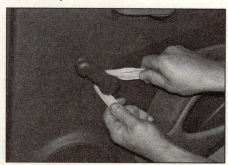

11.8b . . . or improvise with a rag

11.8c Remove the handle . . .

11.8d . . . and recover the washer

11.9 Remove the handle cover trim

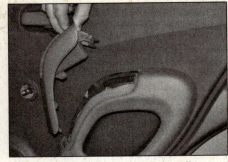

11.10a Remove the door pull

11.10b Panel screw location

11.11a Release the lower edge of the panel

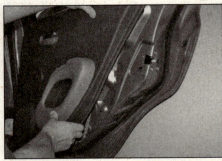

11.11b Pull the panel free from the door

9 Carefully prise free the pull handle escutcheon and then push back and lift up the handle trim piece to remove it **(see illustration)**.
10 Using a suitable tool and working from the rear of the door-pull insert prise the assembly free. Disconnect the wiring plug if electric

windows are fitted. Remove the screw now exposed **(see illustrations)**.
11 The door trim panel is now secured by a number of plastic clips, all round the sides and base. Start at one of the bottom corners, and prise the panel with a wide-bladed tool to

release the first few clips. Work along the base of the panel, then up the sides, releasing the clips as you go. Finally, the panel should be lifted to unhook the top edge from the door glass channel **(see illustrations)**.
12 If required, remove the door membrane using a similar method to that described in paragraph 6.

Refitting

13 Refitting is a reversal of removal. Before starting, check to see whether any trim clips have been left on the door, and transfer them to the trim panel.

12 Door handles and locks – removal and refitting

Front doors

Interior handle

1 Remove the door inner trim panel as described in Section 11.
2 Remove the screw securing the handle and then slide the handle to the rear of the door to remove it **(see illustration)**.
3 Unhook the cable end from the handle, and the handle can be removed.
4 To remove the cable, the plastic membrane will also have to be peeled off, as described in Section 11. Unclip the cable from the door clip, then unhook the end fitting from the lock assembly.
5 Refitting is a reversal of removal. Refit the door trim panel with reference to Section 11.

Exterior handle and lock

6 Remove the door inner trim panel as described in Section 11, and peel back the plastic membrane.
7 Unbolt and remove the window rear guide channel **(see illustrations)**.
8 If fitted unhook the key cylinder link rod. On vehicles fitted with the intelligent key system disconnect the wiring to the door handle antenna.
9 Remove the grommets from the side of the door to access the T30 Torx screw. Remove the screw **(see illustrations)**.
10 Working from the outside pull up the handle assembly and remove the key cylinder.

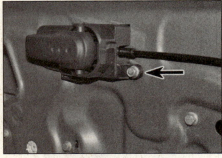

12.2 Remove the screw

12.7a Five-door vehicles have a reinforcement bar fitted

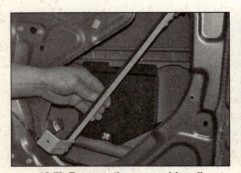

12.7b Remove the rear guide rail

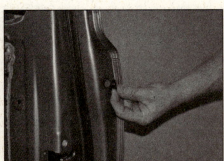

12.9a Remove the grommet . . .

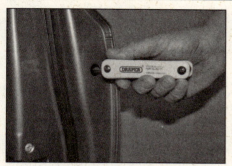

12.9b . . . and then remove the screw

12.10a Remove the cylinder cover . . .

12.10b . . . and remove the handle

Pull the handle up and slide it to the rear of the car to remove it. Collect the two gaskets from the handle and key cylinder **(see illustrations)**.

11 Next remove the three T30 Torx fittings from the door lock assembly and then slide forward and remove the door handle inner bracket. Unhook the cable from the handle inner bracket and remove from the door. Remove the lock mechanism at the same time **(see illustrations)**.

12 Refitting is a reversal of removal, bearing in mind the following points:
a) Lubricate the moving parts of the lock assembly with multipurpose grease before refitting.
b) The three lock securing screws on the back edge of the door should have their threads cleaned and coated with thread-locking fluid before refitting them.
c) Check the operation of the lock mechanism before refitting the door inner trim panel.
d) Refit the door trim panel with reference to Section 11.

Rear doors

Interior handle

13 Remove the door inner trim panel as described in Section 11.
14 Remove the screw securing the handle and then slide the handle to the rear of the door to remove it.
15 Unhook the cable end from the handle, and the handle can be removed.
16 To remove the cable, the plastic membrane

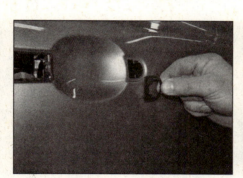

12.10c Recover the front gasket . . .

will also have to be peeled off, as described in Section 11. Unclip the cable from the door clip, then unhook the end fitting from the lock assembly.
17 Refitting is a reversal of removal. Refit the door trim panel with reference to Section 11

Exterior handle and lock

18 Remove the door inner trim panel as described in Section 11, and peel back the plastic membrane.
19 Unbolt and remove the window rear guide channel.
20 Remove the grommets from the side of the door to access the T30 Torx screw. Remove the screw.
21 Working from the outside pull up the handle assembly and remove the cover plate at the rear of the handle. Pull the handle up and slide it to the rear of the car to remove it. Collect the two gaskets from the handle and cover plate.

12.10d . . . and the rear

22 Next remove the three T30 Torx fittings from the door lock assembly and then slide forward and remove the door handle inner bracket. Unhook the cable from the handle inner bracket and remove from the door. Remove the lock mechanism at the same time.

22 Refitting is a reversal of removal, bearing in mind the following points:
a) Lubricate the moving parts of the lock assembly with multi-purpose grease before refitting.
b) The three lock securing screws on the back edge of the door should have their threads cleaned and coated with thread-locking fluid before refitting them.
c) Check the operation of the lock mechanism before refitting the door inner trim panel.
d) Refit the door trim panel with reference to Section 11.

12.11a Remove the lock screws

12.11b Unhook the cable

12.11c Unplug and remove the lock

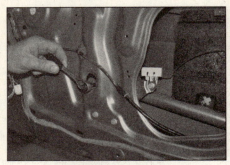

13.5a Remove the bolts . . .

13.5b . . . and then the glass

13.8 Unplug the wiring to the motor

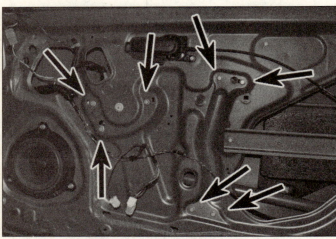

13.9a Remove the bolts . . .

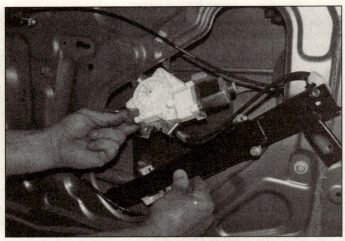

13.9b . . . and then manoeuvre the motor and regulator from the door

13 Door window glass and regulator – removal and refitting

Front door window

Removal

1 Remove the door trim panel as described in Section 11, and then remove the plastic membrane.

2 On 5-door models unbolt and remove the support bar. Models with the intelligent key system also have a buzzer fitted. Remove this if fitted.

3 Remove the rear glass guide channel, noting how it slots into the door frame at the top.

4 Reconnect the electric window switch and while supporting the glass lower the window until the retaining bolts are visible in the access holes in the inner panel.

5 Unscrew the glass retaining bolts, then lift the glass and remove it from the door **(see illustrations)**.

Refitting

6 Refitting is a reversal of removal, noting the following points:

a) Tighten the glass retaining bolts securely.
b) Refit the door trim panel as described in Section 11.

Front regulator

Removal

7 Remove the door window glass as described previously in this Section.

8 Disconnect the wiring plug from the power window motor **(see illustration)**.

9 The window regulator and motor are removed as a complete unit. Remove the seven fixing bolts and withdraw the regulator from the door **(see illustrations)**.

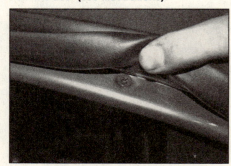

13.12 Locate the fixing screw

Refitting

10 Refitting is a reversal of removal, noting the following points:

a) Lubricate the moving parts of the regulator with multipurpose grease before refitting.
b) Check the operation of the window regulator mechanism before refitting the door trim panel.

Rear window

Removal

11 Remove the door trim panel as described in Section 11, then open the window as far as possible.

12 Unplug the electrical connection to the loudspeaker (where fitted) and then lift up the door seal at the top of the door frame to reveal the screw that secures the window guide rail. Remove the screw **(see illustration)**.

13 Remove the two bolts securing the lower half of the guide channel.

14 Push the guide channel to the front of the door and remove it.

15 Slide the rear fixed quarterlight glass and its rubber seal forwards, and remove it from the door **(see illustration)**. If required, the rubber seal can then be removed from the glass.

13.15 Remove the quarterlight

13.16a The front glass securing bolt . . .

13.16b . . . and the rear

13.16c Removing the rear door glass

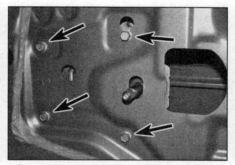

13.19a The regulator mounting bolts

13.19b Withdraw the regulator

16 Refit the winder handle and lower the glass to a position where the fixings can be accessed. Remove the bolts and manoeuvre the glass out of the door frame **(see illustrations)**.

Refitting

17 Refitting is a reversal of removal, noting the following points:
a) *Check the operation of the window regulator mechanism before refitting the door trim panel.*
b) *Refit the door trim panel as described in Section 11.*

Rear regulator

Removal

18 Remove the door window glass as described previously in this Section.
19 The window regulator is secured by four bolts. Remove the bolts and withdraw the regulator from the door **(see illustration)**.

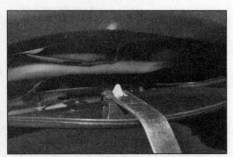

14.1a The safest way to remove the clips is pull out the clips directly and not tug on the panel itself

Refitting

20 Refitting is a reversal of removal, noting the following points:
a) *Lubricate the moving parts of the regulator with multipurpose grease before refitting.*
b) *Check the operation of the window regulator mechanism before refitting the door trim panel.*

14 Tailgate and support struts – removal, refitting and adjustment

Tailgate

Removal

1 Open the tailgate and remove the trim panel. This is secured with eight trim clips. Using the correct tool or a broad blade, remove the tailgate trim panel by prising it free. We found the panel very flexible and managed to fit the tool directly onto the trim clip **(see illustrations)**.
2 With reference to Chapter 12, disconnect the wiring from the rear wiper motor and tailgate lock.
3 Remove the high-level brake lamp as described in Chapter 12.
4 As far as possible, release all the tailgate wiring from any clips or ties, as it must all be fed back through the top of the tailgate and removed.
5 Disconnect the washer tube from the jet, and feed it back into the tailgate. Taking care

not to damage the paintwork, prise out the tailgate washer jet.
6 Using a pencil or marker pen; mark the position of the hinges on the tailgate to aid refitting.
7 Support the tailgate, and disconnect the support struts as described later in this Section.
8 Prise out the rubber gaiters at the top of the tailgate, and carefully start to pull through the wiring and washer tube. If the same tailgate is being refitted, tie on some lengths of string to the various wiring plugs beforehand – the string can then be untied when it emerges from the top of the tailgate, and left in place to pull the wires back through.
9 Ensure that the tailgate is adequately supported, ideally with the aid of an assistant, then unscrew the bolts securing the hinges to the tailgate and lift the tailgate from the car.

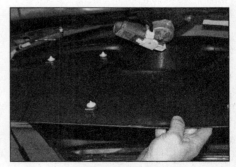

14.1b Remove the panel

15.2 Remove the electrical plug and recover the lock

15.5a Remove the nuts . . .

15.5b . . . and then disconnect the wiring plug

Refitting

10 Refitting is a reversal of removal, bearing in mind the following points:

a) *Make sure that the hinges are aligned with the marks made before removal.*

b) *Where applicable, use the string to pull the wiring harness and the washer fluid hose into position in the tailgate.*

c) *On completion, check the alignment of the tailgate with the surrounding body panels and, if necessary, adjust the position of the tailgate hinges within the elongated holes until satisfactory alignment is achieved.*

Support struts

Removal

11 Open the tailgate, and support it in the open position, using a wooden prop or similar tool. Note that the tailgate is heavy, and will fall closed if either of the support struts are disconnected.

12 Working at the car body end of the strut, remove the two bolts and detach the strut mounting plate.

13 At the tailgate end, either prise off the ball-stud fitting to remove the strut, or remove two further bolts and take off the mounting bracket.

Refitting

14 Refitting is a reversal of removal.

15 Tailgate lock components – removal and refitting

Lock

Removal

1 Open the tailgate, and remove the inner

trim panel, which is secured by a total of eight push-in clips **(see illustration 14.1a)**.

2 Remove the two bolts and then disconnect the wiring **(see illustration)**.

Refitting

3 Refitting is a reversal of removal, but check the operation of the lock mechanism before refitting the tailgate trim panel.

Lock handle

Removal

4 Open the tailgate, and remove the inner trim panel, which is secured by a total of eight clips.

5 Disconnect the electrical supply to the handle and remove the two securing nuts **(see illustrations)**.

Refitting

6 Refitting is a reversal of removal.

16 Central locking system components – general information

Door lock motor

1 The door lock motors are an integral part of the lock assemblies. Removal and refitting is part of the door lock removal and refitting procedure in Section 12.

Door lock switch

2 The door lock switches are integrated into the lock assembly. Note that the interior light switches in the door posts are also part of the system. Removal and refitting is described in Section 12.

Remote control battery renewal

3 Remove the small screw from the key fob, and separate the two halves **(see illustrations)**. On intelligent key models depress the tab and remove the end cover to reveal the emergency access key. Use a small screwdriver to separate the two halves and then remove the battery.

4 The battery is held in place (negative side up) by four separate retaining clips. Use a small screwdriver at the marked point and prise up to release the battery **(see illustrations)**.

16.3a Remove the screw . . .

16.3b and separate the key fob

16.4a Insert a screwdriver at the point shown . . .

16.4b . . . and lever out the battery

5 Fit the new battery (CR2016 for standard remotes and CR2032 for intelligent key models) the same way up as the old one, and ensure it is held securely by the clips.

6 Reassemble the key fob, and test the operation (the key indicator light should come on when the key is pressed).

Door lock control unit

7 The door lock control is managed by the body control module (BCM). Remove the dash upper panel as described in Section 25 of this Chapter.

8 Disconnect the wiring plug, then unbolt and remove the unit from the crossmember.

9 Refitting is a reversal of removal.

Remote locking receiver unit

10 The remote locking receiver unit is fitted to the ignition lock assembly. Remove it as described in Chapter 12.

11 Intelligent key models also have an antenna fitted to the driver's door handle, centre console and under the rear seat squab.

Emergency key access

12 Should the remote key fob or the intelligent key unit fail, Nissan have provided an emergency feature. Use the key tip to prise off the door barrel cover. Store the cover safely and then use the key in the now exposed barrel **(see illustrations)**.

13 Cars fitted with the intelligent key system have a key blade in the fob. Remove the end cover to access the key. In the car prise free the cover from the start button to expose the key cylinder.

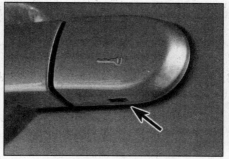

16.12a The key access point

16.12b Prise the cover free . . .

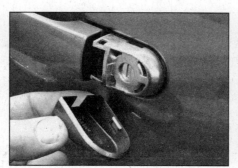

16.12c . . . remove it . . .

16.12d . . . and insert the key

---

17 Electric window components – removal and refitting

Window switches

1 Refer to Chapter 12, Section 4.

Window motors

2 Remove the regulator as described in Section 13. Unscrew the three motor securing screws, and withdraw the motor from the regulator.

3 Refitting is a reversal of removal.

---

18 Exterior mirrors and associated components – removal and refitting

Mirror

Removal

1 Remove the door trim panel as described in Section 11. With care and a broad lever it is just possible to remove the mirror without removing the panel.

2 Carefully unclip the triangular trim panel from inside the mirror base **(see illustration)**.

---

3 Disconnect the mirror wiring plug if fitted.

4 Remove the three mirror mounting screws, supporting the mirror from outside as the last is removed, and withdraw the mirror (and wiring if fitted) from the door **(see illustration)**.

Refitting

5 Refitting is a reversal of removal, noting the following points:

a) Check the condition of the mirror-to-body seal – any damage here could result in water entering the car.

b) Tighten the mirror mounting nuts securely.

c) Refit the door trim panel as described in Section 11.

Mirror motor

6 The motor is integral with the mirror, and cannot be renewed separately. If faulty, the complete mirror assembly must be renewed.

18.2 Remove the interior trim piece

18.4 The mirror retaining screws

Mirror switch

Removal

7 Carefully prise the door mirror switch panel from the facia – use a piece of card, or wrap the tool blade in tape, to prevent damage to the facia.

8 Disconnect the switch wiring plug, and remove the switch.

Refitting

9 Refitting is a reversal of removal. Check the operation of the switch before clipping the panel back into place.

Mirror glass

⚠ **Warning: If the mirror glass is broken, wear gloves to protect your hands.**

Removal

10 The mirror glass can be removed with

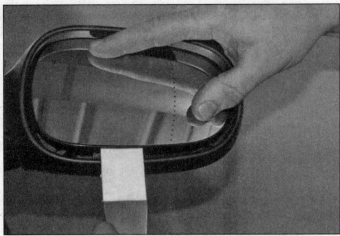

18.11a Release the mirror glass

18.11b The glass removed

the mirror in place if preferred (this avoids removing the door trim panel as described in Section 11).

11 Using a screwdriver or broad blade, release the mirror glass from below. With the glass pulled forwards there is just enough space to see the locking tabs from below **(see illustrations)**.

Refitting

12 Refitting is a reversal of removal. Hook the glass in at the top, then press it firmly on the bottom edge to engage the clips. Use a flat-bladed screwdriver under the glass mounting plate to provide a surface to bear against when engaging the clips.

19 Windscreen, side and tailgate glass – general information

These areas of glass are secured by the tight fit of the weatherseal in the body aperture, and are bonded in position with a special adhesive. Renewal of such fixed glass is a difficult, messy and time-consuming task, which is considered beyond the scope of the home mechanic. It is difficult, unless one has plenty of practice, to obtain a secure, waterproof fit. Furthermore, the task carries a high risk of breakage; this applies especially

to the laminated glass windscreen. In view of this, owners are strongly advised to have this sort of work carried out by one of the many specialist windscreen fitters.

Removal of the fixed rear door quarterlight glass on 5-door models is covered in Section 13.

20 Body exterior fittings – removal and refitting

Bumpers

1 Refer to Section 6.

Scuttle cover panel

2 Refer to the windscreen wiper motor removal procedure in Chapter 12.

Wheel arch liners

3 The wheel arch liners are secured by a combination of self-tapping screws and push-fit clips.
4 Jack up the front, or the rear of the car, and support it on axle stands (see *Jacking and vehicle support*).
5 At the front remove the roadwheel and then remove the single bolt at the front and three screws at the rear. Next remove the four trim clips from the wheel arch **(see illustrations)**.
6 With all the fasteners removed, pull the liner down from the arch and remove it **(see illustration)**.
7 At the rear follow the same procedure to the front.

Body trim strips and badges

8 The various body trim strips and badges are held in position with a special adhesive. Removal requires the trim/badge to be heated, to soften the adhesive, and then cut away from the surface. Due to the high risk of damage to the paintwork during this operation, it is recommended that this task should be entrusted to a Nissan dealer or bodyshop.

20.5a The three rear fixings

20.5b Remove the front trim clip and two screws . . .

20.5c . . . and then remove the trim clips from the wheel arch

20.6 Remove the liner

Fuel filler flap and operating cable

Note: *This procedure assumes the flap can still be opened. The cable operates a spring-loaded plunger inside the flap, at the rear – provided the cable hasn't broken right at the flap end, the plunger can be operated by pulling on the inner cable, at any point along its length.*

Removal

9 The filler flap is held in place by two screws. Prise free the fuel cap security cable and remove the two screws **(see illustration)**.

10 The operating cable can be removed as follows. Inside the filler flap, twist the locking collar on the cable end/plunger, and push the cable into the rear wing. Alternatively reach the release mechanism from the inside.

11 Remove the right-hand parcel shelf support panel as described in Section 23. Pull the cable from the wing and remove the catch from the cable **(see illustration)**.

12 Remove the inner sill cover panel and the driver's kick panel.

13 Lift up the lever and remove the fixing screw. Release the cable from the lever and then work back along the inner sill, unclipping and removing the cable.

Refitting

14 Refitting is a reversal of removal. Make sure the cable is not kinked or twisted, and check its operation before refitting the parts removed for access.

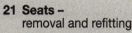

21 Seats – removal and refitting

Front seat

⚠ **Warning: On models with side airbags (denoted by SRS AIRBAG tags on the outside of the seat back), disconnect the battery negative lead (see Disconnecting the battery), then wait for five minutes before proceeding. If this waiting period is not observed, there is danger of activating the airbag system.**

1 Slide the seat fully rearwards, then unplug

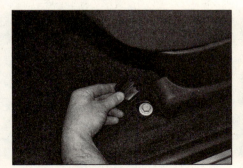

21.3 . . . and the rears

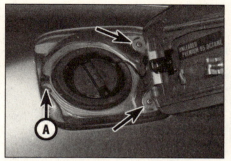

20.9 The filler flap fixings showing release lever (A)

the wiring connectors to the seatbelt buckle and side airbag (if fitted) **(see illustration)**.

2 Remove the covers from the mounting bolts and remove the bolts **(see illustration)**.

3 Slide the seat fully forwards, use a screwdriver to prise off the seat sliding rail rear covers (note which fits where, as they are not interchangeable), then unscrew the two rear bolts **(see illustration)**.

4 Lift the seat, complete with mounting rails, and remove it from the car.

5 Refitting is a reversal of removal, but tighten the seat mounting bolts to the specified torque.

Rear seat

Bench seat

6 Early models feature a standard rear bench seat.

7 Pull up the seat squab at the front and free

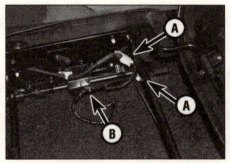

21.1 Remove the plugs (A) and then the cable support (B)

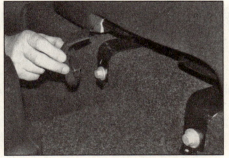

21.11 Remove the front covers and bolts . . .

20.11 Release the cable from the catch

it from the two locating pegs. Once released pull it forward and remove it from the car.

8 Release the tilt lever and lower the seat back and the working from in the boot remove the bolts from the hinge mechanism and remove the seat back from the car.

9 Refitting is a reversal of removal, but tighten the seat hinge bolts securely.

Sliding bench seat

10 Slide the seat to its furthest back position.

11 Prise free the trim panels at the front and remove the bolts **(see illustration)**.

12 Next push the seat forwards and remove the rear bolt covers and then remove the bolts **(see illustration)**.

13 The seat unit is very heavy and an assistant will be required to manoeuvre it out of the car.

14 Refitting is a reversal of removal, but tighten the seat rail bolts to the specified torque.

21.2 Remove the front bolt covers . . .

21.12 . . . and then the rears

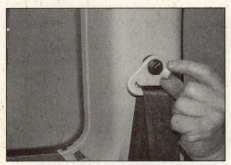

22.1 Remove the cover and then the bolt

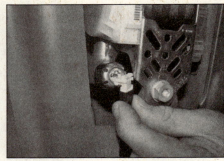

22.3 Disconnect the electrical supply . . .

22.4a . . . and remove the bolt

22.4b Remove the seatbelt inertia reel and pretensioner

22 Seat belt components – removal and refitting

Front belt

> ⚠ **Warning: Disconnect the battery negative lead (see Disconnecting the battery), then wait for five minutes before proceeding. If this waiting period is not observed, there is danger of activating the seat belt tensioner.**

Removal

1 Prise free the upper cover from the door pillar and remove the bolt **(see illustration)**.
2 Remove the door pillar lower trim on 5-door models and the rear side panel on 3-door models, as described in Section 23.
3 Remove the electrical connector to the seatbelt pretensioner **(see illustration)**.

22.16 The rear seat belt mountings

4 On 3-door models, unscrew the lower bolt and the upper screw on the belt reel and then remove the strap mounting bolt **(see illustrations)**.
5 On 5-door models, the belt and reel are held in place by a single anchor bolt. Remove the bolt noting the order of the washers and spacers.

Refitting

6 Refitting is a reversal of removal, but tighten the seat belt bolts to the specified torque.

Front belt stalk

Removal

7 Remove the seat as described in Section 21.
8 Prise the trim clip free from the side moulding and remove the moulding.
9 Free the wiring loom from the support clip and then unbolt the seat belt stalk.

22.17 The floor mounting

Refitting

10 Refitting is a reversal of removal, bearing in mind the following points:
  a) *Make sure that the stalk is angled towards the seat.*
  b) *Tighten the securing bolt to the specified torque.*

Front belt height adjuster

Removal

11 Remove the door pillar trim on 5-door models or rear side panel on 3-door models as described in Section 23.
12 The height adjuster is secured by two bolts, one top and one bottom. Remove the bolts and withdraw the adjuster from the car.

Refitting

13 Refitting is a reversal of removal. Tighten the bolts to the specified torque.

Rear inertia reel belt

Removal

14 Remove the rear seats as described in Section 21.
15 Remove the boot side panels to access the mounting bolts as described in Section 23.
16 Remove the bolt from the upper mounting on the rear door pillar and then remove the screw and bolt from the inertia reel **(see illustration)**.
17 Unbolt the belt mounting on the floor and remove the belt **(see illustration)**.

Refitting

18 Refitting is a reversal of removal. Tighten the bolts to the specified torque.

Rear buckles and centre belt

Removal

19 Remove the rear seat as described in Section 21.
20 The buckles and lap belt are bolted to the floor on early models, and they are integrated into the seat assembly on sliding bench seat models.
21 On sliding seat models remove the seat back cover to access the reel mechanism and seatbelt stalks **(see illustration)**.
22 Unbolt the inertia reel and work the belt free from the seat back, and then unbolt the

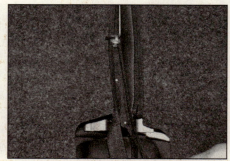

22.21 A pull tab for the zip will have to be improvised

22.22a Remove the bolt . . .

22.22b . . . and work the reel free from the seat back

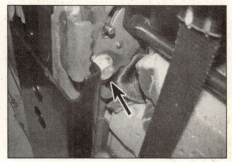

22.22c One of the stalk mounting bolts

seat belt stalks from the lower seat frame **(see illustrations)**.

Refitting

23 Refitting is a reversal of removal. Tighten the bolts to the specified torque.

---

23 Interior trim and fittings – removal and refitting

General

1 The interior trim panels are secured by a combination of clips and screws, with easily-broken plastic clips featuring heavily. Removal and refitting is generally self-

explanatory, noting that it may be necessary to remove or loosen surrounding panels to allow a particular panel to be removed. The following paragraphs describe the removal and refitting of the major panels in more detail.

Door inner trim panels

2 Refer to Section 11.

Steering column shrouds

Lower shroud

3 Remove the three screws securing the steering column lower shroud, and lower it out **(see illustration)**.

Upper shroud

4 The upper shroud will come free when the lower section is removed.

Both shrouds

5 Refitting is a reversal of removal. If both shrouds have been removed, refit the upper one first.

Glovebox

6 Open the glovebox and remove the two hinge pins, then remove the door **(see illustrations)**.

7 Some models have a sliding tray fitted. Pull the tray forward to access the two screws behind it. Remove these screws and the five other screws from the perimeter of the glovebox and then remove the glovebox **(see illustrations)**.

8 Refitting is a reversal of removal.

23.3 The lower shroud screws

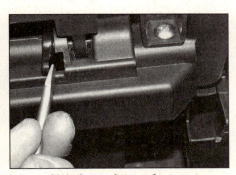

23.6a Lever the peg free . . .

23.6b . . . and remove it

23.6c Remove the glovebox door

23.7a Remove the tray support . . .

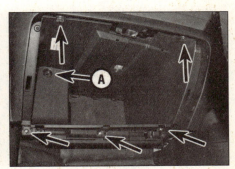

23.7b . . . and then the five remaining screws. Push free the cable clip at point A

23.7c Remove the glovebox

23.9a Pull back the weatherseal . . .

23.9b . . . and pull the trim free

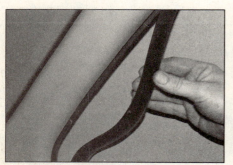

23.12a Pull back the weatherseal . . .

23.12b . . . and prise free the trim panel

23.21 The lower trim panel being removed

Footwell trim panels

9 Prise up the front edge of the weatherseal, to free the footwell trim panel. Work round the edges of the panel, freeing the clips, until the panel can be lifted out (see illustrations).

10 Refitting is a reversal of removal.

A-pillar trim panel

11 Open the door, and carefully prise the rubber door seal from the edge of the door aperture.

12 The A-pillar trim panels are clipped in place. Two clips near the top hold it in place, the lower edge tucks into the side of the facia. Pull the panel backwards to remove it (see illustrations). Check whether any of the clips pull out of the panel, to be left on the car – transfer them back to the panel before refitting.

13 Refitting is a reversal of removal.

B-pillar trim panels (5-door)

Note: The B-pillar trim is in two sections.

14 Detach the rubber weatherstrip from the B-pillar as necessary to free the edges of the trim panel.

15 The B-pillar lower trim panel is wrapped around the weatherseal locating flange on the B-pillar. Pull the panel back at its front edge to release it.

16 To remove the upper trim panel, unclip the trim cover, and unscrew the seat belt upper anchor bolt.

17 Unclip the upper trim panel, and remove it.

18 Refitting is a reversal of removal.

Rear trim panels

Rear side trim panel (3-door)

19 Remove the rear seat cushion. Alternatively, remove the rear seat completely, as described in Section 22.

20 Detach the rubber weatherstrip from the B-pillar as necessary to free the edges of the trim panel.

21 Pull the lower trim panel forward, freeing the trim clips and disengage it from the upper trim piece (see illustration).

22 Refitting is a reversal of removal.

Rear window trim panel (3-door)

23 Detach the rubber weatherstrip from the B-pillar as necessary to free the edges of the trim panel.

24 The window trim panel is overlapped by the rear side trim panel below it, so remove the panel as described earlier in this Section.

25 Similarly, the window trim panel is overlapped by the parcel shelf support panel – either remove the panel as described in later in this Section, or just free the top edge.

26 Unscrew the front seat belt upper mounting bolt.

27 Prise free the lower trim clips and then pull the panel down to free the upper metal clips. When these are free gently rock the panel -whilst pulling inwards – to free the remaining plastic trim clips.

28 Refitting is a reversal of removal. Tighten the rear seat belt lower anchor bolt to the specified torque.

Parcel shelf support panel

29 Detach the rubber weatherstrip from the tailgate aperture as necessary to free the edges of the trim panel.

30 Remove the parcel shelf and the boot floor carpet.

31 Fold the rear seat (backrest and cushion) fully forwards. Alternatively, remove the rear seat completely, as described in Section 22.

32 Prise the clip free from the boot side trim and remove the trim piece (see illustrations).

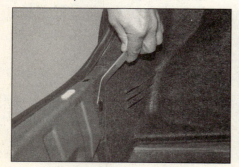

23.32a Prise the trim clip free. . .

23.32b . . . and remove the trim piece

33 On 5-door vehicles remove the panel work up from the bottom to release the plastic and metal clips.

34 On 3-door models remove the clips and then pull the trim forward to unhook it from the rear side window trim piece **(see illustration)**.

35 Where required work the seatbelt through the slot in the panel and then remove the panel.

Carpets

36 The passenger compartment floor carpet is one piece, and is secured along the edges by various types of clips, the door weatherstrips and inner trim panels.

37 Carpet removal and refitting is reasonably straightforward, but time-consuming, due to the fact that all adjoining trim panels must be released, and the seats and centre console must be removed.

38 With all the seats and trim removed the carpet will be still trapped under the heater control box. By pulling and rotating the carpet it is possible to reach the centre point and make discrete cuts with a sharp knife to free the carpet. These cuts will be hidden behind the heater box when refitted.

Headlining

39 The headlining is clipped to the roof, and can be withdrawn only once all fittings such as the grab handles, sun visors, sunroof, front, centre and rear pillar trim panels, and associated components have been removed. The door, tailgate and sunroof aperture weatherstrips will also have to be prised clear.

40 Note that headlining removal requires considerable skill and experience if it is to be carried out without damage, and is therefore best entrusted to an expert. Nissan recommend that it is renewed when removed.

Sun visors

41 Remove the two sun visor hinge screws,

23.34 The support panel partly removed

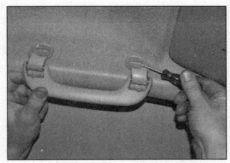

23.43a Lever the pins free . . .

and remove the sun visor from the roof **(see illustration)**. The holding clips are secured by just one screw.

42 Refitting is a reversal of removal.

Grab handles

43 Carefully prise free the locking pegs and the remove the grab handle from the roof **(see illustrations)**.

44 Refitting is a reversal of removal.

Interior mirror

45 On models not fitted with a rain sensor, carefully push the base cover upwards to release it from the mirror base. On models fitted with a rain sensor (for automatic wipers),

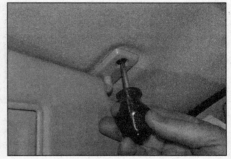

23.41 Removing the sun visor

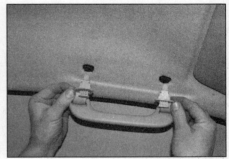

23.43b . . . and remove the handle

carefully slide the base cover downwards off of the base.

46 Refitting is a reversal of removal.

24 Centre console – removal and refitting

Removal

1 On manual transmission models, push the seats forward and remove the two rear screws **(see illustration)**.

2 Prise free the small trim insert in below the gear lever **(see illustrations)**.

3 Pull the gear lever gaiter free.

4 Prise free and then remove the two trim

24.1 Remove the rear fixing screws

24.2a Lever out the trim piece . . .

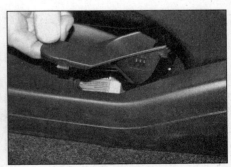

24.2b . . . and remove it

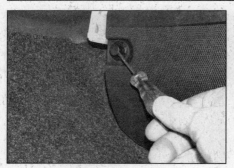

24.4a Lever out the clip . . .

24.4b . . . and remove it

24.4c On automatic transmission models pull the front up to free the clips

clips at the front of the console. On automatic models the front is simply clipped into place **(see illustrations)**.

5 Lift the console off its mounting clips, and lift it over the handbrake lever. On manual transmission models, feed the gaiter up over the gear lever. Disconnect the wiring plugs from the console switches as necessary, and remove the console from the car.

Refitting

6 Refitting is a reversal of removal.

25 Facia assembly – removal and refitting

Note: *Depending on the other work being carried out, not all of the facia sections may need to be removed. It is strongly recommended that this Section is read through thoroughly before starting the procedure.*

General information

1 The most likely reason the facia assembly will require removal is to access the heater module. This is the first item to be fitted on the production line, and consequently the entire dashboard assemble must be removed to repair the heater. The most likely fault needing attention will be the heater matrix, blower motor or the air conditioning evaporator.

2 The facia assembly is made up of over twenty five components. This is just the plastic trim parts and does not include any mechanical or electronic components. Whilst the removal process is not particularly hard it is very time consuming and often very frustrating.

3 Before starting, gather together some masking tape, marker pens and parcel tags. Everything should be labelled and marked as it is removed. If possible store the items in the logical order they were removed.

4 The order of work will depend on which component requires attention. Below we have set out a suggested work order, based on the assumption that the aim is to remove the heater module:

 a) A-pillar trim panels.
 b) Dashboard upper panel.
 c) Steering wheel (see Chapter 10).
 d) Steering column cover tray.
 e) Driver's airbag and combination switch (see Chapter 12).
 f) Steering column (see Chapter 10).
 g) Switch panel (see Chapter 12).
 h) Instrument cluster surround.
 i) Instrument cluster (see Chapter 12).
 j) Audio unit trim panel.
 k) Heater control panel (see Chapter 3).
 l) Audio unit (see Chapter 12).
 m) Centre cover trim.
 n) Glovebox.
 o) Facia side panels.
 p) Facia side vents.
 q) Passenger airbag.

 r) Upper instrument panel and lower panel.
 s) Dashboard support beam.

Removal

Facia section

5 Disconnect the battery negative lead, with reference to Chapter 5A, then wait for five minutes before proceeding. If this waiting period is not observed, there is danger of activating the airbags.

6 Prise free the A-pillar trim panels (as described in Section 23) and then remove the upper dash panel **(see illustration)**. On models with climate control remove the sunlight sensor from the upper panel.

7 Pull free the trim panel below the column **(see illustration)**.

8 Remove the steering wheel as described in Chapter 10.

9 Remove the airbag rotary connector ('clockspring') as described in Chapter 12.

10 Also referring to Chapter 12, remove the steering column switches, and the switch panel to the right of the steering column.

11 Prise free the instrument panel surround and remove the cluster as described in Chapter 12.

12 Remove the vent and trim panel, complete with the audio unit next and then remove the audio unit. Some models have a blanking plate in front of the top screws. The two lower screws may not be present on all models **(see illustrations)**.

25.6 Remove the upper facia panel

25.7 Pull the shelf free

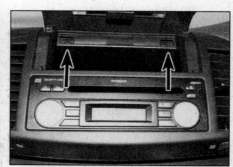

25.12a Remove the screws from the front . . .

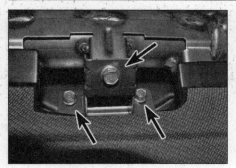

25.12b . . . and from the top

25.12c Removing the audio unit

25.14a Remove the air vents . . .

13 Remove the heater control panel as described in Chapter 3, then remove glovebox as described in Section 23.

14 Remove the dashboard side covers and the fresh air vents at the end of the facia. Unplug the wiring to the passenger airbag switch on the left-hand panel **(see illustrations)**.

15 Remove the passenger airbag as described in Chapter 12.

16 Remove the screws from the fusebox and free it from the dash panel, and then remove the bonnet release cable. The fuel filler cap release lever should also be removed **(see illustrations)**.

17 Work round the facia panel and remove the screws holding it in place **(see illustrations)**. If possible have an assistant support the panel as it is removed. The panel is not heavy, but could easily be scratched or damaged without careful handling. Remove the facia from the car.

Crossmember

18 Working along the crossmember, remove the loom fixing clips. These are awkward to remove and it may be more convenient to cut them off and fit new ones, given their low cost. Remove the clips that retain the ductwork for the heater **(see illustration)**.

19 Unbolt the earth connections on the crossmember and then unplug and remove the body control module (BCM).

25.14b . . . and the end covers

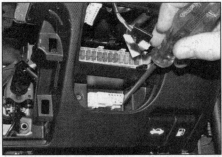

25.16a Remove the fusebox screws . . .

25.16b . . . and the bonnet and fuel filler cap release screws

25.17a There are fixings in the end of the panel . . .

25.17b . . . on the top . . .

25.17c . . . and below

25.18 Lever out the clip

25.20a Remove the support bracket

25.20b Prise free the blanking grommets . . .

25.20c . . . and remove the bolts

20 Remove the heater support bracket and the crossmember bolts **(see illustrations)**. Note the location of the special bolts on removal.

21 The crossmember is now supported by the two locating pegs **(see illustration)**. Release the wiring harness from the crossmember, and move it clear, noting how it is routed and attached.

22 Check that everything is clear and remove the crossmember from the car **(see illustration)**.

Refitting

23 Refitting is a reversal of removal, bearing in mind the following points:

a) *If the facia is being refitted at a later date,* ensure that the battery is disconnected before starting. It is dangerous, for example, to reconnect the airbag wiring with the battery connected.

b) *Ensure that the wiring harness is securely reconnected to the facia crossmember, and is routed as before.*

c) *Tighten all bolts securely.*

25.21 The locating pegs will support the crossmember

25.22 Manoeuvre the crossmember from the car

Chapter 12
Body electrical system

Contents

Airbag system – general information, precautions and system
 de-activation... 20
Airbag system components – removal and refitting.............. 21
Anti-theft immobiliser – general information 19
Bulbs (exterior lights) – renewal 5
Bulbs (interior lights) – renewal. 6
Electrical fault finding – general information 2
Electrical systems check ....See *Weekly checks*
Exterior light units – removal and refitting 7
Fuses and relays – general information 3
General information and precautions......................... 1
Headlight adjuster components – removal and refitting 8
Headlight beam alignment – general information. 9
Horn – removal and refitting................................. 11

Instrument panel – removal and refitting 10
Multiplex wiring modules – general information. 23
Parking aid components - general information, removal and refitting .. 22
Radio aerial – removal and refitting 18
Radio unit – removal and refitting. 16
Speakers – removal and refitting 17
Switches – removal and refitting 4
Tailgate wiper motor – removal and refitting 14
Washer fluid level check.....................See *Weekly checks*
Windscreen wiper motor and linkage – removal and refitting 13
Windscreen/tailgate washer system components – removal and
 refitting 15
Wiper arms – removal and refitting......................... 12
Wiper blades check ....See *Weekly checks*

Degrees of difficulty

| **Easy,** suitable for novice with little experience | 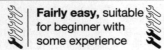 | **Fairly easy,** suitable for beginner with some experience | | **Fairly difficult,** suitable for competent DIY mechanic | | **Difficult,** suitable for experienced DIY mechanic | | **Very difficult,** suitable for expert DIY or professional | |

Specifications

General
System type .... 12 volt, negative-earth

Fuses
Refer to label inside fusebox lid or wiring diagrams

Bulbs

	Type	Wattage
Direction indicator light:		
Front (amber)	Bayonet-fit	21
Side repeater	Push-fit	5
Rear	Bayonet-fit	21
Foglight:		
Front	H11	55
Rear	Bayonet-fit	21
Headlight	H4	55/60
High-level stop-light	Push-fit	21
Interior light	Festoon	10
Luggage compartment light	Festoon	10
Map reading lights	Push-fit	5
Number plate light	Push-fit	10
Reversing light	Bayonet-fit	21
Sidelight	Push-fit	5
Stop/tail light	Bayonet-fit	21/5

Torque wrench settings

	Nm	lbf ft
Airbag sensor mounting bolts	12	9
Driver's airbag mounting bolts	10	7
Passenger's airbag mounting bolts	6	4

1 General information and precautions

⚠️ **Warning: Before carrying out any work on the electrical system, read through the precautions given in Safety first! at the beginning of this manual, and in Chapter 5A.**

The electrical system is of 12 volt negative-earth type. Power for the lights and all electrical accessories is supplied by a lead-acid type battery, which is charged by the alternator.

This Chapter covers repair and service procedures for the various electrical components not associated with the engine. Information on the battery, alternator and starter motor can be found in Chapter 5A.

It should be noted that, prior to working on any component in the electrical system, the battery negative terminal should first be disconnected, to prevent the possibility of electrical short-circuits and/or fires.

Caution: Before disconnecting the battery, refer to Disconnecting the battery in the Reference Section.

Certain later models may be equipped with an automatic headlight system. This system uses the light and rain sensor to detect outside brightness and automatically turn the headlights, parking lights and foglights on or off. Later models may also be equipped with a convenience 'Friendly Lighting' facility which enables the driver to provide lighting from the headlights for 30 seconds to 2 minutes after the ignition has been switched off. Both systems are controlled by the Body Control Module.

2 Electrical fault finding – general information

Note: *Refer to the precautions given in Safety first! and at the beginning of Chapter 5A before starting work. The following tests relate to testing of the main electrical circuits, and should not be used to test delicate electronic circuits (such as anti-lock braking systems), particularly where an electronic control module is used.*

General

1 A typical electrical circuit consists of an electrical component, any switches, relays, motors, fuses, fusible links or circuit breakers related to that component, and the wiring and connectors which link the component to both the battery and the chassis. To help to pinpoint a problem in an electrical circuit, wiring diagrams are included at the end of this Chapter.

2 Before attempting to diagnose an electrical fault, first study the appropriate wiring diagram, to obtain a more complete understanding of the components included in the particular circuit concerned. The possible sources of a fault can be narrowed down by noting whether other components related to the circuit are operating properly. If several components or circuits fail at one time, the problem is likely to be related to a shared fuse or earth connection.

3 Later models are fitted with Multiplex wiring which makes traditional electrical fault finding more difficult, as inter-related circuits are connected together as required by the BCM (Body Control Module). The BCM works in conjunction with the IPDM (Intelligent Power Distribution Module) to respond to information from the vehicle's switches and sensors, and acts as a communication system between the individual control units (see Section 3 for additional information). All of the vehicle's control units and modules are inter-connected by the multiplex Controller Area Network (CAN), which is identified by a two-wire twisted loom (the loom is twisted for 'noise' immunity). This system makes tracing faults from one end of the car to the other almost impossible, with the added factor that the BCM or IPDM may also be at fault in not switching/connecting the circuits correctly. Once testing has passed beyond the very basic stage, it may be more time-efficient to have the system fault diagnosed by a Nissan dealer.

⚠️ **Warning: Since with the multiplex wiring system every circuit in the car passes through at least one 'ECU', it is inadvisable to use any kind of self-powered test equipment, as this may cause damage to the electronic modules fitted.**

4 Electrical problems usually stem from simple causes, such as loose or corroded connections, a faulty earth connection, a blown fuse, a melted fusible link, or a faulty relay (refer to Section 3 for details of testing relays). Visually inspect the condition of all fuses, wires and connections in a problem circuit before testing the components. Use the wiring diagrams to determine which terminal connections will need to be checked, in order to pinpoint the trouble-spot.

5 The basic tools required for electrical fault-finding include a circuit tester or voltmeter (a 12 volt bulb with a set of test leads can also be used for certain tests); a self-powered test light (sometimes known as a continuity tester); an ohmmeter (to measure resistance); a battery and set of test leads; and a jumper wire, preferably with a circuit breaker or fuse incorporated, which can be used to bypass suspect wires or electrical components. Before attempting to locate a problem with test instruments, use the wiring diagram to determine where to make the connections.

6 To find the source of an intermittent wiring fault (usually due to a poor or dirty connection, or damaged wiring insulation), a 'wiggle' test can be performed on the wiring. This involves wiggling wiring by hand, to see if the fault occurs as the wiring is moved. It should be possible to narrow down the source of the fault to a particular section of wiring. This method of testing can be used in conjunction with any of the tests described in the following sub-Sections.

7 Apart from problems due to poor connections, two basic types of fault can occur in an electrical circuit – open-circuit, or short-circuit.

8 Open-circuit faults are caused by a break somewhere in the circuit, which prevents current from flowing. An open-circuit fault will prevent a component from working, but will not cause the relevant circuit fuse to blow.

9 Short-circuit faults are caused by a 'short' somewhere in the circuit, which allows the current flowing in the circuit to 'escape' along an alternative route, usually to earth. Short-circuit faults are normally caused by a breakdown in wiring insulation, which allows a feed wire to touch either another wire, or an earthed component such as the bodyshell. A short-circuit fault will normally cause the relevant circuit fuse to blow.

Finding an open-circuit

10 To check for an open-circuit, connect one lead of a circuit tester or voltmeter to either the negative battery terminal or a known good earth.

11 Connect the other lead to a connector in the circuit being tested, preferably nearest to the battery or fuse.

12 Switch on the circuit, bearing in mind that some circuits are live only when the ignition switch is moved to a particular position.

13 If voltage is present (indicated either by the tester bulb lighting or a voltmeter reading, as applicable), this means that the section of the circuit between the relevant connector and the battery is problem-free.

14 Continue to check the remainder of the circuit in the same fashion.

15 When a point is reached at which no voltage is present, the problem must lie between that point and the previous test point with voltage. Most problems can be traced to a broken, corroded or loose connection.

Finding a short-circuit

16 To check for a short-circuit, first disconnect the load(s) from the circuit (loads are the components which draw current from a circuit, such as bulbs, motors, heating elements, etc).

17 Remove the relevant fuse from the circuit, and connect a circuit tester or voltmeter to the fuse connections.

18 Switch on the circuit, bearing in mind that some circuits are live only when the ignition switch is moved to a particular position.

19 If voltage is present (indicated either by the tester bulb lighting or a voltmeter reading, as applicable), this means that there is a short-circuit.

20 If no voltage is present, but the fuse still blows with the load(s) connected, this indicates an internal fault in the load(s).

Finding an earth fault

21 The battery negative terminal is connected to 'earth' – the metal of the engine/transmission unit and the car body – and most systems are wired so that they only receive a positive feed, the current returning via the metal of the car body. This means that the component mounting

3.2a The interior fusebox and diagnostic socket

3.2b The IPDM fuses

3.2c The relay, fusible link and fusebox adjacent to the battery

and the body form part of that circuit. Loose or corroded mountings can therefore cause a range of electrical faults, ranging from total failure of a circuit, to a puzzling partial fault.

22 In particular, lights may shine dimly (especially when another circuit sharing the same earth point is in operation), motors (eg, wiper motors or the radiator cooling fan motor) may run slowly, and the operation of one circuit may have an apparently-unrelated effect on another.

23 Note that on many vehicles, earth straps are used between certain components, such as the engine/transmission and the body, usually where there is no metal-to-metal contact between components, due to flexible rubber mountings, etc.

24 To check whether a component is properly earthed, disconnect the battery, and connect one lead of an ohmmeter to a known good earth point. Connect the other lead to the wire or earth connection being tested. The resistance reading should be zero; if not, check the connection as follows.

25 If an earth connection is thought to be faulty, dismantle the connection, and clean back to bare metal both the bodyshell and the wire terminal or the component earth connection mating surface. Be careful to remove all traces of dirt and corrosion, then use a knife to trim away any paint, so that a clean metal-to-metal joint is made.

26 On reassembly, tighten the joint fasteners securely; if a wire terminal is being refitted, use serrated washers between the terminal and the bodyshell, to ensure a clean and secure connection.

27 When the connection is remade, prevent the onset of corrosion in the future by applying

a coat of petroleum jelly or silicone-based grease, or by spraying on (at regular intervals) a proprietary ignition sealer.

3 Fuses and relays – general information

Fuses

1 Fuses are designed to break a circuit when a predetermined current is reached, in order to protect the components and wiring which could be damaged by excessive current flow. Any excessive current flow will be due to a fault in the circuit, usually a short-circuit (see Section 2).

2 The main fuses are located in the fusebox, behind a panel in the driver's side of the dashboard. Additional fuses are located in the 'intelligent power distribution module' (IPDM) in the engine compartment, under the left-hand headlight. Further fuses and fusible links can also be found adjacent to the battery **(see illustrations)**.

3 Pull the fusebox cover and remove it for access to the fuses **(see illustration)**. In the case of the IPDM fuses, the left hand headlight will need to be removed first.

4 A blown fuse can be recognised from its melted or broken wire.

5 To remove a fuse, first ensure that the relevant circuit is switched off. Taking out the ignition key is a start, but several circuits are live even with the ignition off – for maximum safety, disconnect the battery (see *Disconnecting the battery*).

6 Pull the fuse from its location, using the

provided fuse puller or thin-nosed pliers if necessary **(see illustration)**.

7 Before renewing a blown fuse, trace and rectify the cause, and always use a fuse of the correct rating. Never substitute a fuse of a higher rating, or make temporary repairs using wire or metal foil; more serious damage, or even fire, could result.

8 Note that the fuses are colour-coded as follows. Refer to the markings on the back of the fusebox lids for details of the circuits protected.

Colour	Rating
Orange	5A
Red	10A
Blue	15A
Yellow	20A
Clear or white	25A
Green	30A

9 Larger fusible links will also be found in the fuse and relay box next to the battery. Since many of these are rated in excess of 30 amps, if any of these is found to have blown, it indicates a serious wiring fault, which should be investigated – just fitting a new fuse may cause further problems.

Relays

10 A relay is an electrically-operated switch, which is used for the following reasons:
  a) A relay can switch a heavy current remotely from the circuit in which the current is flowing, allowing the use of lighter-gauge wiring and switch contacts.
  b) A relay can receive more than one control input, unlike a mechanical switch.
  c) A relay can have a timer function – for example, the intermittent wiper relay.

11 The relays are divided between the under-facia fusebox and the fusible link/relay box next to the battery. However most of the switching functions normally controlled by individual relays are part of the IPDM. The IPDM controls the following:
  a) Main beam and dipped beam.
  b) Sidelights and number plate lamp.
  c) Front wipers.
  d) Headlight washers and front foglights – where fitted.
  e) Rear screen heater.
  f) Air conditioning compressor.
  g) Radiator cooling fan.

3.3 Pull the cover to access the fusebox

3.6 Removing a fuse

12 Other relay functions are controlled by the Body Control Module (BCM). These include:
a) *Central locking control.*
b) *Electric window systems.*
c) *Interior lights.*
d) *Indicators and hazard warning lights.*
e) *Rear foglight.*
f) *Rear wiper and washer.*

13 If a circuit or system controlled by a relay develops a fault, and the relay is suspect, operate the system. If the relay is functioning, it should be possible to hear it 'click' as it is energised. If this is the case, the fault lies with the components or wiring of the system.

14 If the relay is not being energised, then either the relay is not receiving a main supply or a switching voltage, or the relay itself is faulty. Testing is by the substitution of a known good unit, but be careful – while some relays are identical in appearance and in operation, others look similar but perform different functions.

15 To remove a relay, first ensure that the relevant circuit is switched off. The relay can then simply be pulled out from the socket, and pushed back into position.

---

4 Switches –
   removal and refitting
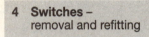

Note: *Before removing any switch, disconnect the battery negative lead, and position the lead away from the battery (also see Disconnecting the battery).*

Ignition switch/steering lock

Steering column lock cylinder

1 The lock assembly is retained by 'shear bolts' to the column assembly. These bolts have a narrower section below the head of the bolt. They are fitted by tightening until the head of the bolt falls off. This is a very effective anti-theft device since the bolts will require drilling out to remove the lock and cylinder.

2 Remove the steering column assembly as described in Chapter 10.

3 With the column on the bench, remove the pick-up coil for the anti-theft system and the ignition switch.

4 It is always worth seeing if the bolts can be tapped free before resorting to drilling out the bolt. To do this, use a centre punch on the edge of the bolt and attempt to unscrew the bolt.

5 If this fails then the only alternative will be to drill out the shear bolts.

Ignition switch

Caution: Do not remove the ignition switch whilst the steering column lock cylinder is removed.

6 Remove the steering column shrouds as described in Chapter 11, Section 23, and the lower panel below the column.

7 Disconnect the wiring to the column switch, key antenna and ignition switch and then remove the wiring support clip from the steering column.

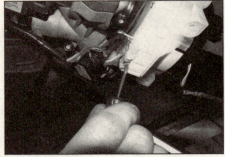
4.12a A small screwdriver will help depress the locking tab . . .

8 Using a long cross-head screwdriver remove the two screws that retain the switch.

9 Refitting is a reversal of removal, but make sure that switch engages correctly.

Steering column switches

10 Remove the steering wheel and airbag as described in Chapter 10 and Section 21 of this Chapter.

11 Also remove the steering column shrouds as described in Chapter 11, Section 23 and the spiral cable as described in Section 21.

12 Disconnect the wiring plug at the bottom of the switch (a small screwdriver is useful here) and then remove the screw and pull off the switch assembly **(see illustrations)**.

13 Refitting is a reversal of removal.

Heated rear window switch

14 Remove the heater control panel to access the switch as described in Chapter 3.

15 The heated rear window switch is integral with the heater/air conditioning control panel and cannot be renewed separately.

16 Refitting is a reversal of removal.

4.23 Pull the switch panel free

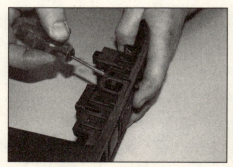
4.25a Lever the tab free . . .

4.12b . . . enabling the connector to be removed

Hazard warning light switch

17 Remove the heater control panel to access the switch as described in Chapter 3.

18 The hazard warning light switch can be removed by levering back the two locking pawls and then pushing the switch out.

19 Refitting is a reversal of removal.

Air conditioning switch

20 Remove the heater control panel to access the switch as described in Chapter 3.

21 The air conditioning switch is integral with the control panel, and cannot be renewed separately.

22 Refitting is a reversal of removal.

Electric mirror switch

23 Taking care not to mark the facia, prise out the switch panel until it is free **(see illustration)**.

24 Disconnect the wiring plug(s) from the back of the switch panel, and withdraw the assembly from the facia **(see illustration)**.

25 The mirror switch can now be removed from the panel **(see illustrations)**.

26 Refitting is a reversal of removal.

4.24 Remove the electrical connectors

4.25b . . . and remove the switch

4.33a Remove the plug . . .

4.33b . . . and lever the switch free

4.36 Disconnect the plug and then prise switch free

Headlight beam adjuster

27 The adjuster switch is part of the same panel as the mirror switch.
28 Disconnect the wiring plug(s) from the back of the switch panel, and withdraw the assembly from the facia.
29 Refitting is a reversal of removal.

Rear foglight switch

30 The switch is part of the column-mounted indicator and wiper switch assembly.

Blower motor switch

31 The switch is part of the heater control panel, which is removed as described in Chapter 3. Renewal requires the renewal of the complete control panel.

Electric window switches

32 Taking care not to mark the trim, prise out the switch panel from the door.
33 Disconnect the wiring plug from the window switch assembly, and withdraw the assembly from the door trim panel. Unscrew the switch panel mounting screws on the underside, and separate the switch proper from its trim piece (see illustrations).
34 Refitting is a reversal of removal.

Centre console switches

35 Remove the centre console as described in Chapter 11.
36 Disconnect the wiring plug(s) from the switch assembly, and withdraw the assembly from the console (see illustration).
37 Refitting is a reversal of removal.

4.38 Remove the screw

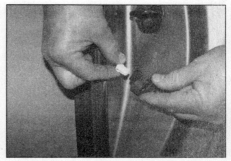

4.39 Pull the switch free and disconnect the wiring plug

Door courtesy light switches

38 Open the relevant door. Remove the screw securing the switch to the door frame, and prise the switch out of its location (see illustration).
39 Disconnect the wiring plug and remove the switch. Make sure that the wiring does not drop back into the aperture by using tape or string to secure it (see illustration).
40 Refitting is a reversal of removal.

Handbrake-on warning switch

41 Refer to Chapter 9.

Stop-light switch

42 Refer to Chapter 9.

Light and rain sensor

43 Remove the interior mirror as described in Chapter 11, Section 23.

44 Release the spring clip and the pawl, then withdraw the sensor and disconnect the wiring. Do not touch the delicate circuit board.
45 Refitting is a reversal of removal.

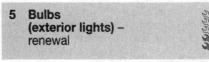

5 Bulbs (exterior lights) – renewal

1 Whenever a bulb is renewed, note the following points:
a) *Disconnect the battery negative lead before starting work (see Disconnecting the battery).*
b) *Remember that, if the light has just been in use, the bulb may be extremely hot.*
c) *Always check the bulb contacts and holder, ensuring that there is clean metal-to metal contact between the bulb and its live(s) and earth. Clean off any corrosion or dirt before fitting a new bulb.*
d) *Wherever bayonet-type bulbs are fitted (see Specifications), ensure that the live contact(s) bear firmly against the bulb contact.*
e) *Always ensure that the new bulb is of the correct rating, and that it is completely clean before fitting it; this applies particularly to headlight/foglight bulbs (see below).*

Headlight

2 Pull the wiring plug from the rear of the bulb, then pull off the rubber cover (see illustrations).

5.2a Remove the wiring plug . . .

5.2b . . . and the rubber seal

5.3a Push the retainer sideways to release . . .

5.3b . . . and then remove the bulb

5.7 Twist the bulbholder to release it

5.8 Pull the bulb free

5.11a Remove the bulbholder from the indicator light . . .

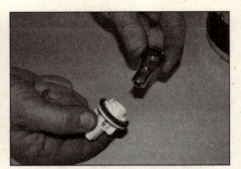

5.11b . . . then depress and twist the bulb anticlockwise to remove it

3 Release the bulb's wire retaining clip by unhooking it sideways at the top, then pivot the clip down. Withdraw the bulb (see illustrations).

4 When handling the new bulb, use a tissue or clean cloth to avoid touching the glass with the fingers; moisture and grease from the skin can cause blackening and rapid failure of this type of bulb. If the glass is accidentally touched, wipe it clean using methylated spirit.

5 Install the new bulb, ensuring that its locating tabs are correctly seated in the light cut-outs. Secure the bulb in position with the spring clip.

6 Refit the rubber cover, ensuring that a good seal is made to the back of the headlight. Reconnect the wiring plug.

Front sidelight

7 Disconnect the wiring plug from the bulbholder. Twist the bulbholder anti-clockwise, and pull it from the rear of the headlight (see illustration).

8 Pull out the wedge-type bulb from the holder, and fit a new one firmly into place (see illustration).

9 Refit the bulbholder, twisting it firmly into place to secure it.

Front direction indicator light

10 Remove the front grille (on the appropriate side) as described in Section 7.

11 Twist the bulbholder anticlockwise to remove it from the light, then depress and twist the bulb anticlockwise to remove it from the bulbholder (see illustrations).

12 Refitting is a reversal of removal.

Front foglight

13 Remove the foglight as described in Section 7. Twist free the bulbholder, and remove the bulb.

14 Refitting is a reversal of removal.

Indicator side repeater light

15 Remove the lamp as described in Section 7, and then twist the bulbholder to remove it from the lamp. Pull the wedge-type bulb free (see illustration).

16 Refitting is a reversal of removal.

Rear lights

17 Remove the appropriate lamp as described in Section 7, and then depress the locating tab to free the bulbholder assembly (see illustrations).

18 All the bulbs are a bayonet-type fitting (see

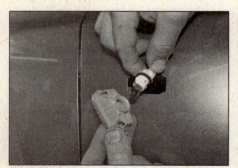

5.15 Twist the bulbholder to release it

5.17a Remove the foam insulator . . .

5.17b . . . and then the bulbholder

5.18 Removing the stop/tail bulb

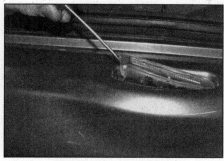

5.20 Prise the lamp free

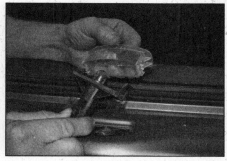

5.21 Remove the lens

5.22 Remove the bulb

5.25 Replacing the high-level stop-light bulb

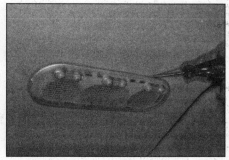

6.2 Prise the lens free

illustration). Pay attention when renewing the stop/tail bulb. It will only fit one way, but it is possible to force it home incorrectly.
19 Refitting is a reversal of removal.

Number plate light

20 Taking care not to damage the paintwork prise the number plate light from the bumper using a small screwdriver **(see illustration)**.
21 Remove the lens **(see illustration)**.
22 Twist the bulb anti-clockwise and remove it from the light **(see illustration)**.
23 Refitting is a reversal of removal.

High-level stop-light

24 Remove the lamp as described in Section 7.
25 Twist free the bulbholder, and then remove the bulb **(see illustration)**.
26 Refitting is a reversal of removal.

6 Bulbs (interior lights) – renewal

General

1 Refer to Section 5, paragraph 1.

Interior light

2 Carefully prise the light unit lens down at the side, using a small screwdriver **(see illustration)**.
3 Pull the festoon-type interior light bulb from the sprung contacts **(see illustration)**.
4 Fit the new bulb using a reversal of the removal procedure.
5 If required, the light unit can be removed completely, by levering free the locating tabs and disconnecting the wiring plug **(see illustrations)**.

Luggage compartment light

6 Carefully prise the light unit out from the trim panel **(see illustration)**.
7 Pull the festoon-type interior light bulb from the sprung contacts.

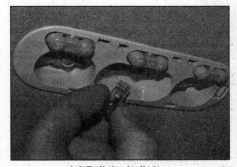

6.3 Pull the bulb free

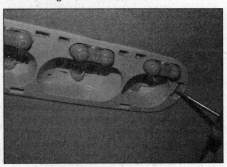

6.5a Release the tab . . .

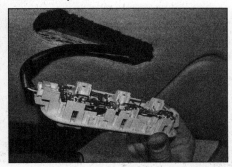

6.5b . . . and remove the light

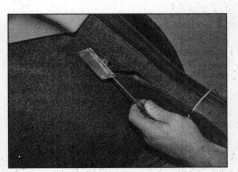

6.6 Prise the light free

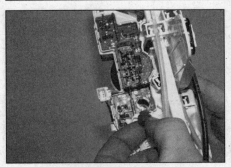

6.14a Twist the bulbholder free . . .

6.14b . . . and remove the bulb

8 Fit the new bulb using a reversal of the removal procedure.

Instrument panel illumination

9 Remove the instrument panel as described in Section 10.

7.3a Unscrew the upper . . .

7.3b . . . and inner lower headlight mounting bolts . . .

10 Twist the relevant bulbholder anti-clockwise and remove it from the rear of the panel. Depending on type, the instrument panel bulbs will either be one-piece items (with integral bulbs), or will have a wedge-type bulb, which can be pulled out.

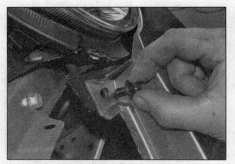

7.3c . . . then remove the bumper-to-headlight fastener . . .

7.3d . . . and reach in behind the bumper to unscrew the lower outer bolt

7.4a Disconnect the wiring plugs from the sidelight . . .

7.4b . . . headlight . . .

11 Refit the instrument panel as described in Section 10.

Switch illumination

12 The bulbs are integral with the switches, and cannot be renewed separately.

Heater control illumination

13 Remove the heater control panel as described in Chapter 3.
14 Twist the relevant bulbholder anti-clockwise, and remove it from the rear of the panel. The bulb is a push-fit in the holder **(see illustrations)**.
15 Refit the heater control panel (Chapter 3).

---

7 Exterior light units – removal and refitting

Note: *Before removing any switch, disconnect the battery negative lead, and position the lead away from the battery (also see Disconnecting the battery).*

Headlight

1 If you are only working on one headlight, then remove the fixings from the appropriate side only, however access to the outer headlight mounting bolt is difficult and also the bumper has to be flexed considerably in order to remove the headlight, so if you are removing both headlights, consider removing the complete front bumper first.
2 If not already done, remove the grille from the appropriate side as described in paragraph 7 of this Section.
3 Remove the three headlight mounting bolts. The upper and inner bolts are easily accessible, however the outer bolt is hidden behind the front bumper. First, remove the upper and inner bolts, then remove the bumper-to-headlight mounting fastener. Reach in behind the bumper and unscrew the headlight outer bolt from the body crossmember **(see illustrations)**.
4 Disconnect the three wiring plugs from the rear of the headlight, then carefully release the outer headlight extension/peg from the crossmember and withdraw the headlight while flexing the front bumper slightly outwards **(see illustrations)**.

7.4c . . . and headlight adjuster . . .

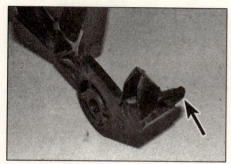

7.4d . . . then release the extension/peg to remove the headlight

7.7a Remove the clips . . .

7.7b . . . and free the lower locating tabs

7.8a Remove the Torx type screw (early) or screws (later) . . .

7.8b . . . and recover the light

7.8c Front direction indicator light mounting screws on later models

5 Refitting is a reversal of removal.

Front direction indicator light

6 The front indicator is fitted to the front grille.

7 Remove the two trim clips from both ends, and then reach behind the grille to free the three locating tabs at the lower edge **(see illustrations)**. Disconnect the wiring plug from the indicator light. If required, twist the bulbholder anticlockwise to remove it.

8 With the grille on the bench, remove the single screw (early models) or two screws (later models) and release the light from the grille **(see illustrations)**.

9 Refitting is a reversal of removal.

Front foglight

10 Remove the front bumper as described in Chapter 11.

11 Disconnect the wiring to the front foglights as the bumper is removed.

12 Take precautions to avoid damage to the bumper paintwork and then remove the two mounting bolts to free the lamp assembly.

13 Refitting is a reversal of removal.

Indicator side repeater light

14 Before attempting to remove the repeater protect the wing paintwork with masking tape.

15 Pull the rear of the lamp out, while pushing it forward to release the locating pawl. A small screwdriver may be helpful

here. We found this difficult to do; and for fear of damaging the paintwork we opted to remove the wing liner and push the lamp free from the rear **(see illustrations)**. Disconnect the wiring plug

16 Refitting is a reversal of removal, but make sure the ribbed surface of the light is upwards.

Rear lights

17 Open the tailgate and remove the two screws **(see illustration)**.

18 Pull out the rear light cluster unit directly from its outer edge to release the clip. This clip can be particularly tight and care must be taken to keep the light unit level with the rear of the car while pulling on it, to prevent the clip breaking off. With the light unit removed, check if the cushion rubber has

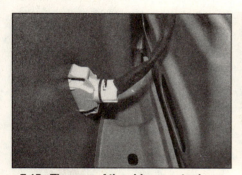

7.15a The rear of the side repeater lamp

7.15b Pushing the lamp free from the rear

7.17 Rear light cluster retaining screws

7.18a Outer clip and location hole

7.18b Make sure the cushion rubber is located on the clip before refitting

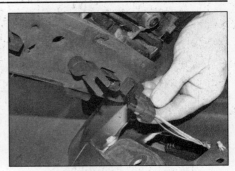

7.19 Disconnect the wiring from the rear light cluster

been displaced and if necessary refit it to the clip **(see illustrations)**.

19 Disconnect the wiring plug from the light unit **(see illustration)**.

Rear number plate light

20 The procedure is described as part of the bulb renewal procedure in Section 5.

High-level stop-light

21 Open the tailgate and then release the lamp cover. Do this by pulling it horizontally with both hands **(see illustration)**.

22 Push the mounting clip down and then in, to free the lamp **(see illustration)** and then disconnect the wiring plug.

7.21 Pull the cover free

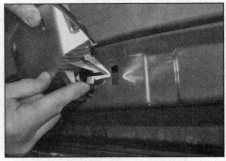

7.22 Depress the tab to free the lamp

8 Headlight adjuster components – removal and refitting

Adjuster switch

1 Refer to Section 4.

Adjuster motor

2 The motor is integral with the headlight, and is not available separately. The headlight is removed as described in Section 7.

9 Headlight beam alignment – general information

1 All models are equipped with an electrical vertical beam adjuster unit – this can be used to adjust the headlight beam, to compensate for

the relevant load which the car is carrying. An adjuster switch is provided on the facia. Refer to the car's handbook for further information.

2 Accurate adjustment of the headlight beam is only possible using optical beam-setting equipment, and this work should therefore be carried out by a Nissan dealer or suitably-equipped workshop. Headlight aim is part of the MOT test, so any MOT test centre will have the equipment to do this.

3 For reference, the headlights can be finely adjusted by rotating the adjuster screws fitted to the rear of each light unit. The vertical adjustment screw is mounted at the outer end of the headlight. The horizontal adjustment screw is mounted at the inner end of the headlight.

10 Instrument panel – removal and refitting

1 The instrument display fitted to Micra

models contains very few traditional bulbs. All warning lights use light emitting diodes (LEDs) for illumination. Bulbs are fitted for the indicator lights, main beam and panel illumination.

Removal

2 Disconnect the battery negative lead, and position the lead away from the battery (also see *Disconnecting the battery*).

3 With reference to Chapter 11, remove the steering column shrouds and the dashboard upper panel.

4 Gently work free the panel trim. This is retained by a combination of metal clips and five locating tabs **(see illustration)**.

5 Disconnect the wiring plug from the rear of the panel **(see illustration)**.

6 Remove the two front mounting screws and one at the rear and withdraw it **(see illustration)**.

Refitting

7 Refitting is a reversal of removal.

10.4 Prise the trim piece free

10.5 Remove the connector plug

10.6a Remove the rear screw . . .

10.6b . . . one front screw . . .

10.6c . . . and the other

10.6d Removing the panel

11.2 Remove the mounting bolt

12.2 Remove the nut cover

12.3 Remove the wiper arm

11 Horn – removal and refitting

Removal

1 Open the bonnet, and remove the right-hand side grille complete with the indicator lamp.
2 Unscrew the single horn mounting bolt, and withdraw the horn from its mounting **(see illustration)**.
3 Disconnect the wiring to the horn.

Refitting

4 Refitting is a reversal of removal.

12 Wiper arms – removal and refitting

Removal

1 Operate the wiper motor, and then switch it off so that the wiper arm returns to the park position.
2 Prise off the wiper arm spindle nut cover, then slacken and remove the spindle nut **(see illustration)**.
3 Lift the blade off the glass, and pull the wiper arm off its spindle **(see illustration)**.
4 Note that on some models, the wiper arms may be very tight on the spindle splines – it should be possible to lever the arm off the spindle, using a flat-bladed screwdriver (take

care not to damage the scuttle cover panel). In extreme cases, it may even be necessary to use a small puller to free the arm **(see illustration)**.

Refitting

5 Ensure that the wiper arm and spindle splines are clean and dry, and then refit the arm to the spindle. Where applicable, align the wiper blade with the tape fitted on removal.
6 Refit the spindle nut, tightening it securely, and clip the nut cover back into position.

13 Windscreen wiper motor and linkage – removal and refitting

Note: *After removal of the wiper and linkage the support panel can also be removed. Removing this panel provides clear access to the rear of the engine and the braking system.*

Removal

1 Remove the wiper arms as described in Section 12.

> **HAYNES HiNT** *Stick a piece of masking tape along the edge of the wiper blade, to use as an alignment aid on refitting.*

2 Remove the rubber weatherstrip along the front edge of the windscreen lower cover panel **(see illustration)**.

12.4 A small puller may help free the wiper arm

13.2 Pull the weatherstrip clips free

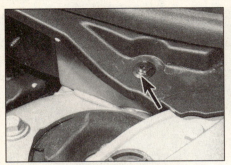

13.3a One of the cowl screws

13.3b Pull the cowl forward

13.4 Remove the wiring plug

HAYNES HINT

With the cowl removed the lower edge of the screen is exposed and liable to cracking from dropped and mishandled tools. A length of split hose (arrowed) protects the screen.

13.6 Remove the motor and linkage

3 Remove the two screws and pull the panel forward to remove it **(see illustrations)**.
4 Disconnect the wiper motor wiring plug **(see illustration)**, and collect the seals from the wiper arm spindles.
5 Remove the three bolts and single nut **(see Haynes Hint)**.
6 Lift out the wiper motor and linkage from below the windscreen **(see illustration)**. If the wiper motor and linkage is being removed for access to another component, this is all the dismantling which is required. To separate the motor and linkage, proceed as follows.
7 Remove the nut (and recover the washer) from the motor spindle.
8 Before removing the wiper motor itself, paint or scribe a mark across the motor spindle and the mounting frame.
9 Remove the three screws, and separate the wiper motor from the frame.

Refitting

10 Refitting is a reversal of removal, bearing in mind the following points:
a) *Ensure that the motor spindle is in the 'parked' position (align the marks made before removal), then refit the washer and tighten the nut.*
b) *Tighten all fasteners securely.*
c) *Refit the wiper arms with reference to Section 12.*

14 Tailgate wiper motor – removal and refitting

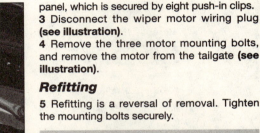
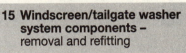

Removal

1 Remove the wiper arm as described in Section 12, and collect the seal from the spindle.
2 Open the tailgate, and remove the inner trim

panel, which is secured by eight push-in clips.
3 Disconnect the wiper motor wiring plug **(see illustration)**.
4 Remove the three motor mounting bolts, and remove the motor from the tailgate **(see illustration)**.

Refitting

5 Refitting is a reversal of removal. Tighten the mounting bolts securely.

15 Windscreen/tailgate washer system components – removal and refitting

Washer fluid reservoir

Removal

1 Remove the front bumper as described in Chapter 11.
2 Remove the filler neck from the radiator support panel by removing the filler cap and then pushing down on the filler neck.
3 Disconnect the wiring plug from the washer pump.
4 Anticipate some spillage of washer fluid (have a suitable container ready), then disconnect the washer hoses, noting their fitted locations **(see illustration)**.
5 Remove the two reservoir mounting bolts and single nut, and then remove the reservoir.

Refitting

6 Refitting is a reversal of removal. Make sure the washer hoses are securely reconnected to their original positions.

14.3 Remove the wiring plug

14.4 Remove the motor

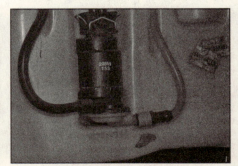

15.4 The screen washer pump

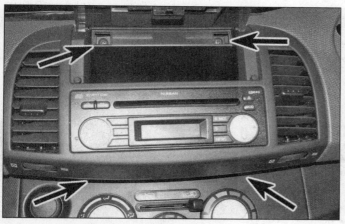

16.3 Remove the upper and lower screws

16.4a Remove the three bolts below the upper dash panel . . .

Washer fluid pump

Removal

7 Proceed as described in paragraphs 1 to 4.
8 Push the pump up from the reservoir, and recover the rubber sealing grommet.

Refitting

9 Examine the rubber sealing grommet, and renew if necessary.
10 Refitting is a reversal of removal, but take care not to push the grommet into the reservoir when refitting the pump. Make sure that the pump is securely fitted in its sealing grommet, and make sure that the fluid hose(s) are securely reconnected.

Windscreen washer jet

Removal

11 Taking care not to damage the paintwork, carefully prise the washer jet from the inside of the bonnet.
12 Disconnect the washer hose from the jet, and remove it completely. Check the operation of the one-way valve by blowing through the washer jet.

Refitting

13 Refitting is a reversal of removal, but make sure that the fluid hose connections are securely remade.

Tailgate washer jet

Removal

14 Remove the high-level stop-light as described in Section 7.
15 Anticipating some fluid spillage, disconnect the fluid hose from the base of the jet. Tape the hose to the tailgate if possible, to stop it dropping down inside.
16 Taking care not to damage the paintwork, carefully prise the washer jet from the top of the tailgate.

Refitting

17 Refitting is a reversal of removal, but make sure that the fluid hose connection is securely re-made.

16 Radio unit –
removal and refitting

Removal

1 If removing the original audio unit, ensure you have the security code before proceeding.
2 Remove the dashboard upper panel as described in Chapter 11.
3 Remove the two upper and two lower mounting screws **(see illustration)**.
4 Working from the top of the dashboard remove the three screws holding the audio unit to the crossmember and remove the unit complete with the centre vents **(see illustrations)**. Disconnect the wiring as the unit is pulled free.
5 With the unit on the bench remove the screws and separate the audio unit from its support cage **(see illustrations)**.

Refitting

6 Refitting is a reversal of removal, but enter the security code. Do this by using the preset radio station buttons. If the code is 3624 for example press the preset button 1 three times, and then the preset station button 2 six times. Continue for the remaining station preset buttons and then press the TA button on the unit to confirm the code selection. The audio unit should now work.

16.4b . . . and remove the audio unit

16.5a First remove the air vents . . .

16.5b . . . and then the front panel screws

16.5c Remove the screws that secure the audio unit to the cage

17 Speakers – removal and refitting

Removal

1 Remove the front door trim, rear door trim or rear panel (on 3-door models) as described in Chapter 11.
2 The door speakers are secured to the inner door panel by three or four screws **(see illustrations)**.
3 Disconnect the speaker wiring plug.

Refitting

4 Refitting is a reversal of removal.

18 Radio aerial – removal and refitting

Removal

1 If only the aerial mast is to be removed, this can be unscrewed from the aerial base.
2 Removing the aerial base requires that the headlining must be unclipped and lowered at the front, which is not a job to be undertaken lightly. It is advisable to remove the grab handles and sun visors (as described in Chapter 11), and even the interior light (Section 6). The front door rubber seals will also need to be pulled away from the door frames.
3 Remove the radio unit as described in Section 16.
4 The aerial lead runs across the top of the lower section of the facia (remove the upper section for access, as described in Chapter 11). From there, it runs up the left hand A-pillar, and across to the base of the aerial, where it is secured by a nut.
5 Once the aerial lead has been disconnected, remove the aerial base fasteners, and remove the base from the roof. Recover the sealing grommet.

Refitting

6 Refitting is a reversal of removal.

19 Anti-theft immobiliser – general information

An engine immobiliser system is fitted as standard to all models, and the system is operated automatically every time the ignition key is inserted/removed. The latest version of the Nissan Anti-Theft System is sophisticated in that the key must be recognised not only by the main ECU, but also by the Body Control Module (BCM), the Intelligent Power Distribution Module (IPDM) and the instrument panel.

The immobiliser system ensures that the car can only be started using the original Nissan keys supplied with the car when

17.2a Remove the screws and disconnect the wiring from the front door speaker

new. Each key contains an electronic chip (transponder) which is programmed with a code. When the key is inserted into the ignition switch, it uses the current present in the sensor coil (which is fitted to the switch housing) to send a signal to the various electronic control units. When the key is recognised by all modules in the system the car will start.

The security indicator light on the facia panel indicates when the system is active. Should the light continue to flash once the ignition key has been inserted, the engine will not start – the most likely reason for this being the use of an uncoded key.

If the ignition key is lost, a new one can be obtained from a Nissan dealer. They have access to the correct key code for the immobiliser system of your car, and will be able to supply a new coded key.

If you have any spare keys cut, and they are not coded correctly, they will only open the doors, etc, and will not be capable of starting the engine. For this reason, it may be best to have any spare keys supplied by your Nissan dealer.

20 Airbag system – general information, precautions and system de-activation

General information

Driver's and front seat passenger's airbags are fitted as standard equipment on most models. The driver's airbag is fitted to the steering wheel centre pad, while the passenger's unit is fitted to the top of the facia. These airbags are intended to deploy in the event of a head-on collision.

Higher specification models also have side airbags which fire from modules built into the front seats. The side airbags are only supposed to be triggered in the event of a lateral impact. Some models also feature curtain airbags fitted above the front and rear doors, again these are designed to deploy in side impacts.

The system is armed only when the ignition is switched on. However, a reserve power source maintains a power supply to the

17.2b The rear speakers (3-door models) are retained by four screws

system in the event of a break in the main electrical supply. The system is activated by 'g' sensors (deceleration sensors), incorporated in the electronic control unit. All models have a separate sensor, bolted to the engine bay front panel, while models with side airbags have further sensors in the B-pillars. Note that the electronic control unit also controls the front seat belt tensioners, fitted to all models.

The airbags are inflated by gas generators, which force the bags out from their locations. Although these are safety items, their deployment is violently rapid, and this may cause injury if they are triggered unintentionally.

Precautions

⚠ *Warning: The following precautions must be observed when working on vehicles equipped with an airbag system, to prevent the possibility of personal injury.*

General precautions

The following precautions must be observed when carrying out work on a vehicle equipped with an airbag:
a) *Do not disconnect the battery with the engine running.*
b) *Before carrying out any work in the vicinity of the airbag, removal of any of the airbag components, or any welding work on the car, de-activate the system as described in the following sub-Section.*
c) *Do not attempt to test any of the airbag system circuits using test meters or any other test equipment.*
d) *If the airbag warning light comes on, or any fault in the system is suspected, consult a Nissan dealer without delay. Do not attempt to carry out fault diagnosis, or any dismantling of the components.*

Precautions when handling an airbag
a) *Transport the airbag by itself, bag upwards.*
b) *Do not put your arms around the airbag.*
c) *Carry the airbag close to the body, bag outwards.*
d) *Do not drop the airbag or expose it to impacts.*
e) *Do not attempt to dismantle the airbag unit.*

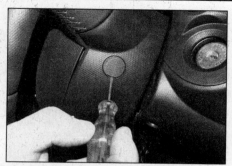

21.2 Remove the bolt covers to access the Torx fittings

21.3a Lever the locking catch up . . .

21.3b . . . and then lift up the plug

f) *Do not connect any form of electrical equipment to any part of the airbag circuit.*

Precautions when storing an airbag

a) *Store the unit in a cupboard with the airbag upwards.*
b) *Do not expose the airbag to temperatures above 80°C.*
c) *Do not expose the airbag to flames.*
d) *Do not attempt to dispose of the airbag – consult a Nissan dealer.*
e) *Never refit an airbag which is known to be faulty or damaged.*

De-activation of airbag system

The system must be de-activated as follows, before carrying out any work on the airbag components or surrounding area.
a) *Switch off the ignition.*
b) *Remove the ignition key.*
c) *Switch off all electrical equipment.*
d) *Disconnect the battery negative lead (see Disconnecting the battery).*
e) *Insulate the battery negative terminal and the end of the battery negative lead to prevent any possibility of contact.*
f) **Wait for at least five minutes** *before carrying out any further work.*

21 Airbag system components – removal and refitting

> **Warning: Refer to the precautions given in Section 20 before attempting to carry out work on the airbag components.**

Driver's airbag

Removal

1 De-activate the airbag system as described in Section 20. The airbag unit is an integral part of the steering wheel centre pad.
2 The airbag's two Torx screws are fitted to the back of the steering wheel centre pad, and are hidden by plastic trim covers **(see illustration)**. It is likely the screws will be quite tight, especially if they have not been disturbed recently – use only the proper tools to remove them (T30 Torx).

3 Turn the unit over, and working from the side, remove the electrical connector by levering free the locking catch and then lifting out the plug **(see illustrations)**.
4 Remove the airbag and store it in a safe place, with reference to the precautions in Section 20.

Refitting

5 Refitting is a reversal of removal, noting the following points:
a) *The battery must still be disconnected when reconnecting the airbag wiring.*
b) *Ensure that the airbag wiring plug is securely reconnected.*
c) *Fit new bolts and tighten to the correct torque.*

Passenger's airbag

Removal

6 De-activate the airbag system as described in Section 20, and remove the glovebox as described in Chapter 11, Section 23.
7 Remove the upper section of the facia panel as described in Chapter 11.
8 Disconnect the wiring plug **(see illustration)**.
9 Remove the two airbag retaining nuts and single bolt **(see illustration)** and then carefully remove the airbag.

Refitting

10 Refitting is a reversal of removal, bearing in mind the following points:
a) *The battery must still be disconnected when reconnecting the airbag wiring.*
b) *Make sure that the wiring harness is*

21.8 Lever up the catch and remove the plug

routed as noted before removal, and that the connectors are reconnected to their original positions.
c) *Make sure that the wiring connectors are securely reconnected.*
d) *Fit new nuts and bolt and tighten the to the specified torque.*

Airbag clockspring (rotary connector)

Removal

11 Remove the driver's airbag unit as described previously in this Section.
12 Remove the steering wheel as described in Chapter 10.
13 Remove the steering column shrouds as described in Chapter 11, Section 23.
14 If the clockspring will be off the car for any length of time, secure it using tape so that it is not turned.
15 Release the electrical connectors to the switch assembly, and then remove the screws.
16 Remove the clockspring complete with the switch assembly, and separate the clockspring on the bench.

Refitting

17 Refitting is a reversal of removal.
18 Before refitting the steering wheel, the clockspring unit should be centralised (unless it is known absolutely that the steering wheel was centralised before removal, and that the clockspring has not been turned during or since its removal).
19 First, turn the clockspring clockwise

21.9 Remove the nuts and bolt

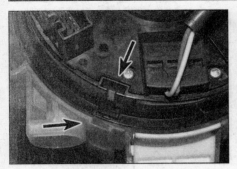

21.19 The clockspring alignment marks

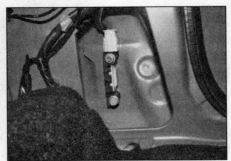

21.32 The side impact sensor

gently, until resistance is felt. Now turn the clockspring about two and a half turns anti-clockwise, until the arrowhead markings on the front face and outer cover are aligned **(see illustration)**. **Note:** *It is not enough to simply align the marks – the unit must be centralised first, with the marks as confirmation.*

20 Refit the steering wheel as described in Chapter 10.

Side airbags

21 The side airbags are located internally within the front seat backrest, and no attempt should be made to remove them. Any suspected problems with the side airbag system should be referred to a Nissan dealer. The side airbags are supplied as a complete seat back, since deployment damages the seat back.

Airbag control unit

Removal

22 The airbag control unit is located underneath the centre console. Before removing the control unit, de-activate the airbag system as described in Section 20.

23 Remove the centre console as described in Chapter 11.

24 Disconnect the wiring plugs from the front of the control unit. If there is any chance of incorrectly refitting them, mark them for position first.

25 Remove the bolts used to secure the sensor, and remove it from the floor.

Refitting

26 Refitting is a reversal of removal, bearing in mind the following points:

a) *The battery must still be disconnected when reconnecting the airbag wiring.*

b) *Make sure that the wiring connectors are securely reconnected.*

c) *Tighten the mounting bolts to the specified torque – this is essential if the sensors inside the unit are to operate correctly.*

Airbag sensors

Front impact sensor

27 The sensor are located under the bonnet,

behind the front slam panel. Before removing the sensors, de-activate the airbag system as described in Section 20.

28 Remove the front right-hand grille.

29 Disconnect the sensor wiring plug.

30 Unscrew the two sensor mounting bolts, and withdraw the sensor.

31 Refitting is a reversal of removal, bearing in mind the following points:

a) *The battery must still be disconnected when reconnecting the wiring.*

b) *Make sure that the wiring connectors are securely reconnected.*

c) *Replace the mounting bolts and tighten the bolts to the specified torque*

Side impact sensors

32 The sensors are located in the B-pillars, behind the seat belt inertia reel **(see illustration)**. Before removing the sensors, de-activate the airbag system as described in Section 20.

33 On 3-door models, remove either the door trim panel or the rear side trim panel (depending on which side impact sensor is being worked on), as described in Chapter 11.

34 On 5-door models, remove the B-pillar trim panel as described in Chapter 11, Section 23.

35 Remove the seatbelt as described in Chapter 11.

36 Disconnect the sensor wiring plug.

37 Unscrew the two sensor mounting bolts, and withdraw the sensor.

38 Refitting is a reversal of removal, bearing in mind the following points:

a) *The battery must still be disconnected when reconnecting the wiring.*

b) *Make sure that the wiring connectors are securely reconnected.*

c) *Fit new bolts and tighten the mounting bolts to the specified torque.*

22 Parking aid components – general information, removal and refitting

General information

1 The parking aid system is available as a standard fitment on some models, and

optional on other models. Four ultrasound sensors located in the rear bumper measure the distance to the closest object behind the car, and inform the driver using acoustic signals from a buzzer located under the right-hand rear luggage compartment trim. The nearer the object, the more frequent the acoustic signals.

2 The system includes a control unit and self-diagnosis program, and therefore, in the event of a fault, the vehicle should be taken to a Nissan dealer.

Control unit

Removal

3 The control unit is located beneath the rear luggage right-hand side trim. First, adjust the rear seat fully forward and fold down the backrest.

4 Remove the luggage compartment right-hand rear trim panel as described in Chapter 11.

5 Disconnect the wiring from the control unit, then prise out the 2 securing clips and remove the unit from inside the car.

Refitting

6 Refitting is a reversal of removal.

Buzzer

7 The buzzer is located next to the control unit. Follow the procedure described in paragraphs 3 and 4.

8 Disconnect the wiring from the buzzer, then prise out the 2 securing clips and remove the buzzer from inside the car.

9 Refitting is a reversal of removal.

Range/distance sensor

Removal

10 The rear bumper must be removed as described in Chapter 11 in order to remove the sensors.

11 Squeeze together the retaining clips, then press out the sensor from the outside of the bumper.

Refitting

12 Refitting is a reversal of removal. Press the sensor firmly into position until the retaining clips engage.

23 Multiplex wiring modules – general information

1 The Intelligent Power Distribution Module (IPDM) forms part of the engine compartment fuse/relay box and is located behind the left-hand headlight. The Body Control Module (BCM) is located beneath the dashboard upper panel. Neither of these modules can be renewed without specialised electronic equipment so it is recommended that this work be carried out by a Nissan dealer.

Nissan Micra wiring diagrams

Diagram 1

WARNING: This vehicle is fitted with a supplemental restraint system (SRS) consisting of a combination of driver (and passenger) airbag(s), side impact protection airbags and seatbelt pre-tensioners. The use of electrical test equipment on any SRS wiring systems may cause the seatbelt pre-tensioners to abruptly retract and airbags to explosively deploy, resulting in potentially severe personal injury. Extreme care should be taken to correctly identify any circuits to be tested to avoid choosing any of the SRS wiring in error.
For further information see airbag system precautions in body electrical systems chapter.
Note: The SRS wiring harness can normally be identified by yellow and/or orange harness or harness connectors.

Key to symbols

Link-A — Fusible link

Fuse-1 — Fuse

Bulb

1 Amp — Heating element with indicated current rating

M — Electric motor

6 / 4 — Dotted outline indicate the item (bulb) is part of a larger assembly. Number indicate pin numbers

6 / 4 — Solid outline indicates the item is an individual part and not part of a larger assembly

Ganged switch with multiple contacts

Single switch with multiple contacts

Momentary switch

Relay

CPU — Graphical representation of a component for which no additional data is provided

ABS ECU 6 — Link to another circuit; where appropriate the interfacing pin numbers are shown

7 — Item reference; refering to key at top of diagram page

Connecting wires

Wire splice, soldered or connectorised junction

Alternative layout depending on model / year

O/G — Wire colour (orange with green stripe)

Diode

Light emitting diode

Light sensitive diode

Models with ABS
ABS ECU 6 — Chain dashed box indicates item specific to a particular varient

Earth point

E1 — Earth point with reference (see earth locations on this page)

Key to circuits

Diagram 1 — Information on wiring diagrams

Diagram 2 — Power distribution system

Diagram 3 — Starting system, charging system. radiator fan, cigar lighter, horn, indicators and hazard warning

Diagram 4 — Headlamps, rear fog lights, brake lights, numberplate lights, sidelights, front fog lights

Diagram 5 — Headlamp levelling, reversing light, interior lights

Diagram 6 — Windscreen wipers, screen washers, rear screen wiper, headlight washer, rear screen and door mirror heaters

Diagram 7 — Central locking, motorised door mirrors, powered windows

Diagram 8 — Blower and air conditioning, instrument illumination

Diagram 9 — Heated seats, motorised sunroof, ABS/ESP system

Diagram 10 — Typical audio system

Diagram 11 — Instruments

Diagram 12 — Fuse details

Key to earth points

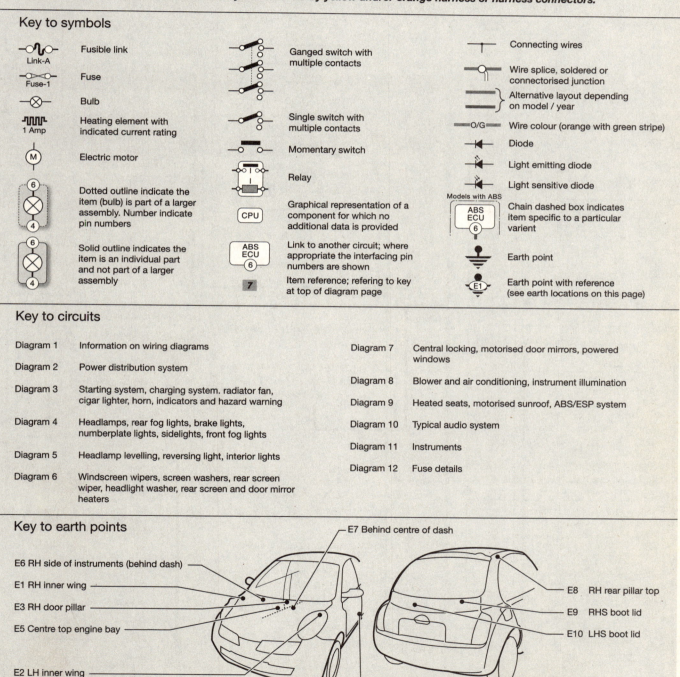

E7 Behind centre of dash

E6 RH side of instruments (behind dash)

E1 RH inner wing

E3 RH door pillar

E5 Centre top engine bay

E2 LH inner wing

E4 LH door pillar

E8 RH rear pillar top

E9 RHS boot lid

E10 LHS boot lid

H33749

Wire colours

B	Black	P	Purple
G	Green	R	Red
K	Pink	S	Grey
Lg	Light green	L	Blue
N	Brown	W	White
O	Orange	Y	Yellow
Lu	Light blue		

Key to items

1 Battery
2 Ignition switch
3 Fusible link holder
4 Fuse box
5 Fuse and relay box
  a) accessory relay
  b) blower motor relay

6 Intelligent power
   distribution module
  a) starter relay
  b) cooling fan hi relay
  c) cooling fan lo relay
  d) fuel pump relay
  e) ignition relay
  f) ECM relay

  g) throttle control motor relay
  h) rear window heater relay
  j) front wiper hi/lo relay
  k) front wiper main relay
  l) A/C relay
  m) tail lamp relay
  n) headlamp lo relay
  o) LH headlamp hi relay

  p) RH headlamp hi relay
  q) front fog light relay

7 Park/neutral switch
8 Auto transmission
   selector switch

Diagram 2

H33750

Note (1) 2005 onward

Power distribution system

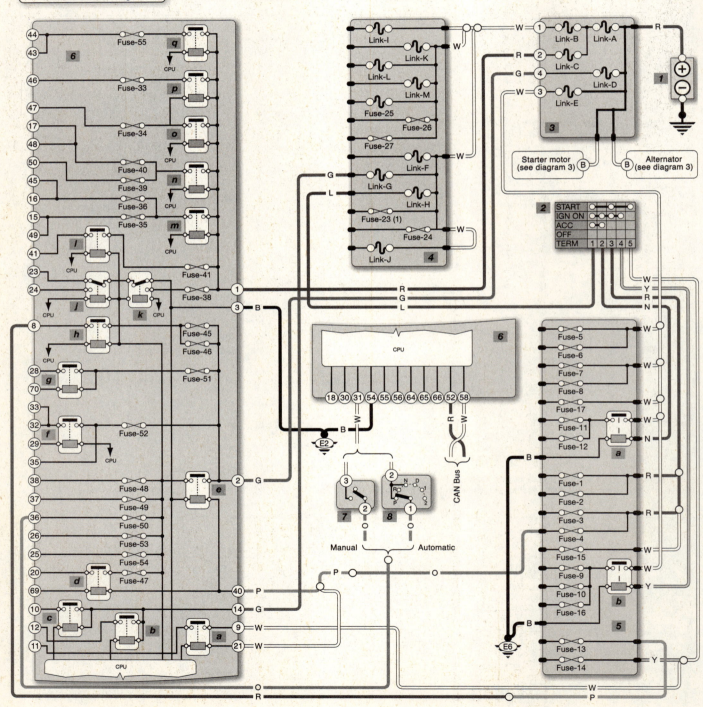

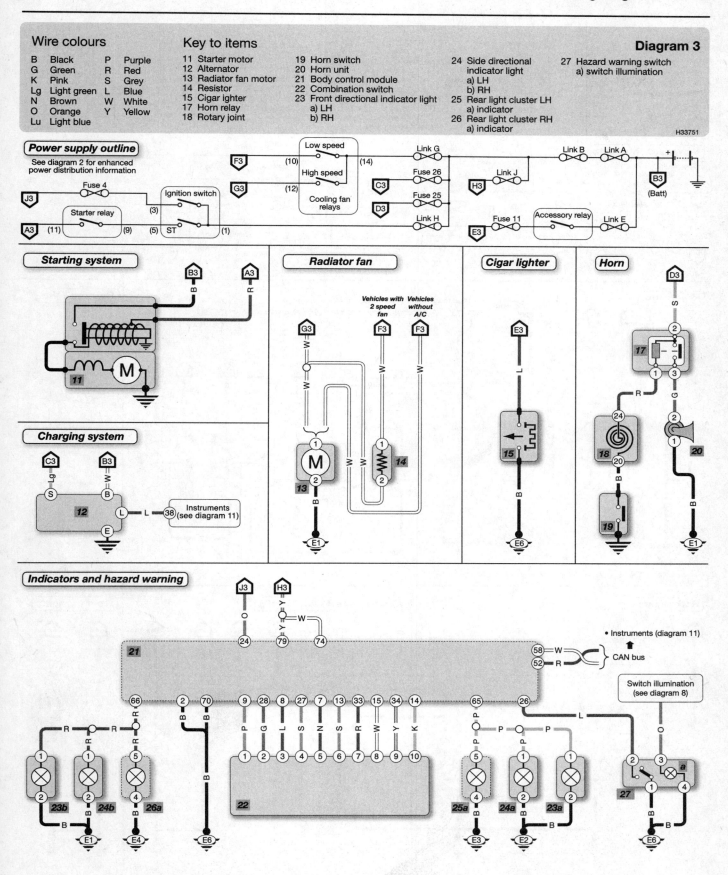

Wire colours

B	Black	P	Purple
G	Green	R	Red
K	Pink	S	Grey
Lg	Light green	L	Blue
N	Brown	W	White
O	Orange	Y	Yellow
Lu	Light blue		

Key to items

11 Starter motor
12 Alternator
13 Radiator fan motor
14 Resistor
15 Cigar ighter
17 Horn relay
18 Rotary joint

19 Horn switch
20 Horn unit
21 Body control module
22 Combination switch
23 Front directional indicator light
   a) LH
   b) RH

24 Side directional
   indicator light
   a) LH
   b) RH
25 Rear light cluster LH
   a) indicator
26 Rear light cluster RH
   a) indicator

27 Hazard warning switch
   a) switch illumination

H33751

Diagram 3

Power supply outline
See diagram 2 for enhanced power distribution information

Starting system

Charging system

Radiator fan

Cigar lighter

Horn

Indicators and hazard warning

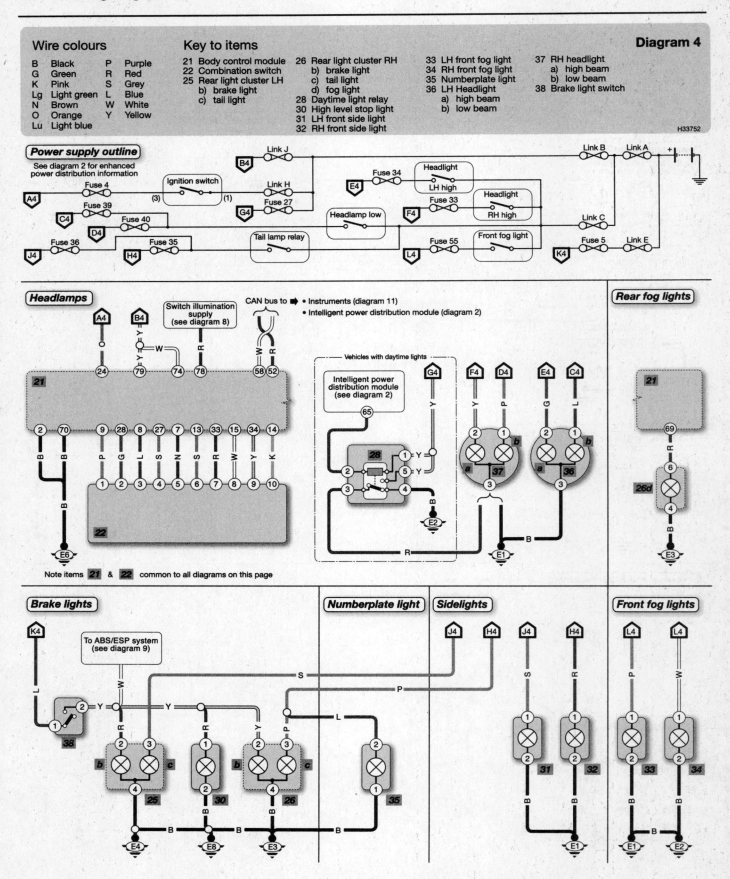

Wire colours

B	Black	P	Purple
G	Green	R	Red
K	Pink	S	Grey
Lg	Light green	L	Blue
N	Brown	W	White
O	Orange	Y	Yellow
Lu	Light blue		

Key to items

21 Body control module
22 Combination switch
25 Rear light cluster LH
  b) brake light
  c) tail light
26 Rear light cluster RH
  b) brake light
  c) tail light
  d) fog light
28 Daytime light relay
30 High level stop light
31 LH front side light
32 RH front side light

33 LH front fog light
34 RH front fog light
35 Numberplate light
36 LH Headlight
  a) high beam
  b) low beam

37 RH headlight
  a) high beam
  b) low beam
38 Brake light switch

Diagram 4

H33752

Power supply outline
See diagram 2 for enhanced power distribution information

Headlamps

Rear fog lights

CAN bus to ➡ • Instruments (diagram 11)
• Intelligent power distribution module (diagram 2)

Switch illumination supply (see diagram 8)

Vehicles with daytime lights

Intelligent power distribution module (see diagram 2)

Note items **21** & **22** common to all diagrams on this page

Brake lights

To ABS/ESP system (see diagram 9)

Numberplate light

Sidelights

Front fog lights

Wire colours

B	Black	P	Purple
G	Green	R	Red
K	Pink	S	Grey
Lg	Light green	L	Blue
N	Brown	W	White
O	Orange	Y	Yellow
Lu	Light blue		

Key to items

6 Intelligent fuse box
7 Park/neutral switch
8 Auto transmission selector switch
21 Body control module
22 Combination switch
25 Rear light cluster LH
   d) reversing light
40 LH Headlight aiming motor
41 RH Headlight aiming motor
42 Headlight aiming switch
43 Key switch
44 Key switch and ignition knob switch
45 LH front door switch
46 LH rear door switch
47 RH front door switch
48 RH rear door switch
49 Interior light
50 Luggage space light
51 Rear door release actuator

Diagram 5

H33753

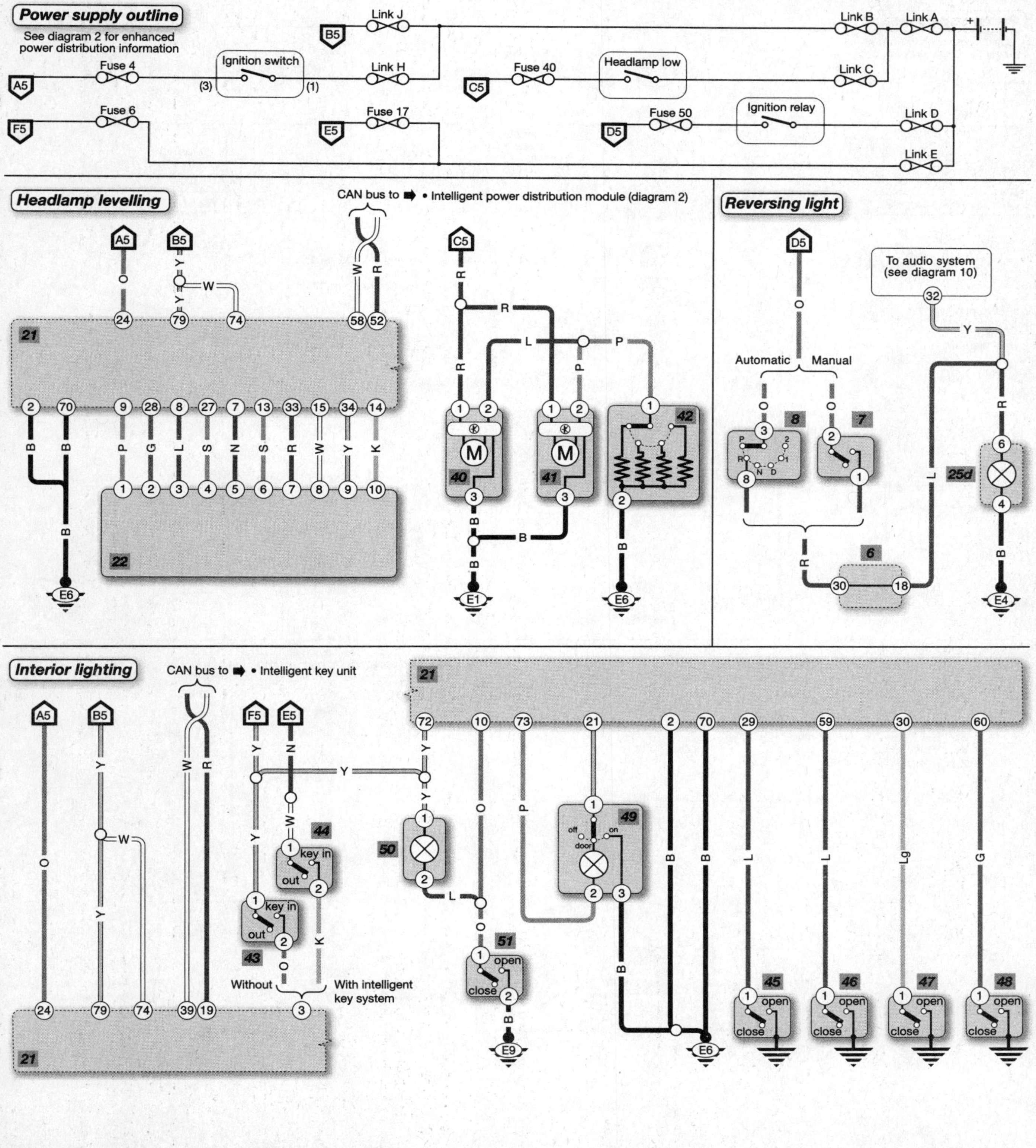

Power supply outline

See diagram 2 for enhanced power distribution information

Link J Link B Link A
Ignition switch
Fuse 4 Link H Fuse 40 Headlamp low Link C
Fuse 6 Fuse 17 Fuse 50 Ignition relay Link D
Link E

Headlamp levelling

CAN bus to ➡ • Intelligent power distribution module (diagram 2)

Reversing light

To audio system (see diagram 10)

Automatic   Manual

Interior lighting

CAN bus to ➡ • Intelligent key unit

key in / out
key in / out
Without   With intelligent key system

off / on / door
open / close

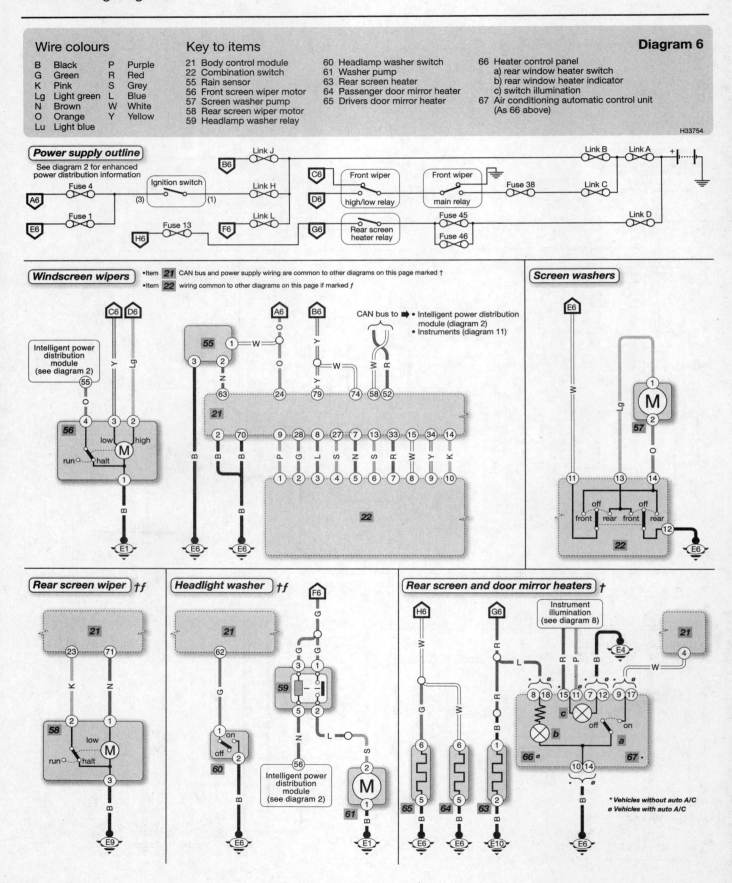

Diagram 6

Wire colours

B   Black   P   Purple
G   Green   R   Red
K   Pink   S   Grey
Lg Light green L   Blue
N   Brown   W   White
O   Orange   Y   Yellow
Lu Light blue

Key to items

21 Body control module
22 Combination switch
55 Rain sensor
56 Front screen wiper motor
57 Screen washer pump
58 Rear screen wiper motor
59 Headlamp washer relay
60 Headlamp washer switch
61 Washer pump
63 Rear screen heater
64 Passenger door mirror heater
65 Drivers door mirror heater
66 Heater control panel
    a) rear window heater switch
    b) rear window heater indicator
    c) switch illumination
67 Air conditioning automatic control unit
    (As 66 above)

H33754

Power supply outline

See diagram 2 for enhanced power distribution information

Windscreen wipers

• Item 21 CAN bus and power supply wiring are common to other diagrams on this page marked †
• Item 22 wiring common to other diagrams on this page if marked ƒ

Screen washers

Rear screen wiper ††ƒ

Headlight washer ††ƒ

Rear screen and door mirror heaters †

* Vehicles without auto A/C
ø Vehicles with auto A/C

Wire colours

B Black
G Green
K Pink
Lg Light green
N Brown
O Orange
Lu Light blue

P Purple
R Red
S Grey
L Blue
W White
Y Yellow

Key to items

21 Body control module
43 Key switch
44 Key switch and ignition knob switch
68 Intelligent key unit
69 Door lock/unlock switch
 a) lock status indicator
 b) interior switch illuminator
70 External boot lid release switch

71 Boot lid switch
 a) switch
 b) release actuator
72 Drivers door lock actuator
73 Passenger door lock actuator
74 RH rear door lock actuator
75 LH rear door lock actuator

76 Door mirror adjustment switch
 a) position adjustment switch
 b) mirror selector switch
77 Drivers door mirror actuator
78 Passenger door mirror actuator
79 Power window main switch (drivers side)
80 Front passenger window switch
81 Drivers side window motor
82 Passenger side window motor

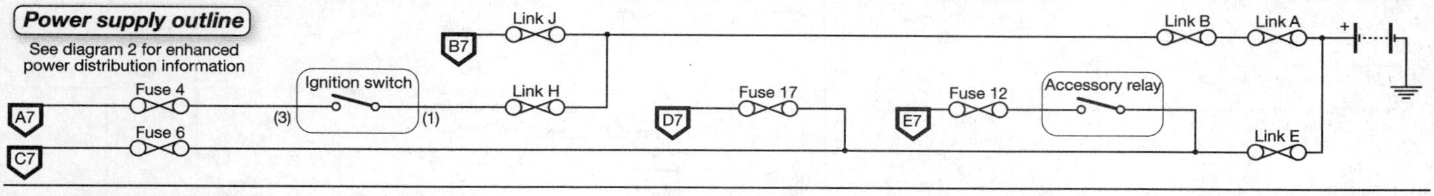

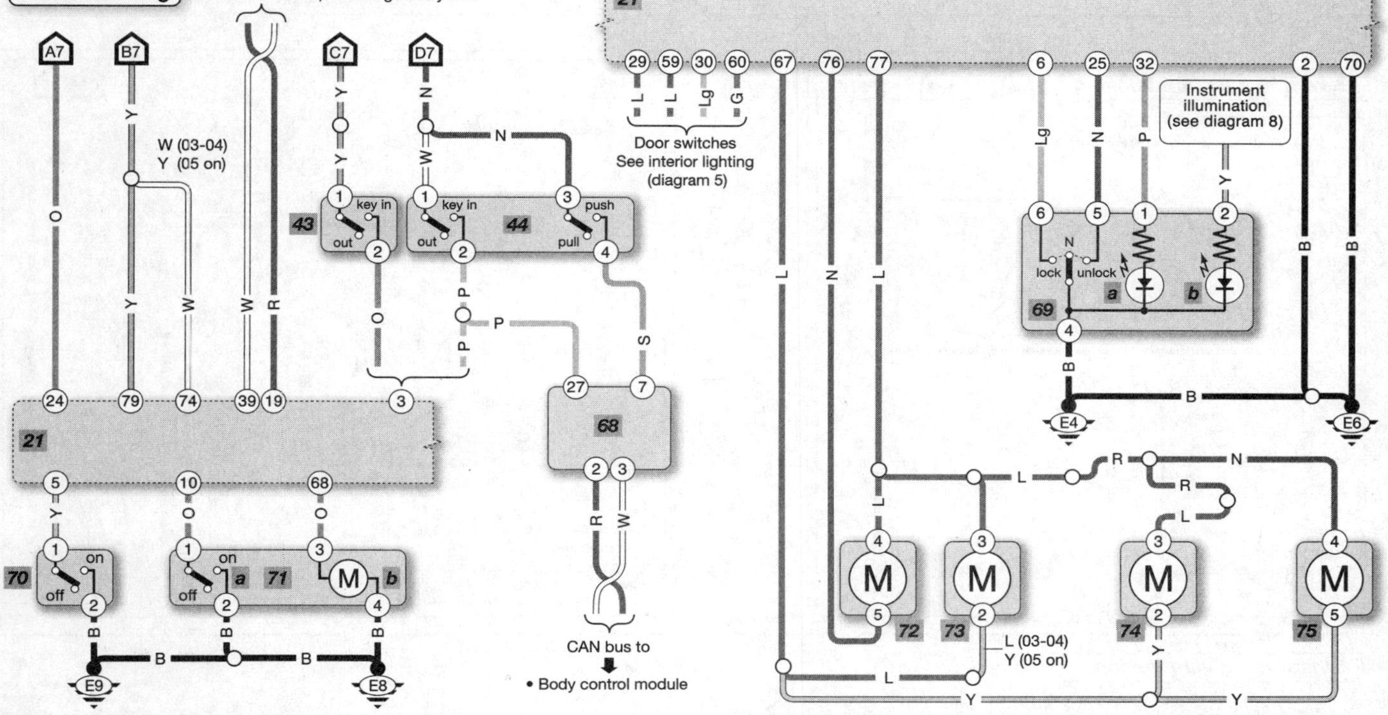

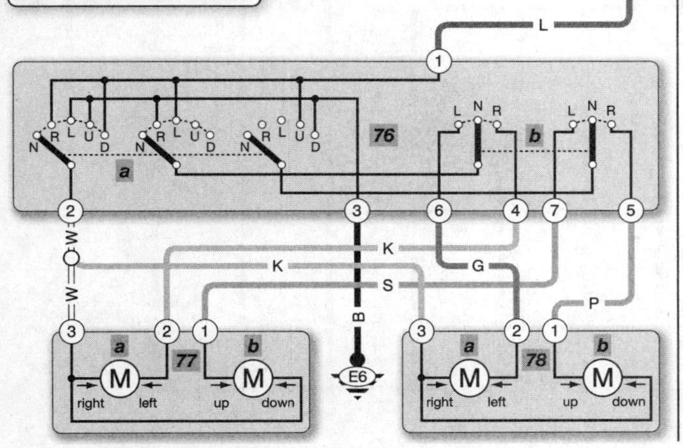

Diagram 7

H33755

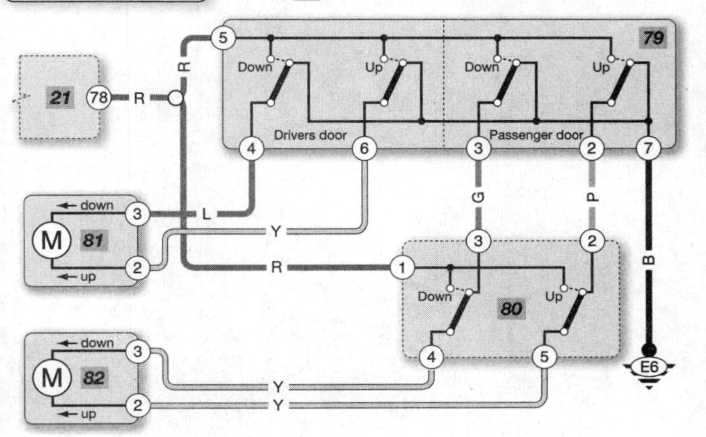

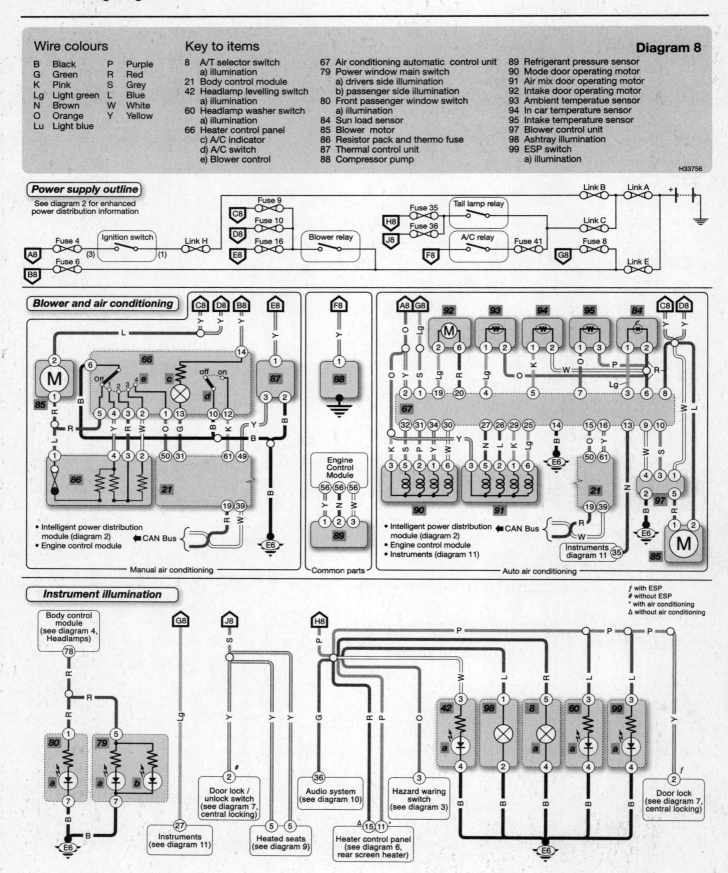

Wire colours

B	Black	P	Purple
G	Green	R	Red
K	Pink	S	Grey
Lg	Light green	L	Blue
N	Brown	W	White
O	Orange	Y	Yellow
Lu	Light blue		

Key to items

8 A/T selector switch
  a) illumination
21 Body control module
42 Headlamp levelling switch
  a) illumination
60 Headlamp washer switch
  a) illumination
66 Heater control panel
  c) A/C indicator
  d) A/C switch
  e) Blower control

67 Air conditioning automatic control unit
79 Power window main switch
  a) drivers side illumination
  b) passenger side illumination
80 Front passenger window switch
  a) illumination
84 Sun load sensor
85 Blower motor
86 Resistor pack and thermo fuse
87 Thermal control unit
88 Compressor pump

89 Refrigerant pressure sensor
90 Mode door operating motor
91 Air mix door operating motor
92 Intake door operating motor
93 Ambient temperature sensor
94 In car temperature sensor
95 Intake temperature sensor
97 Blower control unit
98 Ashtray illumination
99 ESP switch
  a) illumination

Diagram 8

H33756

Power supply outline

See diagram 2 for enhanced power distribution information

Blower and air conditioning

- Intelligent power distribution module (diagram 2)
- Engine control module

Manual air conditioning

Engine Control Module

Common parts

- Intelligent power distribution module (diagram 2)
- Engine control module
- Instruments (diagram 11)

Auto air conditioning

Instrument illumination

f with ESP
without ESP
*** with air conditioning
Δ without air conditioning

Body control module (see diagram 4, Headlamps)

Door lock / unlock switch (see diagram 7, central locking)

Instruments (see diagram 11)

Heated seats (see diagram 9)

Audio system (see diagram 10)

Heater control panel (see diagram 6, rear screen heater)

Hazard waring switch (see diagram 3)

Door lock (see diagram 7, central locking)

Wire colours

B	Black	P	Purple
G	Green	R	Red
K	Pink	S	Grey
Lg	Light green	L	Blue
N	Brown	W	White
O	Orange	Y	Yellow
Lu	Light blue		

Key to items

21	Body control module	104	LH seat heater
99	ESP switch		a) cushion heater and sub
102	LH seat heater switch		heater
	a) indicator sitch		b) seat back heater and
	b) switch illumination		sub heater
103	RH seat heater switch		c) thermoswitch
	(as 102 above)	105	RH seat heater
			(as 104 above)
		106	Sunroof motor

107	Sunroof switch
108	ABS actuator and electronics unit
109	Yaw rate/side G sensor
110	Electronic power steering control unit (EPS)
111	LH front wheel sensor
112	RH front wheel sensor
113	LH rear wheel sensor
114	RH rear wheel sensor

Diagram 9

H33757

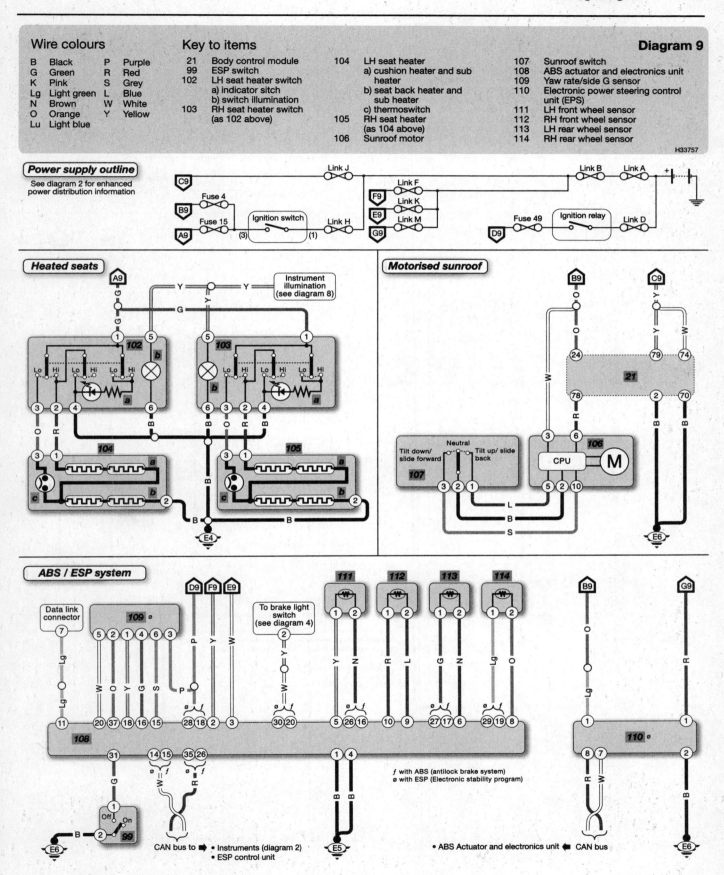

Power supply outline
See diagram 2 for enhanced power distribution information

Heated seats

Motorised sunroof

ABS / ESP system

f with ABS (antilock brake system)
ø with ESP (Electronic stability program)

CAN bus to ➡ • Instruments (diagram 2)
• ESP control unit

• ABS Actuator and electronics unit ⬅ CAN bus

Wire colours

B	Black	P	Purple
G	Green	R	Red
K	Pink	S	Grey
Lg	Light green	L	Blue
N	Brown	W	White
O	Orange	Y	Yellow
Lu	Light blue		

Key to items

18   Rotary joint
117 Audio control unit (and navigation where applicable)
118 LH front door speaker
119 LH door tweeter
120 RH front door speaker
121 RH door tweeter
122 LH rear door speaker
123 RH rear door speaker

124 Steering wheel control switches
    a) mode switch
    b) seek switch
    c) volume switch
125 GPS antenna

Diagram 10

H33758

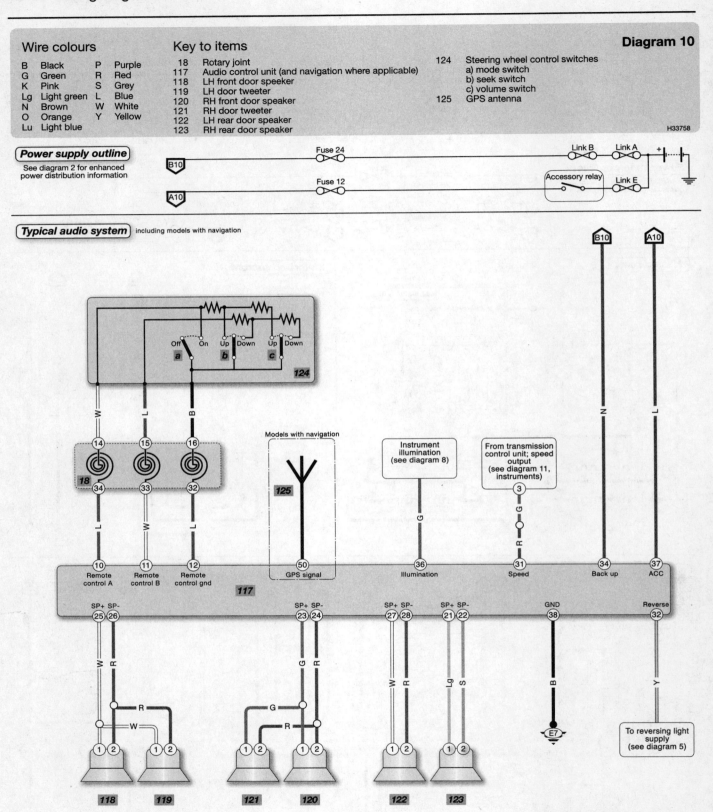

Power supply outline

See diagram 2 for enhanced power distribution information

Typical audio system including models with navigation

Diagram 11

Wire colours

B	Black	P	Purple
G	Green	R	Red
K	Pink	S	Grey
Lg	Light green	L	Blue
N	Brown	W	White
O	Orange	Y	Yellow
Lu	Light blue		

Key to items

18   Rotary joint
38   Brake light switch
124 Steering wheel control switches
     d) drive computer on/off switch
128 Main instrument unit
129 Seatbelt switch
130 Brake fluid level switch
131 Ambient temperature sensor
133 A/T overdrive switch

134 Parking brake switch
135 Fuel level sensor

H33759

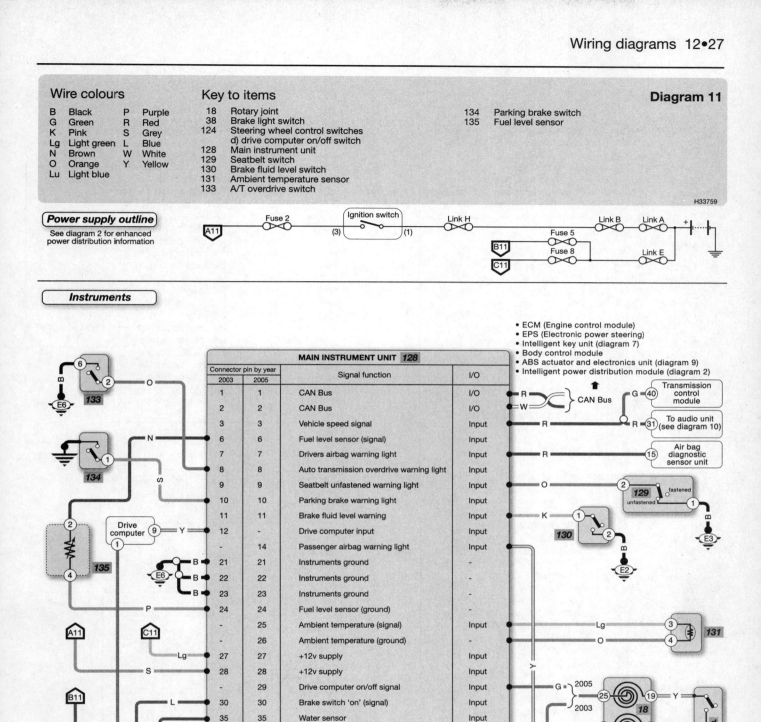

Power supply outline

See diagram 2 for enhanced power distribution information

Instruments

- ECM (Engine control module)
- EPS (Electronic power steering)
- Intelligent key unit (diagram 7)
- Body control module
- ABS actuator and electronics unit (diagram 9)
- Intelligent power distribution module (diagram 2)

MAIN INSTRUMENT UNIT 128			
Connector pin by year		Signal function	I/O
2003	2005		
1	1	CAN Bus	I/O
2	2	CAN Bus	I/O
3	3	Vehicle speed signal	Input
6	6	Fuel level sensor (signal)	Input
7	7	Drivers airbag warning light	Input
8	8	Auto transmission overdrive warning light	Input
9	9	Seatbelt unfastened warning light	Input
10	10	Parking brake warning light	Input
11	11	Brake fluid level warning	Input
12	-	Drive computer input	Input
-	14	Passenger airbag warning light	Input
21	21	Instruments ground	-
22	22	Instruments ground	-
23	23	Instruments ground	-
24	24	Fuel level sensor (ground)	-
-	25	Ambient temperature (signal)	Input
-	26	Ambient temperature (ground)	-
27	27	+12v supply	Input
28	28	+12v supply	Input
-	29	Drive computer on/off signal	Input
30	30	Brake switch 'on' (signal)	Input
35	35	Water sensor	Input
38	38	Charge warning lamp	Input

Air conditioning
(see diagram 8)

Alternator
(see diagram 3
starting and charging)

Air bag
diagnostic sensor
unit

Remote control gnd
(see diagram 10
Audio system)

Diagram 12

Fusible link holder `3` (engine bay)

Link	Rating	Function
A	250A	Main link fuse
B	80A	Supply to fuse box
C	80A	Supply to intelligent power distribution module
D	80A	Supply to intelligent power distribution module
E	60A	Supply to fuse and relay box

Fuse box `4` (engine bay)

Link	Rating	Function
F	40A	ABS and ESP systems
G	40A	Cooling fan
H	40A	Ignition switch supply
I	40A	Folding roof and PTC heaters (option)
J	40A	Body control module
K	30A	ABS and ESP systems
L	30A	Headlamp washer
M	60A	ESP and EPS systems

Fuse	Rating	Function
23	15A	Windows and folding roof
24	15A	Audio and Navi system
25	10A	Horn
26	10A	Charging system
27	10A	Daytime lights

Fuseblock junction box `5` (engine bay)

Fuse	Rating	Function
1	15A	Front/rear washer/wiper system
2	10A	Instruments
3	10A	Supplemental restraint system
4	10A	Body control module, A/C auto control module EPS system
5	10A	Brake lights
6	10A	Central locking
7	10A	Combination switch
8	10A	Instrument illumination
9	15A	Heater blower, A/C
10	15A	Heater blower, A/C
11	15A	Cigar lighter
12	10A	Door mirrors, Audio system
13	10A	Door mirror heaters
14	10A	Daytime lights
15	10A	Heated seats
16	10A	PTC heaters (option)
17	10A	Central locking

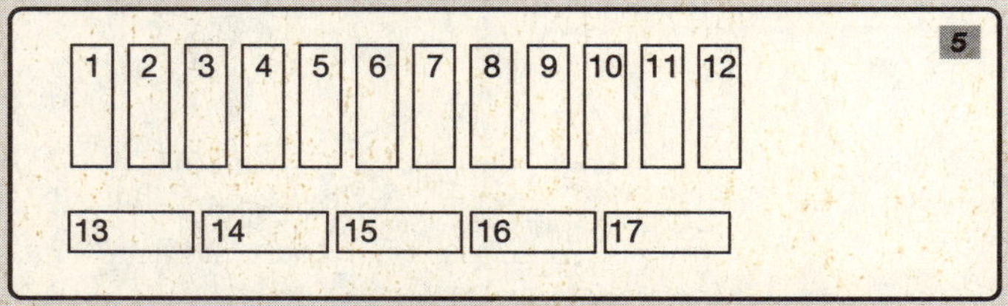

Intelligent power distribution module `6` (engine bay)

Fuse	Rating	Function
33	10A	Headlamp high beam RH
34	10A	Headlamp high beam LH
35	10A	Sidelights, interior illumination
36	10A	Sidelights, interior illumination
38	20A	Windscreen wipers
39	15A	Headlamp low beam
40	15A	Headlamp low beam
41	10A	Air conditioning (A/C)
45	15A	Heated rear screen
46	15A	Heated rear screen
47	15A	Fuel pump
48	10A	Engine electronics
49	10A	ABS/ESP
50	10A	Starting system, reversing light
51	20A	Engine electronics
52	20A	Engine electronics
53	10A	Engine electronics
54	10A	Engine electronics
55	20A	Front fog lights

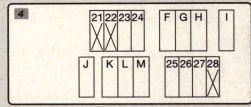

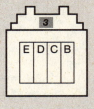

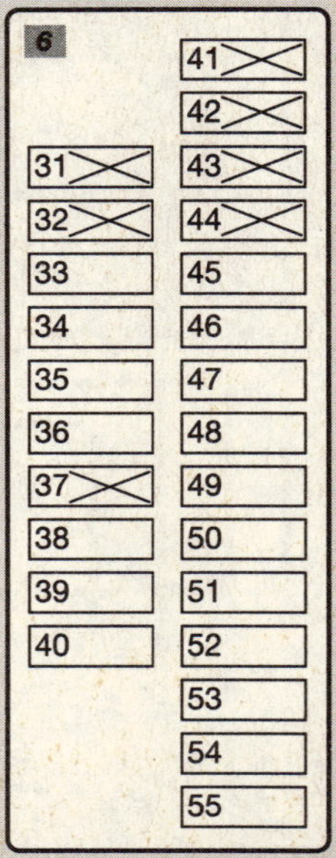

H33760

Dimensions and weights . . . . **REF•1**
Conversion factors . . . . **REF•2**
Buying spare parts . . . . **REF•3**
Jacking and vehicle support . . . . **REF•4**
Disconnecting the battery . . . . **REF•5**
General repair procedures . . . . **REF•6**

Vehicle identification . . . . **REF•7**
Tools and working facilities . . . . **REF•8**
MOT test checks . . . . **REF•10**
Fault finding . . . . **REF•14**
Glossary of technical terms . . . . **REF•26**
Index . . . . **REF•31**

Dimensions and weights

Note: *All figures are approximate, and may vary according to model. Refer to manufacturer's data for exact figures.*

Dimensions

Overall length	3715 mm
Overall width	1660 mm
Overall height (unladen)	1540 mm
Wheelbase	2432 mm

Weights

Kerb weight	946 to 1056 kg
Maximum gross vehicle weight	1475 kg
Maximum towing weight	510 kg

Conversion factors

Length (distance)

Inches (in)	x 25.4	= Millimetres (mm)	x 0.0394	= Inches (in)	
Feet (ft)	x 0.305	= Metres (m)	x 3.281	= Feet (ft)	
Miles	x 1.609	= Kilometres (km)	x 0.621	= Miles	

Volume (capacity)

Cubic inches (cu in; in³)	x 16.387	= Cubic centimetres (cc; cm³)	x 0.061	= Cubic inches (cu in; in³)	
Imperial pints (Imp pt)	x 0.568	= Litres (l)	x 1.76	= Imperial pints (Imp pt)	
Imperial quarts (Imp qt)	x 1.137	= Litres (l)	x 0.88	= Imperial quarts (Imp qt)	
Imperial quarts (Imp qt)	x 1.201	= US quarts (US qt)	x 0.833	= Imperial quarts (Imp qt)	
US quarts (US qt)	x 0.946	= Litres (l)	x 1.057	= US quarts (US qt)	
Imperial gallons (Imp gal)	x 4.546	= Litres (l)	x 0.22	= Imperial gallons (Imp gal)	
Imperial gallons (Imp gal)	x 1.201	= US gallons (US gal)	x 0.833	= Imperial gallons (Imp gal)	
US gallons (US gal)	x 3.785	= Litres (l)	x 0.264	= US gallons (US gal)	

Mass (weight)

Ounces (oz)	x 28.35	= Grams (g)	x 0.035	= Ounces (oz)	
Pounds (lb)	x 0.454	= Kilograms (kg)	x 2.205	= Pounds (lb)	

Force

Ounces-force (ozf; oz)	x 0.278	= Newtons (N)	x 3.6	= Ounces-force (ozf; oz)	
Pounds-force (lbf; lb)	x 4.448	= Newtons (N)	x 0.225	= Pounds-force (lbf; lb)	
Newtons (N)	x 0.1	= Kilograms-force (kgf; kg)	x 9.81	= Newtons (N)	

Pressure

Pounds-force per square inch (psi; lbf/in²; lb/in²)	x 0.070	= Kilograms-force per square centimetre (kgf/cm²; kg/cm²)	x 14.223	= Pounds-force per square inch (psi; lbf/in²; lb/in²)
Pounds-force per square inch (psi; lbf/in²; lb/in²)	x 0.068	= Atmospheres (atm)	x 14.696	= Pounds-force per square inch (psi; lbf/in²; lb/in²)
Pounds-force per square inch (psi; lbf/in²; lb/in²)	x 0.069	= Bars	x 14.5	= Pounds-force per square inch (psi; lbf/in²; lb/in²)
Pounds-force per square inch (psi; lbf/in²; lb/in²)	x 6.895	= Kilopascals (kPa)	x 0.145	= Pounds-force per square inch (psi; lbf/in²; lb/in²)
Kilopascals (kPa)	x 0.01	= Kilograms-force per square centimetre (kgf/cm²; kg/cm²)	x 98.1	= Kilopascals (kPa)
Millibar (mbar)	x 100	= Pascals (Pa)	x 0.01	= Millibar (mbar)
Millibar (mbar)	x 0.0145	= Pounds-force per square inch (psi; lbf/in²; lb/in²)	x 68.947	= Millibar (mbar)
Millibar (mbar)	x 0.75	= Millimetres of mercury (mmHg)	x 1.333	= Millibar (mbar)
Millibar (mbar)	x 0.401	= Inches of water (inH₂O)	x 2.491	= Millibar (mbar)
Millimetres of mercury (mmHg)	x 0.535	= Inches of water (inH₂O)	x 1.868	= Millimetres of mercury (mmHg)
Inches of water (inH₂O)	x 0.036	= Pounds-force per square inch (psi; lbf/in²; lb/in²)	x 27.68	= Inches of water (inH₂O)

Torque (moment of force)

Pounds-force inches (lbf in; lb in)	x 1.152	= Kilograms-force centimetre (kgf cm; kg cm)	x 0.868	= Pounds-force inches (lbf in; lb in)
Pounds-force inches (lbf in; lb in)	x 0.113	= Newton metres (Nm)	x 8.85	= Pounds-force inches (lbf in; lb in)
Pounds-force inches (lbf in; lb in)	x 0.083	= Pounds-force feet (lbf ft; lb ft)	x 12	= Pounds-force inches (lbf in; lb in)
Pounds-force feet (lbf ft; lb ft)	x 0.138	= Kilograms-force metres (kgf m; kg m)	x 7.233	= Pounds-force feet (lbf ft; lb ft)
Pounds-force feet (lbf ft; lb ft)	x 1.356	= Newton metres (Nm)	x 0.738	= Pounds-force feet (lbf ft; lb ft)
Newton metres (Nm)	x 0.102	= Kilograms-force metres (kgf m; kg m)	x 9.804	= Newton metres (Nm)

Power

Horsepower (hp)	x 745.7	= Watts (W)	x 0.0013	= Horsepower (hp)

Velocity (speed)

Miles per hour (miles/hr; mph)	x 1.609	= Kilometres per hour (km/hr; kph)	x 0.621	= Miles per hour (miles/hr; mph)

Fuel consumption*

Miles per gallon, Imperial (mpg)	x 0.354	= Kilometres per litre (km/l)	x 2.825	= Miles per gallon, Imperial (mpg)
Miles per gallon, US (mpg)	x 0.425	= Kilometres per litre (km/l)	x 2.352	= Miles per gallon, US (mpg)

Temperature

Degrees Fahrenheit = (°C x 1.8) + 32   Degrees Celsius (Degrees Centigrade; °C) = (°F - 32) x 0.56

It is common practice to convert from miles per gallon (mpg) to litres/100 kilometres (l/100km), where mpg x l/100 km = 282

Spare parts are available from many sources, including maker's appointed garages, accessory shops, and motor factors. To be sure of obtaining the correct parts, it will sometimes be necessary to quote the vehicle identification number (see *Vehicle identification*). If possible, it can also be useful to take the old parts along for positive identification. Items such as starter motors and alternators may be available under a service exchange scheme – any parts returned should always be clean.

Our advice regarding spare part sources is as follows.

Officially-appointed garages

This is the best source of parts which are peculiar to your car, and which are not otherwise generally available (eg, badges, interior trim, certain body panels, etc). It is also the only place at which you should buy parts if the car is still under warranty.

Accessory shops

These are very good places to buy materials and components needed for the maintenance of your car (oil, air and fuel filters, spark plugs, light bulbs, drivebelts, oils and greases, brake pads, touch-up paint, etc). Components of this nature sold by a reputable shop are of the same standard as those used by the car manufacturer.

Besides components, these shops also sell tools and general accessories, usually have convenient opening hours, charge lower prices, and can often be found not far from home. Some accessory shops have parts counters where the components needed for almost any repair job can be purchased or ordered.

Motor factors

Good factors will stock all the more important components which wear out comparatively quickly, and can sometimes supply individual components needed for the overhaul of a larger assembly (eg, brake seals and hydraulic parts, bearing shells, pistons, valves, alternator brushes). They may also handle work such as cylinder block reboring, crankshaft regrinding and balancing, etc.

Tyre and exhaust specialists

These outlets may be independent, or members of a local or national chain. They frequently offer competitive prices when compared with a main dealer or local garage, but it will pay to obtain several quotes before making a decision. When researching prices, also ask what 'extras' may be added – for instance, fitting a new valve and balancing the wheel are both commonly charged on top of the price of a new tyre.

Other sources

Beware of parts or materials obtained from market stalls, car boot sales or similar outlets. Such items are not invariably sub-standard, but there is little chance of compensation if they do prove unsatisfactory. In the case of safety-critical components such as brake pads, there is the risk not only of financial loss but also of an accident causing injury or death.

Second-hand components or assemblies obtained from a car breaker can be a good buy in some circumstances, but this sort of purchase is best made by the experienced DIY mechanic.

Jacking and vehicle support

The jack supplied with the car's tool kit should only be used for changing the roadwheels – see *Wheel changing* at the front of this book. When carrying out any other kind of work, raise the car using a hydraulic (or 'trolley') jack, and always supplement the jack with axle stands positioned under the jacking/support points. If the roadwheels do not have to be removed, consider using wheel ramps – if wished, these can be placed under the wheels once the car has been raised using a hydraulic jack, and then lowered onto the ramps so that it is resting on its wheels.

Only ever jack the car up on a solid, level surface. If there is even a slight slope, take great care that the car cannot move as the wheels are lifted off the ground. Jacking up on an uneven or gravelled surface is not recommended, as the weight of the car will not be evenly distributed, and the jack may slip as the car is raised.

As far as possible, do not leave the car unattended once it has been raised, particularly if children are playing nearby.

Before jacking up the front of the car, ensure that the handbrake is firmly applied. When jacking up the rear of the car, place wooden chocks in front of the front wheels, and engage first gear **(see illustration)**.

To raise the front and/or rear of the car, use the jacking/support points at the front and rear ends of the door sills, which are easily identified by the welded on support bracket. Position a block of wood with a groove cut in it on the jack head to prevent the car's weight resting on the sill edge; align the sill edge with the groove in the wood so that the car's weight is spread evenly over the surface of the block. Supplement the jack with axle stands (also with slotted blocks of wood) positioned as close as possible to the jacking points.

When using a hydraulic jack or axle stands, always try to position the jack head or axle stand head under one of the relevant jacking points.

Providing care is taken (and a block of wood is used to spread the load), the centre of the front subframe, and the centre of the rear axle beam, may be used as support points **(see illustration)**. It may be safe also to use reinforced areas of the floor pan ('chassis legs'), particularly those in the region of suspension mountings, as support points – consult a Nissan dealer for advice before using anything other than the approved jacking points, however.

Do not jack the car under any other part of the sill, sump, floorpan, or directly under any of the steering or suspension components. Avoid trapping cables, fuel pipes and brake pipes, and do not compress the suspension.

Never work under, around, or near a raised vehicle, unless it is adequately supported on stands. Do not rely on a jack alone, as even a hydraulic jack could fail under load.

Wheel chocks should be used when jacking the rear of the car

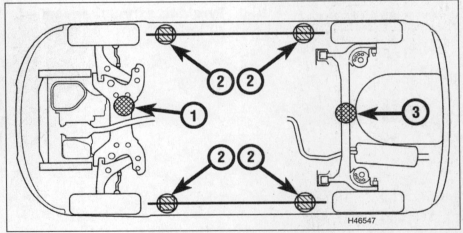

H46547

Vehicle jacking and support points

1 *Centre of front subframe*
2 *Door sill front and rear jacking points*
3 *Centre of the rear axle*

Several systems fitted to the car require battery power to be available at all times, either to ensure that their continued operation (such as the clock) or to maintain control unit memories (such as that in the engine management system's ECU) which would be wiped if the battery were to be disconnected. Whenever the battery is to be disconnected therefore, first note the following, to ensure that there are no unforeseen consequences of this action:

a) *First, on any vehicle with central locking, it is a wise precaution to remove the key from the ignition, and to keep it with you, so that it does not get locked in if the central locking should engage accidentally when the battery is reconnected.*

b) *The engine management system's ECU will lose the information stored in its memory when the battery is disconnected. This includes idling and operating values, and any fault codes detected – in the case of the fault codes, if it is thought likely that the system has developed a fault for which the corresponding code has been logged, the car must be taken to a Nissan dealer for the codes to be read, using the special diagnostic equipment necessary for this. Whenever the battery is disconnected, the information relating to idle speed control and other operating values will have to be reprogrammed into the unit's memory. The ECU does this automatically, but until then there may be surging, hesitation, erratic idle and a generally inferior level of performance. To allow the ECU to relearn these values, start the engine and run it as close to idle speed as possible until it reaches its normal operating temperature, then run it for approximately two minutes at 1200 rpm. Next, drive the car as far as necessary – approximately 5 miles of varied driving conditions is usually sufficient – to complete the relearning process.*

Devices known as 'memory-savers' (or 'code-savers') can be used to avoid some of the above problems. Precise details vary according to the device used. Typically, it is plugged into the cigarette lighter, and is connected by its own wires to a spare battery; the car's own battery is then disconnected from the electrical system, leaving the 'memory-saver' to pass sufficient current to maintain audio unit security codes and ECU memory values, and also to run permanently-live circuits such as the clock, all the while isolating the battery in the event of a short-circuit occurring while work is carried out.

⚠️ **Warning: Some of these devices allow a considerable amount of current to pass, which can mean that many of the car's systems are still operational when the main battery is disconnected. If a 'memory-saver' is used, ensure that the circuit concerned is actually 'dead' before carrying out any work on it!**

Whenever servicing, repair or overhaul work is carried out on the car or its components, observe the following procedures and instructions. This will assist in carrying out the operation efficiently and to a professional standard of workmanship.

Joint mating faces and gaskets

When separating components at their mating faces, never insert screwdrivers or similar implements into the joint between the faces in order to prise them apart. This can cause severe damage which results in oil leaks, coolant leaks, etc upon reassembly. Separation is usually achieved by tapping along the joint with a soft-faced hammer in order to break the seal. However, note that this method may not be suitable where dowels are used for component location.

Where a gasket is used between the mating faces of two components, a new one must be fitted on reassembly; fit it dry unless otherwise stated in the repair procedure. Make sure that the mating faces are clean and dry, with all traces of old gasket removed. When cleaning a joint face, use a tool which is unlikely to score or damage the face, and remove any burrs or nicks with an oilstone or fine file.

Make sure that tapped holes are cleaned with a pipe cleaner, and keep them free of jointing compound, if this is being used, unless specifically instructed otherwise.

Ensure that all orifices, channels or pipes are clear, and blow through them, preferably using compressed air.

Oil seals

Oil seals can be removed by levering them out with a wide flat-bladed screwdriver or similar implement. Alternatively, a number of self-tapping screws may be screwed into the seal, and these used as a purchase for pliers or some similar device in order to pull the seal free.

Whenever an oil seal is removed from its working location, either individually or as part of an assembly, it should be renewed.

The very fine sealing lip of the seal is easily damaged, and will not seal if the surface it contacts is not completely clean and free from scratches, nicks or grooves. If the original sealing surface of the component cannot be restored, and the manufacturer has not made provision for slight relocation of the seal relative to the sealing surface, the component should be renewed.

Protect the lips of the seal from any surface which may damage them in the course of fitting. Use tape or a conical sleeve where possible. Where indicated, lubricate the seal lips with oil before fitting and, on dual-lipped seals, fill the space between the lips with grease.

Unless otherwise stated, oil seals must be fitted with their sealing lips toward the lubricant to be sealed.

Use a tubular drift or block of wood of the appropriate size to install the seal and, if the seal housing is shouldered, drive the seal down to the shoulder. If the seal housing is unshouldered, the seal should be fitted with its face flush with the housing top face (unless otherwise instructed).

Screw threads and fastenings

Seized nuts, bolts and screws are quite a common occurrence where corrosion has set in, and the use of penetrating oil or releasing fluid will often overcome this problem if the offending item is soaked for a while before attempting to release it. The use of an impact driver may also provide a means of releasing such stubborn fastening devices, when used in conjunction with the appropriate screwdriver bit or socket. If none of these methods works, it may be necessary to resort to the careful application of heat, or the use of a hacksaw or nut splitter device. Before resorting to extreme methods, check that you are not dealing with a left-hand thread!

Studs are usually removed by locking two nuts together on the threaded part, and then using a spanner on the lower nut to unscrew the stud. Studs or bolts which have broken off below the surface of the component in which they are mounted can sometimes be removed using a stud extractor.

Always ensure that a blind tapped hole is completely free from oil, grease, water or other fluid before installing the bolt or stud. Failure to do this could cause the housing to crack due to the hydraulic action of the bolt or stud as it is screwed in.

For some screw fastenings, notably cylinder head bolts or nuts, torque wrench settings are no longer specified for the latter stages of tightening, "angle-tightening" being called up instead. Typically, a fairly low torque wrench setting will be applied to the bolts/nuts in the correct sequence, followed by one or more stages of tightening through specified angles.

When checking or retightening a nut or bolt to a specified torque setting, slacken the nut or bolt by a quarter of a turn, and then retighten to the specified setting. However, this should not be attempted where angular tightening has been used.

Locknuts, locktabs and washers

Any fastening which will rotate against a component or housing during tightening should always have a washer between it and the relevant component or housing.

Spring or split washers should always be renewed when they are used to lock a critical component such as a big-end bearing retaining bolt or nut. Locktabs which are folded over to retain a nut or bolt should always be renewed.

Self-locking nuts can be re-used in non-critical areas, providing resistance can be felt when the locking portion passes over the bolt or stud thread. However, it should be noted that self-locking stiffnuts tend to lose their effectiveness after long periods of use, and should then be renewed as a matter of course.

Split pins must always be replaced with new ones of the correct size for the hole.

When thread-locking compound is found on the threads of a fastener which is to be re-used, it should be cleaned off with a wire brush and solvent, and fresh compound applied on reassembly.

Special tools

Some repair procedures in this manual entail the use of special tools such as a press, two or three-legged pullers, spring compressors, etc. Wherever possible, suitable readily-available alternatives to the manufacturer's special tools are described, and are shown in use. In some instances, where no alternative is possible, it has been necessary to resort to the use of a manufacturer's tool, and this has been done for reasons of safety as well as the efficient completion of the repair operation. Unless you are highly-skilled and have a thorough understanding of the procedures described, never attempt to bypass the use of any special tool when the procedure described specifies its use. Not only is there a very great risk of personal injury, but expensive damage could be caused to the components involved.

Environmental considerations

When disposing of used engine oil, brake fluid, antifreeze, etc, give due consideration to any detrimental environmental effects. Do not, for instance, pour any of the above liquids down drains into the general sewage system, or onto the ground to soak away. Many local council refuse tips provide a facility for waste oil disposal, as do some garages. You can find your nearest disposal point by calling the Environment Agency on 08708 506 506 or by visiting www.oilbankline.org.uk.

OIL CARE
FOLLOW THE CODE

Note: It is illegal and anti-social to dump oil down the drain. To find the location of your local oil recycling bank, call 08708 506 506 or visit www.oilbankline.org.uk.

Modifications are a continuing and unpublicised process in car manufacture, quite apart from major model changes. Spare parts manuals and lists are compiled upon a numerical basis, the individual vehicle identification numbers being essential to correct identification of the component concerned.

When ordering spare parts always provide as much information as possible. Quote the car model, year of manufacture, body and engine numbers as appropriate.

The *vehicle identification plates* are located behind a cover on the front cowl, and on a self-adhesive label on the door post **(see illustrations)**. In addition to many other details, it carries the Vehicle Identification Number (VIN), maximum vehicle weight information, and codes for interior trim and body colours.

The *engine number* is stamped on the front of the engine at the gearbox end **(see illustrations)**.

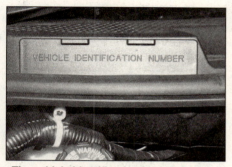

The vehicle identification plate is located behind the cover on the cowl . . .

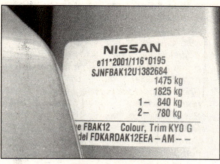

. . . and on the door post

Engine number location

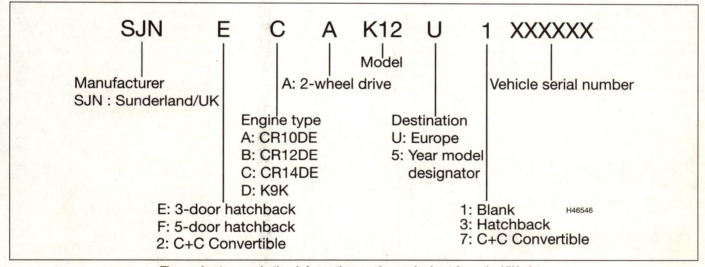

SJN E C A K12 U 1 XXXXXX

Model

Manufacturer
SJN : Sunderland/UK

A: 2-wheel drive

Engine type
A: CR10DE
B: CR12DE
C: CR14DE
D: K9K

E: 3-door hatchback
F: 5-door hatchback
2: C+C Convertible

Destination
U: Europe
5: Year model designator

1: Blank
3: Hatchback
7: C+C Convertible

Vehicle serial number

H46546

The engine type and other information can be worked out from the VIN plate

Tools and working facilities

Introduction

A selection of good tools is a fundamental requirement for anyone contemplating the maintenance and repair of a motor vehicle. For the owner who does not possess any, their purchase will prove a considerable expense, offsetting some of the savings made by doing-it-yourself. However, provided that the tools purchased meet the relevant national safety standards and are of good quality, they will last for many years and prove an extremely worthwhile investment.

To help the average owner to decide which tools are needed to carry out the various tasks detailed in this manual, we have compiled three lists of tools under the following headings: *Maintenance and minor repair*, *Repair and overhaul*, and *Special*. Newcomers to practical mechanics should start off with the *Maintenance and minor repair* tool kit, and confine themselves to the simpler jobs around the vehicle. Then, as confidence and experience grow, more difficult tasks can be undertaken, with extra tools being purchased as, and when, they are needed. In this way, a *Maintenance and minor repair* tool kit can be built up into a *Repair and overhaul* tool kit over a considerable period of time, without any major cash outlays. The experienced do-it-yourselfer will have a tool kit good enough for most repair and overhaul procedures, and will add tools from the *Special* category when it is felt that the expense is justified by the amount of use to which these tools will be put.

Maintenance and minor repair tool kit

The tools given in this list should be considered as a minimum requirement if routine maintenance, servicing and minor repair operations are to be undertaken. We recommend the purchase of combination spanners (ring one end, open-ended the other); although more expensive than open-ended ones, they do give the advantages of both types of spanner.

- ☐ *Combination spanners:*
  Metric - 8 to 19 mm inclusive
- ☐ *Adjustable spanner - 35 mm jaw (approx.)*
- ☐ *Spark plug spanner (with rubber insert) - petrol models*
- ☐ *Spark plug gap adjustment tool - petrol models*
- ☐ *Set of feeler gauges*
- ☐ *Brake bleed nipple spanner*
- ☐ *Screwdrivers:*
  Flat blade - 100 mm long x 6 mm dia
  Cross blade - 100 mm long x 6 mm dia
  Torx - various sizes (not all vehicles)
- ☐ *Combination pliers*
- ☐ *Hacksaw (junior)*
- ☐ *Tyre pump*
- ☐ *Tyre pressure gauge*
- ☐ *Oil can*
- ☐ *Oil filter removal tool (if applicable)*
- ☐ *Fine emery cloth*
- ☐ *Wire brush (small)*
- ☐ *Funnel (medium size)*
- ☐ *Sump drain plug key (not all vehicles)*

Repair and overhaul tool kit

These tools are virtually essential for anyone undertaking any major repairs to a motor vehicle, and are additional to those given in the *Maintenance and minor repair* list. Included in this list is a comprehensive set of sockets. Although these are expensive, they will be found invaluable as they are so versatile - particularly if various drives are included in the set. We recommend the half-inch square-drive type, as this can be used with most proprietary torque wrenches.

The tools in this list will sometimes need to be supplemented by tools from the *Special* list:

- ☐ *Sockets to cover range in previous list (including Torx sockets)*
- ☐ *Reversible ratchet drive (for use with sockets)*
- ☐ *Extension piece, 250 mm (for use with sockets)*
- ☐ *Universal joint (for use with sockets)*
- ☐ *Flexible handle or sliding T "breaker bar" (for use with sockets)*
- ☐ *Torque wrench (for use with sockets)*
- ☐ *Self-locking grips*
- ☐ *Ball pein hammer*
- ☐ *Soft-faced mallet (plastic or rubber)*
- ☐ *Screwdrivers:*
  Flat blade - long & sturdy, short (chubby), and narrow (electrician's) types
  Cross blade - long & sturdy, and short (chubby) types
- ☐ *Pliers:*
  Long-nosed
  Side cutters (electrician's)
  Circlip (internal and external)
- ☐ *Cold chisel - 25 mm*
- ☐ *Scriber*
- ☐ *Scraper*
- ☐ *Centre-punch*
- ☐ *Pin punch*
- ☐ *Hacksaw*
- ☐ *Brake hose clamp*
- ☐ *Brake/clutch bleeding kit*
- ☐ *Selection of twist drills*
- ☐ *Steel rule/straight-edge*
- ☐ *Allen keys (inc. splined/Torx type)*
- ☐ *Selection of files*
- ☐ *Wire brush*
- ☐ *Axle stands*
- ☐ *Jack (strong trolley or hydraulic type)*
- ☐ *Light with extension lead*
- ☐ *Universal electrical multi-meter*

Sockets and reversible ratchet drive

Brake bleeding kit

Torx key, socket and bit

Hose clamp

Angular-tightening gauge

Special tools

The tools in this list are those which are not used regularly, are expensive to buy, or which need to be used in accordance with their manufacturers' instructions. Unless relatively difficult mechanical jobs are undertaken frequently, it will not be economic to buy many of these tools. Where this is the case, you could consider clubbing together with friends (or joining a motorists' club) to make a joint purchase, or borrowing the tools against a deposit from a local garage or tool hire specialist.

The following list contains only those tools and instruments freely available to the public, and not those special tools produced by the vehicle manufacturer specifically for its dealer network. You will find occasional references to these manufacturers' special tools in the text of this manual. Generally, an alternative method of doing the job without the vehicle manufacturers' special tool is given. However, sometimes there is no alternative to using them. Where this is the case and the relevant tool cannot be bought or borrowed, you will have to entrust the work to a dealer.

☐ *Angular-tightening gauge*
☐ *Valve spring compressor*
☐ *Valve grinding tool*
☐ *Piston ring compressor*
☐ *Piston ring removal/installation tool*
☐ *Cylinder bore hone*
☐ *Balljoint separator*
☐ *Coil spring compressors (where applicable)*
☐ *Two/three-legged hub and bearing puller*
☐ *Impact screwdriver*
☐ *Micrometer and/or vernier calipers*
☐ *Dial gauge*
☐ *Tachometer*
☐ *Fault code reader*
☐ *Cylinder compression gauge*
☐ *Hand-operated vacuum pump and gauge*
☐ *Clutch plate alignment set*
☐ *Brake shoe steady spring cup removal tool*
☐ *Bush and bearing removal/installation set*
☐ *Stud extractors*
☐ *Tap and die set*
☐ *Lifting tackle*

Buying tools

Reputable motor accessory shops and superstores often offer excellent quality tools at discount prices, so it pays to shop around.

Remember, you don't have to buy the most expensive items on the shelf, but it is always advisable to steer clear of the very cheap tools. Beware of 'bargains' offered on market stalls, on-line or at car boot sales. There are plenty of good tools around at reasonable prices, but always aim to purchase items which meet the relevant national safety standards. If in doubt, ask the proprietor or manager of the shop for advice before making a purchase.

Care and maintenance of tools

Having purchased a reasonable tool kit, it is necessary to keep the tools in a clean and serviceable condition. After use, always wipe off any dirt, grease and metal particles using a clean, dry cloth, before putting the tools away. Never leave them lying around after they have been used. A simple tool rack on the garage or workshop wall for items such as screwdrivers and pliers is a good idea. Store all normal spanners and sockets in a metal box. Any measuring instruments, gauges, meters, etc, must be carefully stored where they cannot be damaged or become rusty.

Take a little care when tools are used. Hammer heads inevitably become marked, and screwdrivers lose the keen edge on their blades from time to time. A little timely attention with emery cloth or a file will soon restore items like this to a good finish.

Working facilities

Not to be forgotten when discussing tools is the workshop itself. If anything more than routine maintenance is to be carried out, a suitable working area becomes essential.

It is appreciated that many an owner-mechanic is forced by circumstances to remove an engine or similar item without the benefit of a garage or workshop. Having done this, any repairs should always be done under the cover of a roof.

Wherever possible, any dismantling should be done on a clean, flat workbench or table at a suitable working height.

Any workbench needs a vice; one with a jaw opening of 100 mm is suitable for most jobs. As mentioned previously, some clean dry storage space is also required for tools, as well as for any lubricants, cleaning fluids, touch-up paints etc, which become necessary.

Another item which may be required, and which has a much more general usage, is an electric drill with a chuck capacity of at least 8 mm. This, together with a good range of twist drills, is virtually essential for fitting accessories.

Last, but not least, always keep a supply of old newspapers and clean, lint-free rags available, and try to keep any working area as clean as possible.

Micrometers

Dial test indicator ("dial gauge")

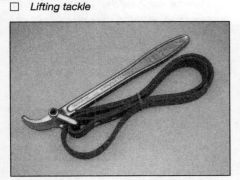

Oil filter removal tool (strap wrench type)

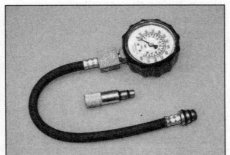

Compression tester

Bearing puller

This is a guide to getting your vehicle through the MOT test. Obviously it will not be possible to examine the vehicle to the same standard as the professional MOT tester. However, working through the following checks will enable you to identify any problem areas before submitting the vehicle for the test.

It has only been possible to summarise the test requirements here, based on the regulations in force at the time of printing. Test standards are becoming increasingly stringent, although there are some exemptions for older vehicles.

An assistant will be needed to help carry out some of these checks.

The checks have been sub-divided into four categories, as follows:

1 Checks carried out **FROM THE DRIVER'S SEAT**

2 Checks carried out **WITH THE VEHICLE ON THE GROUND**

3 Checks carried out **WITH THE VEHICLE RAISED AND THE WHEELS FREE TO TURN**

4 Checks carried out on **YOUR VEHICLE'S EXHAUST EMISSION SYSTEM**

---

1 Checks carried out **FROM THE DRIVER'S SEAT**

Handbrake (parking brake)

☐ Test the operation of the handbrake. Excessive travel (too many clicks) indicates incorrect brake or cable adjustment.
☐ Check that the handbrake cannot be released by tapping the lever sideways. Check the security of the lever mountings.

☐ If the parking brake is foot-operated, check that the pedal is secure and without excessive travel, and that the release mechanism operates correctly.
☐ Where applicable, test the operation of the electronic handbrake. The brake should engage and disengage without excessive delay. If the warning light does not extinguish when the brake is disengaged, this could indicate a fault which will need further investigation.

Footbrake

☐ Depress the brake pedal and check that it does not creep down to the floor, indicating a master cylinder fault. Release the pedal,

wait a few seconds, then depress it again. If the pedal travels nearly to the floor before firm resistance is felt, brake adjustment or repair is necessary. If the pedal feels spongy, there is air in the hydraulic system which must be removed by bleeding.

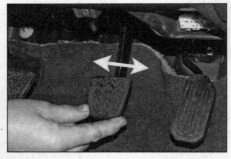

☐ Check that the brake pedal is secure and in good condition. Check also for signs of fluid leaks on the pedal, floor or carpets, which would indicate failed seals in the brake master cylinder.
☐ Check the servo unit (when applicable) by operating the brake pedal several times, then keeping the pedal depressed and starting the engine. As the engine starts, the pedal will move down slightly. If not, the vacuum hose or the servo itself may be faulty.

Steering wheel and column

☐ Examine the steering wheel for fractures or looseness of the hub, spokes or rim.
☐ Move the steering wheel from side to side and then up and down. Check that the steering wheel is not loose on the column, indicating wear or a loose retaining nut. Continue moving the steering wheel as before, but also turn it slightly from left to right.

☐ Check that the steering wheel is not loose on the column, and that there is no abnormal movement of the steering wheel, indicating wear in the column support bearings or couplings.
☐ Check that the ignition lock (where fitted) engages and disengages correctly.
☐ Steering column adjustment mechanisms (where fitted) must be able to lock the column securely in place with no play evident.

Windscreen, mirrors and sunvisor

☐ The windscreen must be free of cracks or other significant damage within the driver's field of view. (Small stone chips are acceptable.) Rear view mirrors must be secure, intact, and capable of being adjusted.

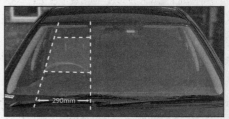

☐ The driver's sunvisor must be capable of being stored in the "up" position.

Seat belts and seats

Note: *The following checks are applicable to all seat belts, front and rear.*

☐ Examine the webbing of all the belts (including rear belts if fitted) for cuts, serious fraying or deterioration. Fasten and unfasten each belt to check the buckles. If applicable, check the retracting mechanism. Check the security of all seat belt mountings accessible from inside the vehicle, ensuring any height adjustable mountings lock securely in place.

☐ Seat belts with pre-tensioners, once activated, have a "flag" or similar showing on the seat belt stalk. This, in itself, is not a reason for test failure.

☐ The front seats themselves must be securely attached and the backrests must lock in the upright position.

Doors

☐ Both front doors must be able to be opened and closed from outside and inside, and must latch securely when closed.

Bonnet and boot/tailgate

☐ The bonnet and boot/tailgate must latch securely when closed.

2 Checks carried out WITH THE VEHICLE ON THE GROUND

Vehicle identification

☐ Number plates must be in good condition, secure and legible, with letters and numbers correctly spaced – spacing at (A) should be 33 mm and at (B) 11 mm. At the front, digits must be black on a white background and at the rear black on a yellow background. Other background designs (such as honeycomb) are not permitted.

☐ The VIN plate and/or homologation plate must be permanently displayed and legible.

Electrical equipment

☐ Switch on the ignition and check the operation of the horn.

☐ Check the windscreen washers and wipers, examining the wiper blades; renew damaged or perished blades. Also check the operation of the stop-lights.

☐ Check the operation of the sidelights and number plate lights. The lenses and reflectors must be secure, clean and undamaged.

☐ Check the operation and alignment of the headlights. The headlight reflectors must not be tarnished and the lenses must be undamaged.

☐ Switch on the ignition and check the operation of the direction indicators (including the instrument panel tell-tale) and the hazard warning lights. Operation of the sidelights and stop-lights must not affect the indicators - if it does, the cause is usually a bad earth at the rear light cluster. Indicators should flash at a rate of between 60 and 120 times per minute – faster or slower than this could indicate a fault with the flasher unit or a bad earth at one of the light units.

☐ Check the operation of the rear foglight(s), including the warning light on the instrument panel or in the switch.

☐ The warning lights must illuminate in accordance with the manufacturer's design. For most vehicles, the ABS and other warning lights should illuminate when the ignition is switched on, and (if the system is operating properly) extinguish after a few seconds. Refer to the owner's handbook.

Footbrake

☐ Examine the master cylinder, brake pipes and servo unit for leaks, loose mountings, corrosion or other damage. If ABS is fitted, this unit should also be examined for signs of leaks or corrosion.

☐ The fluid reservoir must be secure and the fluid level must be between the upper (A) and lower (B) markings.

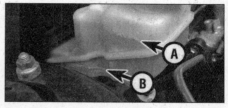

☐ Inspect both front brake flexible hoses for cracks or deterioration of the rubber. Turn the steering from lock to lock, and ensure that the hoses do not contact the wheel, tyre, or any part of the steering or suspension mechanism. With the brake pedal firmly depressed, check the hoses for bulges or leaks under pressure.

Steering and suspension

☐ Have your assistant turn the steering wheel from side to side slightly, up to the point where the steering gear just begins to transmit this movement to the roadwheels. Check for excessive free play between the steering wheel and the steering gear, indicating wear or insecurity of the steering column joints, the column-to-steering gear coupling, or the steering gear itself.

☐ Have your assistant turn the steering wheel more vigorously in each direction, so that the roadwheels just begin to turn. As this is done, examine all the steering joints, linkages, fittings and attachments. Renew any component that shows signs of wear or damage. On vehicles with power steering, check the security and condition of the steering pump, drivebelt and hoses.

☐ Check that the vehicle is standing level, and at approximately the correct ride height.

Shock absorbers

☐ Depress each corner of the vehicle in turn, then release it. The vehicle should rise and then settle in its normal position. If the vehicle continues to rise and fall, the shock absorber is defective. A shock absorber which has seized will also cause the vehicle to fail.

Exhaust system

☐ Start the engine. With your assistant holding a rag over the tailpipe, check the entire system for leaks. Repair or renew leaking sections.

3 Checks carried out **WITH THE VEHICLE RAISED AND THE WHEELS FREE TO TURN**

Jack up the front and rear of the vehicle, and securely support it on axle stands. Position the stands clear of the suspension assemblies. Ensure that the wheels are clear of the ground and that the steering can be turned from lock to lock.

Steering mechanism

☐ Have your assistant turn the steering from lock to lock. Check that the steering turns smoothly, and that no part of the steering mechanism, including a wheel or tyre, fouls any brake hose or pipe or any part of the body structure.

☐ Examine the steering rack rubber gaiters for damage or insecurity of the retaining clips. If power steering is fitted, check for signs of damage or leakage of the fluid hoses, pipes or connections. Also check for excessive stiffness or binding of the steering, a missing split pin or locking device, or severe corrosion of the body structure within 30 cm of any steering component attachment point.

Front and rear suspension and wheel bearings

☐ Starting at the front right-hand side, grasp the roadwheel at the 3 o'clock and 9 o'clock positions and rock gently but firmly. Check for free play or insecurity at the wheel bearings, suspension balljoints, or suspension mount-ings, pivots and attachments.

☐ Now grasp the wheel at the 12 o'clock and 6 o'clock positions and repeat the previous inspection. Spin the wheel, and check for roughness or tightness of the front wheel bearing.

☐ If excess free play is suspected at a component pivot point, this can be confirmed by using a large screwdriver or similar tool and levering between the mounting and the component attachment. This will confirm whether the wear is in the pivot bush, its retaining bolt, or in the mounting itself (the bolt holes can often become elongated).

☐ Carry out all the above checks at the other front wheel, and then at both rear wheels.

Springs and shock absorbers

☐ Examine the suspension struts (when applicable) for serious fluid leakage, corrosion, or damage to the casing. Also check the security of the mounting points.

☐ If coil springs are fitted, check that the spring ends locate in their seats, and that the spring is not corroded, cracked or broken.

☐ If leaf springs are fitted, check that all leaves are intact, that the axle is securely attached to each spring, and that there is no deterioration of the spring eye mountings, bushes, and shackles.

☐ The same general checks apply to vehicles fitted with other suspension types, such as torsion bars, hydraulic displacer units, etc. Ensure that all mountings and attachments are secure, that there are no signs of excessive wear, corrosion or damage, and (on hydraulic types) that there are no fluid leaks or damaged pipes.

☐ Inspect the shock absorbers for signs of serious fluid leakage. Check for wear of the mounting bushes or attachments, or damage to the body of the unit.

Driveshafts (fwd vehicles only)

☐ Rotate each front wheel in turn and inspect the constant velocity joint gaiters for splits or damage. Also check that each driveshaft is straight and undamaged.

Braking system

☐ If possible without dismantling, check brake pad wear and disc condition. Ensure that the friction lining material has not worn excessively, (A) and that the discs are not fractured, pitted, scored or badly worn (B).

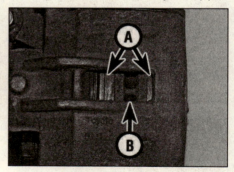

☐ Examine all the rigid brake pipes underneath the vehicle, and the flexible hose(s) at the rear. Look for corrosion, chafing or insecurity of the pipes, and for signs of bulging under pressure, chafing, splits or deterioration of the flexible hoses.

☐ Look for signs of fluid leaks at the brake calipers or on the brake backplates. Repair or renew leaking components.

☐ Slowly spin each wheel, while your assistant depresses and releases the footbrake. Ensure that each brake is operating and does not bind when the pedal is released.

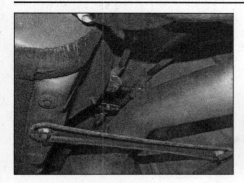

☐ Examine the handbrake mechanism, checking for frayed or broken cables, excessive corrosion, or wear or insecurity of the linkage. Check that the mechanism works on each relevant wheel, and releases fully, without binding.

☐ It is not possible to test brake efficiency without special equipment, but a road test can be carried out later to check that the vehicle pulls up in a straight line.

Fuel and exhaust systems

☐ Inspect the fuel tank (including the filler cap), fuel pipes, hoses and unions. All components must be secure and free from leaks. Locking fuel caps must lock securely and the key must be provided for the MOT test.

☐ Examine the exhaust system over its entire length, checking for any damaged, broken or missing mountings, security of the retaining clamps and rust or corrosion.

Wheels and tyres

☐ Examine the sidewalls and tread area of each tyre in turn. Check for cuts, tears, lumps, bulges, separation of the tread, and exposure of the ply or cord due to wear or damage. Check that the tyre bead is correctly seated on the wheel rim, that the valve is sound and properly seated, and that the wheel is not distorted or damaged.

☐ Check that the tyres are of the correct size for the vehicle, that they are of the same size and type on each axle, and that the pressures are correct.

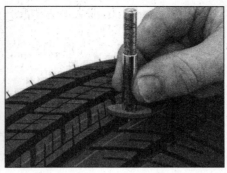

☐ Check the tyre tread depth. The legal minimum at the time of writing is 1.6 mm over the central three-quarters of the tread width. Abnormal tread wear may indicate incorrect front wheel alignment or wear in steering or suspension components.

☐ If the spare wheel is fitted externally or in a separate carrier beneath the vehicle, check that mountings are secure and free of excessive corrosion.

Body corrosion

☐ Check the condition of the entire vehicle structure for signs of corrosion in load-bearing areas. (These include chassis box sections, side sills, cross-members, pillars, and all suspension, steering, braking system and seat belt mountings and anchorages.) Any corrosion which has seriously reduced the thickness of a load-bearing area (or is within 30 cm of safety-related components such as steering or suspension) is likely to cause the vehicle to fail. In this case professional repairs are likely to be needed.

☐ Damage or corrosion which causes sharp or otherwise dangerous edges to be exposed will also cause the vehicle to fail.

Towbars

☐ Check the condition of mounting points (both beneath the vehicle and within boot/hatchback areas) for signs of corrosion, ensuring that all fixings are secure and not worn or damaged. There must be no excessive play in detachable tow ball arms or quick-release mechanisms.

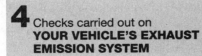

4 Checks carried out on **YOUR VEHICLE'S EXHAUST EMISSION SYSTEM**

Petrol models

☐ The engine should be warmed up, and running well (ignition system in good order, air filter element clean, etc).

☐ Before testing, run the engine at around 2500 rpm for 20 seconds. Let the engine drop to idle, and watch for smoke from the exhaust. If the idle speed is too high, or if dense blue or black smoke emerges for more than 5 seconds, the vehicle will fail. Typically, blue smoke signifies oil burning (engine wear);

black smoke means unburnt fuel (dirty air cleaner element, or other fuel system fault).

☐ An exhaust gas analyser for measuring carbon monoxide (CO) and hydrocarbons (HC) is now needed. If one cannot be hired or borrowed, have a local garage perform the check.

CO emissions (mixture)

☐ The MOT tester has access to the CO limits for all vehicles. The CO level is measured at idle speed, and at 'fast idle' (2500 to 3000 rpm). The following limits are given as a general guide:

At idle speed – Less than 0.5% CO
At 'fast idle' – Less than 0.3% CO
Lambda reading – 0.97 to 1.03

☐ If the CO level is too high, this may point to poor maintenance, a fuel injection system problem, faulty lambda (oxygen) sensor or catalytic converter. Try an injector cleaning treatment, and check the vehicle's ECU for fault codes.

HC emissions

☐ The MOT tester has access to HC limits for all vehicles. The HC level is measured at 'fast idle' (2500 to 3000 rpm). The following limits are given as a general guide:

At 'fast idle' – Less then 200 ppm

☐ Excessive HC emissions are typically caused by oil being burnt (worn engine), or by a blocked crankcase ventilation system ('breather'). If the engine oil is old and thin, an oil change may help. If the engine is running badly, check the vehicle's ECU for fault codes.

Diesel models

☐ The only emission test for diesel engines is measuring exhaust smoke density, using a calibrated smoke meter. The test involves accelerating the engine at least 3 times to its maximum unloaded speed.

Note: *On engines with a timing belt, it is VITAL that the belt is in good condition before the test is carried out.*

☐ With the engine warmed up, it is first purged by running at around 2500 rpm for 20 seconds. A governor check is then carried out, by slowly accelerating the engine to its maximum speed. After this, the smoke meter is connected, and the engine is accelerated quickly to maximum speed three times. If the smoke density is less than the limits given below, the vehicle will pass:

Non-turbo vehicles: 2.5m-1
Turbocharged vehicles: 3.0m-1

☐ If excess smoke is produced, try fitting a new air cleaner element, or using an injector cleaning treatment. If the engine is running badly, where applicable, check the vehicle's ECU for fault codes. Also check the vehicle's EGR system, where applicable. At high mileages, the injectors may require professional attention.

Engine

- [ ] Engine fails to rotate when attempting to start
- [ ] Engine rotates, but will not start
- [ ] Engine difficult to start when cold
- [ ] Engine difficult to start when hot
- [ ] Starter motor noisy or excessively-rough in engagement
- [ ] Engine starts, but stops immediately
- [ ] Engine misfires, or idles unevenly
- [ ] Engine stalls, or lacks power
- [ ] Engine backfires
- [ ] Engine noises
- [ ] Oil consumption excessive
- [ ] Oil pressure warning light illuminated with engine running

Cooling system

- [ ] Overheating
- [ ] Overcooling
- [ ] External coolant leakage
- [ ] Internal coolant leakage
- [ ] Corrosion

Fuel and exhaust systems

- [ ] Fuel consumption excessive
- [ ] Fuel leakage and/or fuel odour
- [ ] Black smoke in exhaust
- [ ] Blue or white smoke in exhaust
- [ ] Excessive noise or fumes from exhaust system

Clutch

- [ ] Pedal travels to floor – no pressure or very little resistance
- [ ] Clutch fails to disengage (unable to select gears)
- [ ] Clutch slips (engine speed increases, with no increase in vehicle speed)
- [ ] Judder as clutch is engaged
- [ ] Noise when depressing or releasing clutch pedal

Manual transmission

- [ ] Noisy in neutral with engine running
- [ ] Noisy in one particular gear
- [ ] Difficulty engaging gears
- [ ] Jumps out of gear
- [ ] Vibration
- [ ] Lubricant leaks

Automatic transmission

- [ ] Fluid leakage
- [ ] Transmission fluid brown, or has burned smell
- [ ] General gear selection problems
- [ ] Transmission will not downshift (kickdown) with accelerator fully depressed
- [ ] Engine will not start in any gear, or starts in gears other than Park or Neutral
- [ ] Transmission slips, shifts roughly, is noisy, or has no drive in forward or reverse gears

Driveshafts

- [ ] Vibration when accelerating or decelerating
- [ ] Clicking or knocking noise on turns (at slow speed on full-lock)

Braking system

- [ ] Car pulls to one side under braking
- [ ] Noise (grinding or high-pitched squeal) when brakes applied
- [ ] Excessive brake pedal travel
- [ ] Brake pedal feels spongy when depressed
- [ ] Excessive brake pedal effort required to stop vehicle
- [ ] Judder felt through brake pedal or steering wheel when braking
- [ ] Brakes binding
- [ ] Rear wheels locking under normal braking

Suspension and steering

- [ ] Car pulls to one side
- [ ] Wheel wobble and vibration
- [ ] Excessive pitching and/or rolling around corners, or during braking
- [ ] Wandering or general instability
- [ ] Excessively-stiff steering
- [ ] Excessive play in steering
- [ ] Lack of power assistance
- [ ] Tyre wear excessive

Electrical system

- [ ] Battery will only hold a charge for a few days
- [ ] Ignition (no-charge) warning light remains illuminated with engine running
- [ ] Ignition (no-charge) warning light fails to come on
- [ ] Lights inoperative
- [ ] Instrument readings inaccurate or erratic
- [ ] Horn faults
- [ ] Windscreen/tailgate wiper faults
- [ ] Windscreen/tailgate washer faults
- [ ] Electric window faults
- [ ] Central locking system faults

Introduction

The car owner who does his or her own maintenance according to the recommended service schedules should not have to use this section of the manual very often. Modern component reliability is such that, provided those items subject to wear or deterioration are inspected or renewed at the specified intervals, sudden failure is comparatively rare. Faults do not usually just happen as a result of sudden failure, but develop over a period of time. Major mechanical failures in particular are usually preceded by characteristic symptoms over hundreds or even thousands of miles. Those components which do occasionally fail without warning are often small and easily carried in the car.

With any fault-finding, the first step is to decide where to begin investigations. Sometimes this is obvious, but on other occasions, a little detective work will be necessary. The owner who makes half a dozen haphazard adjustments or replacements may be successful in curing a fault (or its symptoms), but will be none the wiser if the fault recurs, and ultimately may have spent more time and money than was necessary. A calm and logical approach will be found to be more satisfactory in the long run. Always take into account any warning signs or abnormalities that may have been noticed in the period preceding the fault – power loss, high or low gauge readings, unusual smells, etc – and remember that failure of components such as fuses may only be pointers to some underlying fault.

The pages which follow provide an easy-reference guide to the more common problems which may occur during the operation of the vehicle. These problems and their possible causes are grouped under headings denoting various components or systems, such as Engine, Cooling system, etc. The general Chapter which deals with the problem is also shown in brackets; refer to the relevant part of that Chapter for system-specific information. Whatever the fault, certain basic principles apply. These are as follows:

Verify the fault. This is simply a matter of being sure that you know what the symptoms are before starting work. This is particularly important if you are investigating a fault for someone else, who may not have described it very accurately.

Don't overlook the obvious. For example, if the car won't start, is there fuel in the tank? (Don't take anyone else's word on this particular point, and don't trust the fuel gauge either!) If an electrical fault is indicated, look for loose or broken wires before using the test gear.

Cure the disease, not the symptom. Substituting a flat battery with a fully-charged one will get you off the hard shoulder, but if the underlying cause is not attended to, the new battery will go the same way.

Don't take anything for granted. Particularly, don't forget that a 'new' component may itself be defective (especially if it's been rattling around in the boot for months), and don't leave components out of a fault diagnosis sequence just because they are new or recently fitted. When you do finally diagnose a difficult fault, you'll probably realise that all the evidence was there from the start.

Consider what work, if any, has recently been carried out. Many faults arise through careless or hurried work. For instance, if any work has been performed under the bonnet, could some of the wiring have been dislodged or incorrectly routed, or a hose trapped? Have all the fasteners been properly tightened? Were new, genuine parts and new gaskets used? There is often a certain amount of detective work to be done in this case, as an apparently-unrelated task can have far-reaching consequences.

Engine

Engine fails to rotate when attempting to start

- [ ] Battery terminal connections loose or corroded (*Weekly checks*).
- [ ] Battery discharged or faulty (Chapter 5A).
- [ ] Broken, loose or disconnected wiring in the starting circuit (Chapter 5A).
- [ ] Defective starter solenoid or ignition switch (Chapter 5A or 12).
- [ ] Defective starter motor (Chapter 5A).
- [ ] Flywheel ring gear or starter pinion teeth loose or broken (Chapter 2A or 5A).
- [ ] Engine earth strap broken or disconnected.
- [ ] Engine suffering 'hydraulic lock' (eg, from water ingested after traversing flooded roads, or from a serious internal coolant leak) – consult a Nissan dealer for advice.
- [ ] Automatic transmission shift lock fault, footbrake not depressed, or faulty stop-light switch (Chapter 7B or 9).

Engine rotates, but will not start

- [ ] Fuel tank empty.
- [ ] Battery discharged or inadequate capacity (engine rotates slowly) (Chapter 5A).
- [ ] Battery terminal connections loose or corroded (*Weekly checks*).
- [ ] Ignition components damp or damaged (Chapter 1 or 5B)
- [ ] Worn, faulty or incorrectly-gapped spark plugs (Chapter 1)
- [ ] Immobiliser faulty or incorrectly used, or 'uncoded' ignition key being used (Chapter 12).
- [ ] Crankshaft sensor, or other engine management system sensor, fault (Chapter 4A)
- [ ] Air filter element dirty or clogged (Chapter 1).
- [ ] Blockage in exhaust system (Chapter 4B).
- [ ] Low cylinder compressions (Chapter 2A)
- [ ] Valve timing incorrect, possibly through a poorly-fitted timing chain (Chapter 2A).
- [ ] Major mechanical failure (eg, camshaft drive) (Chapter 2A).

Engine difficult to start when cold

- [ ] Battery discharged (Chapter 5A).
- [ ] Battery terminal connections loose or corroded (see *Weekly checks*).
- [ ] Worn, faulty or incorrectly-gapped spark plugs (Chapter 1).
- [ ] Other ignition system fault (Chapter 5B).
- [ ] Fuel system fault (Chapter 4A).
- [ ] Wrong grade of engine oil used (*Weekly checks* or Chapter 1).
- [ ] Low cylinder compressions (Chapter 2A)

Engine (continued)

Engine difficult to start when hot

- [ ] Air filter element dirty or clogged (Chapter 1).
- [ ] Fuel system fault (Chapter 4A).
- [ ] Low cylinder compressions (Chapter 2A).

Starter motor noisy or excessively-rough

- [ ] Starter pinion or flywheel ring gear teeth loose or broken (Chapter 2A or 5A).
- [ ] Starter motor mounting bolts loose or missing (Chapter 5A).
- [ ] Starter motor internal components worn or damaged (Chapter 5A).

Engine starts, but stops immediately

- [ ] Loose or faulty electrical connections in the ignition circuit (Chapter 1 or 5B).
- [ ] Vacuum leak at the throttle body, inlet manifold or associated hoses (Chapter 4A).
- [ ] Blocked injectors/fuel system fault (Chapter 4A).
- [ ] Fuel very low in tank.
- [ ] Restriction in fuel feed.
- [ ] Air cleaner dirty, or blockage in air intake system (Chapter 1 or 4A).
- [ ] Blockage in exhaust system (Chapter 4B).

Engine misfires, or idles unevenly

- [ ] Air cleaner dirty or blockage in air intake system (Chapter 1 or 4A).
- [ ] Vacuum leak at the throttle body, inlet manifold or associated hoses (Chapter 4A).
- [ ] Worn, faulty or incorrectly-gapped spark plugs (Chapter 1).
- [ ] Valve clearances incorrect (Chapter 2A).
- [ ] Uneven or low cylinder compressions (Chapter 2A).
- [ ] Camshaft lobes worn (Chapter 2A).
- [ ] Timing chain incorrectly fitted (Chapter 2A).
- [ ] Blocked injectors/fuel injection system fault (Chapter 4A).
- [ ] Valve(s) sticking, valve spring(s) weak or broken, or poor compressions (Chapter 2A).
- [ ] Overheating (Chapter 3).
- [ ] Cylinder head gasket blown (Chapter 2A).

Engine stalls, or lacks power

- [ ] Fuel filter choked (Chapter 4A).
- [ ] Fuel pump faulty, or delivery pressure low (Chapter 4A).
- [ ] Valve clearances incorrect (Chapter 2A).
- [ ] Vacuum leak at the throttle body, inlet manifold or associated hoses (Chapter 4A).
- [ ] Worn, faulty or incorrectly-gapped spark plugs (Chapter 1).
- [ ] Faulty ignition coils (Chapter 5B).
- [ ] Uneven or low cylinder compressions (Chapter 2A).
- [ ] Blocked injector/fuel system fault (Chapter 4A).
- [ ] Blocked catalytic converter (Chapter 4B).
- [ ] Engine overheating (Chapter 3).
- [ ] Air filter element blocked (Chapter 1).
- [ ] Accelerator cable problem (Chapter 4A).
- [ ] Throttle position sensor fault (Chapter 4A).
- [ ] Engine management warning light on (fault code in system) (Chapter 4A).
- [ ] Timing chain worn, or incorrectly fitted (Chapter 2A).
- [ ] Brakes binding (Chapter 1 or 9).
- [ ] Clutch slipping (Chapter 6).

Engine backfires

- [ ] Timing chain incorrectly fitted (Chapter 2A).
- [ ] Vacuum leak at the throttle body, inlet manifold or associated hoses (Chapter 4A).
- [ ] Blocked catalytic converter (Chapter 4B).
- [ ] Ignition coil(s) faulty (Chapter 5B).

Engine noises

Pre-ignition (pinking) or knocking during acceleration or under load

- [ ] Ignition system fault (Chapter 1 or 5B).
- [ ] Incorrect grade of spark plug (Chapter 1).
- [ ] Incorrect grade (or type) of fuel used (Chapter 4A).
- [ ] Vacuum leak at the throttle body, inlet manifold or associated hoses (Chapter 4A).
- [ ] Excessive carbon build-up in cylinder head/pistons (Chapter 2A or 2B).
- [ ] Blocked injector/fuel injection system fault (Chapter 4A).

Whistling or wheezing noises

- [ ] Leaking inlet manifold or throttle body gasket (Chapter 4A).
- [ ] Leaking exhaust manifold gasket, or pipe-to-manifold joint (Chapter 4B).
- [ ] Leaking vacuum hose (Chapter 4 or 9).
- [ ] Blowing cylinder head gasket (Chapter 2A).
- [ ] Partially blocked or leaking crankcase ventilation system (Chapter 4B).

Tapping or rattling noises

- [ ] Worn camshaft(s) (Chapter 2A)
- [ ] Ancillary component fault (coolant pump, alternator, etc) (Chapter 3, 5A, etc).
- [ ] Valve clearances incorrect (Chapter 2A).

Knocking or thumping noises

- [ ] Worn big-end bearings (regular heavy knocking, perhaps less under load) (Chapter 2B).
- [ ] Worn main bearings (rumbling and knocking, perhaps worsening under load) (Chapter 2B).
- [ ] Piston slap – most noticeable when cold, caused by piston/bore wear (Chapter 2B).
- [ ] Ancillary component fault (coolant pump, alternator, etc) (Chapter 3, 5A, etc).
- [ ] Engine mountings worn or defective (Chapter 2A).
- [ ] Front suspension or steering components worn (Chapter 10).

Oil consumption excessive

- [ ] External leakage (standing or running) – eg, timing chain cover, crankshaft oil seals (Chapter 2A).
- [ ] New engine not yet run-in.
- [ ] Engine oil incorrect grade/poor quality, or oil level too high (*Weekly checks*).
- [ ] Crankcase ventilation system obstructed (Chapter 1 or 4B).
- [ ] Burning oil due to general engine wear – pistons and/or bores, valve stem oil seals, etc (Chapter 2B).

Oil pressure warning light illuminated with engine running

- [ ] Low oil level or incorrect oil grade (*Weekly checks*).
- [ ] Engine oil and filter change overdue (Chapter 1).
- [ ] Faulty oil pressure warning light switch (Chapter 2A).
- [ ] Worn engine bearings and/or oil pump (Chapter 2A or 2B).
- [ ] High engine operating temperature (Chapter 3).
- [ ] Oil pick-up strainer clogged – remove sump to check (Chapter 2A).

Cooling system

Overheating

- [ ] Insufficient coolant in system (*Weekly checks*).
- [ ] Thermostat faulty (Chapter 3).
- [ ] Radiator core blocked or grille restricted (Chapter 3).
- [ ] Radiator electric cooling fan or coolant temperature sensor faulty (Chapter 3).
- [ ] Pressure cap faulty (Chapter 3).
- [ ] Inaccurate coolant temperature gauge sender (Chapter 3).
- [ ] Airlock in cooling system (Chapter 1).
- [ ] Engine management system fault (Chapter 4A).
- [ ] Blockage in exhaust system (Chapter 4B).
- [ ] Cylinder head gasket blown (Chapter 2A).

Overcooling

- [ ] Thermostat faulty (Chapter 3).
- [ ] Inaccurate coolant temperature gauge sender (Chapter 3).

External coolant leakage

- [ ] Deteriorated or damaged hoses or hose clips (Chapter 1).
- [ ] Radiator core or heater matrix leaking (Chapter 3).
- [ ] Pressure cap faulty (Chapter 1).
- [ ] Water pump or thermostat housing leaking (Chapter 3).
- [ ] Boiling due to overheating (Chapter 3).
- [ ] Core plug leaking (Chapter 2B).

Internal coolant leakage

- [ ] Leaking cylinder head gasket (Chapter 2A).
- [ ] Cracked cylinder head or cylinder bore (Chapter 2A or 2B).

Corrosion

- [ ] Infrequent draining and flushing (Chapter 1).
- [ ] Incorrect antifreeze mixture, or inappropriate antifreeze type (*Weekly checks* and Chapter 1).

Fuel and exhaust systems

Fuel consumption excessive

- [ ] New engine not yet run-in.
- [ ] Air cleaner element dirty, or blockage in air intake system (Chapter 1 or 4A).
- [ ] Fuel system fault (Chapter 4A).
- [ ] Crankcase ventilation system blocked (Chapter 4B).
- [ ] Unsympathetic driving style, or adverse conditions.
- [ ] Tyres under-inflated (see *Weekly checks*).
- [ ] Brakes binding (Chapter 1 or 9).
- [ ] Fuel leak, causing apparent high consumption (Chapter 1 or 4A).
- [ ] Valve timing incorrect, possibly through a poorly-fitted timing chain (Chapter 2A).

Fuel leakage and/or fuel odour

- [ ] Damaged or corroded fuel tank, pipes or connections (Chapter 1).
- [ ] Evaporative emissions system fault (Chapter 4B).

Black smoke in exhaust

- [ ] Air cleaner element dirty, or blockage in air intake system (Chapter 1 or 4A).
- [ ] Fuel system fault (Chapter 4A).

Blue or white smoke in exhaust

- [ ] Engine oil incorrect grade or poor quality, or fuel passing into sump (worn piston rings/bores).
- [ ] Air cleaner element dirty, or blockage in air intake system (Chapter 1 or 4A).
- [ ] Injector(s) faulty (Chapter 4A).
- [ ] Blocked or damaged emissions system hoses or components (Chapter 4B).
- [ ] General engine wear – pistons and/or bores, valve stem oil seals, etc (Chapter 2B).
- [ ] Cylinder head gasket blown – white smoke (Chapter 2A).

Excessive noise or fumes from exhaust system

- [ ] Leaking exhaust system or manifold joints (Chapter 1 or 4B).
- [ ] Leaking, corroded or damaged silencers or pipe (Chapter 1 or 4B).
- [ ] Oxygen sensors loose or damaged (Chapter 4B).
- [ ] Broken mountings, causing body or suspension contact (Chapter 1 or 4B).

Clutch

Pedal travels to floor – no pressure or very little resistance

☐ Air in hydraulic system/faulty master or slave cylinder (Chapter 6).
☐ Faulty hydraulic release system (Chapter 6).
☐ Clutch pedal return spring detached or broken (Chapter 6).
☐ Broken clutch release bearing or fork (Chapter 6).
☐ Broken diaphragm spring in clutch pressure plate (Chapter 6).

Clutch fails to disengage (unable to select gears)

☐ Air in hydraulic system/faulty master or slave cylinder (Chapter 6).
☐ Faulty hydraulic release system (Chapter 6).
☐ Clutch disc sticking on transmission input shaft splines (Chapter 6).
☐ Clutch disc sticking to flywheel or pressure plate (Chapter 6).
☐ Faulty pressure plate assembly (Chapter 6).
☐ Clutch release mechanism worn or incorrectly assembled (Chapter 6).

Clutch slips (engine speed increases, with no increase in vehicle speed)

☐ Faulty hydraulic release system (Chapter 6).
☐ Clutch disc linings excessively worn (Chapter 6).
☐ Clutch disc linings contaminated with oil or grease (Chapter 6).
☐ Faulty pressure plate or weak diaphragm spring (Chapter 6).

Judder as clutch is engaged

☐ Clutch disc linings contaminated with oil or grease (Chapter 6).
☐ Clutch disc linings excessively worn (Chapter 6).
☐ Faulty or distorted pressure plate or diaphragm spring (Chapter 6).
☐ Worn or loose engine/transmission mountings (Chapter 2A).
☐ Clutch disc hub or transmission input shaft splines worn (Chapter 6 or 7A).

Noise when depressing or releasing clutch pedal

☐ Worn clutch release bearing (Chapter 6).
☐ Worn or dry clutch pedal bushes (Chapter 6).
☐ Worn or dry clutch master cylinder piston (Chapter 6).
☐ Faulty pressure plate assembly (Chapter 6).
☐ Pressure plate diaphragm spring broken (Chapter 6).
☐ Broken clutch disc cushioning springs (Chapter 6).

Manual transmission

Noisy in neutral with engine running

☐ Lack of oil (Chapter 1).
☐ Input shaft bearings worn (noise apparent with clutch pedal released, but not when depressed) (Chapter 7A).*
☐ Clutch release bearing worn (noise apparent with clutch pedal depressed, possibly less when released) (Chapter 6).

Noisy in one particular gear

☐ Worn, damaged or chipped gear teeth (Chapter 7A).*

Difficulty engaging gears

☐ Clutch fault (Chapter 6).
☐ Worn or damaged gear cables (Chapter 7A).
☐ Worn synchroniser assemblies (Chapter 7A).*

Jumps out of gear

☐ Worn or damaged gear cables (Chapter 7A).
☐ Worn synchroniser assemblies (Chapter 7A).*
☐ Worn selector forks (Chapter 7A).*

Vibration

☐ Lack of oil (Chapter 1).
☐ Worn bearings (Chapter 7A).*

Lubricant leaks

☐ Leaking differential side gear oil seal (Chapter 7A).
☐ Leaking housing joint (Chapter 7A).*
☐ Leaking input shaft oil seal (Chapter 7A).*
☐ Leaking selector shaft oil seal (Chapter 7A).

Although the corrective action necessary to remedy the symptoms described is beyond the scope of the home mechanic, the above information should be helpful in isolating the cause of the condition, so that the owner can communicate clearly with a professional mechanic.

Automatic transmission

Note: *Due to the complexity of the automatic transmission, it is difficult for the home mechanic to properly diagnose and service this unit. For problems other than the following, the car should be taken to a dealer service department or automatic transmission specialist. Do not be too hasty in removing the transmission if a fault is suspected, as most of the testing is carried out with the unit still fitted.*

Fluid leakage

- [ ] Automatic transmission fluid is usually dark (and often red) in colour. Fluid leaks should not be confused with engine oil, which can easily be blown onto the transmission by airflow.
- [ ] To determine the source of a leak, first remove all built-up dirt and grime from the transmission housing and surrounding areas using a degreasing agent, or by steam-cleaning. Drive the car at low speed, so airflow will not blow the leak far from its source. Raise and support the car, and determine where the leak is coming from.

General gear selection problems

- [ ] Chapter 7B deals with the shift lock and selector cable on the automatic transmission. The following are common problems which may be cable-related:
  - a) Engine starting in gears other than Park or Neutral.
  - b) Indicator panel indicating a gear other than the one actually being used.
  - c) Car moves when in Park or Neutral.
  - d) Poor gear shift quality or erratic gear changes.
- [ ] Refer to Chapter 7B to check, and possibly renew, the cables.

Transmission will not downshift (kickdown) with accelerator pedal fully depressed

- [ ] Low transmission fluid level (Chapter 1).
- [ ] Throttle position sensor faulty (Chapter 4A).
- [ ] Engine management system problem (Chapter 4A).
- [ ] Selector cable stretched (Chapter 7B).

Engine will not start in any gear, or starts in gears other than Park or Neutral

- [ ] Shift lock system faulty (Chapter 7B).
- [ ] Selector cable stretched (Chapter 7B).

Transmission slips, shifts roughly, is noisy, or has no drive in forward or reverse gears

- [ ] There are many probable causes for the above problems, but unless there is a very obvious reason (such as a loose or corroded wiring plug connection on or near the transmission), the car should be taken to a Nissan dealer for the fault to be diagnosed. The transmission control unit incorporates a self-diagnosis facility, and any fault codes can quickly be read and interpreted by a Nissan dealer with the proper diagnostic equipment.

Driveshafts

Vibration when accelerating or decelerating

- [ ] Worn inner constant velocity joint (Chapter 1 or 8).
- [ ] Bent or distorted driveshaft (Chapter 8).
- [ ] Right-hand driveshaft vibration damper loose or missing (Chapter 8).
- [ ] Loose or damaged driveshaft nut (Chapter 1 or 8).

Clicking or knocking noise on turns (at slow speed on full-lock)

- [ ] Lack of constant velocity joint lubricant (Chapter 8).
- [ ] Worn outer constant velocity joint (Chapter 1 or 8).
- [ ] Loose or damaged driveshaft nut (Chapter 1 or 8).

Braking system

Note: *Before assuming that a brake problem exists, make sure that the tyres are in good condition and correctly inflated, that the front wheel alignment is correct, and that the car is not loaded with weight in an unequal manner. Apart from checking the condition of all pipe and hose connections, any faults occurring on the Anti-lock Braking System (ABS) should be referred to a Nissan dealer for diagnosis.*

Car pulls to one side under braking

☐ Worn, defective, damaged or contaminated front or rear brake pads/shoes on one side (Chapter 1).
☐ Seized or partially-seized front caliper, or leaking rear wheel cylinder (Chapter 9).
☐ A mixture of brake pad/shoe lining materials fitted between sides (Chapter 1).
☐ Brake caliper mounting bolts loose (Chapter 9).
☐ Rear hub/brake backplate mounting bolts loose (Chapter 9).
☐ Worn or damaged steering or suspension components (Chapter 10).

Noise (grinding or high-pitched squeal) when brakes applied

☐ Brake pad or shoe friction lining material worn down to metal backing Chapter 1.
☐ Excessive corrosion of brake disc or drum (may be apparent after the car has been standing for some time) (Chapter 1).

Excessive brake pedal travel

☐ Inoperative rear brake self-adjust mechanism (Chapter 9).
☐ Rear wheel cylinders leaking (Chapter 9).
☐ Faulty master cylinder (Chapter 9).
☐ Air in hydraulic system (Chapter 9).

Brake pedal feels spongy when depressed

☐ Air in hydraulic system (Chapter 9).
☐ Rear wheel cylinders leaking (Chapter 9).
☐ Deteriorated flexible rubber brake hoses (Chapter 9).
☐ Master cylinder mounting nuts loose (Chapter 9).
☐ Faulty master cylinder (Chapter 9).

Excessive brake pedal effort required to stop car

☐ Faulty vacuum servo unit (Chapter 9).
☐ Disconnected, damaged or insecure brake servo vacuum hoses (Chapter 9).
☐ Primary or secondary hydraulic circuit failure (Chapter 9).
☐ Seized brake caliper or wheel cylinder piston(s) (Chapter 9).
☐ Brake pads or brake shoes incorrectly fitted (Chapter 9).
☐ Incorrect grade of brake pads or brake shoes fitted (Chapter 1).
☐ Brake pads or brake shoe linings contaminated (Chapter 1).

Judder felt through brake pedal or steering wheel when braking

☐ Excessive run-out or distortion of front discs or rear discs/drums (Chapter 9).
☐ Brake pad or brake shoe linings worn (Chapter 1).
☐ Brake caliper or rear brake backplate mounting bolts loose (Chapter 9).
☐ Wear in suspension or steering components or mountings (Chapter 10).

Brakes binding

☐ Seized brake caliper or wheel cylinder piston(s) (Chapter 9).
☐ Faulty handbrake mechanism (Chapter 9).
☐ Faulty master cylinder (Chapter 9).

Rear wheels locking under normal braking

☐ Rear brake pad/shoe linings contaminated (Chapter 1).
☐ Faulty brake pressure regulator valves, or ABS unit (Chapter 9).

Suspension and steering

Note: *Before diagnosing suspension or steering faults, be sure that the trouble is not due to incorrect tyre pressures, mixtures of tyre types, or binding brakes.*

Car pulls to one side

- [ ] Defective tyre (Chapter 1).
- [ ] Excessive wear in suspension or steering components (Chapter 10).
- [ ] Incorrect front wheel alignment (Chapter 10).
- [ ] Accident damage to steering or suspension components (Chapter 10).

Wheel wobble and vibration

- [ ] Front roadwheels out of balance (vibration felt mainly through the steering wheel) (Chapter 1).
- [ ] Rear roadwheels out of balance (vibration felt throughout the car) (Chapter 1).
- [ ] Roadwheels damaged or distorted (Chapter 1).
- [ ] Faulty or damaged tyre (*Weekly checks*).
- [ ] Worn steering or suspension joints, bushes or components (Chapter 10).
- [ ] Roadwheel nuts loose (Chapter 1).
- [ ] Wear in driveshaft joint, or loose driveshaft nut (vibration worst when under load) (Chapter 1 or 8).

Excessive pitching and/or rolling around corners, or during braking

- [ ] Defective shock absorbers (Chapter 10).
- [ ] Broken or weak coil spring and/or suspension components (Chapter 10).
- [ ] Worn or damaged anti-roll bar or mountings (Chapter 10).

Wandering or general instability

- [ ] Incorrect front wheel alignment (Chapter 10).
- [ ] Worn steering or suspension joints, bushes or components (Chapter 10).
- [ ] Tyres out of balance (*Weekly checks*).
- [ ] Faulty or damaged tyre (*Weekly checks*).
- [ ] Roadwheel nuts loose (Chapter 1).
- [ ] Defective shock absorbers (Chapter 10).

Excessively-stiff steering

- [ ] Lack of steering gear lubricant (Chapter 10).
- [ ] Seized track-rod end balljoint or suspension balljoint (Chapter 10).
- [ ] Broken or slipping auxiliary drivebelt (hydraulic power steering) (Chapter 1).
- [ ] Faulty power steering motor, blown fuse, or damaged wiring (electric power steering) (Chapter 10).
- [ ] Incorrect front wheel alignment (Chapter 10).
- [ ] Steering rack or column bent or damaged (Chapter 10).

Excessive play in steering

- [ ] Worn steering column universal joint (Chapter 10).
- [ ] Worn steering track-rod end balljoints (Chapter 10).
- [ ] Worn rack-and-pinion steering gear (Chapter 10).
- [ ] Worn steering or suspension joints, bushes or components (Chapter 10).

Lack of power assistance

- [ ] Broken or slipping auxiliary drivebelt (hydraulic power steering) (Chapter 1).
- [ ] Faulty power steering motor, blown fuse, or damaged wiring (electric power steering) (Chapter 10).
- [ ] Incorrect power steering hydraulic fluid level (*Weekly checks*).
- [ ] Restriction in power steering hydraulic fluid hoses (Chapter 10).
- [ ] Faulty power steering pump (hydraulic power steering) (Chapter 10).
- [ ] Faulty rack-and-pinion steering gear (Chapter 10).

Tyre wear excessive

Tyres worn on inside or outside edges

- [ ] Tyres under-inflated (wear on both edges) (*Weekly checks*).
- [ ] Incorrect camber or castor angles (wear on one edge only) (Chapter 10).
- [ ] Worn steering or suspension joints, bushes or components (Chapter 10).
- [ ] Excessively-hard cornering.
- [ ] Accident damage.

Tyre treads exhibit feathered edges

- [ ] Incorrect toe setting (Chapter 10).

Tyres worn in centre of tread

- [ ] Tyres over-inflated (*Weekly checks*).

Tyres worn on inside and outside edges

- [ ] Tyres under-inflated (*Weekly checks*).

Tyres worn unevenly

- [ ] Tyres out of balance (*Weekly checks*).
- [ ] Excessive wheel or tyre run-out (Chapter 1).
- [ ] Worn shock absorbers (Chapter 10).
- [ ] Faulty tyre (*Weekly checks*).

Electrical system

Note: *For problems associated with the starting system, refer to the faults listed under Engine earlier in this Section.*

Battery will only hold a charge for a few days

- [ ] Battery defective internally (Chapter 5A).
- [ ] Battery electrolyte level low (Chapter 5A).
- [ ] Battery terminal connections loose or corroded (*Weekly checks*).
- [ ] Auxiliary drivebelt worn or slipping (Chapter 1).
- [ ] Alternator not charging at correct output (Chapter 5A).
- [ ] Alternator or voltage regulator faulty (Chapter 5A).
- [ ] Short-circuit causing continual battery drain (Chapters 5A and 12).

Ignition (no-charge) warning light remains illuminated with engine running

- [ ] Auxiliary drivebelt broken, worn, or slipping (Chapter 1).
- [ ] Alternator brushes worn, sticking, or dirty (Chapter 5A).
- [ ] Alternator brush springs weak or broken (Chapter 5A).
- [ ] Internal fault in alternator or voltage regulator (Chapter 5A).
- [ ] Disconnected or loose wiring in charging circuit (Chapter 5A).

Ignition (no-charge) warning light fails to come on

- [ ] Warning light bulb blown (Chapter 12).
- [ ] Broken, disconnected, or loose wiring in warning light circuit (Chapters 5A and 12).
- [ ] Alternator faulty (Chapter 5A).

Lights inoperative

- [ ] Bulb blown (Chapter 12).
- [ ] Corrosion of bulb or bulbholder contacts (Chapter 12).
- [ ] Blown fuse (Chapter 12).
- [ ] Faulty relay (Chapter 12).
- [ ] Broken, loose, or disconnected wiring (Chapter 12).
- [ ] Faulty switch (Chapter 12).

Instrument readings inaccurate or erratic

Gauges give no reading

- [ ] Faulty gauge sender unit (Chapter 3 or 4A).
- [ ] Wiring open-circuit (Chapter 12).
- [ ] Faulty gauge (Chapter 12).

Gauges give continuous maximum reading

- [ ] Faulty gauge sender unit (Chapter 3 or 4A).
- [ ] Wiring short-circuit (Chapter 12).
- [ ] Faulty gauge (Chapter 12).

Horn faults

Horn fails to operate

- [ ] Blown fuse (Chapter 12).
- [ ] Cable or cable connections loose or disconnected (Chapter 12).
- [ ] Faulty switch (Chapter 12).
- [ ] Faulty horn (Chapter 12).

Horn emits intermittent or unsatisfactory sound

- [ ] Cable connections loose (Chapter 12).
- [ ] Horn mountings loose (Chapter 12).
- [ ] Faulty horn (Chapter 12).

Horn operates all the time

- [ ] Horn push either earthed or stuck down (Chapter 12).
- [ ] Horn cable to horn push earthed (Chapter 12).

Windscreen/tailgate wiper faults

Wipers fail to operate, or operate very slowly

- [ ] Wiper blades stuck to screen, or linkage seized (Chapter 12).
- [ ] Blown fuse (Chapter 12).
- [ ] Cable or cable connections loose or disconnected (Chapter 12).
- [ ] Faulty switch (Chapter 12).
- [ ] Faulty relay (Chapter 12).
- [ ] Faulty wiper motor (Chapter 12).

Wiper blades sweep over the wrong area of glass

- [ ] Wiper arms incorrectly-positioned on spindles (Chapter 12).
- [ ] Excessive wear of wiper linkage (Chapter 12).
- [ ] Wiper motor or linkage mountings loose or insecure (Chapter 12).

Wiper blades fail to clean the glass effectively

- [ ] Wiper blade rubbers worn or perished (*Weekly checks*).
- [ ] Wiper arm tension springs broken, or arm pivots seized (Chapter 12).
- [ ] Insufficient windscreen washer additive to adequately remove road film (*Weekly checks*).

Windscreen/tailgate washer faults

One or more washer jets inoperative

- [ ] Blocked washer jet (*Weekly checks* or Chapter 12).
- [ ] Disconnected, kinked or restricted fluid hose (Chapter 12).
- [ ] Insufficient fluid in washer reservoir (*Weekly checks*).

Washer pump fails to operate

- [ ] Broken or disconnected wiring or connections (Chapter 12).
- [ ] Blown fuse (Chapter 12).
- [ ] Faulty washer switch (Chapter 12).
- [ ] Faulty washer pump (Chapter 12).

Washer pump runs for some time before fluid is emitted from jets

- [ ] Faulty one-way valve in fluid supply hose (Chapter 12).

Electric window faults

Window glass will only move in one direction

- [ ] Faulty switch (Chapter 12).

Window glass slow to move

- [ ] Regulator seized or damaged, or lack of lubrication (Chapter 11).
- [ ] Door internal components or trim fouling regulator (Chapter 11).
- [ ] Faulty motor (Chapter 12).

Window glass fails to move

- [ ] Blown fuse (Chapter 12).
- [ ] Faulty relay (Chapter 12).
- [ ] Broken or disconnected wiring or connections (Chapter 12).
- [ ] Faulty motor (Chapter 12).

Central locking system faults

Complete system failure

- [ ] Blown fuse (Chapter 12).
- [ ] Faulty control unit or relay (Chapter 11).
- [ ] Broken or disconnected wiring or connections (Chapter 12).

Latch locks but will not unlock, or unlocks but will not lock

- [ ] Faulty master switch (Chapter 12).
- [ ] Faulty lock (Chapter 11).
- [ ] Faulty relay (Chapter 12).

One lock motor fails to operate

- [ ] Broken or disconnected wiring or connections (Chapter 12).
- [ ] Faulty lock motor (Chapter 11).
- [ ] Fault in door latch (Chapter 11).

A

ABS (Anti-lock brake system) A system, usually electronically controlled, that senses incipient wheel lockup during braking and relieves hydraulic pressure at wheels that are about to skid.

Air bag An inflatable bag hidden in the steering wheel (driver's side) or the dash or glovebox (passenger side). In a head-on collision, the bags inflate, preventing the driver and front passenger from being thrown forward into the steering wheel or windscreen.

Air cleaner A metal or plastic housing, containing a filter element, which removes dust and dirt from the air being drawn into the engine.

Air filter element The actual filter in an air cleaner system, usually manufactured from pleated paper and requiring renewal at regular intervals.

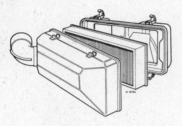

Air filter

Allen key A hexagonal wrench which fits into a recessed hexagonal hole.

Alligator clip A long-nosed spring-loaded metal clip with meshing teeth. Used to make temporary electrical connections.

Alternator A component in the electrical system which converts mechanical energy from a drivebelt into electrical energy to charge the battery and to operate the starting system, ignition system and electrical accessories.

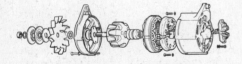

Alternator (exploded view)

Ampere (amp) A unit of measurement for the flow of electric current. One amp is the amount of current produced by one volt acting through a resistance of one ohm.

Anaerobic sealer A substance used to prevent bolts and screws from loosening. Anaerobic means that it does not require oxygen for activation. The Loctite brand is widely used.

Antifreeze A substance (usually ethylene glycol) mixed with water, and added to a vehicle's cooling system, to prevent freezing of the coolant in winter. Antifreeze also contains chemicals to inhibit corrosion and the formation of rust and other deposits that would tend to clog the radiator and coolant passages and reduce cooling efficiency.

Anti-seize compound A coating that reduces the risk of seizing on fasteners that are subjected to high temperatures, such as exhaust manifold bolts and nuts.

Anti-seize compound

Asbestos A natural fibrous mineral with great heat resistance, commonly used in the composition of brake friction materials. Asbestos is a health hazard and the dust created by brake systems should never be inhaled or ingested.

Axle A shaft on which a wheel revolves, or which revolves with a wheel. Also, a solid beam that connects the two wheels at one end of the vehicle. An axle which also transmits power to the wheels is known as a live axle.

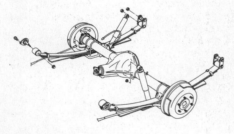

Axle assembly

Axleshaft A single rotating shaft, on either side of the differential, which delivers power from the final drive assembly to the drive wheels. Also called a driveshaft or a halfshaft.

B

Ball bearing An anti-friction bearing consisting of a hardened inner and outer race with hardened steel balls between two races.

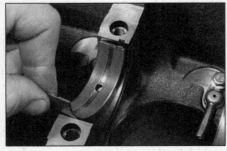

Bearing

Bearing The curved surface on a shaft or in a bore, or the part assembled into either, that permits relative motion between them with minimum wear and friction.

Big-end bearing The bearing in the end of the connecting rod that's attached to the crankshaft.

Bleed nipple A valve on a brake wheel cylinder, caliper or other hydraulic component that is opened to purge the hydraulic system of air. Also called a bleed screw.

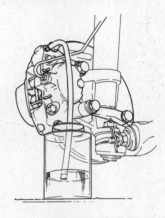

Brake bleeding

Brake bleeding Procedure for removing air from lines of a hydraulic brake system.

Brake disc The component of a disc brake that rotates with the wheels.

Brake drum The component of a drum brake that rotates with the wheels.

Brake linings The friction material which contacts the brake disc or drum to retard the vehicle's speed. The linings are bonded or riveted to the brake pads or shoes.

Brake pads The replaceable friction pads that pinch the brake disc when the brakes are applied. Brake pads consist of a friction material bonded or riveted to a rigid backing plate.

Brake shoe The crescent-shaped carrier to which the brake linings are mounted and which forces the lining against the rotating drum during braking.

Braking systems For more information on braking systems, consult the *Haynes Automotive Brake Manual*.

Breaker bar A long socket wrench handle providing greater leverage.

Bulkhead The insulated partition between the engine and the passenger compartment.

C

Caliper The non-rotating part of a disc-brake assembly that straddles the disc and carries the brake pads. The caliper also contains the hydraulic components that cause the pads to pinch the disc when the brakes are applied. A caliper is also a measuring tool that can be set to measure inside or outside dimensions of an object.

Camshaft A rotating shaft on which a series of cam lobes operate the valve mechanisms. The camshaft may be driven by gears, by sprockets and chain or by sprockets and a belt.

Canister A container in an evaporative emission control system; contains activated charcoal granules to trap vapours from the fuel system.

Canister

Carburettor A device which mixes fuel with air in the proper proportions to provide a desired power output from a spark ignition internal combustion engine.

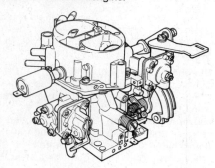

Carburettor

Castellated Resembling the parapets along the top of a castle wall. For example, a castellated balljoint stud nut.

Castellated nut

Castor In wheel alignment, the backward or forward tilt of the steering axis. Castor is positive when the steering axis is inclined rearward at the top.

Catalytic converter A silencer-like device in the exhaust system which converts certain pollutants in the exhaust gases into less harmful substances.

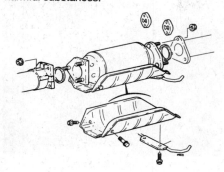

Catalytic converter

Circlip A ring-shaped clip used to prevent endwise movement of cylindrical parts and shafts. An internal circlip is installed in a groove in a housing; an external circlip fits into a groove on the outside of a cylindrical piece such as a shaft.

Clearance The amount of space between two parts. For example, between a piston and a cylinder, between a bearing and a journal, etc.

Coil spring A spiral of elastic steel found in various sizes throughout a vehicle, for example as a springing medium in the suspension and in the valve train.

Compression Reduction in volume, and increase in pressure and temperature, of a gas, caused by squeezing it into a smaller space.

Compression ratio The relationship between cylinder volume when the piston is at top dead centre and cylinder volume when the piston is at bottom dead centre.

Constant velocity (CV) joint A type of universal joint that cancels out vibrations caused by driving power being transmitted through an angle.

Core plug A disc or cup-shaped metal device inserted in a hole in a casting through which core was removed when the casting was formed. Also known as a freeze plug or expansion plug.

Crankcase The lower part of the engine block in which the crankshaft rotates.

Crankshaft The main rotating member, or shaft, running the length of the crankcase, with offset "throws" to which the connecting rods are attached.

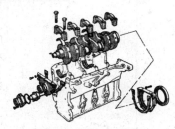

Crankshaft assembly

Crocodile clip See Alligator clip

D

Diagnostic code Code numbers obtained by accessing the diagnostic mode of an engine management computer. This code can be used to determine the area in the system where a malfunction may be located.

Disc brake A brake design incorporating a rotating disc onto which brake pads are squeezed. The resulting friction converts the energy of a moving vehicle into heat.

Double-overhead cam (DOHC) An engine that uses two overhead camshafts, usually one for the intake valves and one for the exhaust valves.

Drivebelt(s) The belt(s) used to drive accessories such as the alternator, water pump, power steering pump, air conditioning compressor, etc. off the crankshaft pulley.

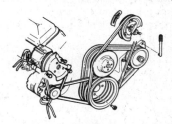

Accessory drivebelts

Driveshaft Any shaft used to transmit motion. Commonly used when referring to the axleshafts on a front wheel drive vehicle.

Driveshaft

Drum brake A type of brake using a drum-shaped metal cylinder attached to the inner surface of the wheel. When the brake pedal is pressed, curved brake shoes with friction linings press against the inside of the drum to slow or stop the vehicle.

Drum brake assembly

E

EGR valve A valve used to introduce exhaust gases into the intake air stream.

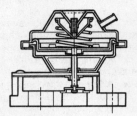

EGR valve

Electronic control unit (ECU) A computer which controls (for instance) ignition and fuel injection systems, or an anti-lock braking system. For more information refer to the *Haynes Automotive Electrical and Electronic Systems Manual*.

Electronic Fuel Injection (EFI) A computer controlled fuel system that distributes fuel through an injector located in each intake port of the engine.

Emergency brake A braking system, independent of the main hydraulic system, that can be used to slow or stop the vehicle if the primary brakes fail, or to hold the vehicle stationary even though the brake pedal isn't depressed. It usually consists of a hand lever that actuates either front or rear brakes mechanically through a series of cables and linkages. Also known as a handbrake or parking brake.

Endfloat The amount of lengthwise movement between two parts. As applied to a crankshaft, the distance that the crankshaft can move forward and back in the cylinder block.

Engine management system (EMS) A computer controlled system which manages the fuel injection and the ignition systems in an integrated fashion.

Exhaust manifold A part with several passages through which exhaust gases leave the engine combustion chambers and enter the exhaust pipe.

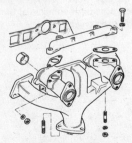

Exhaust manifold

F

Fan clutch A viscous (fluid) drive coupling device which permits variable engine fan speeds in relation to engine speeds.

Feeler blade A thin strip or blade of hardened steel, ground to an exact thickness, used to check or measure clearances between parts.

Feeler blade

Firing order The order in which the engine cylinders fire, or deliver their power strokes, beginning with the number one cylinder.

Flywheel A heavy spinning wheel in which energy is absorbed and stored by means of momentum. On cars, the flywheel is attached to the crankshaft to smooth out firing impulses.

Free play The amount of travel before any action takes place. The "looseness" in a linkage, or an assembly of parts, between the initial application of force and actual movement. For example, the distance the brake pedal moves before the pistons in the master cylinder are actuated.

Fuse An electrical device which protects a circuit against accidental overload. The typical fuse contains a soft piece of metal which is calibrated to melt at a predetermined current flow (expressed as amps) and break the circuit.

Fusible link A circuit protection device consisting of a conductor surrounded by heat-resistant insulation. The conductor is smaller than the wire it protects, so it acts as the weakest link in the circuit. Unlike a blown fuse, a failed fusible link must frequently be cut from the wire for replacement.

G

Gap The distance the spark must travel in jumping from the centre electrode to the side

Adjusting spark plug gap

electrode in a spark plug. Also refers to the spacing between the points in a contact breaker assembly in a conventional points-type ignition, or to the distance between the reluctor or rotor and the pickup coil in an electronic ignition.

Gasket Any thin, soft material - usually cork, cardboard, asbestos or soft metal - installed between two metal surfaces to ensure a good seal. For instance, the cylinder head gasket seals the joint between the block and the cylinder head.

Gasket

Gauge An instrument panel display used to monitor engine conditions. A gauge with a movable pointer on a dial or a fixed scale is an analogue gauge. A gauge with a numerical readout is called a digital gauge.

H

Halfshaft A rotating shaft that transmits power from the final drive unit to a drive wheel, usually when referring to a live rear axle.

Harmonic balancer A device designed to reduce torsion or twisting vibration in the crankshaft. May be incorporated in the crankshaft pulley. Also known as a vibration damper.

Hone An abrasive tool for correcting small irregularities or differences in diameter in an engine cylinder, brake cylinder, etc.

Hydraulic tappet A tappet that utilises hydraulic pressure from the engine's lubrication system to maintain zero clearance (constant contact with both camshaft and valve stem). Automatically adjusts to variation in valve stem length. Hydraulic tappets also reduce valve noise.

I

Ignition timing The moment at which the spark plug fires, usually expressed in the number of crankshaft degrees before the piston reaches the top of its stroke.

Inlet manifold A tube or housing with passages through which flows the air-fuel mixture (carburettor vehicles and vehicles with throttle body injection) or air only (port fuel-injected vehicles) to the port openings in the cylinder head.

J

Jump start Starting the engine of a vehicle with a discharged or weak battery by attaching jump leads from the weak battery to a charged or helper battery.

L

Load Sensing Proportioning Valve (LSPV) A brake hydraulic system control valve that works like a proportioning valve, but also takes into consideration the amount of weight carried by the rear axle.

Locknut A nut used to lock an adjustment nut, or other threaded component, in place. For example, a locknut is employed to keep the adjusting nut on the rocker arm in position.

Lockwasher A form of washer designed to prevent an attaching nut from working loose.

M

MacPherson strut A type of front suspension system devised by Earle MacPherson at Ford of England. In its original form, a simple lateral link with the anti-roll bar creates the lower control arm. A long strut - an integral coil spring and shock absorber - is mounted between the body and the steering knuckle. Many modern so-called MacPherson strut systems use a conventional lower A-arm and don't rely on the anti-roll bar for location.

Multimeter An electrical test instrument with the capability to measure voltage, current and resistance.

N

NOx Oxides of Nitrogen. A common toxic pollutant emitted by petrol and diesel engines at higher temperatures.

O

Ohm The unit of electrical resistance. One volt applied to a resistance of one ohm will produce a current of one amp.

Ohmmeter An instrument for measuring electrical resistance.

O-ring A type of sealing ring made of a special rubber-like material; in use, the O-ring is compressed into a groove to provide the sealing action.

O-ring

Overhead cam (ohc) engine An engine with the camshaft(s) located on top of the cylinder head(s).

Overhead valve (ohv) engine An engine with the valves located in the cylinder head, but with the camshaft located in the engine block.

Oxygen sensor A device installed in the engine exhaust manifold, which senses the oxygen content in the exhaust and converts this information into an electric current. Also called a Lambda sensor.

P

Phillips screw A type of screw head having a cross instead of a slot for a corresponding type of screwdriver.

Plastigage A thin strip of plastic thread, available in different sizes, used for measuring clearances. For example, a strip of Plastigage is laid across a bearing journal. The parts are assembled and dismantled; the width of the crushed strip indicates the clearance between journal and bearing.

Plastigage

Propeller shaft The long hollow tube with universal joints at both ends that carries power from the transmission to the differential on front-engined rear wheel drive vehicles.

Proportioning valve A hydraulic control valve which limits the amount of pressure to the rear brakes during panic stops to prevent wheel lock-up.

R

Rack-and-pinion steering A steering system with a pinion gear on the end of the steering shaft that mates with a rack (think of a geared wheel opened up and laid flat). When the steering wheel is turned, the pinion turns, moving the rack to the left or right. This movement is transmitted through the track rods to the steering arms at the wheels.

Radiator A liquid-to-air heat transfer device designed to reduce the temperature of the coolant in an internal combustion engine cooling system.

Refrigerant Any substance used as a heat transfer agent in an air-conditioning system. R-12 has been the principle refrigerant for many years; recently, however, manufacturers have begun using R-134a, a non-CFC substance that is considered less harmful to the ozone in the upper atmosphere.

Rocker arm A lever arm that rocks on a shaft or pivots on a stud. In an overhead valve engine, the rocker arm converts the upward movement of the pushrod into a downward movement to open a valve.

Rotor In a distributor, the rotating device inside the cap that connects the centre electrode and the outer terminals as it turns, distributing the high voltage from the coil secondary winding to the proper spark plug. Also, that part of an alternator which rotates inside the stator. Also, the rotating assembly of a turbocharger, including the compressor wheel, shaft and turbine wheel.

Runout The amount of wobble (in-and-out movement) of a gear or wheel as it's rotated. The amount a shaft rotates "out-of-true." The out-of-round condition of a rotating part.

S

Sealant A liquid or paste used to prevent leakage at a joint. Sometimes used in conjunction with a gasket.

Sealed beam lamp An older headlight design which integrates the reflector, lens and filaments into a hermetically-sealed one-piece unit. When a filament burns out or the lens cracks, the entire unit is simply replaced.

Serpentine drivebelt A single, long, wide accessory drivebelt that's used on some newer vehicles to drive all the accessories, instead of a series of smaller, shorter belts. Serpentine drivebelts are usually tensioned by an automatic tensioner.

Serpentine drivebelt

Shim Thin spacer, commonly used to adjust the clearance or relative positions between two parts. For example, shims inserted into or under bucket tappets control valve clearances. Clearance is adjusted by changing the thickness of the shim.

Slide hammer A special puller that screws into or hooks onto a component such as a shaft or bearing; a heavy sliding handle on the shaft bottoms against the end of the shaft to knock the component free.

Sprocket A tooth or projection on the periphery of a wheel, shaped to engage with a chain or drivebelt. Commonly used to refer to the sprocket wheel itself.

Starter inhibitor switch On vehicles with an automatic transmission, a switch that prevents starting if the vehicle is not in Neutral or Park.

Strut See MacPherson strut.

T

Tappet A cylindrical component which transmits motion from the cam to the valve stem, either directly or via a pushrod and rocker arm. Also called a cam follower.

Thermostat A heat-controlled valve that regulates the flow of coolant between the cylinder block and the radiator, so maintaining optimum engine operating temperature. A thermostat is also used in some air cleaners in which the temperature is regulated.

Thrust bearing The bearing in the clutch assembly that is moved in to the release levers by clutch pedal action to disengage the clutch. Also referred to as a release bearing.

Timing belt A toothed belt which drives the camshaft. Serious engine damage may result if it breaks in service.

Timing chain A chain which drives the camshaft.

Toe-in The amount the front wheels are closer together at the front than at the rear. On rear wheel drive vehicles, a slight amount of toe-in is usually specified to keep the front wheels running parallel on the road by offsetting other forces that tend to spread the wheels apart.

Toe-out The amount the front wheels are closer together at the rear than at the front. On front wheel drive vehicles, a slight amount of toe-out is usually specified.

Tools For full information on choosing and using tools, refer to the *Haynes Automotive Tools Manual*.

Tracer A stripe of a second colour applied to a wire insulator to distinguish that wire from another one with the same colour insulator.

Tune-up A process of accurate and careful adjustments and parts replacement to obtain the best possible engine performance.

Turbocharger A centrifugal device, driven by exhaust gases, that pressurises the intake air. Normally used to increase the power output from a given engine displacement, but can also be used primarily to reduce exhaust emissions (as on VW's "Umwelt" Diesel engine).

U

Universal joint or U-joint A double-pivoted connection for transmitting power from a driving to a driven shaft through an angle. A U-joint consists of two Y-shaped yokes and a cross-shaped member called the spider.

V

Valve A device through which the flow of liquid, gas, vacuum, or loose material in bulk may be started, stopped, or regulated by a movable part that opens, shuts, or partially obstructs one or more ports or passageways. A valve is also the movable part of such a device.

Valve clearance The clearance between the valve tip (the end of the valve stem) and the rocker arm or tappet. The valve clearance is measured when the valve is closed.

Vernier caliper A precision measuring instrument that measures inside and outside dimensions. Not quite as accurate as a micrometer, but more convenient.

Viscosity The thickness of a liquid or its resistance to flow.

Volt A unit for expressing electrical "pressure" in a circuit. One volt that will produce a current of one ampere through a resistance of one ohm.

W

Welding Various processes used to join metal items by heating the areas to be joined to a molten state and fusing them together. For more information refer to the *Haynes Automotive Welding Manual*.

Wiring diagram A drawing portraying the components and wires in a vehicle's electrical system, using standardised symbols. For more information refer to the *Haynes Automotive Electrical and Electronic Systems Manual*.

Note: *References throughout this index are in the form* **"Chapter number"** • **"Page number"**. *So, for example, 2C•15 refers to page 15 of Chapter 2C.*

A

A-pillar trim panel – 11•18
Accelerator pedal – 4A•7
Accessory shops – REF•3
Acknowledgements – 0•6
Aerial – 12•14
Air conditioning system – 3•8
    refrigerant leaks – 1•7
    switch – 12•4
Air filter – 1•14, 4A•8
Air mix cables – 3•7
Airbags – 0•5, 12•14, 12•15
    clockspring (rotary connector) – 12•15
    control unit – 12•16
    sensors – 12•16
Airlocks – 1•17
Alternator – 5A•3, 5A•4
Antifreeze – 0•12, 0•17, 1•16
Anti-lock braking system (ABS) – 9•11
Anti-roll bar – 10•7
Anti-theft immobiliser – 12•14
Asbestos – 0•5
Automatic transmission – 7B•1 *et seq*
    control module – 7B•5
    fault finding – REF•19
    fluid – 0•17, 1•11, 1•13
    switches/sensors – 7B•4
Auxiliary drivebelts – 1•8
Axle – 10•10

B

B-pillar trim panels – 11•18
Badges – 11•14
Battery – 0•5, 0•15, 5A•2, REF•5
    remote control – 11•12
Big-end bearings – 2B•14, 2B•16
Bleeding
    brakes – 9•9
    clutch – 6•3
Blower motor – 3•6, 3•8
    switch – 12•5
Body corrosion – REF•13
Body electrical system – 12•1 *et seq*
Body trim strips – 11•14
Bodywork and fittings – 11•1 *et seq*
Bonnet – 11•5
    lock – 11•6
    release cable – 11•5
Brake fluid – 0•13, 0•17, 1•15
    leaks – 1•8
Brake pedal – 1•10, 9•8
Braking system – 1•12, 9•1 *et seq*, REF•10, REF•11, REF•12
    fault finding – REF•20
Bulbs – 12•5, 12•7

Bumpers – 11•4
Burning – 0•5
Buying spare parts – REF•3

C

Cables
    air mix – 3•7
    bonnet release – 11•5
    fuel filler flap – 11•15
    gear lever and gearchange – 7A•2
    handbrake – 9•13
    mode control – 3•7
    recirculation control – 3•6
    selector – 7B•2
Calipers – 9•3
Camshafts – 2A•9
    position sensor – 4A•7
Carpets – 11•2, 11•19
Catalytic converter – 4B•5
Central locking system – 11•12
Centre console – 11•19
    switches – 12•5
Charcoal canister – 1•13, 4B•2
Charging – 5A•2, 5A•3
Clutch – 6•1 *et seq*
    fault finding – REF•18
    fluid – 0•13, 0•17
    fluid leaks – 1•8
    pedal – 1•10, 6•3
Coils – 5B•2
Compression test – 2A•4
Compressor – 3•9
Condenser – 3•9
Connecting rods – 2B•11, 2B•13, 2B•16
Console – 11•19
    switches – 12•5
Conversion factors – REF•2
Coolant – 0•12, 0•17, 1•16
    leaks – 1•7
    pump – 3•5
    temperature sensor – 3•5
Cooling fan – 3•4
Cooling, heating and ventilation systems – 3•1 *et seq*
    fault finding – REF•17
Courtesy light – 12•7
    switches – 12•5
Crankcase – 2B•12
    emission control – 4B•1, 4B•2
Crankshaft – 2B•11, 2B•13, 2B•15
    oil seals – 2A•12
    position sensor – 4A•7
    pulley – 2A•6
Crushing – 0•5
Cylinder block – 2B•12
Cylinder head – 2A•10, 2B•6, 2B•7

Note: *References throughout this index are in the form* **"Chapter number"** • **"Page number"**. *So, for example, 2C•15 refers to page 15 of Chapter 2C.*

D

Dents – 11•2
Depressurising fuel system – 4A•2
Dimensions – REF•1
Direction indicator light – 12•6, 12•9
Disconnecting the battery – REF•5
Discs – 1•11, 9•4
Distance sensor – 12•16
Doors – 11•6, REF•11
   courtesy light switches – 12•5
   handles and locks – 11•8
   inner trim panel – 11•6
   lock control unit – 11•13
   lock motor – 11•12
   lock switch – 11•12
   window glass and regulator – 11•10
Drivebelts – 1•8
Driveplate – 2A•12
Driveshafts – 8•1 *et seq*, REF•12
   fault finding – REF•19
   gaiters – 1•11, 8•3, 8•4
   oil seals – 7A•4, 7B•5
Drivetrain – 1•12
Drums – 1•13, 9•5

E

Earth fault – 12•2
ECU (fuel system) – 4A•7
Electric shock – 0•5
Electric windows – 11•13
   switches – 12•5
Electrical systems – 0•16, 1•12, REF•11
   fault finding – 12•2, REF•22
Emergency key access – 11•13
Emission control and exhaust systems – 4B•1 *et seq*, REF•13
Engine in-car repair procedures – 2A•1 *et seq*
   fault finding – REF•15, REF•16
Engine oil – 0•12, 0•17, 1•6
   leaks – 1•7
Engine removal and overhaul procedures – 2B•1 *et seq*
Environmental considerations – REF•6
Evaporative emission control – 4B•1, 4B•2
Evaporator – 3•9
Exhaust emission control – 4B•1
Exhaust manifold – 4B•3
Exhaust specialists – REF•3
Exhaust system – 1•8, 1•12, 4B•2, 4B•4, REF•12, REF•13
Expansion valve – 3•9

F

Facia assembly – 11•20

Fan – 3•4
Fault codes (automatic transmission) – 7B•2
Fault finding – REF•14 *et seq*
   automatic transmission – REF•19
   braking system – REF•20
   clutch – REF•18
   cooling system – REF•17
   driveshafts – REF•19
   electrical system – 12•2, REF•22
   engine – REF•15, REF•16
   fuel and exhaust systems – REF•17
   manual transmission – REF•18
   suspension and steering – REF•21
Filling – 11•3
Filters
   air – 1•14, 4A•8
   oil – 1•6
   pollen – 1•12
Fire – 0•5
Fluids – 0•17
Flywheel – 2A•12
Foglight – 12•6, 12•9
   switch – 12•5
Followers – 2A•9
Footwell trim panels – 11•18
Fuel filler cap – 4B•2
   operating cable – 11•15
Fuel gauge sender unit – 4A•4
Fuel injection system – 4A•5
Fuel injectors – 4A•6
Fuel leaks – 1•7
Fuel pressure regulator – 4A•7
Fuel pump – 4A•3, 4A•4
Fuel rail – 4A•6
Fuel system – 4A•1 *et seq*, REF•13
   fault finding – REF•17
Fuel tank – 4A•3
Fume or gas intoxication – 0•5
Fuses – 12•3

G

Gaiters
   driveshaft – 1•11, 8•3, 8•4
   steering rack – 10•12
Garages – REF•3
Gashes – 11•3
Gaskets – REF•6
Gear lever and gearchange cables – 7A•2
General repair procedures – REF•6
Glossary of technical terms – REF•26 *et seq*
Glovebox – 11•17
Grab handles – 11•19

Note: *References throughout this index are in the form* **"Chapter number"** • **"Page number"**. *So, for example, 2C•15 refers to page 15 of Chapter 2C.*

H

Handbrake – 1•10, REF•10
   cables – 9•13
   lever – 9•12
   warning light switch – 9•13
Handles
   door – 11•8
   grab – 11•19
   tailgate lock – 11•12
Hazard warning light switch – 12•4
Headlight – 12•5, 12•8
   adjuster components – 12•10
   beam adjuster – 12•5
   beam alignment – 12•10
Headlining – 11•19
Heated rear window switch – 12•4
Heater/ventilation system – 3•6
   blower motor – 3•6, 3•8
   blower motor switch – 12•5
   control illumination – 12•8
   control panel – 3•6
   matrix – 3•7
High-level stop-light – 12•7, 12•10
Hinge lubrication – 1•10
Horn – 12•11
Hoses – 3•3, 6•2, 9•9
   leaks – 1•7
HT coils – 5B•2
Hub – 10•3, 10•8
   bearings – 10•4, 10•8
Hydraulic unit (ABS) – 9•11
Hydrofluoric acid – 0•5

I

Identifying leaks – 0•10
Ignition system – 5B•1 *et seq*
   switch – 12•4
Immobiliser – 12•14
Impact sensor – 12•16
Indicator light – 12•6, 12•9
   side repeater light – 12•6
Injectors – 4A•6
Inlet manifold – 4A•8
Instrument panel – 1•12, 12•10
   illumination – 12•8
Interior light – 12•7
   switches – 12•5

J

Jacking and vehicle support – REF•4
Joint mating faces – REF•6
Jump starting – 0•8

K

Knock sensor – 5B•3

L

Leaks – 0•10, 1•7
Light sensor – 12•5
Light units – 12•8
Limited Operation Strategy – 4A•5
Liquid gasket – 2A•4
Locknuts, locktabs and washers – REF•6
Locks
   bonnet – 11•6
   central locking system – 11•12
   door – 11•8, 11•12, 11•13
   lubrication – 1•10
   remote locking receiver unit – 11•13
   steering column – 12•4
   tailgate – 11•12
Lower arm – 10•7, 10•8
Lubricants and fluids – 0•17
Luggage compartment light – 12•7

M

Main bearings – 2B•14, 2B•15
Manifold absolute pressure sensor – 4A•5
Manifolds
   exhaust – 4B•3
   inlet – 4A•8
Manual transmission – 7A•1 *et seq*
   fault finding – REF•18
   oil – 0•17, 1•15, 7A•2
Master cylinder
   brake – 9•8
   clutch – 6•2
Matrix – 3•7
Mirrors – 11•13, 11•19, REF•10
   switch – 12•4
Mode control cables – 3•7
MOT test checks – REF•10 *et seq*
Motor factors – REF•3
Mountings – 2A•13
Multiplex wiring modules – 12•16

Note: References throughout this index are in the form **"Chapter number"** • **"Page number"**. *So, for example, 2C•15 refers to page 15 of Chapter 2C.*

N

Neutral position switch – 7B•4
Nissan Micra manual – 0•6
Number plate light – 12•7

O

Oil
    engine – 0•12, 0•17, 1•6
    manual transmission – 0•17, 1•15, 7A•2
Oil filter – 1•6
Oil leaks – 1•7
Oil pan – 7B•5
Oil pump – 2B•11
Oil seals – REF•6
    crankshaft – 2A•12
    driveshafts – 7A•4, 7B•5
Open-circuit – 12•2
Oxygen sensors – 4B•2

P

Pads – 1•11, 9•2
Parking aid – 12•16
Parcel shelf support panel – 11•18
Park/neutral position switch – 7B•4
Parts – REF•3
Pedals
    accelerator – 4A•7
    brake – 1•10, 9•8
    clutch – 1•10, 6•3
Pipes – 4A•3, 6•2, 9•9
Piston rings – 2B•14
Pistons – 2B•11, 2B•13, 2B•16
Plastic components – 11•3
Poisonous or irritant substances – 0•5
Pollen filter – 1•12
Power steering – 10•11
Pressure cap – 1•17
Puncture repair – 0•9
Purge valve – 4B•2

Q

Quick-release couplings – 4A•3

R

Radiator – 1•16, 3•3
    cap – 1•17
Radio unit – 12•13
    aerial – 12•14

Rain sensor – 12•5
Range/distance sensor – 12•16
Rear axle – 10•10
Rear lights – 12•6, 12•9
Rear trim panels – 11•18
Rear window switch – 12•4
Recirculation control cable – 3•6
Refrigerant leaks – 1•7
Relays – 12•3
Release bearing – 6•2
Remote control
    battery – 11•12
    receiver unit – 11•13
Repeater light – 12•6, 12•9
Respraying – 11•3
Reversing light switch – 7A•3
Revolution sensor – 7B•4
Road test – 1•12
Roadside repairs – 0•7 *et seq*
Roadwheel nut tightness – 1•11
Rocker cover – 2A•5
Routine maintenance & servicing – 1•1 *et seq*
    bodywork and underframe – 11•2
    upholstery and carpets – 11•2
Rust holes – 11•3

S

Safety first! – 0•5, 0•13
Scalding – 0•5
Scratches – 11•2
Screenwasher fluid – 0•13
Screw threads and fastenings – REF•6
Scuttle cover panel – 11•14
Seat belts – 1•10, 11•16
Seats – 11•15
Selector
    cable – 7B•2
    lever – 7B•3
Service interval display – 1•5
Servo unit – 9•10, 9•11
Shift lock system – 7B•4
Shock absorbers – 1•11, 10•9, REF•11, REF•12
Shoes – 1•13, 9•6
Short-circuit – 12•2
Side airbags – 12•16
Side glass – 11•14
Side trim panel – 11•18
Sidelight – 12•6
Silencer – 4B•4
Slave cylinder/release bearing – 6•2
Spare parts – REF•3
Spark plugs – 1•14

Note: *References throughout this index are in the form* "**Chapter number**" • "**Page number**". *So, for example, 2C•15 refers to page 15 of Chapter 2C.*

Speakers – 12•14
Speed sensor – 7A•3
Springs – 10•10, REF•12
Sprockets – 2A•6
Starting and charging systems – 5A•1 *et seq*
Start-up after overhaul – 2B•17
Steering – 1•11, 1•12, REF•11, REF•12
   angles – 10•13
   angle sensor – 9•12
Steering column – 10•11, REF•10
   lock – 12•4
   shrouds – 11•17
   switches – 12•4
Steering rack – 10•12
   gaiters – 10•12
Steering wheel – 10•10, REF•10
Stop-light – 12•7, 12•10
   switch – 9•12
Strut
   suspension – 10•6
   tailgate – 11•11
Subframe – 10•8
Sump – 2A•11
Sun visors – 11•19
Support struts tailgate – 11•11
Suspension and steering – 1•11, 1•12, 10•1 *et seq*, REF•11, REF•12
   fault finding – REF•21
Switches – 12•4
   door lock – 11•12
   handbrake warning light – 9•13
   illumination – 12•8
   mirror – 11•13
   park/neutral position – 7B•4
   reversing light – 7A•3
   stop-light – 9•12
   transmission – 7B•4
Swivel hub – 10•3

T

Tailgate – 11•11
   glass – 11•14
   lock – 11•12
   support struts – 11•11
   washer jet – 12•13
   washer system – 12•12
   wiper motor – 12•12
Technical terms – REF•26 *et seq*
Temperature sensor – 3•5
Thermostat – 3•4
Throttle body – 4A•6
Throttle position sensor – 4A•7
Timing chain – 2B•8
   tensioner and sprockets – 2A•6
Timing ignition – 5B•3
Tools and working facilities – REF•6, REF•8 *et seq*
Top dead centre (TDC) location – 2A•4
Towing – 0•10
Track rod end – 10•12
Trim panels – 11•6, 11•14, 11•17
Turbine revolution sensor – 7B•4

Tyres – REF•13
   condition and pressure – 0•14
   pressures – 0•17
   specialists – REF•3

U

Underbonnet check points – 0•11
Underframe – 11•2
Unleaded petrol – 4A•2
Upholstery – 11•2

V

Vacuum hoses leaks – 1•8
Vacuum servo unit – 9•10, 9•11
Valves – 2B•6, 2B•7
   clearances – 2A•8
Vehicle identification – REF•7, REF•11
Vehicle speed sensor – 7A•3
Vehicle support – REF•4
Ventilation system – 3•6

W

Washer fluid – 0•13
   pump – 12•13
   reservoir – 12•12
Washer jet – 12•13
Water pump – 3•5
Weekly checks – 0•11 *et seq*
Weights – REF•1
Wheels – REF•13
   alignment – 10•13
   bearings – 10•4, 10•8, REF•12
   changing – 0•9
Wheel arch liners – 11•14
Wheel cylinders – 9•7
Wheel sensors (ABS) – 9•11
Windows – 11•13
   glass and regulator – 11•10
   switches – 12•5
   trim panel – 11•18
Windscreen – 11•14, REF•10
   washer jet – 12•13
   washer system – 12•12
   wiper motor – 12•11
Wipers
   arms – 12•11
   blades – 0•15
   motor – 12•11, 12•12
Wiring diagrams – 12•17 *et seq*
Working facilities – REF•9

Y

Yaw rate sensor – 9•12

Haynes Manuals – The Complete **UK Car** List

Title	Book No.
ALFA ROMEO Alfasud/Sprint (74 - 88) up to F *	0292
Alfa Romeo Alfetta (73 – 87) up to E *	0531
AUDI 80, 90 & Coupe Petrol (79 – Nov 88) up to F	0605
Audi 80, 90 & Coupe Petrol (Oct 86 – 90) D to H	1491
Audi 100 & A6 Petrol & Diesel (May 91 – May 97) H to P	3504
Audi A3 Petrol & Diesel (96 – May 03) P to 03	4253
Audi A3 Petrol & Diesel (June 03 – Mar 08) 03 to 08	4884
Audi A4 Petrol & Diesel (95 – 00) M to X	3575
Audi A4 Petrol & Diesel (01 – 04) X to 54	4609
Audi A4 Petrol & Diesel (Jan 05 – Feb 08) 54 to 57	4885
AUSTIN A35 & A40 (56 – 67) up to F *	0118
Mini (59 – 69) up to H *	0527
Mini (69 – 01) up to X	0646
Austin Healey 100/6 & 3000 (56 – 68) up to G *	0049
BEDFORD/Vauxhall Rascal & Suzuki Supercarry (86 – Oct 94) C to M	3015
BMW 1-Series 4-cyl Petrol & Diesel (04 – Aug 11) 54 to 11	4918
BMW 316, 320 & 320i (4-cyl)(75 – Feb 83) up to Y *	0276
BMW 3- & 5- Series Petrol (81 – 91) up to J	1948
BMW 3-Series Petrol (Apr 91 – 99) H to V	3210
BMW 3-Series Petrol (Sept 98 – 06) S to 56	4067
BMW 3-Series Petrol & Diesel (05 – Sept 08) 54 to 58	4782
BMW 5-Series 6-cyl Petrol (April 96 – Aug 03) N to 03	4151
BMW 5-Series Diesel (Sept 03 – 10) 53 to 10	4901
BMW 1500, 1502, 1600, 1602, 2000 & 2002 (59 – 77) up to S *	0240
CHRYSLER PT Cruiser Petrol (00-09) W to 09	4058
CITROEN 2CV, Ami & Dyane (67 – 90) up to H	0196
Citroen AX Petrol & Diesel (87- 97) D to P	3014
Citroen Berlingo & Peugeot Partner Petrol & Diesel (96 – 10) P to 60	4281
Citroen C1 Petrol (05 – 11) 05 to 11	4922
Citroen C3 Petrol & Diesel (02 – 09) 51 to 59	4890
Citroen C4 Petrol & Diesel (04 – 10) 54 to 60	5576
Citroen C5 Petrol & Diesel (01 – 08) Y to 08	4745
Citroen C15 Van Petrol & Diesel (89 – Oct 98) F to S	3509
Citroen CX Petrol (75 – 88) up to F	0528
Citroen Saxo Petrol & Diesel (96 – 04) N to 54	3506
Citroen Visa Petrol (79 – 88) up to F	0620
Citroen Xantia Petrol & Diesel (93 – 01) K to Y	3082
Citroen XM Petrol & Diesel (89 – 00) G to X	3451
Citroen Xsara Petrol & Diesel (97 – Sept 00) R to W	3751
Citroen Xsara Picasso Petrol & Diesel (00 – 02) W to 52	3944
Citroen Xsara Picasso (Mar 04 – 08) 04 to 58	4784
Citroen ZX Diesel (91 – 98) J to S	1922
Citroen ZX Petrol (91 – 98) H to S	1881
FIAT 126 (73 – 87) up to E *	0305
Fiat 500 (57 – 73) up to M *	0090
Fiat 500 & Panda (04 – 12) 53 to 61	5558
Fiat Bravo & Brava Petrol (95 – 00) N to W	3572
Fiat Cinquecento (93 – 98) K to R	3501
Fiat Panda (81 – 95) up to M	0793
Fiat Punto Petrol & Diesel (94 – Oct 99) L to V	3251
Fiat Punto Petrol (Oct 99 – July 03) V to 03	4066
Fiat Punto Petrol (03 – 07) 03 to 07	4746

Title	Book No.
Fiat Punto Petrol (Oct 99 – 07) V to 07	5634
Fiat X1/9 (74 – 89) up to G *	0273
FORD Anglia (59 – 68) up to G *	0001
Ford Capri II (& III) 1.6 & 2.0 (74 – 87) up to E *	0283
Ford Capri II (& III) 2.8 & 3.0 V6 (74 – 87) up to E	1309
Ford C-Max Petrol & Diesel (03 – 10) 53 to 60	4900
Ford Escort Mk I 1100 & 1300 (68 – 74) up to N *	0171
Ford Escort Mk I Mexico, RS 1600 & RS 2000 (70 – 74) up to N *	0139
Ford Escort Mk II Mexico, RS 1800 & RS 2000 (75 – 80) up to W *	0735
Ford Escort (75 – Aug 80) up to V *	0280
Ford Escort Petrol (Sept 80 – Sept 90) up to H	0686
Ford Escort & Orion Petrol (Sept 90 – 00) H to X	1737
Ford Escort & Orion Diesel (Sept 90 – 00) H to X	4081
Ford Fiesta Petrol (Feb 89 – Oct 95) F to N	1595
Ford Fiesta Petrol & Diesel (Oct 95 – Mar 02) N to 02	3397
Ford Fiesta Petrol & Diesel (Apr 02 – 08) 02 to 58	4170
Ford Fiesta Petrol & Diesel (08 – 11) 58 to 11	4907
Ford Focus Petrol & Diesel (98 – 01) S to Y	3759
Ford Focus Petrol & Diesel (Oct 01 – 05) 51 to 05	4167
Ford Focus Petrol (05 – 09) 54 to 09	4785
Ford Focus Diesel (05 – 09) 54 to 09	4807
Ford Fusion Petrol & Diesel (02 – 11) 02 to 61	5566
Ford Galaxy Petrol & Diesel (95 – Aug 00) M to W	3984
Ford Galaxy Petrol & Diesel (00 – 06) X to 06	5556
Ford Granada Petrol (Sept 77 – Feb 85) up to B *	0481
Ford Ka (96 – 08) P to 58	5567
Ford Mondeo Petrol (93 – Sept 00) K to X	1923
Ford Mondeo Petrol & Diesel (Oct 00 – Jul 03) X to 03	3990
Ford Mondeo Petrol & Diesel (July 03 – 07) 03 to 56	4619
Ford Mondeo Petrol & Diesel (Apr 07 – 12) 07 to 61	5548
Ford Mondeo Diesel (93 – Sept 00) L to X	3465
Ford Sierra V6 Petrol (82 – 91) up to J	0904
Ford Transit Connect Diesel (02 – 11) 02 to 11	4903
Ford Transit Diesel (Feb 86 – 99) C to T	3019
Ford Transit Diesel (00 – Oct 06) X to 56	4775
Ford 1.6 & 1.8 litre Diesel Engine (84 – 96) A to N	1172
HILLMAN Imp (63 – 76) up to R *	0022
HONDA Civic (Feb 84 – Oct 87) A to E	1226
Honda Civic (Nov 91 – 96) J to N	3199
Honda Civic Petrol (Mar 95 – 00) M to X	4050
Honda Civic Petrol & Diesel (01 – 05) X to 55	4611
Honda CR-V Petrol & Diesel (02 – 06) 51 to 56	4747
Honda Jazz (02 to 08) 51 to 58	4735
JAGUAR E-Type (61 – 72) up to L *	0140
Jaguar Mk I & II, 240 & 340 (55 – 69) up to H *	0098
Jaguar XJ6, XJ & Sovereign, Daimler Sovereign (68 – Oct 86) up to D	0242
Jaguar XJ6 & Sovereign (Oct 86 – Sept 94) D to M	3261
Jaguar XJ12, XJS & Sovereign, Daimler Double Six (72 – 88) up to F	0478
JEEP Cherokee Petrol (93 – 96) K to N	1943
LAND ROVER 90, 110 & Defender Diesel (83 – 07) up to 56	3017
Land Rover Discovery Petrol & Diesel (89 – 98) G to S	3016

Title	Book No.
Land Rover Discovery Diesel (Nov 98 – Jul 04) S to 04	4606
Land Rover Discovery Diesel (Aug 04 – Apr 09) 04 to 09	5562
Land Rover Freelander Petrol & Diesel (97 – Sept 03) R to 53	3929
Land Rover Freelander (97 – Oct 06) R to 56	5571
Land Rover Series II, IIA & III 4-cyl Petrol (58 – 85) up to C	0314
Land Rover Series II, IIA & III Petrol & Diesel (58 – 85) up to C	5568
MAZDA 323 (Mar 81 – Oct 89) up to G	1608
Mazda 323 (Oct 89 – 98) G to R	3455
Mazda B1600, B1800 & B2000 Pick-up Petrol (72 – 88) up to F	0267
Mazda MX-5 (89 – 05) G to 05	5565
Mazda RX-7 (79 – 85) up to C *	0460
MERCEDES-BENZ 190, 190E & 190D Petrol & Diesel (83 – 93) A to L	3450
Mercedes-Benz 200D, 240D, 240TD, 300D & 300TD 123 Series Diesel (Oct 76 – 85) up to C	1114
Mercedes-Benz 250 & 280 (68 – 72) up to L *	0346
Mercedes-Benz 250 & 280 123 Series Petrol (Oct 76 – 84) up to B *	0677
Mercedes-Benz 124 Series Petrol & Diesel (85 – Aug 93) C to K	3253
Mercedes-Benz A-Class Petrol & Diesel (98 – 04) S to 54	4748
Mercedes-Benz C-Class Petrol & Diesel (93 – Aug 00) L to W	3511
Mercedes-Benz C-Class (00 – 07) X to 07	4780
Mercedes-Benz Sprinter Diesel (95 – Apr 06) M to 06	4902
MGA (55 – 62)	0475
MGB (62 – 80) up to W	0111
MGB 1962 to 1980 (special edition) *	4894
MG Midget & Austin-Healey Sprite (58 – 80) up to W *	0265
MINI Petrol (July 01 – 06) Y to 56	4273
MINI Petrol & Diesel (Nov 06 – 13) 56 to 13	4904
MITSUBISHI Shogun & L200 Pick-ups Petrol (83 – 94) up to M	1944
MORRIS Minor 1000 (56 – 71) up to K	0024
NISSAN Almera Petrol (95 – Feb 00) N to V	4053
Nissan Almera & Tino Petrol (Feb 00 – 07) V to 56	4612
Nissan Micra (83 – Jan 93) up to K	0931
Nissan Micra (93 – 02) K to 52	3254
Nissan Micra Petrol (03 – Oct 10) 52 to 60	4734
Nissan Primera Petrol (90 – Aug 99) H to T	1851
Nissan Qashqai Petrol & Diesel (07 – 12) 56 to 62	5610
OPEL Ascona & Manta (B-Series) (Sept 75 – 88) up to F *	0316
Opel Ascona Petrol (81 – 88)	3215
Opel Ascona Petrol (Oct 91 – Feb 98)	3156
Opel Corsa Petrol (83 – Mar 93)	3160
Opel Corsa Petrol (Mar 93 – 97)	3159
Opel Kadett Petrol (Oct 84 – Oct 91)	3196
Opel Omega & Senator Petrol (Nov 86 – 94)	3157
Opel Vectra Petrol (Oct 88 – Oct 95)	3158
PEUGEOT 106 Petrol & Diesel (91 – 04) J to 53	1882
Peugeot 107 Petrol (05 – 11) 05 to 11	4923
Peugeot 205 Petrol (83 – 97) A to P	0932
Peugeot 206 Petrol & Diesel (98 – 01) S to X	3757

* Classic reprint

Title	Book No.
Peugeot 206 Petrol & Diesel (02 – 06) 51 to 06	4613
Peugeot 207 Petrol & Diesel (06 – July 09) 06 to 09	4787
Peugeot 306 Petrol & Diesel (93 – 02) K to 02	3073
Peugeot 307 Petrol & Diesel (01 – 08) Y to 58	4147
Peugeot 308 Petrol & Diesel (07 – 12) 07 to 12	5561
Peugeot 405 Diesel (88 – 97) E to P	3198
Peugeot 406 Petrol & Diesel (96 – Mar 99) N to T	3394
Peugeot 406 Petrol & Diesel (Mar 99 – 02) T to 52	3982
Peugeot 407 Diesel (04 -11) 53 to 11	5550
PORSCHE 911 (65 – 85) up to C	0264
Porsche 924 & 924 Turbo (76 – 85) up to C	0397
RANGE ROVER V8 Petrol (70 – Oct 92) up to K	0606
RELIANT Robin & Kitten (73 – 83) up to A *	0436
RENAULT 4 (61 – 86) up to D *	0072
Renault 5 Petrol (Feb 85 – 96) B to N	1219
Renault 19 Petrol (89 – 96) F to N	1646
Renault Clio Petrol (91 – May 98) H to R	1853
Renault Clio Petrol & Diesel (May 98 – May 01) R to Y	3906
Renault Clio Petrol & Diesel (June 01 – 05) Y to 55	4168
Renault Clio Petrol & Diesel (Oct 05 – May 09) 55 to 09	4788
Renault Espace Petrol & Diesel (85 – 96) C to N	3197
Renault Laguna Petrol & Diesel (94 – 00) L to W	3252
Renault Laguna Petrol & Diesel (Feb 01 – May 07) X to 07	4283
Renault Megane & Scenic Petrol & Diesel (96 – 99) N to T	3395
Renault Megane & Scenic Petrol & Diesel (Apr 99 – 02) T to 52	3916
Renault Megane Petrol & Diesel (Oct 02 – 08) 52 to 58	4284
Renault Scenic Petrol & Diesel (Sept 03 – 06) 53 to 06	4297
Renault Trafic Diesel (01 – 11) Y to 11	5551
ROVER 216 & 416 Petrol (89 – 96) G to N	1830
Rover 211, 214, 216, 218 & 220 Petrol & Diesel (Dec 95 – 99) N to V	3399
Rover 25 & MG ZR Petrol & Diesel (Oct 99 – 06) V to 06	4145
Rover 414, 416 & 420 Petrol & Diesel (May 95 – 99) M to V	3453
Rover 45 / MG ZS Petrol & Diesel (99 – 05) V to 55	4384
Rover 618, 620 & 623 Petrol (93 – 97) K to P	3257
Rover 75 / MG ZT Petrol & Diesel (99 – 06) S to 06	4292
Rover 820, 825 & 827 Petrol (86 – 95) D to N	1380
Rover 3500 (76 – 87) up to E *	0365
Rover Metro, 111 & 114 Petrol (May 90 – 98) G to S	1711
SAAB 95 & 96 (66 – 76) up to R *	0198
Saab 90, 99 & 900 (79 – Oct 93) up to L	0765
Saab 900 (Oct 93 – 98) L to R	3512
Saab 9000 4-cyl (85 – 98) C to S	1686
Saab 9-3 Petrol & Diesel (98 – Aug 02) R to 02	4614
Saab 9-3 Petrol & Diesel (92 – 07) 52 to 57	4749
Saab 9-3 Petrol & Diesel (07-on) 57 on	5569
Saab 9-5 4-cyl Petrol (97 – 05) R to 55	4156
Saab 9-5 (Sep 05 – Jun 10) 55 to 10	4891
SEAT Ibiza & Cordoba Petrol & Diesel (Oct 93 – Oct 99) L to V	3571
Seat Ibiza & Malaga Petrol (85 – 92) B to K	1609
Seat Ibiza Petrol & Diesel (May 02 – Apr 08) 02 to 08	4889

Title	Book No.
SKODA Fabia Petrol & Diesel (00 – 06) W to 06	4376
Skoda Felicia Petrol & Diesel (95 – 01) M to X	3505
Skoda Octavia Petrol (98 – April 04) R to 04	4285
Skoda Octavia Diesel (May 04 – 12) 04 to 61	5549
SUBARU 1600 & 1800 (Nov 79 – 90) up to H *	0995
SUNBEAM Alpine, Rapier & H120 (68 – 74) up to N *	0051
SUZUKI SJ Series, Samurai & Vitara 4-cyl Petrol (82 – 97) up to P	1942
Suzuki Supercarry & Bedford/Vauxhall Rascal (86 – Oct 94) C to M	3015
TOYOTA Avensis Petrol (98 – Jan 03) R to 52	4264
Toyota Aygo Petrol (05 – 11) 05 to 11	4921
Toyota Carina E Petrol (May 92 – 97) J to P	3256
Toyota Corolla (80 – 85) up to C	0683
Toyota Corolla (Sept 83 – Sept 87) A to E	1024
Toyota Corolla (Sept 87 – Aug 92) E to K	1683
Toyota Corolla Petrol (Aug 92 – 97) K to P	3259
Toyota Corolla Petrol (July 97 0 Feb 02) P to 51	4286
Toyota Corolla Petrol & Diesel (02 – Jan 07) 51 to 56	4791
Toyota Hi-Ace & Hi-Lux Petrol (69 – Oct 83) up to A	0304
Toyota RAV4 Petrol & Diesel (94 – 06) L to 55	4750
Toyota Yaris Petrol (99 – 05) T to 05	4265
TRIUMPH GT6 & Vitesse (62 0 74) up to N *	0112
Triumph Herald (59 – 71) up to K *	0010
Triumph Spitfire (62 – 81) up to X	0113
Triumph Stag (70 – 78) up to T *	0441
Triumph TR2, TR3, TR3A, TR4 & TR4A (52 – 67) up to F *	0028
Triumph TR5 & TR6 (67 – 75) up to P *	0031
Triumph TR7 (75 – 82) up to Y *	0322
VAUXHALL Astra Petrol (Oct 91 – Feb 98) J to R	1832
Vauxhall/Opel Astra & Zafira Petrol (Feb 98 – Apr 04) R to 04	3758
Vauxhall/Opel Astra & Zafira Diesel (Feb 98 – Apr 04) R to 04	3797
Vauxhall/Opel Astra Petrol (04 – 08)	4732
Vauxhall/Opel Astra Diesel (04 – 08)	4733
Vauxhall/Opel Astra Petrol & Diesel (Dec 09 – 13) 59 to 13	5578
Vauxhall/Opel Calibra (90 – 98) G to S	3502
Vauxhall Cavalier Petrol (Oct 88 0 95) F to N	1570
Vauxhall/Opel Corsa Diesel (Mar 93 – Oct 00) K to X	4087
Vauxhall Corsa Petrol (Mar 93 – 97) K to R	1985
Vauxhall/Opel Corsa Petrol (Apr 97 – Oct 00) P to X	3921
Vauxhall/Opel Corsa Petrol & Diesel (Oct 03 – Aug 06) 53 to 06	4617
Vauxhall/Opel Corsa Petrol & Diesel (Sept 06 – 10) 56 to 10	4886
Vauxhall/Opel Corsa Petrol & Diesel (00 – Aug 06) X to 06	5577
Vauxhall/Opel Frontera Petrol & Diesel (91 – Sept 98) J to S	3454
Vauxhall/Opel Insignia Petrol & Diesel (08 – 12) 08 to 61	5563
Vauxhall/Opel Meriva Petrol & Diesel (03 – May 10) 03 to 10	4893
Vauxhall/Opel Omega Petrol (94 – 99) L to T	3510
Vauxhall/Opel Vectra Petrol & Diesel (95 – Feb 99) N to S	3396

Title	Book No.
Vauxhall/Opel Vectra Petrol & Diesel (Mar 99 – May 02) T to 02	3930
Vauxhall/Opel Vectra Petrol & Diesel (June 02 – Sept 05) 02 to 55	4618
Vauxhall/Opel Vectra Petrol & Diesel (Oct 05 – Oct 08) 55 to 58	4887
Vauxhall/Opel Vivaro Diesel (01 – 11) Y to 11	5552
Vauxhall/Opel Zafira Petrol & Diesel (05 -09) 05 to 09	4792
Vauxhall/Opel 1.5, 1.6 & 1.7 litre Diesel Engine (82 – 96) up to N	1222
VW Beetle 1200 (54 – 77) up to S	0036
VW Beetle 1300 & 1500 (65 – 75) up to P	0039
VW 1302 & 1302S (70 – 72) up to L *	0110
VW Beetle 1303, 1303S & GT (72 – 75) up to P	0159
VW Beetle Petrol & Diesel (Apr 99 – 07) T to 57	3798
VW Golf & Jetta Mk 1 Petrol 1.1 & 1.3 (74 – 84) up to A	0716
VW Golf, Jetta & Scirocco Mk 1 Petrol 1.5, 1.6 & 1.8 (74 – 84) up to A	0726
VW Golf & Jetta Mk 1 Diesel (78 – 84) up to A	0451
VW Golf & Jetta Mk 2 Petrol (Mar 84 – Feb 92) A to J	1081
VW Golf & Vento Petrol & Diesel (Feb 92 – Mar 98) J to R	3097
VW Golf & Bora Petrol & Diesel (Apr 98 – 00) R to X	3727
VW Golf & Bora 4-cyl Petrol & Diesel (01 – 03) X to 53	4169
VW Golf & Jetta Petrol & Diesel (04 – 09) 53 to 09	4610
VW LT Petrol Vans & Light Trucks (76 – 87) up to E	0637
VW Passat 4-cyl Petrol & Diesel (May 88 – 96) E to P	3498
VW Passat 4-cyl Petrol & Diesel (Dec 96 – Nov 00) P to X	3917
VW Passat Petrol & Diesel (Dec 00 – May 05) X to 05	4279
VW Passat Diesel (June 05 – 10) 05 to 60	4888
VW Polo Petrol (Nov 90 – Aug 94) H to L	3245
VW Polo Hatchback Petrol & Diesel (94 – 99) M to S	3500
VW Polo Hatchback Petrol (00 – Jan 02) V to 51	4150
VW Polo Petrol & Diesel (02 – May 05) 51 to 05	4608
VW Transporter 1600 (68 – 79) up to V	0082
VW Transporter 1700, 1800 & 2000 (72 – 79) up to V *	0226
VW Transporter (air cooled) Petrol (79 – 82) up to Y *	0638
VW Transporter (water cooled) Petrol (82 – 90) up to H	3452
VW Type 3 (63 – 73) up to M *	0084
VOLVO 120 & 130 Series (& P1800) (61 – 73) up to M *	0203
Volvo 142, 144 & 145 (66 – 74) up to N *	0129
Volvo 240 Series Petrol (74 – 93) up to K	0270
Volvo 440, 460 & 480 Petrol (87 – 97) D to P	1691
Volvo 740 & 760 Petrol (82 – 91) up to J	1258
Volvo 850 Petrol (92 – 96) J to P	3260
Volvo 940 Petrol (90 – 98) H to R	3249
Volvo S40 & V40 Petrol (96 – Mar 04) N to 04	3569
Volvo S40 & V50 Petrol & Diesel (Mar 04 – Jun 07) 04 to 07	4731
Volvo S60 Petrol & Diesel (01 – 08) X to 09	4793
Volvo S70, V70 & C70 Petrol (96 – 99) P to V	3573
Volvo V70 / S80 Petrol & Diesel (98 – 07) S to 07	4263
Volvo V70 Diesel (June 07 – 12) 07 to 61	5557
Volvo XV60 / 90 Diesel (03 – 12) 52 to 62	5630

* Classic reprint

CL 27.08.13

Preserving Our Motoring Heritage

< *The Model J Duesenberg Derham Tourster. Only eight of these magnificent cars were ever built – this is the only example to be found outside the United States of America*

Almost every car you've ever loved, loathed or desired is gathered under one roof at the Haynes Motor Museum. Over 300 immaculately presented cars and motorbikes represent every aspect of our motoring heritage, from elegant reminders of bygone days, such as the superb Model J Duesenberg to curiosities like the bug-eyed BMW Isetta. There are also many old friends and flames. Perhaps you remember the 1959 Ford Popular that you did your courting in? The magnificent 'Red Collection' is a spectacle of classic sports cars including AC, Alfa Romeo, Austin Healey, Ferrari, Lamborghini, Maserati, MG, Riley, Porsche and Triumph.

A Perfect Day Out

Each and every vehicle at the Haynes Motor Museum has played its part in the history and culture of Motoring. Today, they make a wonderful spectacle and a great day out for all the family. Bring the kids, bring Mum and Dad, but above all bring your camera to capture those golden memories for ever. You will also find an impressive array of motoring memorabilia, a comfortable 70 seat video cinema and one of the most extensive transport book shops in Britain. The Pit Stop Cafe serves everything from a cup of tea to wholesome, home-made meals or, if you prefer, you can enjoy the large picnic area nestled in the beautiful rural surroundings of Somerset.

> *John Haynes O.B.E., Founder and Chairman of the museum at the wheel of a Haynes Light 12.*

< *Graham Hill's Lola Cosworth Formula 1 car next to a 1934 Riley Sports.*

The Museum is situated on the A359 Yeovil to Frome road at Sparkford, just off the A303 in Somerset. It is about 40 miles south of Bristol, and 25 minutes drive from the M5 intersection at Taunton.
Open 9.30am - 5.30pm (10.00am - 4.00pm Winter) 7 days a week, *except Christmas Day, Boxing Day and New Years Day*
Special rates available for schools, coach parties and outings Charitable Trust No. 292048